VISIONS OF CULTURE AND THE MODE...

POZNAŃ STUDIES
IN THE PHILOSOPHY OF THE SCIENCES AND THE HUMANITIES

VOLUME 15

Editors

Jerzy Brzeziński   Tomasz Maruszewski
Andrzej Klawiter   Leszek Nowak (editor-in-chief)
Andrzej Kupracz (technical assistant)   Ryszard Stachowski
Krzysztof Łastowski

Advisory Committee

Joseph Agassi (Boston)   Theo A.F. Kuipers (Groningen)
Etienne Balibar (Paris)   Ilkka Niiniluoto (Helsinki)
Piotr Buczkowski (Poznań)   Günter Patzig (Göttingen)
Mario Bunge (Montreal)   Marian Przełęcki (Warszawa)
Robert S. Cohen (Boston)   Jan Such (Poznań)
Francesco Coniglione (Catania)   Klemens Szaniawski (Warszawa)
Andrzej Falkiewicz (Wrocław)   Jerzy Topolski (Poznań)
Dymitrij Gorskij (Moscow)   Johannes Witt-Hansen (Copenhagen)
Jaakko Hintikka (Helsinki)   Ryszard Wójcicki (Łódź)
Jerzy Kmita (Poznań)   Georg H. von Wright (Helsinki)
Władysław Krajewski (Warszawa)   Zygmunt Ziembiński (Poznań)

The principal task of the book series "Poznań Studies in the Philosophy of the Sciences and the Humanities" is to promote the development of the philosophy which would respect both the tradition of great philosophical ideas and the manner of philosophical thinking introduced by analytical philosophy. Our aim is to contribute to practicing philosophy as deep as Marxism and as rationally justified as positivism.

Address of the editors:

Krzysztof Łastowski
Department of Philosophy
A. Mickiewicz University
Szamarzewskiego 89c
60-569 Poznań, Poland

VISIONS OF CULTURE
AND
THE MODELS OF CULTURAL SCIENCES

Edited by

Jerzy Kmita and Krystyna Zamiara

AMSTERDAM - ATLANTA, GA 1989

CIP-GEGEVENS KONINKLIJKE BIBLIOTHEEK, DEN HAAG

Visions

Visions of culture and the models of cultural sciences /
ed. by Jerzy Kmita and Krystyna Zamiara. — Amsterdam - Atlanta, Ga :
Rodopi. — (Poznań studies in the philosophy of the
sciences and the humanities, ISSN 0303-8157 ; vol. 15)
ISBN 90-5183-093-9
SISO 905.2 UDC 316.7
Trefw.: cultuursociologie.
©Editions Rodopi B.V., Amsterdam - Atlanta, GA 1989
Printed in The Netherlands

Part Three: On culture and cultural participation

INTRODUCTION

All papers collected in this volume share a common interest in the phenomena of culture, i.e. in various spheres and domains of culture and in the process of individual participation in it. Theoretical reflection is conducted here at least on two levels: objective, referring directly to cultural phenomena, and meta-theoretical or methodological metalevel. The volume is divided into three parts. In the first one papers of methodological character are included whereas the second and third one contain papers in which theoretical problems referring to culture dominate.

Part One (Methodological orientations in the studies on culture) comprises papers devoted to methodological investigations of cultural studies of culture. The methodological problems analysed here are on the one hand connected with the way in which cultural phenomena are expressed in the theoretical conceptions formulated in the sociology of culture, literary studies, cultural anthropology, art studies and on the other hand they encompass issues related to certain methodological conceptions concerning investigations of culture and representing various epistemological orientations. Positivism, sociologism of the L'Année Sociologique school, neostructuralism and Marxism in the Frankfurt School version are the epistemological orientations taken into account. Problems of the first type are represented for example by J. Grad, who analyses critically the way in which Polish sociologists of culture understand culture and the process of participation in it, or E. Rewers, whose essay deals with the approach to a literary work in the sociological conception of S. Ossowski. T. Jerzak-Gierszewska, who analyses the discrimination between magic and religion in the conceptions of E. Durkheim, H. Hubert and M. Mauss and reconstructs the epistemological assumptions underlying this discrimination also belongs here. In turn, the paper by B. Kotowa distinctly shows the essence of the other kind of methodological problems. The author considers different versions of methodological antinaturalism determining various models of studies of culture — she analyses the function of the so-called understanding intuition ascribed to them which consists in the systematization of assertions in art studies. In certain papers the considerations comprise both kinds of problems. This happens when methodological analysis pertains to heterogeneous concepts which comprise certain theoretical options crucial to ethnomethodological issues, project a new research practice, and on its assumptions criticize traditional models of studies on culture. Theoretical and methodological propositions of J. Habermas are a standard example of such a conception. They become the object of analysis in the papers of A. Szahaj and E. Kobylińska. In a certain sense it refers also to the neostructuralistic semiotics of A.J. Greimas which is methodologically analysed by A. Grzegorczyk.

Part Two (Science as a domain of culture) contains papers which in spite of their subject diversity, share a specific idea about science as a part of symbolic culture that is in various relationships with its other domains or spheres. The paper of J. Kmita is a pattern example of such an attitude to science. Science is considered in the context of the concepts of the development of culture where history is treated as a gradually weakening relationship between methonimic, symbolic and evaluating way of perceiving the world. It is assumed here that this relationship was the strongest in the primitive syncretic magic reasoning; the regulative "force" of culture is connected with it (gradual weakening of this relationship simultaneously means a weakening of the regulative "force" of culture). Contemporary science whose aim is to discover the methonimic order without reference to *sacrum,* in fact cannot exist without combining these two orders. The idea of science as a domain of culture is also characteristic for the philosophical conceptions of E. Cassirer which are the object of J. Sójka's reflections. The author presents certain consequences of this idea stating, among others, that it does not have to entail the extreme form of historical and cultural relativism. The problem of cultural relativism is analyzed in a detailed way by W.J. Burszta whereas the paper of M. Buchowski concerns the problem of ethnocentrism, an attitude whose various forms have been accepted in the humanistic investigations of strange cultures. It turns out that these two problems gain a new manifestation by situating them within perspective where science is regarded as an element of culture. This aspect decided about including these two essays into this part of the volume in spite of the fact that they contain also a considerable amount of methodological reflections. Another essay devoted to cultural relativism, whose author is Z. Gierszewski, is included in turn in part one as it contains exclusively methodological analysis of certain relativistic conceptions. The problem of developing historical materialism by incorporating into it the ideas worked out outside this doctrine is discussed by A. Pałubicka who illustrates her considerations by comparing the structuralistic concept of overdetermination with the idea of functional explanation assumed in a certain interpretation of Marxist theory.

Part Three (On culture and cultural participation) comprises papers which also abound in methodological reflection. However, this time it is subordinated to essential questions referring to culture or the process of individual participation in it which constitute either the starting-point for proposing one's own theoretical solutions to these problems or serve to manifest the accepted methodological standpoint.

The paper by K. Zamiara contains relatively the most considerations of methodological character. The author points out in what way the idea of participation in culture is determined by a psychologistic and individualistic epistemological perspective on the one hand and by its opposition, i.e. antipsychological and at the same time antiindividualistic perspective on the other. These considerations aim at revealing, above all, the epistemological perspective leading to cognitively the most profitable investigations of the phenomena of participation in culture. This is attributed to the complex of epistemological assumptions comprising antipsychologism and a moderate or relatively radical version of methodological antipsychologism. It enables a proper combination of the cultural approach to cultural participation (referring to a proper features of the participation process which depend on the properties of the object of participation, i.e. on culture, its spheres or domains) with investigations representing mainly the psychological approach to cultural participation (referring to features of the participation process which depend mostly on the features of the participating subject). The paper by A. Pluta brings in turn a critical analysis of the conceptions of pedagogical culture accepted in pedagogy. These considerations, however, constitute only the starting-point for sketching the theoretical basis of the problem of initiating pupils into participation in culture. In the essay of P. Ozdowski one can find an attempt at defining various kinds of an individual's psychic processes in terms of propositions (judgements) and assumptions of the semantics of cultural communication. The task of reformulating the concepts and assertions of cognitive psychology has been undertaken because of the projected theory of individual participation in culture. Considerations of an epistemological character serve distinctly to mark the author's own attitude. The problem of the nonprofessional status of language is raised by T. Zgółka who points out that this issue is no longer univocally settled when one takes into account the relationship of linguistic communication with other domains of culture. The author notices the phenomenon of the "fusion" of language as a specific form of social consciousness with other forms — domains of culture; it changes the hitherto opinions on the characteristics of language considered in isolation. In turn, G. Banaszak, who focuses his attention on music, reconstructs the forms of contemporary musical culture, and also notices the phenomenon of "fusion" of this culture with other domains of symbolic culture.

In this introduction only those authors have been taken into consideration whose papers either dominate in a particular part of the volume or contain diversified reflections and thus the decision of including them in a given part requires additional justification. Finally, it is worth noting that besides the diversity of undertaken problems and individual styles of reasoning, mostly all authors share a common theoretical and methodological paradigm. They constitute a group of researchers connected with Jerzy Kmita whose basic concepts and assertions of the so-called historical epistemology and the so-called socio-regulative theory of culture[1] are assumed and creatively developed by them. Both mentioned theories are mutually related by a certain interpretation of historical materialism assumed at their basis. Besides, the descriptive part of the first theory is in fact an element of the second, which is essentially expressed by the assertion qualifying science as one of the domains of symbolic culture (this assertion additionally justifies the title accepted for Part Two).

Krystyna Zamiara

1. Cf. J. Kmita, "Epistemological cognition as historical cognition", *The Polish Sociological Bulletin* 3/1979; J. Kmita, "Humanistic interpretation", *Poznań Studies in the Philosophy of the Sciences and the Humanities,* vol. 1, no. 1, 1975.

PART ONE: METHODOLOGICAL ORIENTATIONS IN THE STUDIES ON CULTURE

Jan Grad

THEORIES OF CULTURE AND STUDIES OF
PARTICIPATION IN CULTURE IN POLISH SOCIOLOGY

The aims of the present paper are: a critical review of conceptions of culture worked out by Polish sociologists, of the notions of cultural participation which those theories imply, and of the experimental studies which have been applied within them.

The theoretical assumptions which underlie the analysis come from the social regulative theory of culture and from the historical epistemology which is connected with the former. I shall not define the basic concepts underlying both theories (i.e. of culture and of historical epistemology) on account of easy access to relevant literature[1] and because the concepts will be used in self-explanatory contexts.

1.   Culture and Participation in Culture in Statistical-Descriptive Analyses

1.1. A characteristic feature of Polish sociology of culture is its interest in cultural participation and in its social conditions. This is best shown by the number of studies appearing each year which describe the results of empirical studies of various aspects of participation in culture by Poles coming from different groups and communities.

This choice of the field of sociological research seems to have been influenced by specific historical factors, namely, by the ideological and cultural policy of the state, which on its way to socialism, aims at "cultural enfranchisement of the masses" or, in other words, at "democratization of culture". Sociological studies are to report on a currently achieved degree of democratization, i.e. on an extent to which broad social circles, in particular "culturally handicapped" workers' and peasants' classes, participate in "higher" (national) culture. At the same time, sociology should point out positive and negative factors which

---

1. See J. Kmita, *On symbolic culture,* Warsaw 1982 (in Polish); J. Kmita, *Culture and cognition,* Warsaw 1985 (in Polish); J. Kmita, *Essays on the theory of scientific cognition,* Warsaw 1976 (in Polish); J. Kmita, *Problems of historical epistemology,* Warsaw 1978 (in Polish).

influence the participation of various social groups. The practical motivation of Polish sociology was already noted by A. Kłoskowska, who claimed that various branches of the discipline which developed in Poland after 1956 (among them, sociology of culture) were the result of empirical studies which had practical origins and aims.[2]

Empirical sociology of culture and, to a great extent, also pedagogy (so-called pedagogy of culture and education, social pedagogy) are meant to provide data illustrating effectiveness of initiatives undertaken by various institutions which were founded in order to "disseminate culture". This is to be done by reporting on the actual (quantitative) participation in culture of various social groups. Accordingly, the studies cover, on one hand, "cultural initiatives" (i.e. the entirety of institutional ventures to organize and direct participation in such places as industrial plants, housing complexes, villages, towns and regions), on the other hand, they cover "cultural life" (i.e. empirically recorded behavioural evidence of participation in culture) of people living in those housing complexes, towns and villages, of workers of the plants as well as of representatives of various social classes and strata, and professional groups. While describing the participation, mainly in artistic culture (fine arts, literature, theatre, music, film), the authors also study conditions which favour "contacts with culture" and facilitate the "cultural reception". By this, they expect to learn what is the reach of influence of the centres of art, of education and of culture. This, in turn, provides evidence how effective the institutional ventures to disseminate culture are.

Studies of the above type consist mainly in recording behavioural signs of participating in various "forms of dissemination of culture" which are offered by the institutions, on the part of members of various social groups, as well as, in recording their frequency.

As the studies use first of all "questionnaire techniques", and statistical methods, they are called statistical-questionnaire studies or quantitative-questionnaire studies. Evaluating them, the sociologists note their usefulness in that they answer the needs of the institutions of "dissemination of culture". The usefulness, however, is of a limited character because of various shortcomings and even errors which do not allow for making on their basis any generalizations and syntheses. They are blamed for simplifying the image of cultural reality, for their one-sidedness and fragmentary character, for the lack of any comparability criteria between

2. Comp. T. Goban-Klas, "On aims and assumptions of the study of cultural participation", *Kultura i Społeczeństwo* 2/1972 (in Polish); A. Kłoskowska, "The sociology of culture in Poland: its perspectives", *Studia Sociologiczne* 3/1971 (in Polish).

their results, and occassionally, also for methodological and organiza-
tional mistakes (e.g. lack of coordination).[3] Above all, studies of that
kind are hardly ever accompanied by sufficient reflections of a methodological and theoretical character, which considerably diminishes their
cognitive value.

Nonetheless, the pursuit of the descriptive-statistical studies is useful
both from the scholarly and practical point of view since they provide
empirical knowledge of: quantitative participation in culture; its "geo-
graphy" both in the spatial (territorial) aspect and from the point of view
of its social stratification; knowledge of social preferences with respect to
particular fields and branches of culture; of the statistics of increase
(decrease) of cultural participation, or in other words, of the so-called
cultural development. It should be kept in mind, however, that the
discussed type of studies should not be undertaken unless their theoretical
and methodological assumptions are clearly stated which define their
cognitive validity, the scope of interpretation of obtained results, and the
applicability of the latter. They merely constitute a basis of further search
for "depth" of cultural participation, i.e. its quality.

1.2. The above emphasized need of theoretical and methodological
reflection in sociological study of cultural participation has long been
neglected, and even now many analysts of "cultural life" are not fully
aware of its significance. Many authors avoid any theoretical discussion
on assumed concept of culture and on other basic notions as participation
in culture, cultural activity, reception and consumption of culture, etc.
Though it is not difficult to infer the concepts of culture, of cultural
activities and events which have been intended by the authors, their clear
statement within a discussion of a theoretical and methodological
character would certainly allow to understand better the authors' arguments for the chosen conception of culture and of cultural participation,
and for intended referents of these concepts as well as it would enable to
delimit the scope of interpretation of the obtained results. It might be
hoped that had some theoretical aspects been taken into account, the
authors would have noticed crucial — in my opinion — distinction
between culture and participation in culture. Thus, it is erroneous to
speak of e.g. the workers' class culture for we are interested in the
workers' participation in culture in general (national, representative or
universal — world culture). What is meant by "cultural activity" (acts of
participation) of the working class during their free time, are such

---

3. Comp. A. Kłoskowska, op. cit., p. 167.

8

activities as watching television, listening to the radio, reading books and newspapers, going to the cinema or to the theatre, taking part in "cultural shows", in amateur theatrical groups and in social gatherings, visiting clubs and coffee-bars, hiking and weekend drives in the countryside, participating in sports and religious practices. The lack of any distinction between culture and cultural participation or, in other words, between the collective and distributive notions of culture, is a cardinal methodological mistake.

Sometimes an author does not go beyond very sketchy "definitions" of the used concepts, and it is difffcult to grasp their meanings outside the relevant contexts. For instance in R. Dyoniziak's *Cultural differentiation of the city community,* the notion of "participation iñ culture" is characterized as follows,

> (...) expression "participation in culture" will be used interchangeably with such phrases as "cultural consumption" and "style of consumption". Cultural differences will be, therefore, differences in cultural participation or in cultural consumption.[4]

Having in mind the common economical notion of consumption understood as providing for one's various needs, we can easily guess what the author means by participation in culture. It depends, according to him, on providing for the so-called cultural needs. Without going into detail, it should be stated in this connection that "cultural needs" are usually related to the notion of cultural values. Providing for one's cultural needs, or in the discussed case cultural consumption, consists in undertaking the actions which lead to realization of the values whose "absence" inspires the actions (we have here a behavioural understanding of needs). The assumed concept of needs results in treating the behaviour of the people who participate in culture as an indicator of the needs which are "felt" by them. Thus, as can be gathered, R. Dyoniziak treats culture in terms of needs and values. But he does not offer its clear definition, stating only that "(...) in scholarly study characteristic 'parameters' (are) patterns of behaviour, attitudes, systems of values and needs (...)"[5]. Unlike A. Siciński, who in *The today and tomorrow of Polish culture* gives a definition of culture which refers to the notion of needs only. Thus, he writes that

> As is known "culture" is an ambiguous term. In this work I use it most often in its "narrow" sense, i.e. with reference to the sphere of fulfilment of so-called "higher" needs, intellectual and aesthetic ones, and also as recreation.[6]

4. R. Dyoniziak, *Cultural differentiation of the city community,* Warsaw 1969, p. 35 (in Polish).
5. Ibid., p. 34.
6. A. Siciński, *The today and tomorrow of Polish culture,* Warsaw 1975, p. 6 (in Polish).

Such concept of culture does not seem to be related to the author's idea of participation in culture which he defines as: "(...) intensity and degree of participation (active and passive) in *national* (emphasis mine) culture."[7] Putting aside the modifier "national", we must note that the above is not a definition at all because of the defined term being repeated in the definiens. Taking for granted that the notion of culture should correspond to the concept of cultural participation, on the basis of the quoted definition of culture "participation in culture" can be understood as fulfilment of the mentioned higher and recreational needs. But such an approach, like many other theories of culture, in fact identifies culture with cultural participation, or to be exact, with its manifestations. This is because in those theories the concept of culture is construed from the point of view of participation in culture, which for a common observer is a sphere of concrete and easily accessible acts of behaviour (so-called external behaviour) and of their products. The point of view of everyday social experience is assumed in some sociological studies, hence those studies treat both culture and participation in culture in terms of behaviour and its results, identifying the two domains. A. Kłoskowska, whose definition of culture is recalled by most authors who are of our present concern, can serve as an illustration. In her words "(...) culture (...) is a relatively integrated whole of acts of human behaviour which follow the common social patterns acquired in education and in social inter-action, and of products of these acts."[8]

J.Szczepański's definition seems more precise, i.e. more elaborate. According to him

> (...) culture is the entirety of the products of human activities, both material and non-material, of values of the patterns of behaviour which have been objectivized and accepted within given communities and are transferred to other communities as well as passed on from generation to generation.[9]

Studies of cultural participation within the above discussed framework must of necessity be limited to observation and to collecting data on the acts of behaviour and their results, to their taxonomy and to inductive generalizations from the data.

The idea of culture conceived in terms of behaviour and its products is sanctioned by the sociology of culture which follows the positivist theory of science, which is a philosophy of everyday social experience. Two of the positivist principles are moved to the fore, namely, phenomenalism and inductionism. I shall not attempt to discuss the positivist heritage of

---

7. Ibid., p. 41.
8. A. Kłoskowska, *The mass culture. A critical study,* Warsaw 1980, p. 40 (in Polish).
9. J. Szczepański, *Elementary concepts of sociology,* Warsaw 1970, p. 78 (in Polish).

sociology of culture,[10] but I would like to point out some of the consequences of the positivist methodology. In agreement with the phenomenalistic conception of empirical facts, the sociologists of culture focus on "the most easily accessible topic", in Kłoskowska's words. This is the primary methodological reason why their studies deal first of all with the institutionalized aspects of "cultural life", which are easy for empirical identification and statistical processing. The most useful tool of such study is a questionnaire. According to Czerwiński, handiness of questionnaires largely contributes to popularity of a statistical-descriptive analysis. Characterizing the empirical ("reductionist" in his terms) sociology of culture, the author writes

> Reductionism in methodology, which is my starting point, consists in attempts to form statements from psychological sentences, to be precise, from the sentences on acts of behaviour. It seems that this general formula would be insufficient to determine the eventual form which prevails in most modern sociological analyses of culture. Out of the many possible models of "science of behaviour", the one which is most often chosen seems to own a lot to a privileged status of the questionnaire, a handy tool of research.[11]

Another consequence of phenomenalism is that sociology of culture calls for an operational character of its used concepts understood as their empirical applicability and verifiability of hypotheses which are formed with their help. Hence come such concepts as "cultural consumption" and others, to which we will return further below.

Our claim is, as follows from the above, that all researchers of "cultural life" apply one and the same methodological principle which comes from the epistemological assumptions of positivism. This is why they are determined in their way of viewing the investigated phenomena of culture and cultural participation, in their interpretation of the obtained results, as well as in assignment of specific literal (semantic) senses to statements made within the framework. And yet, I would not agree with those critics who claim that introducing into this type of studies different methodological principles and assumptions, would make impossible any coherent interpretation, generalizations and comparisons of the studies. Terminological differences are, in their opinion, the evidence of different methodological assumptions. If, however, we consider the referents of the respective terms which are used, it turns out that the differences are largely exaggerated since their extension is usually identical or very close. Thus, the lack of terminological unification is of secondary importance. The lack of comparability between the obtained

10. See W. Śliwczyński, "On the so-called empirical sociology of culture", *Studia Metodologiczne* 24/1985 (in Polish).
11. M. Czerwiński, *Culture and its study,* Warsaw 1985, p. 44 (in Polish).

results seems to come from differences in so-called indicators, and from application of different methods of statistical processing (i.e. different criteria of taxonomy). The indicators are construed with reference to participation in "public cultural life", which is the main field of investigation in sociology of culture.

1.3. It may be the case that a reason that many sociologists of culture abstain from any prior theoretical and methodological reflection on the concepts of culture and cultural participation, results from the fact that the main subject of this branch of sociology has come to be "dissemination of culture" within a social type of institutions. The fields of interest of these institutions have apparently determined the spheres of cultural events which are studied. Accordingly, sociology of culture and cultural pedagogy seem to identify "culture" with forms and manners of its dissemination. What is studied is not, as many authors stipulate, participation in culture but participation of members of various social groups in *institutionalized* "cultural activities". Sometimes this is rendered by the intentional replacement of the broader term "participation in culture" with the narrower one — "cultural participation". The latter, thanks to the everyday positive connotation of the term "cultural", is to refer to the dissemination of professional culture (social, national, universal, and culture of the elites, i.e. so-called "higher" culture). In A. Kłoskowska's term, it refers to the second and third systems of culture. Those systems are known to comprise professional institutions which specialize in dissemination of "cultural values, goods and patterns (they are cultural and educational institutions, and mass-media)". According to J. Kmita, culture is understood here as a practical-administrative notion

> (...) [culture] "is perceived" as a complex of specific ventures such as meetings with men of letters, organized sightseeing trips whose tenaries may occasionally include museums and historical monuments, literary quizes, folklore festivals, etc., as well as organization of amateur choirs, theatrical and dance groups, etc.[12]

Within thus conceived culture, participation consists in acts of social behaviour which are forms and manners of leisure activities offered by the institutions of cultural dissemination. They are such activities as borrowing, buying and reading books, newspapers and magazines, watching TV shows and cinema films, listening to the radio, attending theatres, philharmonic halls, museums, art galleries, public meetings and lectures, social gatherings, taking part in sports and recreation, devoting time to hobbies, participating in amateur groups, etc. Such concept of

---

12. J. Kmita, *Culture and cognition,* op. cit., pp. 5-6.

participation in culture moves to the fore its active component, neglecting the intellectual one. We may find evidence of that in such common phrases as "cultural activities" and "cultural ways of spending free time", as well as in the expression "making use of culture", which is favoured by some sociologists. J. Kądzielski, who is one of them, writes

> We understand by it (making use of culture) the press and book reading, theatre and cinema attendance as well as attendance at some other similar institutions. The phenomenon can be studied from the point of view of its reach and from the point of view of how often members of various social and local communities make use of the cultural institutions and of the media of cultural propaganda.[13]

This is also U. Przybyszewska's idea of participation in culture when in one of her works she says

> In the present work I will limit the notion of cultural participation to making use of cultural institutions and mass-media because these two aspects seem to me most important. They are the basis of free time activities by means of cultural participation.[14]

In sociological writings there is also used another term in the above sense, namely — "cultural consumption", which stands for all possible cultural activities undertaken in free time. The concept of cultural consumption, borrowed from economics, implies practical (empirical) availability of its manifestations as well as their measureability. Thus, the sociologists who use the concept rely on such data illustrating participation in culture which are considered most objective (countable and comparable) and which are ready for statistical processing. They are first of all so-called cultural expenses, which are the basic type of data in economical studies of culture. That kind of information is recalled by U. Małachowska in her study of cultural consumption which she sees as "(...) empirically verifiable cultural participation which is manifested in expenses on cultural goods and cultural services".[15]

Sociology of culture finds still another term useful in its study of participation in culture, often used in place of participation in culture because it renders an active character of thus conceived participation in the most adequate way; it is understood then as a complex of "cultural actions".[16] Also the authors of works dealing with forms of spending free time, speak of cultural activity in the above sense. According to T. Goban-Klas,

---

13. J. Kądzielski, *On models of cultural revolution,* Lódź 1964, p. 67
14. U. Przybyszewska, "Cultural participation today and tendencies of development, in: *Participation in culture and cultural policy,* Warsaw 1981, p. 30 (in Polish).
15. U. Małachowska, "Differences in consumption of daily products and cultural services", *Kultura i Społeczeństwo* 1-2/1982, p. 173 (in Polish).
16. A common use of the word "activity" is known to "action".

13

The term "cultural activity" means undertaking (or readiness to undertake) the activities which aim at learning cultural values such as theatrical plays, works of literature and music, etc. Cultural activities tend in various directions, depending on the kind of values which one wishes to acquire.[17]

Cultural activity can be also understood in a different way, namely, in connection with active "contribution" to dissemination initiatives. In this sense, which functions in everyday use, cultural activity consists of acts of personal involvement in the ventures which aim at organized participation in culture or, in other words, in cultural actions. The common use of the term requires that the involvement should not be professional but "social", unlike that of full time workers of the apparatus of cultural dissemination whose job is "cultural work". The persons who are nonprofessionally involved in organizing cultural ventures are called "cultural activists".

Thus, we can distinguish two concepts of cultural activity, i.e. (1) active participation in the institutionally disseminated forms of participation in culture; this type of participation seems to be preferred in actual dissemination practices; (2) active and nonprofessional participation in disseminating of culture. Individual activities of the latter type most often belong to the first and second system of culture, if we are to follow Kłoskowska's terminology (they are first of all spontaneous theatrical movements, spontaneous informal self-educational groups and other spontaneous initiatives (system I), and formalized institutions of "cultural propaganda" (system II)).

The above concepts of cultural activity should be supplemented, in my opinion, with one more definitional feature which would answer common institutions connected with the term "activity", namely, a non-occasional character of its referents. Hence, the term "cultural activity" (in both of its meanings) should be used exclusively with reference to such individual and group behaviour (within the sphere of our current interest) which is not sporadic but is marked with characteristic regularity, stability or high frequency. Putting it differently, acts of participation in culture must possess some "intensity of making use of cultural means and institutions", as was stated by the author of *On models of cultural revolution*. The same author thinks that intensity of making use of cultural means and institutions can be measured in two ways, i.e. by discovering the number of cultural means and institutions which are used by each person, and by checking frequency of their use.[18] Thus conceived cultural activity

17. T. Goban-Klas, *Young workers of Nowa Huta as recipients and creators of culture*, Wrocław 1971, p. 95 (in Polish).

17. T. Goban-Klas, *Young workers of Nowa Huta as recipients and creators of culture*, Wrocław 1971, p. 95 (in Polish).
18. J. Kądzielski op. cit., p. 111.

would be the quantitatively measured intensity of "cultural contacts" understood as frequent attendance to the institutionalized forms of the dissemination of participation in culture.

Using statistical methods, it is possible to define normative patterns of cultural activity, starting, for instance, either from the average or from the lowest participation, which are empirically verified as regards frequency of "contacts with culture". In this manner, Z. Bokszański seems to have construed one of the elements of his theory of cultural promotion.

Cultural activity is a matter of degree, depending on a sphere of culture which is participated, on forms of its dissemination, and on intensity of participation which is measured by means of regularity and frequency of acts of participation. Differences in cultural participation (often called cultural differentiation) depend, in accordance with the adopted parameters, on the reach of the "cultural field" (in A. Wojciechowska's words), and on changes in "cultural contacts" which are referred to in terms of cultural "fall" and "growth" (or "cultural promotion").

Concluding the section, let us note that the mentioned parameters of cultural activity are at the same time indicators of levels of participation in culture since they show diversity of interests and of types of "cultural needs". Thereby we arrive at the question of how to study "quality" of participation in culture, which is the next topic of our discussion below.

2. *Conceptions of Culture and of Participation in Culture in Studies of the Participation Levels*

2.1. Before projects of studying the "depth" of participation in culture could be endeavoured, it has been necessary to revise the traditional concepts of culture and cultural participation phenomena. To a great extent, this is not so much a matter of revision but of recalling certain ideas conceived already in A. Kłoskowska's theory of culture and in M. Czerwiński's *Culture and its study*. Though sociology of culture has retained the basic "behavioural" concept of culture, it becomes popular nowadays to quote also those parts of Kłoskowska's theory in which she identifies a subsphere of behavioural acts and their results with sphere of symbolic acts, i.e. "symbolic culture". This concept, called by her culture in its narrower sense: "Starts from a diversity of human behaviour acts and does not part with the general conception of culture understood in terms of behaviour".[20] The quotation is not only an expression of

19. Z. Bokszański, *Young workers and cultural promotion*, Warsaw 1976, p. 25 (in Polish).
20. A. Kłoskowska, *The mass culture ...*, op. cit., p. 84.

Kłoskowska's attachment to her own theory, which seems quite natural, but above all it is an evidence of how difficult it is for the whole sociology of culture to get rid of its naturalistic-positivist background.

The concept of symbolic culture postulated by the author of *Sociology of culture,* is still marked by a behavioural approach to culture, due to the fact that symbolic (communicative) acts are treated there as elements of culture whereas in reality they are merely manifestations of participation in the communicative sphere of culture. On the other hand, however, the way Kłoskowska understands symbolic culture is a departure from the radical behavioural approach because some new categories become unavoidable such as certain states of consciousness of the subjects who perform the cultural-symbolic acts whose "contents" are cultural (communicative) beliefs which enable "sending" and "receiving" the senses (meanings) of those acts. The necessity of considering the states of consciousness (in Kłoskowska's words — motivations) of the individuals who perform various acts, should help sociologists become aware that behind human actions stand some messages which may be externalized by means of verbalized norms and rules. Kłoskowska's motivations are nothing else but senses of cultural behaviour acts which are realized by people and which are generated by the "implicit" rules of culture. Had sociology of culture pursued this line, it could have "discovered the world of ideas" which is the universe of culture, the more so that a semiotic perspective must have revealed a conventional character of the relation between the acts of cultural behaviour and their senses (meanings), and the necessity of looking for the rules (conventions) the knowledge of which is indispensable for interpretation of those acts. It is characteristic that already at that time the term "interpretation" finds its place in the studies of participation in culture. As semiotical theories have been gaining more and more insight, and as they have been adopted by the study of culture (in the 1960's and 1970's), the question of participation in culture also becomes better understood.

It is thanks to semiotics that scholars start paying attention to the mental aspect of participation in culture which in semiotical theories consists of "decoding" various cultural signs, i.e. interpreting their underlying senses, and of the complementary process of "sending" those signs, i.e. performing concrete symbolic acts of behaviour such as creating and spreading particular media (works of art, books, radio and television, broadcasts, shows, films, etc.). In this connection, let us quote Kłoskowska once more:

> The idea of cultural participation is in the most intimate way related to the very process of symbolic interaction which lies in the centre of the interests of sociology of culture. Cultural participation consists of acts of construing and receiving, of

interpreting messages. The phenomenon is studied from the point of view of who conveys what to whom and what influence a given message exerts upon its recipient.[21]

In that sense, participation in culture consists in "processes of symbolization".

Referring to Kłoskowska's semiotic conception of culture, A. Tyszka defines participation in culture as follows: "(...) *individual participation in culture* – acquiring its contents, making use of its goods, following its norms and conventions, also creating new values as well as reconstructing the old ones (...)". Concluding, he writes "(...) cultural participation is a *conscious* access which may be an act of cognition or emotion, which is possible thanks to the acquired habits, dispositions and abilities" (emphasis A.T.). It should be noticed in this place that empirical studies in sociology of culture are almost exclusively concerned with the reception aspect of participation in culture, not with the process of cultural creativity (i.e. founding new cultural values).

The mental character of participation in culture is also foregrounded by M. Czerwiński. Though he declares himself for the "reified" rather than "psychological" conception of culture, when discussing "objects of culture", he places them in a context of the accompanying states of consciousness. He does it as follows,

> (objects of culture) are of a symbolic character. That is (...) their function of manifesting, referring cannot be accomplished unless they remain in contact with consciousness which associates them with their meanings and referents (...). It is quite obvious that the sole function of a work of art, object of culture, poem is to modify the states of consciousness (psychological states).[23]

Within thus conceived culture, i.e. mainly as "objects of culture", it is possible to study participation in culture by "reading from" the senses which are inherent in signs (symbols) which, in this instance, are literary works, films, pictures, etc. Hence, studies of this kind are aimed, in Czerwiński's words, at "penetrating the sense", and they are commonly called studies of "reception of culture" or of "quality of participation in culture". Below we shall discuss several examples of such studies.

3. Studies of "Quality" of Participation in Culture

There can be distinguished three main types of such studies, i.e. (1) those

21. A. Kłoskowska, *Social frames of culture. A sociological monograph,* Warsaw 1972, pp. 20.21 (in Polish).
22. A. Tyszka, *Participation in culture, On different life styles,* Warsaw 1971, p. 54 and 72 (in Polish).
23. M. Czerwiński, op. cit., p. 25 and 33.

which, focussing on concrete objects of art, want to discover their "styles
of reception", in other words, they report how their message is understood; (2) those whose aim is to reach directly the so-called states of
cultural awareness of individuals, by learning a type and degree of
people's knowledge of culture, i.e. their acquaintance with artistic
phenomena and cultural competence; (3) those which treat people's
cultural experience as a whole which is acquired by them in the course of
social interaction or, as is said, in their everyday socio-individual "life"-
practice, the experience which is believed to be decisive for how the senses
of symbolic culture are recognized. For lack of space, our discussion of
the three trends may be only fragmentary.

3.1. The first of the above-mentioned types has given rise to the most
thorough empirical studies of reception which have been accomplished so
far. They deal with a number of selected works of art and films. The
conceptual (theoretical) background has been prepared by A. Kłoskowska
within the "general theory of communication" whose central notion is
the communicative act adopted from H.D. Lasswell. One of its integral
components, i.e. communicative result, is reflected in Kłoskowska's
"extended concept of reception" which stands for all the individual
(except physiological) and social states of affairs which are the result of
reception of a certain message.[25] An important role is played in the
discussed type of study by the assumed conception of work of art because
of its interest in levels of understanding of the artistic message, i.e. in
degrees of adequacy of its sense. It is generally assumed that the sense of
work of art is constituted by individual but culturally determined acts of
reception. Additionally, it is believed that at a given time the most
adequate understanding (normative, standard) is a professional one,
called by Kłoskowska the critical reception. Such reception is taken to be
the norm of comparison with the reception by the general public where, if
necessary, degrees of "deviance" are marked. Hence, another notion used
in those studies is "re-creation of the work of art".

The obtained empirical material is usually classified according to the
criteria of adequacy of a given work, next there are postulated stereotypes

24. See A. Kłoskowska, "Common reception of literature on the basis of
Zeromski's works", *Pamiętnik Literacki* 1/1976 (in Polish); A. Kłoskowska and A.
Rokuszewska-Pawełek, "Literary myths and common knowledge. A common re-
ception of the 'Wedding Party'", *Kultura i Społeczeństwo* 1/1977 (in Polish); M.
Gałuszka, "Common reconstruction of films", *Studia Sociologiczne* 1/1984 (in
Polish).
25. Comp. A. Kłoskowska, *Sociology of culture,* Warsaw 1981, p. 418 (in Polish).

of reception and their typology, together with the relevant conditions which are looked for in the so-called characteristics of the investigated persons. The hierarchically ordered "styles of reception" which have been generalized, may be treated as levels of participation in a given branch of culture.

3.2. We shall pass now to the question of the so-called "cultural awareness of individuals"[26] The studies of this type deal, in fact, with the learned knowledge in the domain of artistic (symbolic) culture. Their interest lies rather in theoretical and factual knowledge *about* cultural events (first of all social) which is possessed by selected social groups or by whole society, than in cultural competence which consists of rules of cultural interpretation functioning in society. It is those rules (semantic directives) which determine the senses of cultural activities and cultural objects. Their knowledge is indispensable for "reception of cultural messages". Thus, I would distinguish between the cultural competence which enables to understand "symbolic meanings of metaphors" and so-called artistic messages, and the knowledge of culture. They are both components of individual cultural awareness. Such conception of cultural consciousness may best suit the aims of the studies of the second type.

The studies of cultural awareness (competence) provide information mainly on levels of people's participation in culture because they are not concerned with actual acts of participation but, like the ones discussed above, they must take into account the established and generally accepted form of interpretation of acts and products of symbolic culture in order to reconstruct the rules of cultural interpretation.

3.3. Unlike the authors of the above studies, who deal with cultural knowledge being the result of the planned institutionalized educational ventures, Z. Bokszański suggests investigation of cultural experience of an individual, which is a result of his life-practice in society. His

> (...) formula of studying reception of symbolic culture is to focus on a socially
> diversified fragment of common knowledge which is indispensable in everyday life
> but which also plays a part in "perception" of fictitious interactions (as we assume)
> (...). Our interests exclude a question of aesthetic experience; we are concerned with
> a more elementary level of how "the reality of fiction works".[27]

---

26. See W. Pisarek and T. Goban-Klas, *Cultural activity awareness of culture, and cultural preferences of Polish society,* Cracow 1981 (in Polish); A. Matuchniak-Krasucka, "The knowledge of art and artistic competence as conditions the reception of art", *Kultura i Społeczeństwo* 1/1986 (in Polish).

27. Z. Bokszański, "The reception of symbolic culture and the recipients interactive practices", *Przegląd Socjologiczny* 1/1981 (in Polish).

Thus, the subject of interest is in what way people's common knowledge determines their "mental" participation in symbolic culture. On the basis of some observations, it is believed that "the experience of everyday life" provides conditions on the attitude towards the reality of fiction contained in works of art, and from thus determined point of view, the artistic works are classified as either "easy to understand" or "incomprehensible".

The author recommends this type of study for sociology of knowledge, not for sociology of culture. As far as can be judged, such studies should consist in getting acquainted with individual "biographies", first of all, on the basis of autobiographical materials (memoirs) and interviews, as well as with the help of the so-called "participating observation". A theory of culture, however, must first decide certain questions, such as a clear delimitation of its subject of study, and adopt relevant operational concepts.

It seems that all the above discussed types of studying levels of participation in culture, await insightful theoretical and methodological reflection on participation in culture and on culture itself.

Translated by Nina Nowakowska

Ewa Rewers

THE IMAGE OF THE LITERARY WORK IN PRESENT DAY SOCIOLOGICAL STUDIES

On Stanisław Ossowski's sociology of art.

The aroused expectations of the alliance between sociology and literary studies, so far have not brought any interesting results as the new discipline of sociology of culture might wish to achieve. We may quote here A. Heinz's opinion on the attempts of fusion between two other disciplines, i.e. logic and linguistics which, in his opinion, have failed: "'forceful' integrations of two heterogeneous disciplines without their earlier theoretical delimitation, is a major theoretical mistake which blurs relevance of the studied facts and phenomena; it may merely bring some temporary advantage (coming from the confrontation of two branches of learning), in a long run, however, it must lead to a standstill."[1] Difficulties that sociology of literature faces nowadays and the mentioned standstill, seem to have come, first of all, from the states of the two parent-disciplines, in which sociology of culture cannot get enough support.

The belief that the main reason of the present state of affairs lies in sociology, in particular in sociology of culture, suggests discussing one of the most influential Polish theories of sociology of art, namely the conception which has emerged from the rich sociological thought of S. Ossowski. It is by no means the conception itself that should be blamed for the present situation, on the contrary, many of its claims deserve special attention of those who still believe in the future of sociology of culture. On the other hand, Ossowski's approach provides clear evidence of the basic difficulties, i.e. dubious solutions and inapt assumptions, which make it unable for sociology of art to discover its identity.

It seems that the most troublesome problem for the discussed conception of sociology of art, is methodology of study of individual works of art, in particular, of literary works. Even if we reserve the right to define the literary work as a self-contained phenomenon for theoretical and

---

1. A. Heinz, *An outline of linguistics* (in Polish), Warsaw 1978, p. 32.

historical literary studies, we cannot abstain from the question completely, by confining ourselves to general problems of reception and creative
processes or, which is far more seldom, to discussions of certain historical
literary processes, such as literary trends, schools, groups, and the like.
As it happens, the sociology, though it would like to be called sociology
of literature in the proper sense of the word, not sociology of reception,
creation, and so on, shows astounding helplessness when it is faced with
literature as such, above all, when it must deal with an individual literary
fact.

One of the major problems which must be raised by sociology, is the
question of how to pass from the explanation of social phenomena to
explanation of individual facts. Before we can consider any possible
answers to that question, we should analyse some other cardinal issues
connected with the conception under discussion. As is known, Ossowski's
sociology of art has been a result of his primary concern with aesthetics,
later supplemented by his interests in problems of social life. Among the
writings of the author of *On the basis of aesthetics,* the theory does not
occupy a central position. On the contrary, it seems to be a byproduct of
his aesthetics and general sociological investigations, being an interesting
line of continuation. Thus, Ossowski seems to have viewed the function
of sociology of art as dependent, on the one hand, on the functions
fulfilled by aesthetics and, on the other, on those of sociology. Likewise,
he deals with their subjects and methods of study. As of the two parent
disciplines of sociology of art, it is rather sociology than aesthetics that
gets the upper hand today, the former should be held responsible for
many misunderstandings and failures in application of a sociological
perspective to art study.

A trouble with Ossowski's sociology is its subject matter which is
viewed as the reality of heterogeneous character. In *Zoology and behaviourism,* the author writes

> The phenomena, processes and things which are studied by social sciences, may be
> their subject matter only as the correlates of mental phenomena (...). Not a single
> social institution (marriage, court of justice, church, state, school, theatre), nor any
> social group — unless it is treated as a spatial cluster of bodies — nor a social
> process, can be defined without explicit reference to the states of consciousness.[2]

Thus, in the author's view, social reality (the field of interest of
sociologists) on the one hand, is composed of the observable behaviour
acts of the people who enter social interactions and of their results; on the
other hand, it seems that the autonomy of those acts and their results can

---

2. S. Ossowski, *Zoology and behaviourism,* in: S. Ossowski, *Selected works,* vol. IV
(in Polish), Warsaw 1967, p. 343.

23

be taken for granted only as long as they are supplied with the senses which are determined by the beliefs which constitute social consciousness. It must be remembered that Ossowski has in mind rather dispositions than beliefs, and that their characteristics differ, for instance, from those postulated by Kmita in his normative-directive conception of beliefs which are constituents of the historically relativized social consciousness. Nonetheless, Ossowski's idea of sociology puts to the fore the phenomena of "mental reality" which accompany concrete behavioural acts and their results. What the theory does not include, is a clear demarcation line between the two kinds of reality nor any explanation of their mutual relationships; neither does it answer the question of how a coherent theory could explain such two types of objects.

The quotation which follows may serve as an illustration of the above-mentioned problems.

> My objection to one cover term for dispositions and results, comes from the fact that there cannot be a tenacious category which would stand for both. If dispositions are elements of culture, they stand in such a relation to their results as an argument to its function: k and $f(k)$. Even in ordinary language, which is far from consistent, we do not say that buildings, tools, works of art are parts of culture or constituents of culture, but that they are products of culture or cultural monuments, i.e. $f(k)$.[3]

In other words, although the author defines culture as a function and emphasizes its mental character, he is reluctant to relieve a sociologist of a duality in his study in which he should analyse not only artifacts, but also their belief contexts. Accordingly, Ossowski's conception seems to imply three different sociologies, empirical, humanistic and intermediary, theoretical which would rely on the data and methods of the empirical one.

Empirical sociology dates back to the 19th century. From Comte through Durkheim, Tönnies up to Neurath, there reigned a specific version of empiricism which, in Ossowski's opinion, was as much useful as inconsistently realized. One reason for that state of affairs seems to have lain in that sociology could hardly follow the behaviouristic conception of social action. The latter requires abstracting from certain phenomena, which for instance psychology can easily do, but which for sociology is unthinkable since those phenomena constitute the proper subject of sociological study. Ossowski mentions in this connection communicating, conscious interactions, and others. Besides a behaviour-

---

3. S. Ossowski, "Ossowski's latter of April, OI, 1963" (quoted after A. Kłoskowska, "A conception of autotellic symbolic culture", in: *On society and social theories. The memory of Stanisław Ossowski* (in Polish), Warsaw 1985, p. 418.

istic interpretation of such concepts as society, social interaction and social relations, would deprive them of their sociological significance.

> Narrowing down a study to an analysis in terms of external behaviour, reduces the domain of sociological problems, first of all, because it is practically impossible for behaviourism to adequately account for non-stereotyped verbal behaviour, i.e. such behaviour acts which are determined by memory of the past events, or which aim at achieving goals in the remote future. Imagine, for instance, a behaviouristic interpretation of a law which says that social bonds are tightened in face of some external danger.[4]

In view of the above, Ossowski concludes that a behaviouristic approach to social reality which characterizes the early empirical sociology, inevitably involves reduction in the subject of sociological investigation, and therefore it is unacceptable for a sociologist. In addition, such an approach brings about unlawful violations and lack of consistency in the sociological theories which otherwise tend to be empirical. It is characteristic that his doubts about the epistemology of the above theories, are strengthend when it comes to defining the subject matter of sociology of culture, and in case of sociology of art — even more so.

In Ossowski's writings, however, the term "empirical sociology" is also used in a different meaning which, in a way, contradicts the former one. Thus, modern empirical sociology, which is recalled by the latter use, possesses the following properties. First, it uses new methods of quantitative analysis. Second, it offers precise and reliable directives for social behaviour in concrete situations. According to Ossowski, the precursor of the new approach was *The Polish peasant* by Thomas and Znaniecki. A developed version of the empirical sociology may be found in Lazarsfeld and in Stouffer.

Another trend in sociology, i.e. humanistic, is represented by those studies which cannot be reduced to either of the above variants of sociological empiricism. We come across an interesting version of the present-day humanistic sociology in the works of Laswell and Parsons. In Ossowski's opinion, its primary features are: precision of theses, proofs and definitions — which involves introduction of a formalized language — and proper care about the truly empirical sense of sociological theory. A major difference between empirical and humanistic sociologies, lies in that the former holds the assumption of double naturalism, i.e. onto-logical and methodological, whereas the latter insists on independence of

4. S. Ossowski, *Zoology and behaviourism,* op. cit., p. 345.
5. S. Ossowski, *Natural science patterns in empirical sociology,* in: S. Ossowski, *Collected works,* vol. IV, op. cit., p. 248.

methods and functions of the humanistic studies.

While Ossowski thoroughly and interestingly characterizes the naturalist-positivist methodological model of empirical sociology against which he argues, albeit inconsistently, his discussion on humanistic sociology does not present a clear picture. Thus, we learn that:

1) humanistic sociology adopts the anti-naturalist ontological and methodological assumptions,

2) "A humanistic sociologist, if he is interested in scientific study, must also be an empiricist, in the sense that the experimental data are for him of the highest authority."[6]

3) The humanistic study which is considered, does not allow for a definition in terms of so-called humanistic problems, but only with reference to the type of material which is of the sociologist's interest.

4) A large part of the data collected by a sociologist working in "empiricist" humanistic sociology must by no means be confined to that type of material.

5) Unlike empirical sociology, the humanistic one does not disregard internal evidence, to which it not only refers for heuristic purposes, but of which it also makes use when interpreting such observable data as manifestations of people's attitudes, thoughts and habits; when it explains the relational mechanisms obtained by induction, and when it defends the sociological theses which are based on comparative historical studies. When referring to internal evidence, the sociologist is constrained by some additional conditions which are irrelevant for a sociologist-empiricist. In Ossowski's view, the conditions involve proper intellectual and humanistic rigour, and necessary criticism with respect to one's own interpretations.

6) The theories formed within humanistic sociology should undertake an effort to enable people to understand the world. By no means may they be intended to provide a basis of so-called manipulation.

An interesting property of thus conceived theories of sociology, is their similarity to theories of art, in particular, of literature, which property is strongly emphasized by Ossowski.

Though division of culture into separate branches relies on functional criteria, the functional diversity is valid only in some respects. The criteria of relative independence do not exclude the existence of some concurrent functions. Literary and artistic works may perform various cognitive functions, though the cognitive needs are provided for mainly by science, in accordance with the common definition of the latter.[7]

6. S. Ossowski, *Natural science patterns ...*, op. cit., p. 261.
7. S. Ossowski, *The social sciences and problem of the theory of culture,* in: S. Ossowski, *Collected works,* vol. IV, op. cit., p. 289.

As mentioned above, Ossowski's concern with humanistic sociology becomes more intense when he deals with sociology of culture, and with sociology of art, in particular. That would suggest that his claims concerning the subject matter of the sociological study, should determine its epistemological and methodological options. Below we shall examine his conception of sociology of art from the point of view of such expectations.

Discussing sociology of art vis-à-vis other branches of sociology, Ossowski points to its independent character. When we deal with sociology of family, village, and so on, we have to do with some concrete types of social groups and social relations. "When we speak of 'sociology of art', it is rather the word 'art' than 'sociology' which performs the role of definiens; namely, we point to the fact that art is studied from a certain specific perspective."[8] In Ossowski's words, both art and scientific study are specific types of human activity. No wonder, then, that contrary to our earlier expectations, it is the empirical sociology that deals with art, i.e. human activity.

Its constitutive features vis-à-vis other art studies, such as aesthetics, are: the sociological point of view and the studied material. To tell the truth, they are mutually interrelated and practically inseparable assumptions of the author's conception. For a sociologist, any tendency to isolate some preferable interpretations of artistic works, should be alien by principle. For instance, in his discussions with L. Chwistek, Ossowski lays emphasis on the necessity for the axiologically neutral attitudes whenever problems of aesthetic evaluation become a subject of sociological studies. Setting aside the question of how realistic such a postulate can be, we should be aware of its positivist origin in the discussed variant of sociology of art. The idea of resigning from the value assignment prevails in the entire Polish sociology of culture nowadays, which does not prevent scholars from discussing general problems of evaluation in art. But in Ossowski this abandonment takes an uncommon form. In order to understand this peculiarity, we should begin by recalling a fundamental distinction postulated by aesthetics, i.e. that between artistic and aesthetic values.

For Ossowski, they are two different aspects of aesthetic evaluation. The artistic values, which are properties of human creative acts and of the results of those acts, define the genetic aspect of aesthetic evaluation. The aesthetic values, or more properly values of the aesthetic object, which

---

8. S. Ossowski, *The prospects of sociology in the post-war world,* in: S. Ossowski, *Collected works,* vol. VI (in Polish), Warsaw 1970, p. 251.

cannot be reduced to the sphere of human behaviour, constitute the functional aspect of aesthetic evaluation. The relation between the two is that of cause and effect (the artist's work is an immediate cause of the receiver's emotions). Predicating of artistic values, which does not require any reference to aesthetic emotions, leads to defining the objective value of a given work of art. A necessary condition of the predicating is expertness. In other words, there must be an elite of experts whose duty and privilege will be evaluation of the artist's work from the point of view of the artistic values which it accomplishes.

The question about the aesthetic values of an aesthetic object, should be directed to all its addresses, since these values are of a "democratic" character, and their only confirmation lies in aesthetic emotions. In one of his earlier works S. Morawski argues against Ossowski's conception of aesthetics, because of its psychological character. It seems, however, that the argument does not hold because Ossowski explicitly points to the objective-subjective character of those values.

Returning to the main idea of the sociological study of art, we should state that it consists in discovery and description of "democratic" aesthetic values. Thus, the scholars are interested in opinions about the work of art which come from representatives of various social and cultural groups, and from various historical periods. In other words, first, the expertise of some informers (i.e. extended artistic-literary competence), is not treated by a sociologist as preferable property; the groups of such informers are assigned the same status as other social groups. In this the sociologist's attitude is exactly the opposite to the one which characterizes a literary critic, student of literature, author of a literary programme. The sociological attitude is well motivated. It is meant to supplement literary studies which, presenting a hierarchy of aesthetic values and of works carrying the values, are always dependent on a set of normative beliefs which belong to the accepted (or postulated) theory of literature. The same holds true of literary criticism and of writers themselves. For a sociologist of literature, their opinions are of similar interest as those of representatives of other groups, with different or less extended literary-artistic competence. If we image the social evaluation of literature as an iceberg, the experts opinions will make its top; but for a sociologist the whole is of equal interest. Second, likewise a sociologist does not attempt to provide comparative evaluation of works of art coming from different cultures. Third, he treats all artistic works coming

9. S. Morawski, "Review of the third edition of 'The foundations of aesthetics'", *Studia Filozoficzne* 5/1959 (in Polish).

from one culture alike, independent of their unequal artistic levels.

Such an "egalitarian" approach of sociology of art to its subject-matter, brings up the fundamental question of how a sociologist should know that he is dealing with a piece of literature and not, for instance, with an essay or piece of journalism? How may he even be certain that he studies the opinions about true literature, and not about some pseudo-literary scribbles? Can he rely on the readers' reports of their emotions while he is forming a tentative theory of the literary work which would serve his purpose (i.e. the purpose of his study)? Last but not least, is it possible for sociology of literature to pursue its study regardless of any such theories?

The answers to all the above questions which are offered by Ossowski and by other sociologists of literature, are either evasive or negative. Ossowski suggests that the material should be collected with the help of the expert advice. Sociology of literature seems unable to work out any sociological hypothesis of the literary work, therefore it either turns to problems of cultural reception and participation in culture, or it borrows from theories of literature, strangely enough, mainly from those which are outputs of the 19th century positivism or trivial formalism.

Reconstructing Ossowski's conception of sociology of art, I cannot get rid of a thought that the main reason of inadequacies in the sociological idea of literature, lies in its negligence of the linguistic character of literature. All elements of which the literary work is composed and which are described by norms and rules of various levels lying outside the text, must find their medium in language. While examining levels of the hierarchical text-intention which is the basis of the structural organization of Pushkin's poetry, J. Lotman lists the following types of norms: (1) Norms of correctness within a given natural language; (2) Norms of acceptability from the viewpoint of "common sense" and life experience; (3) Norms of acceptability from the point of view of the writer's philosophy; (4) Norms which guarantee the reception of a given text as a poetic one both by the writer and by his readers; (5) Norms which are determined by the structural properties of a given poetic genre, common for a certain group of texts.[10] It's worth to note that Lotman's classification of norms favours both sociological and linguistic reflection.

The hypothesis of the primacy of the linguistic character of the literary work, opens many possibilities for all kinds of studies, but unlike theory of literature (J. Mukařovsky, M. Głowiński, R. Fowler) sociology of

---

10. J. Lotman, "Early poems by Pasternak and some problems of structural analysis of text" (in Polish transl. from Russian by H. Chłystowski), *Literatura na Świecie* 3/1986, pp. 21-22.

literature has hardly made any use of those possibilities. Instead of what could be expected in accordance with the "common sense" norms, i.e. instead of turning to natural language in all its variety as the only medium between an individual act of creativity and society, sociology has chosen to neglect the problem. Writing on sociology of poetic language (a proper part of sociology of literature), Mukařovsky points to the relations between literary practice and language practice, and consequently — society. "The claim that a piece of poetry contains must go through the medium of language, is at the same time a statement about internal relations between the work of poetry and society."[11] Thus, the author seems to think of the sociological perspective not only with reference to the external conditions of the literary work, i.e. in terms of its production and social functions, which apparently exhaust the actual potential of sociology of literature; but he would also apply a sociological view to the study of the internal structure of the literary work. It is the highest time to observe, in this connection, that also Ossowski's conception of sociology of literature outlines some general but interesting perspectives of crossing the boundary between the work of art and its contexts. The direction which he designs, however, is not the one towards the linguistic structure.

A proper sociology of poetic language should be concerned with discovering and interpreting the relations of analogy (first of all) between three types of structure, i.e. of society, of language and of the work of literature. Sociology has been able to propose its theories only with respect to the first of the structures which are mentioned by Mukařovsky; the remaining two have evaded its methods of study, neither have they found a place among the problems raised by sociology of literature.

The above criticism also holds for Ossowski's sociology of art. His comments on language from the point of view of sociology of culture, have a marginal character; moreover, they are oversimplified, not to say, anachronistic. He distinguishes between three types of language: language of science, language of poetry and language of mysticism. "(...) which are ideal types, hardly ever ment in a pure form; most often elements of one type mixed with those of another."[12] The very idea of the languages as sets of elements some of which are common or may replace one another, goes back to the 19th century atomic conceptions of language which have been rejected by the 20th century structural linguistics.

---

11. J. Mukařovský, "On sociology of poetic language", in: J. Mukařovský, *Among signs and structures* (in Polish transl. from Czech by M.R. Mayenowa), Warsaw 1970, p. 169.
12. S. Ossowski, *The social sciences ...*, op. cit., p. 292.

Each of the three languages can perform any of the basic communicative functions, i.e. descriptive (determined by semantic conventions), expressive (of the emotions which do not constitute the semantic message expressed in words) and impressive (forcing upon the hearer-reader the reactions which go beyond the process of understanding the message) (...). The difference between the three types of a language lie in ways and psychological states with the help of which the languages realize communicative functions.[13]

The above statement from Ossowski calls for a few words of comment.

1) It certainly refers to K. Bühler's theory of speech acts. Ossowski's communicative functions, i.e. descriptive, expressive and impressive, are equivalents of Bühler's representation (*Darstellung*), expression (*Ausdruck*) and *Appell,* respectively. Ossowski also upholds their characteristics, putting emphasis on (a) conventional relation between language signs and reality, (b) indexical (in the sense of humanistic indexes or symptoms) relation between the speach act and its participants (expressive and impressive functions). In 1962, when the statement was formulated, it might have been supplemented with the semantic criteria to distinguish the functions. At that time there appear first versions of generative transformational grammar and theories of speech acts. Semantic descriptions of illocutionary acts, which come later and which, in a way, account for expressive and impressive functions, by all means should be implemented by modern sociology of literature, unless it wants to see its theoretical background in K. Bühler's outdated model of speech acts.

2) Bühler's linguistic theory whose elements are borrowed by Ossowski cannot solve any problems of the special cultural languages. Of its concern are functions of the speech act. Its transplantation to those special languages (the procedure is not uncommon among literary theorists either), is another methodological mistake of Ossowski's theory.

3) A belief that language performs more than one function comes from various, not only linguistic, sources. Linguistics, poetics, as well as sociology, seem to have been under a strong influence of traditional psychology. Both Bühler and R. Jakobson whose model of language communication (often made use of by sociology) is based on Bühler's, are proponents of a much criticized version of linguistic polyfunctionalism, i.e. the psycholinguistic approach. In this approach to external language functions, the primary roles are assigned to the speaker/hearer, whose attitudes to the contents of the message are believed to decide about functions of a speech act. The above quoted remarks by Ossowski may serve as an illustration of such an approach. In addition to obvious terminological inadequacy (both Bühler and Ossowski talk about lan-

13. Ibid., p. 292.

guage functions having in mind, in fact, language practice), there are some other serious consequences of the psycholinguistic basis of the postulated functional organization.

In reality, Bühler does not distinguish between the constitutive language functions and functions of other levels.[14] Ossowski takes all his functions to be of communicative character, by which he eliminates an interesting possibility (in particular for sociology, *vide* sociolinguistic studies) of finding a link between the functionally conditioned internal differentiation of language and the social expectations towards it. The recurrence of the basic types of communicative situations, leads to a conclusion that there must be a finite number of optional functions which bind concrete situations and communicative conditions, which their respective (i.e. regularly recurring) social modes of language use. It turns out, then, that Ossowski's theory of language, because of its psycholinguistic orientation, cannot be of any help in accounting for the use of language as the medium between social structure and the structure of the literary work. For a sociologist of literature who would wish to make use of Mukařovsky's suggestions, it is compelling to have proper judgement about adequacy of the available linguistic theories and their applicability to problems of society and literature.

In the light of the above, Ossowski's idea of language of poetry seems quite interesting. Although the relevant remarks are rather of a marginal character vis-à-vis his reflections on language of science, particularly of social sciences, they are still very suggestive. Thus, he believes that: 1) "Language of poetry does not intend to convey precisely a conceptual message, but rather to arouse live images rich in associations and emotional states." 2) "Its intention is to arouse the reader/listener's imagination, therefore it will contain expressions and phrases of a high degree of novelty, and not the ones which are characteristic of conventional language use". 3) " (....) while using poetic language, we do not assume that the expressed message could not be translated into the language of conventionalized concepts." 4) "Poetic language often makes use of words which are treated as signs belonging to two or more symbolic systems, i.e. its means of communication can be 'multidimensional'." 5) "In language of poetry a symbolic sense often interferes with the literal meaning, and the poet will not renounce either."

Let us have a look at some consequences following from the above. Out of three communicative functions which are mentioned by Ossowski,

14. R.W. Pazuchin, "Language, function, communication", *Woprosy Jazykoznanija* 6/1979 (in Russian).

two are foregrounded in a poetic utterance, i.e. expressive and impressive. Such an approach to functions of poetic utterances is characteristic of pre-structural literary studies, mainly of positivist ones. A result of thus conceived functional organization is shifting attention from the text itself to the participants, which is typical of the sociological approach. In addition, however, the symbolic character of the literary work is backgrounded in favour of its indexical properties. Thus, the sociologist puts aside social conventions which lie at the basis of the work of literature. Their place is taken by individual acts of creativity and reception.

No wonder, then, that many functions which are normally referred to when we deal with language of literature, such as aesthetic, autotellic, and so on, are totally absent. Besides, there is hardly any place for the basic function which the literary work performs, i.e. for the message which it conveys, which is certainly different from conventionalized messages, but which cannot be reduced to "live images rich in associations and emotional states".

The above-mentioned unsystematic atomic conception of language, emerges once more from Ossowski's theory of poetic language which is defined as a set of intentional means to bring about a desired effect in the addressee. As is known for many years, the characteristic property of poetic language does not lie in the most unusually coined verbal expressions and phrases. Neither is it true that language of poetry is highly spontaneous and unconventional. In fact, poetic language is a variety of natural language with a remarkable degree of conventionality. Ossowski simply fails to distinguish between the conventions of colloquial, standard and the like varieties of language, and the conventions which are obligatorily used in literature alone.

Surprise effects of poetic utterances, which are also mentioned by Ossowski, are not so much a result of an escape from language conventions, but they are rather a matter of creating new artistic-aesthetic conventions which start ruling the language substance. The process cannot be handled in terms of stimulus (unconventionally coined expressions) — response (non-stereotyped reaction of the reader). It is worthy to note that this typically behaviouristic conception of the act of literary communication, obliterates the denotation of "convention", which refers to a fact which is impossible to observe but can be inferred from the observed behaviour. The problem of the semantic of poetic language seems to me even more controversial. As is known, norms of

15. S. Ossowski, *The social science ...,* op. cit., p. 292-293.

standard language (likewise, of colloquial and others) can be violated not only in poetry, hence such violations are not a sufficient condition of distinguishing between poetic and some other language variety. Neither are aesthetic motivations, related to foregrounding of the aesthetic language function, the only cause of deviance from the norm. Therefore, the claim that the work of art is intended to provoke non-stereotyped reactions in the reader/hearer, is far from sufficient. On the contrary, we would be inclined to accept a hypothesis that the readers' attitudes to artistic works, are socially conventionalized, with the proviso that the conventions refer to the artistic-aesthetic beliefs, not to some ill-defined imagination.

The novelty which the reader of the literary work encounter, comes not so much from unpredictable language phenomena, but first of all from new, albeit expected, semantic principles. It does not suffice to say that language of poetry is a product of various contexts which give rise to its elements which retain a memory of their literary and extra-literary past uses. Another of Ossowski's opinions that the semantics of poetic language and of standard language, are basically isomorphic, and consequently, that the former can be translated into "the language of conventional concepts", does not seem tenable either, though it is understandable in view of the author's other claims.

Against the expectations which Ossowski's aesthetic inspiration might raise, some properties of his conception of poetic language are clearly paradoxical. Nonetheless, despite our earlier criticism, it seems that the author points out some important conditions under which a sociological theory of the literary work might be proposed, although he never outlines such a theory himself. The conditions I have in mind, are as follows.

First, it is necessary to reconstruct variants of social-literary consciousness, for which we need a far broader perspective than can be offered by the currently available theories of literature alone.

Second, transformations in the social consciousness under the influence of new literary phenomena, should be reconstructed as well. Both types of reconstruction together can be the basis of the new theory of the literary work. It will emerge from a few, possibly alternative, hypotheses of the social-artistic consciousness.

Third, the idea of the work of literature as a knot of social relations binding literary characters to the participants of an act of literary communication, which is explicitly present in Ossowski's sociology of art, calls for a theory in which the literary work would be the centre of a social interaction, and not merely a phenomenon which is by such an interaction conditioned.

Lest the above-mentioned potential of Ossowski's sociology of art remain a mere postulate, the theory must revise its basic assumptions. In the first place, the revision should affect those principles which come from the positivist-naturalist sociology.

Translated by Nina Nowakovska

Teresa Jerzak-Gierszewska

THE THEORETICAL AND METHODOLOGICAL CONTEXT OF THE DIFFERENTIATION BETWEEN MAGIC AND RELIGION IN THE CONCEPTION OF HUBERT, MAUSS AND DURKHEIM

Among the classical concepts for differentiating magic and religion, the approach represented by Hubert, Mauss and Durkheim holds a distinguished position, since unlike most of them it has remained in the main line of discussion on the subject for over a century now. One of the most important reasons undoubtedly lies in the fact that the approach received an explicitly formulated theoretical and methodological context presented by Durkheim in *Les Règles de la Mèthode Sociologique* (1895). The programme of research on social phenomena which the treatise contained was only an expression of the assumptions and rules implicitly used by the author in his earlier studies (see Durkheim 1956, p. 2) but to a large extent decided also about his future research conducted in the school of *L'Année Sociologique*. Both Durkheim and his coworkers developed and sometimes slightly modified the theoretical issues within its framework, but the programme itself did not undergo any essential changes at least in the period when two major works on magic and religion were written, namely, *Théorie générale de la magie* (1902-03) by Hubert and Mauss, and *Les Formes élémentaires de la vie religieuse* (1912) by Durkheim. The theoretical and methodological context of both treatises clearly makes the intentions and course of considerations on the demarcation of magic and religion by Hubert and Mauss, and continued by Durkheim.

1. Durkheim's Programme of Research on Social Phenomena
Social fact is undoubtedly a key concept in Durkheim's research programme, and was defined by him as follows,

> Est fait social toute manière de faire, fixée ou non, susceptible d'exercer sur l'individu une contrainte extérieure; ou bien encore, qui est générale dans l'étendue d'une société donnée tout en ayant une existence propre, indépendante de ses manifestations individuelles (Durkheim 1956, p. 14).

The above definition does not provide the essential features of a social phenomenon (fact) but only the external ones which enable its identification and distinction. These features are objectivity and commonness.

Objectivity is a feature which markedly distinguishes social facts, and makes it able to exert external compulsion on an individual. The existence of such a compulsion is manifested in the sanctions or resistance encountered by individual actions disregarding or contradicting social facts.

Social fact can also be tentatively defined as a phenomenon common in a social group but existing independently of the individual forms which it adopts in the course of becoming common. This definition is actually a reformulation of the former because each social fact existing irrespectively of the consciousness of a particular member of a given society becomes only when it is over these consciousness.

However, commonness of a phenomenon in a given society is not a feature which distinguishes it as a social fact. Even if a phenomenon is experienced or manifested by all the members of a society it still does not assume the character of a social fact but is merely its individual expression, or to use Durkheim's words, its individual embodiment (*incarnation individuelle*) (Durkheim 1956, p. 8).

Social fact is not entirely limited to individual manifestations, but can exist even nobody experiences it at a given point of time. On the other hand, individual manifestations are only partly determined by it, depending largely on the bio-psychic constitution of a person and the conditions in which he or she functions.

Although the division into social facts and their individual embodiments is not directly observable, it can be carried out with the help of appropriate procedures. Such an operations is indispensable for the analysis of social facts in pure form, devoid of any individual traits. Social facts differ in the degree of consolidation attained, displaying in this respect a wide range of variants from fully established phenomena with a rigid and stable form to phenomena which as yet have not adopted any definite form. Facts constituting social structure which are called collective modes of existence (Durkheim 1956, p. 12) are fully consolidated phenomena. Their opposites are social facts in a not yet crystallized form, such as states of collective emotions or trends of public opinion.

Social phenomena understood as modes of acting, thinking, and feeling capable of exerting external compulsion on an individual are ascribed by Durkheim to the category of things,

Est chose, en effet, tout ce qui est donné, tout ce qui s'offre ou, plutôt, s'impose à l'observation (...). Les phénomènes sociaux présentent incontestablement ce caractère (Durkheim 1956, p. 27).

However, ideas possessed by particular members of a society lack this feature. Individual representations are observable indirectly, "through the phenomenal reality in which they are expressed" (Durkheim 1956, p. 28). Thus, Durkheim concludes that if we perceive social phenomena as things, they should be studied as things.

A preliminary characterization of social fact implies a general rule for studying social phenomena: "La première règle et la plus fondamentale est de considérer les faits sociaux comme des choses" (Durkheim 1956, p. 15).

Such a characterization does not determine the ontic status of social phenomena, the thesis that they are things being a necessary though tentative initial assumption.

> (...) alors même que, finalement, ils n'auraient pas tous les caractères intrinsèques de la chose, on doit d'abord les traiter comme s'ils les avaient (Durkheim 1956, p. 28).

The character of this assumption is methodological and not ontological (metaphysical), as usually interpreted by critics of Durkheim's research programme.

The general rule for considering social facts as things was rendered explicit in the form of three detailed rules. The first one says that, "Il faut écarter systématiquement toutes les prénotions" (Durkheim 1956, p. 31). To gain direct access to social phenomena, a scholar should not use commonplace concepts (representations) both when defining or investigating his research object. These representations are shaped by practice, in which they can be effectively used in spite of their theoretical falseness.

> Ce n'est donc pas en les élaborant, de quelque manière qu'on s'y prenne, que l'on arrivera jamais à découvrir les lois de la réalité. Elles sont, au contraire, comme un voile qui s'interpose entre les choses et nous et qui nous les masque d'autant mieux qu'on le croit plus transparent (Durkheim 1956, p. 16).

A scholar should therefore avoid using concepts (representations) originating outside science, although they may not be altogether useless. Being in some way related to phenomena, they can serve as indications signalling the existence of groups of phenomena with common features.

> Dans la pratique (scientifique — T.J.-G.), c'est toujours du concept vulgaire et du mot vulgaire que l'on part. On cherche si, parmi les choses qui connote confusément ce mot, il en est qui présentent des caractère extérieurs communs. S'il y en a et si le concept formé par le groupement des faits ainsi rapprochés coincide, sinon totalement (ce qui est rare), du moins en majeure partie, avec le concept vulgaire, on pourra continuer à désigner le premier par le même mot que le second et garder dans la science l'expression usitée dans la langue courante. Mais si l'écart est trop considérable, si la notion commune confond une pluralité de notions distinctes, la création de termes nouveaux et spéciaux s'impose (Durkheim 1956, p. 37 ff.).

A researcher should reject all popular representations and direct his attention to facts constituting the investigated domain of reality. Subsequent methodological rules warrant his direct contact with the domain.

Rule (2) demands,

> Ne jamais prendre pour objet de recherches qu'un groupe de phénomènes
> préalablement définis par certains caractères extérieurs qui leur sont communs et
> comprendre dans la même recherche tous ceux qui répondent à cette définition
> (Duckheim 1956, p. 35).

Thus, the first and foremost step in any scientific research should be to give the definition of their object phenomena. If the phenomena have not been subject to scientific investigation, their definition can include only those features which are sufficiently external to enable direct observation.

Scientific investigation should also comprise all phenomena which come under the preliminary definition, since at this point a researcher still has no criteria for their selection at his disposal. His knowledge of the investigated domain of reality is limited to features tentatively defining it. Although the essence of phenomena is not expressed in the external, directly observable features, they are the only point of departure for studies aimed at grasping it, as the features do not occur at random. On the contrary, they are linked to the crucial attributes of phenomena,

> (...) à moins que le principe de causalité ne soit un vain mot, quand des caractères
> déterminés se retrouvent identiquement et sans aucune exception dans tous les
> phénomènes d'un certain ordre, on peut être assuré qu'ils tiennent étroitement à la
> nature de ces derniers et qu'ils en sont solidaires (Durkheim 1956, p. 42).

The external features of social phenomena are given to the researcher through impressions, but the acceptance of sensual data as the starting point for scientific recognition may lead to subjectivism. Being aware of this danger, a researcher should keep precautions. The registered features on the basis of which he chooses his field of studies have to be supremely objective.

> (...) une sensation est d'autant plus objective que l'objet auquel elle se rapporte a
> plus de fixité; car la condition de toute objectivité, c'est l'existence d'un point de
> repère, constant et identique, auquel la représentation peut être rapportée et qui
> permet d'éliminer tout ce qu'elle a de variable, partant de subjectif (Durkheim
> 1956, p. 44).

A researcher can find such a point of reference for the concepts (representations) created by him only in those social phenomena which have already crystallized into a definite form. For instance legal and moral codes, religious dogmas, folk proverbs and facts of social structure all possess a stable form, which does not change in the course of usage. Such social facts

> (...) constituent un objet fixe, un étalon constant qui est toujours à la portée de
> observateur et qui ne laisse pas de place aux impressions subjectives et aux
> observations personnelles (Durkheim 1956, p. 45).

The more social phenomena are devoid of the individual manifestation through which they are expressed, the easier it is to formulate them into scientific representations.

Quand, donc, le sociologue entreprend d'explorer un ordre quelconque de faits sociaux, il doit s'efforcer de les considérer par un côté où ils se présentent isolés de leurs manifestations individuelles (Durkheim 1956, p. 45).

The above quoted rule states in precise terms the third, anti-psychologistic aspect of considering social facts as things. Along with detailed implications, the rule constitutes the theoretical and methodological context of studies conducted by Durkheim and his coworkers, and without refering to this context it is impossible to understand fully their impact to studies on magic and religion.

2. The Distinction between Magic and Religion in the Approach of Hubert-Mauss

The evolutionists' studies on magic did not result in a clear and complete image. Even Frazer's voluminous study presented in the second edition of *The golden bough* does not describe magic as a whole but only its one particular kind, namely, sympathetic magic. Dissatisfied with the state of affairs, Hubert and Mauss think it necessary to formulate their own conception comprising all kinds of magic phenomena. An analysis of the various manifestations of magic discovered both in primitive and hetero-geneous societies should lead to the determination of its constitutive elements.

Tentatively assuming that in various societies magic constitutes a quite clearly distinguished sphere of phenomena, both authors are convinced that it can be precisely defined. They see their research task in the formulation of such a definition since they are not contented that some phenomena are popularly called magic. The performers or observers of acts they themselves termed as magic "(...) accept subjective points of view which are not necessary characteristic of scientific perspective" (Hubert and Mauss 1973, p. 11). Thus, for instance the followers of different religions refer to the remains of an old religious cult as magic although the elements still preserve their religious character. A similar attitude is also adopted by some scholars. But Hubert and Mauss think the term magic should be applied only to those phenomena which the whole community and not merely its part considers as such. However, when formulating a scientific definition of magic one may not always refer to popular concepts. Usually, communities practicing magic are not vividly conscious of the acts performed within it. Therefore, a precise definition of magic can be the result of thorough studies of its relation with religion.

For both authors the concept of a rite is the point of departure for the analysis of this relation. According to them the term denotes every act of specific effectiveness, other than mechanical or conventional. Particular ritual acts and means used in them are basically different from the goal of the rite as a whole — they belong to other cause-and-effect sequences. The efficiency of a rite exceeds by far the efficiency of technical or conventional (e.g. legal) acts seeking the same goal. This specific property of rites distinguishes them from other traditional acts; they are "(...) traditional acts of specific efficiency" (Hubert and Mauss 1973, p. 15).

Having defined a rite, one can proceed to show the differences existing between its two kinds: magic and religious rites. According to Hubert and Mauss the criteria for differentiating them proposed by the evolutionists are inadequate. Among others they comprise criteria formulated by Frazer. The first one stating that, "(...) magical act is sympathetic" (Hubert and Mauss 1973, p. 15) does not reflect the actual difference between the two, since not all magic rites are based on the principle of sympathy. What is more, this principle is not a specific characteristic of magic but is present in religion too. The Jewish rite of bringing down rain is an example of a sympathetic religious act: during the feast of Sukkoth, the high priest raising his hand used to pour water on the altar of the temple of Jerusalem. The rite seems to work by itself, and yet it is of a distinctly religious character. The performer, the place, a solemn form of the rite, the intentions of participants leave no room for doubt in this respect.

Also the second criterion proposed by the author of *The golden bough:* "Magical rite acts by itself whereas religious rite is a propitiation or conciliation" (Hubert and Mauss 1973, p. 16) is inadequate. In various religions, rites involve constraint to attain their aims, and gods are compelled to obey rites performed without any transgressions of the form. Moreover, not all magic rites work directly, as in some spirits, and in others even gods are summoned. These beings do not always obey the magician, who finally has to win their favour.

Rejecting the concepts of differentiating magic and religious rites, the authors of *Théorie générale de la magie* propose their own criteria for demarcating the two kinds of rites, taking into consideration only the external features which distinguish them. One of the criteria is based on the fact that every kind of rite usually has a different performer. Magic rites are performed by a magician, whereas the religious ones are fulfilled by a priest. When in exceptional cases the priest performs a magic act, it differs markedly from the acts he normally performs.

Further criteria for distinguishing magic and religious rites involve the circumstances in which they take place. So, first of all their sites are different. A magic rite is always performed in out-of-the-way, remote places at night or in darkness, and even if there are witnesses it still remains secret. A religious rite, on the other hand, is generally fulfilled in public places in broad daylight. Besides, although a magic rite is sometimes periodical (in the case of agrarian magic) or necessary for attaining a goal (e.g. health) it is always considered irregular, abnormal and not very respectable, while a religious rite is usually performed regularly and respected.

The external features of magic and religious rites, from which criteria for distinguishing them originate, enable a preliminary definition of both concepts. Hubert and Mauss explicitly formulate only the definition of a magic rite. "We shall call so every rite, which is not a part of any organized cult" (Hubert and Mauss 1973, p. 21). The definition clearly reveals the concept of a religious rite as a part of organized cult, implicitly assumed by them.

The difference between a magic and religious rite implies a difference between the beliefs associated with those rites.

Magic and religious beliefs are difficult to distinguish in the aspect of content, and they may even be identical in their particulars. Therefore, only indirect distinction is possible, based on the difference between the magic and religious rites, which turns out to be crucial for the delimitation of the entire domains of magic and religion. The feature distinguishing the two domains consists in organized cult, which is characteristic of religion but absent in magic. By organized cult Hubert and Mauss understood an organization comprising both the performers and participants of a rite, but they failed to present its institutional form in greater detail. This would be later done by Durkheim, who called such an organization a Church, and stressed its moral character.

Particular rites and corresponding beliefs are linked into system varying complexity known as cults. A cult is the intrinsic order of magic and religion, and each consists of two aspects — practical, in the form of acts (rite), and theoretical in the form of appropriate belief (beliefs).

In the approach of Hubert and Mauss, magic and religion are separate domains of social phenomena. They are composed of two kinds of phenomena, i.e. beliefs and acts (rites), and specific efficiency attributed to magic and religious rites is their characteristic feature. This efficiency is recognized exclusively by members of that society in which the rites are performed. It is not perceptible to an observer from outside who does not share the same beliefs.

The realm of social phenomena common for magic and religion is determined by features observable only from the point of view of the social group practising them. On the other hand the border separating both domains is also accessible to observation from outside of given social group.

3. The Distinction between Magic and Religion in the Approach of Durkheim

Studies on religion and other domains of social phenomena bordering on it, conducted in the school of *L'Année Sociologique* were to an extent summed up by Durkheim in his *The elementary forms of the religious life.* It contains a wide and detailed analysis of religious phenomena registred among the natives of Australia. Considerations centred around the crucial problem of what is meant by religion are an introduction to the analysis proper. Of course, a preliminary determination of the religious domain from among other social phenomena cannot be treated as a definition comprising all its essential features. The latter can only be ascertained in the course of penetrating studies. Thus, a preliminary characterization of religion,

> is to indicate a certain number of external and easily recognizable signs, which will enable us to recognize religious phenomena wherever they are met with, and which will deter us from confounding them with others (Durkheim 1975, pp. 37-38).

Durkheim states that, "Religious phenomena are naturally arranged in two fundamental categories: beliefs and rites" (Durkheim 1965, p. 51). Religious beliefs are the strongest accepted opinions, with representations as the elementary components, whereas rites are definite modes of action. Between the two categories of basic religious facts there is the extreme difference separating the spheres of thought and activity.

Rites cannot be defined and distinguished from other kinds of human activity otherwise than by the specific nature of their object. The characterization of a rite requires a previous description of its object. The special nature of this object is represented by a respective belief. Thus, it is impossible to define a rite without first defining the belief.

All the religious beliefs have a common denominator, which consists in an assumed division of all the objects both real and ideal represented by them into two opposed spheres, each designated by a different name. The naming attributed to these names is well expressed by two terms: *sacred* (*sacré*) and *profane* (*profane*). The terms *sacré* and *profane* used by the author of *The elementary forms of the religious life* are also sometimes rendered as 'that, which is sacred' and 'that, which is lay'. In such a translation the term *profane* becomes synonymous to the term *laique*. However, Durkheim consciously avoids the word *laique* as a synonym of *profane*. He does not explain the reasons of his choice, suggesting only that the popular understanding of the terms is closest to the meaning he himself accepted.

It is worth noting that the same terminological distinction functions in the phenomenology of religion founded by R. Otto, although there the meaning of the terms is different than in the circle of *L'Année Sociologique*.

Religious beliefs present (represent, embody) the nature of sacred objects, their history, presupposed qualities and powers, their mutual interactions and relations with profane objects. The sacred objects are not only personal beings called gods or spirits, for even rocks, stones, trees, springs or pieces of wood can be considered as such. To an extent, religious rites also have this status. However, it is impossible to determine unequivocally the content of the domain of sacred things, because it may comprise various objects depending on the religious beliefs which decide about it.

An ennumeration of several sacred objects does not indicate at all the general characteristics which oppose them to profane objects. One of such features is the place they are generally attributed in the hierarchy of beings. They are as a rule considered superior in dignity and power to profane objects. However, a distinction of sacred and profane objects strictly on the basis of hierarchy is too general, and what is more, not truly precise. Thus, for instance in the hierarchy of beings determined by religious beliefs, a man belongs either to the sacred or the profane depending on whether he participates in religious rites at a given moment or not.

An absolute heterogenity of the sacred relatively to the profane is a characteristic which fully separates the two domains. They are two different worlds. The sacred and the profane are always and everywhere treated as separate, radically opposed kinds of objects. The opposition adopts various forms in particular religions. In some it is held that the kingdoms of the sacred and the profane are situated in different regions of the physical universe, while others claim that the sacred belongs to the ideal and transcendental world, whereas the profane is identified with the material one. Although the forms of contrast between the two domains change, the very contrast itself is universally accepted.

The sacred and profane objects can pass from one world to the other. The way in which it takes place clearly emphasizes a complete dissimilarity of the two worlds. Upon such a transition each object undergoes an authentic metamorphosis, which is especially evident in the rites of initiation. Initiation is a sequence of rites with the aim of introducing a young man into religious life. The culminating point comes when he crosses the border separating the profane from the sacred because at that moment a complete metamorphosis takes place. It is believed that the initiated man ceases to exist in his hitherto form which belonged to the profane, and is reborn as a new man in the world of the sacred.

Because of their inherent heterogenity, objects from different domains cannot touch or coalesce without losing their true nature. The external separation of the objects is an easily observable manifestation of the contrast between the two classes. The division of the universe of objects expressed (represented) as notions, into two radically opposed classes: the sacred and the profane, constitutes in turn a criterion for distinguishing religious beliefs from all other socially shared opinions. It is a distinctive feature of religious beliefs that they represent the nature of the sacred objects, and their relations both with each other as well as the profane objects. On the other hand, rites connected with beliefs are "the rules of conduct which prescribe how a man should comport himself in the presence of these sacred objects" (Durkheim 1965, p. 56).

A complex of beliefs and rites corresponding to a certain number of ordered sacred objects constitutes a religion. The objects to which religious beliefs and rites refer are thus harmonized and mutually related that they form a homogeneous autonomic system. Religion is not contained in one single idea, nor based on a sole principle varying relatively to the circumstances in which it is expressed, but which in its foundations is everywhere the same. However, religion is a whole composed of distinct, relatively individualized parts.

Groups of related sacred objects as well as single objects of greater importance are organizing centres for systems of beliefs and rites constituting particular cults. For there is no religion which completely excludes a pluralism of sacred objects and as a result is reduced to a single cult. Each religion comprises a number of more or less autonomous cults. In certain religions they are ordered into a hierarchy while in other they are merely united.

The conceptual scheme of Durkheim presented so far is still insufficient for a complete distinction of the phenomenon of religion because they equally pertain to two related domains: magic and religion. Magic too is composed of certain beliefs and rites, but the former are less developed. Because of its technical and utilitarian goals it does not leave room for pure speculation. Like religion, magic includes ceremonies, sacrifices, lustrations, prayers, chants, and dances. The beings invoked by the magician and the powers he makes use of are not simply similar in their nature to the beings and powers present in religion, very often they are identical. In many communities e.g. the souls of the dead are the sacred objects to which religious rites are addressed, but at the same time they also play a crucial role in magic. Demons are considered a means of magic action, and therefore they too are surrounded with interdictions.

Often, they are hardly distinguishable from the gods proper, and what is more, the magician sometimes invokes official deities.

In the light of the above, doubts may arise as to whether it is at all possible to distinguish magic and religion. An apparent reluctance with which religion regards magic on the one hand, and the hostility of magic towards religion on the other, testify that after all they can be separated. The demarcation line between the two domains can be traced as follows.

Religious beliefs are always common to a certain community which shares and practises the rites connected with them. Not only are they recognized by all members of the community but they are also a concern of the whole group, and a uniting factor. Particular individuals feel themselves united into a community because of the very fact of sharing common beliefs;

> A society whose members are united by the fact that they think in the same way in regard to the sacred world and its relations with the profane world, and by the fact that they translate these common ideas into common practices, is what is called a Church (Durkheim 1965, p. 59).

Throughout the history of mankind we do not find a religion without Church. Wherever religious life exists, it is always rooted in a definite community. Even the so-called private cults — i.e. domestic and corporation cults satisfy this condition, since they are always performed by a social group, a family or a corporation.

In magic the situation is altogether different. As a rule, magic beliefs enjoy a wide reception in a given community. In some societies the adherents of magic are not less numerous than the adherents of the religion proper. However, magic does not bind its adherents together, nor does it unite them into a group which leads the same kind of life. "There is no Church of magic" (Durkheim 1965, p. 60). Between the magician and the individuals seeking his advice, as well as between the individuals themselves there are no lasting bonds which make them members of a moral community, comparable to that constituted by adherents of the same god. The magician has clients with whom he maintains random and temporary relations. Even a public and official recognition of his role does not change the situation. However, in some communities, magicians form societies, which meet for the performance of certain rites. But it should be noted that these rare and exceptional societies are not necessary to the functioning of magic. A magician does not have to congregate with other magicians when exercising his art, and usually isolates himself from them, whereas religion is inseparable from the idea of a Church. This is the aspect where the essential difference between magic and religion is revealed. A magic society never involves ordinary followers of magic but only the magicians. A Church, in turn, is not an association of priests, but a moral community encompassing all the believers, both the laymen and priests. This fundamental difference between the two domains is expressed in the second part of the below definition.

> A religion is a unified system of beliefs and practices relative to sacred things, that is to say, things set apart and forbidden — beliefs and practices which unite into one single moral community called a Church, all those who adhere to them (Durkheim 1965, p. 62).

This definition closes Durkheim's general considerations on magic, religion and their mutual relations. His approach can be summed up in a few points:

1. Magic and religion are the domains of two kinds of social phenomena: beliefs and rites.

2. Both magic and religion are made up of cults, which are complexes of corresponding beliefs and rites.

3. The specific characteristic of religious and magic beliefs which distinguishes them from all other social opinions (representations) is the fundamental principle of the division of the universe into the sacred and the profane.

4. The division of the universe into the sacred and the profane is of a bipolar character. Because of their heterogeneity, the domain of the sacred is opposed to the domain of the profane.

5. The essential difference between magic and religion consists in that the latter has an integrative function, which is absent in the former.

6. The integrative function of religion is realized in the moral community of all those who participate in the same cult.

When we compare the conception of Hubert-Mauss with the conception of Durkheim, it is easily noticed that the latter not only draws upon but also develops the former. Durkheim not only accepts the statements of the authors of *Théorie générale de la magie* but expounds them, and makes them more accurate by introducing a number of important modifications. One such example, presented in *The elementary forms of the religious life,* are the notions of the sacred and the profane, which enable a more precise distinction of the sphere common for magic and religion from the entire domain of social phenomena. Another modification is the introduction of the idea of a Church through which the nature of an organized religious cult is explained.

The way Durkheim develops the conception formulated earlier by Hubert and Mauss does not infringe upon its founding principles, because both approaches are based on the same theoretical and methodological assumptions. The most dominant among them is the thesis of methodological antipsychologism in the version known as collectivism or extreme anti-individualism. It says that all social phenomena are irreducible to individual phenomena characteristic for particular members of a given social group. And thus, collective representations, which for instance magic or religious beliefs are made up of, defy reduction to the ideas held by single participants of a religious and magic cult. The thesis of anti-individualism is expressed in the recommendation that social phenomena be treated as things existing irrespectively of the consciousness of particular members of the investigated social group.

Besides antipsychologism and anti-individualism, methodological anti-holism is another determinant of the theoretical and methodological standpoint assumed by representatives of the school of *L'Année Sociologique*. Durkheim formulates it as follows,

> Now a whole cannot be defined except in relation to its parts. It will be more methodical, then, to try to characterize the various elementary phenomena of which all religions are made up, before we attack the system produced by their union (Durkheim 1965, p. 51).

When defining theoretical and methodological approach as positivistic, Durkheim and his coworkers strongly emphasized their difference from the positivism of Comte, Spencer or Mill.

Translated by Stefan Wiertlewski.

REFERENCES

1. Durkheim, E. (1956). *Les Règles de la Méthode Sociologique,* 13th ed. Paris.
2. Durkheim, E. (1965). *The elementary forms of the religious life.* New York: Free Press.
3. Hubert, H. and Mauss, M. (1973). "General theory of magic." In: M. Mauss (Ed.)'. *Sociology and anthropology* (in Polish). Warsaw: PWN.

Anna Grzegorczyk

RECONSTRUCTION OF MYTH IN THE
SEMANTICS OF A.J. GREIMAS

1. Theoretical Context of Greimas' Semiotics

A.J. Greimas is the chief representative of Semiolinguistic Research Group placing its scientific results in the mainstream of post-Lévi-Straussian structuralism, otherwise termed as neo-structuralism or anti-humanistic structuralism. This label though hardly precise, immediately describes the type of the humanities cultivated by the author of *Semanti-que structurale*. Hence, Greimas' declaration asserting that his semiotics concentrates primarily on: "the significance of the world to man as well as of man to man"[1] must be considered in reference to the assumption of this trend and not as isolated, which proves exceptionally misleading.

Thus contrary to what can be inferred from the above declaration it is not the understanding , subject-oriented and dominated by value-oriented type of the humanities. It is rather its scientific, i.e. "anti-humanistic" creation of the socio-cultural world. Greimas' semiolin-guistics is, on the one hand, a continuation of structural linguistics (F. de Saussure, L. Hjelmslev), structural science of culture (W. Propp, C. Lévi-Strauss) which results in its formal complication and specification and, on the other hand, tends toward a scientific epistemology of history, deprived of the antropological view as well as of personalized ways of thinking about culture, i.e. toward Foucault and Althusser.

Paradoxically, the interest in discourse, in the realm of human expression, gives rise to an impersonal view of humanistic phenomena. However, such an attitude does not revive the viewpoint of a natural historian within the frames of a positivistic variant. In neo-structuralism, especially in Greimas' concept, both the natural and the cultural image of the world are conceived of as the effect of an unintentionally structuring mind. Hence, here the impersonal approach to humanistic phenomena means a view beyond the subject-nature, or subject-object opposition. It is an approach which, in a peculiar way, annihilates the nineteenth century controversy within the humanities: the problem of a subjective

---

1. *Entretien avec A.J. Greimas,* Dilbilim 1976, p. 27.

versus a naturalistic concept of culture, in favour of a rival concept considering the subject/object opposition as groundless. A structure both unintentional and unrelated to any form of consciousness, becomes the original source of cognition, and otherwise, of the non-scientific world-picture.

Therefore, despite the difficulties, it is worth considering the author's aim, the thoughts and paths followed so persistently by him.

The history of contemporary linguistics, rooted in the theoretical reflection of F. de Saussure forms a point of departure; although remote — yet inspiring. De Saussure's definition of language as a system of signs, the differentiation of *langue* as a scheme opposed to *parole*-custom, the discrimination of form and substance as well as the distinction between the two components of *sign – signifiant* and *signifié* – all this amounts to the concept of meaning as inherent in language and contradicting the referential concepts. It is widely acknowledged that these facts were responsible for a new trend in linguistics. The ideas of the Genevian scholar were soon adopted by the Russian formalists, by the Prague structuralists as well as by the French structuralists who extrapolated the theoretical-linguistic assumptions upon other humanities, also by the Kopenhagen School which frequently developed the ideas through revision.

Disregarding the often considerable differences among the theoretical and methodological assumptions of the above schools, it can be generally stated that the previously enumerated assumptions survived and contributed to the establishment of structural semantics and semiotics. The extrapolation of these assumptions, a process of broadening the field of academic study, and their development were essentially based on:

(1) acceptance of the two homological planes of sign-*signifiant* and *signifié;*
(2) transposition of analytical methods applied to *signifiant* upon the plane of *signifié;*
(3) subdivision of lexical units into so-called minimal units, i.e. the isolation of semantic features following the example of distinctive features;

The above indicated contexts of scholarly tradition are crucial for Greimas theory, consciously derived from L. Hjelmslev, W. Propp and C. Lévi-Strauss.

2. A.J. Greimas: Semiotics

Semiotism, or even pansemiotism, is the assumption which underlies Greimas' theory and research. Reality is defined as meaningful, i.e. definable as an arrangement or group of various semiotic systems. Hence, there is no extralinguistic reality as an absolute reference; it has to be interpreted then as a certain articulation of reality delimited by a definite code. Evidently, this formulation of the assumption reflects only the very general idea of Greimas' semiotic reflection and it renders neither its historical complexity nor the theoretical nuances in which it was entangled. Its complete reconstruction would require more references to the tradition of semiotics. For the purpose of a lucid argument our choice concentrates on the crucial links pertinent to this proposition. There are three current definitions of semiotics[2] and Greimas chooses the definition which allows for widest theoretical perspective. Thus semiotics is defined as a meaningful set with a supposed autonomous internal organization. Such a definition of a meaningful set coincides with the notion of object-semiotics (*sémiotique-object*). On the other hand, the notion of subject-semiotics points to the problem of the dichotomy between the "natural" and the "constructed". Further on it leads to the subdivision of natural semiotics, comprising two large meaningful sets: a) natural languages, and b) extralinguistic contexts — semiotics of the natural world.

The priority of natural semiotics in relation to man appears as the chief argument supporting the classification above-mentioned. It means that man is "immersed" in the natural language and that he has been "projected" into the world of universal sense since the day of his birth. Man experiences these facts but he does not construct them. Still, Greimas concludes that the borderline between the natural and the constructed is not clear. It is frequently difficult to discern, within the semiotics of space, between the "constructed" and the "natural" space. The idea of a "natural" landscape is a cultural notion and is meaningful only in relation to space communicated by man. Therefore Greimas suggests the notion of macrosemiotics, comprising both natural languages and natural worlds, within which the particular semiotics are organized. The idea of natural worlds denotes "nature" as communicated by culture which renders them as relativistic and allows for the use of plural forms. As a consequence the notion of macrosemiotics is to be applied to various object-semiotics exclusively and their classification is to take into account the two following assumptions: 1) the natural world can be translated into natural languages; 2) other semiotics can be translated into natural languages only, a reverse process is impossible.

And so Greimas includes the following ideas traditionally related to

2. There are several meanings of the term "semiotics", e.g.: 1) any manifesting itself object of cognition, 2) object of cognition as it appears during and after its description, 3) a set of tools enabling its cognition; according to A.J. Greimas and J. Courtès, Sémiotique raisonnée de la théorie langage, vol. I, p. 339.

the notion of semiotics: the considerably altered idea of criterion of the natural *versus* the constructes with macrosemiotics and the idea of object-semiotics. He relates to the latter an important condition of the necessity of an explicit semiotic theory as semiotics requires both object-semiotics and a formulating, communicating and articulating semiotic theory. By this path, the relation of object-semiotics to a describing theory. Greimas follows Hjelmslev, especially his typology of semiotics. According to this typology the opposition of a natural *versus* a constructed criterion is substituted by the: a) criterion of "scientificity" ("descriptivity") resulting in a differentiation of object-semiotics and theoretical semiotics, i.e. a theoretical discourse about the object-semiotics; b) criterion of the number of planes of speech deciding on what planes of object-semiotics are considered and constituted by a given theoretical semiotics.[3] Here, a certain illusory duplicity growing around the Greimas' notion of semantics should be dissipated — one can speak. On the one hand, it denotes a theoretical discourse describing a given system of sign, i.e. the plane of expression and the plane of content. In consequence, it is a description assuming a parallelism of the two planes imposed by its organizing structure (a complex of relations). Already Hjelmslev asserted the preservation of structure during the passage from one plane to another and it is, in turn, his particular "generale". On the other hand, the notion of semiotics denotes the object of this theoretical discourse — the "twofold" system of signs it characterizes. It appears as a "duplicity" from a point of view external to Hjelmslev's concepts while within the concept it stands for identity. Both ways of understanding semiotics are supposed to have the same object of reference. Apparently, this identity

---

3. Referring to Hjelmslev one can differentiate: 1) single-plane semiotics (systems of symbols for Hjelmslev), scientific (e.g. algebra) and non-scientific (e.g. games); 2) double-plane semiotics (for Hjelmslev semiotics *sensu stricto*), scientific and non-scientific; 3) multi-plane semiotics — they are double-plane semiotics with object-semiotics forming one of the planes at least. They are classified according to their and the object-semiotics' scientific or non-scientific quality:

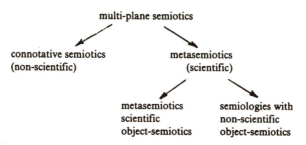

seems worth considering. Thus object-semiotics is derived from semiotics as theoretical discourse; it is created by the "logic" of a system of notions — by their structure — applied by, but independent of a scholar. This "logic" or structure imposes the object of discourse which, in turn, reproduces the same "logic" of structure. Hence object-semiotics is identical with semiotics as theoretical discourse and an analogical identity occurs for the planes of expression and content. It is an identity prejudged by the peculiar Hjelmslevian "generale".

3. Greimas: Semantics

The semiotic theory is, primarily, a theory of meaning, formulating the conditions of understanding and producing sense, i.e. semantics. At this point the concept of the author of *Du sens* enters the traditional linguistic field of semantics itself as well as its history. Thus again our argument requires a retrospective survey of the Saussure's and Hjelmslev's statements furnishing the basis of structural semantics. De Saussure's declaration that "language is form but not substance" is accepted by Hjelmslev as crucial for it renders possible the differentiation between *langue* and *parole,* and this opposition, in turn, allows for an intra-systemic concept of meaning — consequently, a conquest over its referential concept.

The discrimination of *langue* (language as system) from *parole* (concrete utterance, individual use of language) is of historical importance, contributing to the definition of language as an autonomous object of linguistic study. This differentiation, together with the acceptance of *langue* as language itself and *parole* as its external context, is an attempt at the liberation of language from heterogeneous elements (reference, substance). Simultaneously, it is an effort to discover the essence of language — its uniqueness, and to define it as an autonomous object of linguistic investigations. Language as *langue* becomes a "system of oppositions" devoid of any external context. Consequently, a sign is treated as something specific, not to be reduced to any physical or psychological phenomena, and its meaning — derived from the linkage of *signifiant* and *signifié,* defined by the position within language — emerges as intrasystemic. And this is the meaning of Saussurian "generale" — language is form and not substance — which Hjelmslev both assume and radically strengthens.

For the purpose of elucidating Hjelmslev's radicalization it is indispensable to specify, the so far seemingly obvious, notion of substance. Many scholars thought that the use of this concept in de Saussure's theory was open to doubt both due to its different applications in the philosophical tradition and to the sometimes unclear formulations of the author of *Cours de linguistique générale.* Questions arise mainly around the terms in which it should be defined: physical, notional, psychological or non-psychological. However the introduction of Hjelmslev's terminological precisions allows for a fairly explicit definition of the notion. Evidently, it is de Saussure from whom the author of *Prolegomena* derives his subdivision of speech (*langage*) into language (langue) *in abstracto* and utterance (*parole*) *in concreto,* the grounds for form-substance differentiation. Moreover, he makes them more specific by distinguishing two planes of speach: the plane of expression and of content, within which he discerns forms and substance.

	Content	Expression
Substance		
Form		

Both forms are "retained" for language in abstracto while both "substances" are removed into *parole in concreto.* Simultaneously the ambiguities concerning the notion of substance are elucidated due to the introduction of a new term — *meritum* – denoting the physical and psychological aspects traditionally associated with this idea. Thus Hjelmslev's terminology becomes much more elaborate than the Saussurian and comprises: content *meritum* (a formless reality, a shapeless continuum), content substance (a notional concept of reality), for of content (a system of designatum features), form of expression (a system of phonological features), substance of expression (concrete sounds) and *meritum* of expression (an unspecified continuum of sounds). The substance of content is achieved by placing the content's form against the meritum of content while the substance of expression by placing the form of expression against its *meritum.* Hjelmslev's example comparing *meritum* to a handful of sand, form to "little moulds" and substance to a mud pie, appears as a very useful illustration of these statements. To support this interpretation let me refer to Hjelmslev's own words: "Substance depends on form to the extent of conditioning its existence and under no circumstances can it be ascribed an independent one" or: "due to the forms of content and expression, and only due to them, there exist the substance of content and the substance of expression, which manifest themselves as the projection of form upon *meritum;* analogically to a net casting its shadow upon an undivided surface".[4]

Hjelmslev's formulation radicalizes de Saussure's statements. Language not only orders substance, as in *Cours* ..., but even calls it into being. Language not only creates the notional system but also, via "formative actions", delimits the borderlines of reality. It is within this context that Hjelmslev's "generale" concerning the determination of substance by form, should be conceived. This "generale" demands the removal of the substances of content and expression beyond linguistic interests as not essential for the definition of the "pure" features of language as a system. On the other hand, both of the planes are linked by a sign function and thus he recognizes the forms of expression and of content as planes upon which the intralinguistic, glossemantic action takes place. Hjelmslev's glossemantics is a concept of linguistics which leaves semantics beyond the borderlines of research, linguistics in which neither is the study of expression phonetics nor — the study of meaning semantics.[5] It concentrates on language as a form of expression and a form of content. They, in turn, define the intralinguistic constitution of meaning. These relations are mainly revealed by the commutation and substitution test. Communication denotes a change in the form of expression accompanied by a change in the form of content or vice versa; communication requires an exchange of two invariant elements (refers to disjunctive paradigmatic relations). There is no analogy between the opposites of both planes in case of substitution and therefore two variants are exchanges (refers to synonymous paradigmatic relations). Thus language becomes a structure in the sense of a network of interdependencies. These links may assume the shape of "functions" — either conjunctive (and-and) or disjunctive (either-or). Meaning is for Hjelmslev a linguistic abstraction to be described only by functions. Hence a sign is for the author of *Prolegomena...* "the function of the mutually assumed forms of content and expression".

The above indicated Saussurian-Hjelmslevian tenets are expressed by the three general statements on: the structural identity of the planes of content and expression (I), language as a form devoid of substance (II), the linguistic creation of substance (III) — and they become the grounds of Greimas' semiotic concept of myth.

Greimas' attitude to Hjelmslev parallels that of the author of *Pro-*

4. L. Hjelmslev, *Prolegomena do teorii języka* (Prolegomena to a theory of language), ed. H. Kurkowska and A. Weinsberg (Polish translation), Warsaw 1979, pp. 76-82.

5. G. Helbig, *Dzieje językoznawstwa nowożytnego* (Contemporary history of linguistics), Wrocław 1982, p. 64.

legomena ... to de Saussure. It results in enrichment and radicalization under the impact of the neorational trend in linguistics. The author of *Semantique structurale* — his theoretical reflection deeply rooted in the neorational tendency, with its tradition of content-oriented grammar (Cartesian linguistics, Humboldt, Sapir-Whorf) was capable of positing anew the problems of content and its description for the purpose of his favoured semiotics of myth.

Due to its background, Greimas' semantics becomes not only another version of the theory of meaning, supervising object-semiotics, but also a definite philosophy of culture. Therefore it is more frequently called general semantics (differently from the way the term functions in Hayakawa's or Korzybski's concept). Greimas' philosophy-semantics contains — as already mentioned — several propositions of the neorational trend in linguistics and assumes that:

(1)   Reflection concerning the world and ourselves is performed in a frame of the linguistic semiotic systems.
(2)   These systems delimit cognition.
(3)   Language organizes and establishes the semantic universe of our reflection and therefore
(4)   the theory of language is a theory of cognition and
(5)   semantic universes of natural languages are essentially determined by the inborn predispositions of species.

Greimas transforms some of the assumptions respectively. The initial assumption is essentially modified: reflection is subjected not only to the exclusively linguistic semantic system but to all possible systems of this type. However, language functions as macrosemiotics (cf. earlier statements) generating the remaining semiotics — it resembles a primary modelling system. The above statements are already supplemented by his own achievements:

(6)   the structure of any cultural text imitates language structure,
(7)   the textual microuniverse forms a textual equivalent of the universe of language,
(8)   the synchronic structure of language, especially of myth, defines the limits of what can be expressed.

The aim of thus formulated semantics is an attempt at constructing a universal model of human abilities to generate texts.

Let us concentrate on this attempt by introducing the characteristic terminology of the author of *Du sens* and by using the already mentioned tenets of our key traditions, i.e. the Hjelmslevian and neorational.

The starting point of structural semantics is its reference to Hjelmslev's first general assumption concerning the analogical construction of the planes of content and expression. This affords the conviction that the system of meanings can be reconstructed by following the "system of sounds" reconstructed within phonology. So the emphasis on the plane of content is to supplement the contemporary linguistic achievements. Greimas' programme focuses consciously on semantics, especially on the structure of content, though it is characterized in non-grammatical terms, i.e. non-Hjelmslevian. And thus the Dane's assumptions are considerably modified. For the purpose of elucidating the structure of content he introduces an elementary unit of meaning — *sème*:

> "Sème", as he remarks, usually defines a "minimal unit" (comparable with the proper feature of the distinctive one in the Prague School) of meaning; situated on the plane of content it counterparts *phème*, a unit of the plane of expression.[6]

Sèmes, minimal units of the semantic plane, are realized by numerous lexemes on the plane of expression. However, a clear distinction should be observed between the semic system and the lexical manifestation of its particular items. The subdivision of a word into semic elements, e.g. of the lexem cow — demonstrates that it consists of the following semes: "animal" + "female" + "domesticated". Lexem is not a simple semic collection but a hierarchically ordered set of semes. The semes within a lexem, are in hierarchical relations belonging to the heterogeneous semic systems. Each lexem contains a constant element, a constant semic minimum, the so-called semic stem (Ns), e.g. in lexem cow the semic stem is "animal" + "female" + "domesticated". Thus, evidently, a semic stem consists of a complex hierarchy of semes originating from mutually independent systems. Semantic shifts within a lexem are produced by semic variables, or otherwise, contextual semes (Cs). Assuming each lexem as constant, it is possible to observe which other lexems, sets of particular semes, can be contextually related to a given lexem, e.g. "a cow chews", but not "a cow turns green". In this way context serves as a system of agreements and disagreements between two semic sets which can, but need not, be related to them. Thus there is an intermediate unit between lexem and sem — semem, i.g. the sum of the semic stem and contextual semes. The notion of seme, semem and lexem enable us to reconstruct Greimas' concept of meaning.

Greimas, as we know, accepts Hjelmslev's general assumption. Therefore, in order to reconstruct the process in which meaning is formed, the notional apparatus of the above structural semantics can be related to these assumptions:

6. A.J. Greimas, *Sémiotique ...*, op cit., p. 332.

58

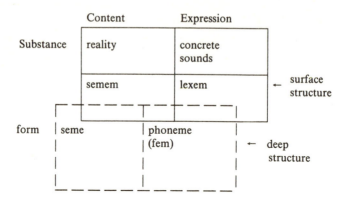

seme — an abstract unit, defined by the relation of a paradygmatic opposition to another such unit; element of the deep structure — form of content; an elementary unit of meaning, i.e. none of its elements enter as it does itself into structural relations;
phoneme — rendering of seme on the plane of expression of the same level; elementary unit;
semem — a unit of the plane of content — surface structure; complex, a combination of semes;
lexem — rendering of seme on the plane of expression of the same level; complex unit, a combination of phonemes.

Though Greimas evidently accepts Hjelmslev's concept of meaning as an intralinguistic category he discerns the twofold structure the forms of content and expression (absent in the author of *Prolegomena* ...) suggesting a structure of meanings with two levels. The importance of surface structure: semem is generated by the elements and relations of the deep structure. Thus semem may become a structural place open to be filled with substance. On the other hand, meanings from the level of deep structure are described in terms of semic oppositions between elementary units; it is a universal level, formed above the given natural languages. The universal element originates from the notion of deep structure used by the generative linguistics. The ambitious attempts at formulating a list of semic universals, follows the list of Jacobson's 12 binary phonemic universals. He suggests that 20 such categories are capable of producing several million of semic combinations, a quantity sufficient for the discovery of the semantic universe co-denotative with a given natural language.[7] Greimas conceives of the universal not in a cummulative sense, i.e. as a occurrence of the same semic oppositions in all languages,

7. Ibid., p. 327.

but in a distributive sense. His intention is to provide a complete list of all such possible oppositions. This repertoire of binary semic categories is not repeated by a given language as a whole but only partially realized. This repertoire contains such categories as, e.g. nature/culture, life/death, sacrum/profanum.

Basic grammar consists of the description of deep structure in terms of general semantics. The elementary structure of meaning, i.e. the already mentioned semic opposition relating the two contradictory terms (semes) S_1 and $S_2 : S_1 \rightleftarrows S_2$, becomes the fundamental notion of this grammar. The development and completion of this elementary structure by introducing the negation of its terms: $S_1 \rightleftarrows \bar{S}_1, S_2 \rightleftarrows \bar{S}_2$ leads to the so-called constitutive element: four-termed, enriched in relation to the elementary structure by the relation of implication and contradiction (cf. Aristotle's logical square). Accordnig to Greimas the constitutive model forms the foundation of our reflection on the world, it generates all meaning: "fournit un modele sémiotique appropriépour rendre compte des promiéres articulations du sens á l'interieur d'un micro-univers sémantique".[8] A complete characteristic of this model comprises, apart from its universal aspect still a) the paradigmatic aspect — links among semes, b) the taxonomic aspect — introduction of classifying order in the realm of object-references, and c) the generative aspect-production of value systems on the level of articulation (axiology, ideology), discursive, non-narrative forms, all dynamic processes and narrative syntax. The generative aspect is responsible for the possibility of transformational operations concerning the terms on the level of basic grammar. The number of these transformations is limited to the so-called algorythms. The syntax of algorythms is defined by the assumptions of interdependencies between paradigmatics and syntagmatics. Later this assumption will occur as fundamental one for the semiotics of myth. Let us propose a precise formulation: the syntagmatic aspect of narrative grammar, is conditioned by the paradigmatic aspect of the basic grammar, i.e. the level of deep narration. For the purpose of completeness, apart from an elementary structure of meaning, Greimas distinguishes — in the deep structure — an elementary axiological structure constituting the paradigmatics for syntactic valuating operations upon the semiotic square. As he claims, this allows for a perfect description of the colliding values in tragedy.

Constructing this comparative study of myth Greimas, as stated above, utilizes the notional apparatus of general semantics. However, he also borrows from the achievements of the founder of a structural approach

8. A.J. Greimas, *Du sens,* Paris 1966, p. 161.

to myth, the author of *Tristes des tropiques* although their adaptation by Greimas hardly can be accepted from the total point of view of Lévi-Strauss. Evidently, a methodological pattern for Lévi-Strauss methodology, including all the advantages, was provided by the Prague School. Therefore this study shares the one-sidedness of this trend in structuralism. This "one-sidedness" emerges in the treatment of the plane of content as the very last resort in the course of defining paradigmatic relations organizing, synonymously or disjunctively, the elements of the plane of expression. Besides similarity to the Prague School, Lévi-Strauss respects only paradigmatic relations. Nevertheless some of his assumptions either inspired Greimas' original concept or seem analogical to its statement despite their completely different origin. The following belong to the former: 1) myth belongs both to *langue* and *parole,* 2) myth tells about past events and formulates norms of understanding the world, 3) on a deeper level of abstraction there is a common code, determined by human predispositions, and which guarantees a free processing of varying information, 4) a chronological order of events — on the level of expression — follows a series of transformations, 5) these are three structural elements of myths: code, fittings (armature) and message. On the other hand, the thesis that myth is derived from the manner in which elements are related is analogical to Greimas' suggestions though, evidently, it can be deduced directly from Hjelmslev's intrasystemic concept of meaning. And these two lines of thought — Hjelmslevian and Lévi-Straussian — are interrelated in his comparative study of myth, where general semantics becomes metasemiotics and the mythic discourse — object-semiotics. The description of the particular levels of mythic discourse, otherwise its generative route — the constitutive process it follows — becomes his task. Let us first quote a metaphorical description from the author of *Du sens:*

la théorie sémiotique est amenée à concevoire le discours comme un dispositif en "pate feuilletée", constitué d'un certain nombre de niveaux de profondeur superposés, et dont le dernier seulement, le plus superficiel, pourra recevoire une représentation sémantique comparable, grosso modo, aux structures linguistiques "profondes" (dans la perspective chomskyenne): de ce point de vue, la grammaire pfrastique apparaitra alors comme le prolongement naturel de la graimmaire du discours.[9]

The introduction of certain explanatory statements concerning myth production is indispensable for the understanding of this metaphor.

Greimas' fundamental assumption refers to the narrativity of myth and, as his original idea, it results from the classification of myth as a

9. A.J. Greimas and J. Courtes, *Sémiotique ...,*

short story. It also affects the total argument of the author of *semantique*
structurale. Out of the numerous approaches to narration he chooses the
one emphasizing syntagmatic coherence, i.e. the necessary connections
between components. The properties of such narration are algorythmic
and transformational aspects. Considering the characterization of myth
Greimas suggests a description in terms of general semantics. Consequently, basic grammar — mentioned above — conditions the deep level
of narration both by providing its fundamental paradigmatics and,
simultaneously, determining its syntagmatics. Hence the terms of basic
grammar supply narration grammar with notions. And thus the elementary structure of meaning, isolated for the purpose of linguistic
expression, is applicable to the analysis of the elementary structure of
myth. The constitutive model, in turn, can be used for the construction of
a narrative deep structure model. Paradigmatic relations determine basic
narrative elements, i.e. actants. Actants are minimal units of narration
defined — analogously to seme — by relation of oppositions. The
elementary semantic structure of myth is defined by the relation of
opposition between two actants: A_1 and A_2. This elementary structure can
be developed due to its description on the basis of a constitutive model.
This model is governed by the rules of logic (implication, contradiction,
opposition) conditioning the syntagmatic model of narration; they
facilitate precisely defined lines of narrative sequence development. The
effect of these sequences depends on a definite choice triggering off a
given transformation while blocking another. The two models of myth,
on a deep level, are defined by paradigmatic disjunction operations
performed on narrative elements — actants: a) the taxonomic model —
obtained via paradigmatic disjunction relating actants in opposition, b)
the narrative model — obtained via syntagmatic conjunction joining
actants by necessary relations into narrative syntagms. Thus the taxonomic model contains a list of 6 binary actants: Subject/ Object,
Helper/Opponent, Sender/Addressee. Actantss in deep structure, can be
related as follows: Sender-Object-Addressee, Helper-Subject-Opponent.
They are the sources of the linear development of plot (action), achieved
due to the introduction of a third element, i.e. mediator, into the
paradigmatic opposition. The list of actants and their relations forms
peculiar semantic — syntactic universals of the deep level. The principles
of transformation comprise substitution, absence, confusion and en-
largement. They allow for a passage from the deep level of narration to
the surface level (form of content) and to the surface level of discourse
(form of expression). The structure of all possible relations concerning
actants and their activity within narrative syntagms is reflected by
combinations of actants and the subjection of the deep level of respective

relations to logical operations, e.g. assertion to attribution (gaining the object of value), negation — to domination (struggle between Subject and Opponent). The model includes three types of narrative syntagms to channel the activities of actants: contract syntagm (entering into contracts), disjunctive syntagm (departures and returns), performative syntagm (attempts). Analogously, on the plane of expression, i.e. the discoursive one, the organization of its units is defined by functions interrelating them, e.g.: 1) orientation (introductory situation or homeostasis), 2) complication (distortion of initial situation), 3) valuation (arrival of the hero and his test), 4) resolution (the salutary action of the hero), 5) coda (re-establishment of the initial situation). The narrative syntagms of the plane of content are realized by two narrative models: deceptive (*deceptif*) and reliable (*veridique*).

They are also responsible for narrative chaos in discourse as reflected, in particular sequences, by various figures of syntactic inversion. Thus, after these introductory commentations, it seems possible to associate the tenets of the comparative study of myth to the notional apparatus of general semantics:

	Content	Expression
Substance	histoire sequence of events	sequence of sentences
Form	narration II	discourse
	combination of actants and narrative syntagms	structure of narrative transfer message -functions narrative modes syntactic figures of sequence
		different levels of abstraction
	narration I taxonomic model constitutive model of narration	

The above scheme requires a brief comment. Evidently, the differentiation of such levels of mythic discourse becomes meaningful only

63

within the context of all the previous statements concerning general semantics, considering both the Hjelmslevian achievements and the inspirations of Lévi-Straussian of ethnology. Only then Greimas' declarations become comprehensible: 1) myth can be defined as "La mise en correlation (...) des cathégories sémiques",[10] 2) a taxonomic model defines the code, i.e. the formal structure constituted by a small number of semic categories; their combination can, by producing semems, report the total content, i.e. a part of given mythological universe, 3) narrative model — comprising both the deep and surface form of content, the so-called fittings (*armature*), go beyond the code and secure the syntactic coherence of myth; the rules of transformation super vise passages from deep to the surface structure; thus the fittings characterize myth as narrative structure, 4) narrative elements both of the plane of expression and content and of both levels (deep and surface) are defined by syntagmatic relations suppervising the intra-systemic formation of the myth's meaning, 5) owing to the analogous structure of both planes, the characterization of the deep structure can be applied to the description of surface form of content-narration as well as to the description of surface form of expression-discourse, 6) interrelation between the two planes can be tested by commutation, 7) the structural semantics of myth emphasizes the structure of content.

By assuming the mythic discourse as multilevel, Greimas prejudges both its method of production and its reading. To read a myth means to pass from one level to another. And here the author of *Sémantique structurale* transgresses the former statements. While reading a concrete myth the constructed intra-systemic notions be "projected" upon the substance of content. Thus it requires a shift from formal semantics — according to Greimas — via semiosis, a passage from the level of *langue* to *parole,* from the description of semio-narrative and discoursive competence to the description of a concrete *histoire* expressed in a defined utterance-discourse. Only at this point the generative route of mythic discourse is terminated.

4. Semeiosis of Myth
As Greimas observes, the meaning of myth depends on the interrelation of its elements. The interpretation of this thesis is ambiguous and should follow at least two lines of thought. The views, so far presented, suggest that message — the third structural element of myth, i.e. its peculiar

10. A.J. Greimas, "La mythologie comparée", in: A.J. Greimas, *Du sens,* op. cit., p. 134.

meaning, results from the co-operation of fittings (narration) and code (semic oppositions) — hence it is produced intra-systemically, structurally. To confirm the above, there appears a new descriptive tool, the so-called isotopy, i.e. "un ensemble de catégories sémantiques qui rend possible la lecture uniform du recit, telle qu'elle résulte des lectures partielles des énoncés et de la résolution de leurs ambiguités qui est guidée par la recherche de la lecture unique".[11]

Two varieties were introduced to specify the notion of isotopy, synonymous to semantic coherence, i.e. first, the discoursive-narrative and thus referring to the surface -lane of the form of content, second, the general-structural subjected to the deep level. This fact determines the two planes of meaning in myth. However it should be noticed that the problem of decoding the message as a particular meaning of myth is not limited to intra-language relations and notional differences. Contrary to Hjelmslev, Greimas is interested in the passage from the level of "pure" linguistics to reality, from form to substance. Hjelmslev was not interested in extralinguistic reality as his semeiosis was constituted by the two interrelated planes: the forms of expression and content. For the founder of these comparative studies the semeiosis connection should occur between the form and substance of content — the mythic language and reality. Semeiosis, generally, is a process of imposing "a notional network" — produced by the forms of expression and content — upon reality, contrary to the Hjelmslevian concept were form is imposed on meritum which, in turn, "creates" substance. Greimas, facing a concrete myth encounters an already formed reality as the primary semeiosis of a natural-cultural world what is done by the myth itself, and supplies the first substance of content. The secondary semeiosis equals the "projection" of intra-systemic notions and relations upon substance I, i.e. the mythological reality. The results of mythic semeiosis, i.e. the form of a given myth, becomes a reality for the comparative study of myth and renders secondary semeiosis as indispensable. The twofold structure of mythic language determines a two-stage semeiosis present in perspective isotopes. The sequence of events ordered according to the actant discoursive model produces narrative-surface isotopy. As a result message equals plot summary. However, deep-structural isotopy leads to the only required reading as resulting from the imposition of a taxonomic — i.e. code and fittings or, otherwise, semic oppositions transformed via the constitutive model — deep narrative model upon a concrete myth (set of

11. A.J. Greimas, "Pour une théorie l'interpretation du récit mythique", in: A.J. Greimas, *Du sens,* op. cit., p. 188.

myths). After the mythic reality had been bestowed with features derived from the semantic model, the concealed meaning of myth, i.e. the norm (set of norms) of viewing reality is discovered.

Translated by Ewa Kębłowska-Ławniczak

Barbara Kotowa

ANTINATURALISTIC PRINCIPLES OF
SYSTEMATIZING STATEMENTS IN ART STUDIES

In the considerations presented below a certain trend in the dispute on methodological model of the humanities is expounded. The dispute started on the turn of the 19th century between adherents of the antinaturalistic conception of the cognitive status of the humanities and their naturalistically oriented opponents. For particular problems this dispute has been continued in the philosophy of science till nowadays. The issue of interest here refers to methodological characterization of definitional determinations of particular models of empirical sciences. It may be formulated as a question about the principle systematizing the "whole", an example of which is a system of statements constituting a given discipline of scientific knowledge. In other words it is a question concerning the way of ordering the informative content accumulated by a given empirical discipline, which in the form of appropriate statements constitutes a certain logically coherent "whole". Depending on the kind of relations combining particular statements of that "whole", one can speak about a higher or lower level of methodological maturity of a given discipline.

The methodological model of 19th century humanities, in the form in which it became the aim of the antinaturalists' attack in the above mentioned dispute, was constituted, as it is known, on the basis of the epistemology of classical positivism, a conception which in an early phase of its development was connected mainly with the practice of natural sciences, functioning as the field of philosophical verbalization of a socio-subjective context of this practice, i.e. of methodological knowledge. The latter is understood here as a certain system of normative and directival beliefs respected by scientists — representatives of a given discipline of knowledge. The positivistic "version" of the humanities formed in this way, gained obviously, as if in consequence, a number of features characteristic for the natural sciences "picture" of scientific knowledge. Therefore, this model should be treated not as an effect of the reconstruction of norms and methodological directives, characterizing the real course of investigations of scientists-humanists, but rather as a normative transposition of the positivistic way of thinking about natural sciences into the domain of the humanities. As it is usually assumed, the methodological "picture" of the humanistic inquiry, as a matter of fact, followed the model of natural sciences, which in turn, it should be stressed, was built according to the positivistic images of its creators about the methodological characteristics of these sciences. This thesis is exemplified by the ideas of J.S. Mill whose methodological conceptions, as belonging to the most widespread at the end of the 19th century as far as the orientation of naturalistic positivism is concerned, were most often the object of the criticism conducted by antinaturalists. In book VI of his *System of logic* devoted to "moral and social sciences", as he calls the humanities, Mill states right out that,

In substance, whatever can be done in a work like this for the Logic of the Moral Sciences, has been or ought to have been accomplished in the five preceding Books; to which the present can be only a kind of supplement or appendix, since the methods of investigation applicable to moral and social science must have been already described, if I have succeeded in enumerating and characterizing those of science in general.[1]

Let us consider again the methodological suggestions of the author of the *System of logic,* this time concentrating mainly on this point of his positivistic model of "the science in general" which in its antinaturalistic version is the leading topic of these considerations, i.e. at the point concerning the way statements are systematized in empirical sciences. According to the declaration of methodological naturalism, contained in the above quotation from the English philosopher, this way is also obligatory in the practice of the humanities. For Mill, explaining is an activity which orders all the statements of a given empirical discipline. He writes that explanation "means resolving an uniformity which is not a law of causation, into the laws of causation from which it results, or a complex law of causation into simpler and more general ones from which it is capable of being deductively inferred".[2] In this case we deal, as can be seen, with a nomothetic ordering of all the statements of a given discipline, the ordering in which the explanatory operation, deductive in character, plays the role of a systematizing factor, referring to positivistically understood laws. However, the factor which, according to Mill distinguishes the application of the explanatory procedure in "moral and social sciences" from its application in other empirical sciences, is the acceptance of psychology as the explanatory basis by representatives of the former disciplines. Of course, it was psychology in its 19th century

1. J.S. Mill, *System logiki* (Polish translation of: *System of logic ratiocinative and intuitive*), Warsaw 1962, vol. 2, p. 536.
2. Ibid., p. 18.

version. That is why, statistic or strictly general statements formulated as psychological laws, generally assumed only implicitly, occur usually in the explanans of the applied deductive explanation.

To sum up the remarks presented so far, let us note that positivistic methodological naturalism (Mill's conception can be accepted as its representative version) prefers such a model of the humanities in which the structure systematizing the whole of the statements of a given discipline is an explanatory structure (so that one statement entails another one in logical sense because of definite laws).

The positivistic attitude towards one of the basic factors constituting the methodological model of the humanities (generally — of empirical sciences), which has only been sketched here, met with a strong opposition of the antinaturalistically oriented adherents of the methodological "vision" of this discipline of knowledge. In particular, they usually reject the conviction about the possibility of occurrence of both laws and theories (as systems of laws) in the humanities ("studies of culture" in the terminology of the majority of them). Therefore, the role of the units of knowledge ordering all the statements constituting a given discipline, is attributed by them to variously characterized and variously called nonnomothetic types of systematizing relationships. In this situation one cannot consider explanation in the sense discussed above; a kind of a psychic operation is an oppositional correlative of this scientific inquiry for antinaturalists. They most often call it "understanding" and it is based on "inner" experience of an intuitive-irrational or intuitive-intellectual character which is opposed to the "outer" experience of the natural scientists.

In the following parts of this paper I will undertake a detailed discussion of some typical ways in which this antinaturalistic (and simultaneously antipositivistic) "understanding" intuition was used in various variants of methodological antinaturalism as a tool for systematizing statements in the "studies of culture" ("cultural sciences"), and particularly in theoretical and methodological reflections on art.

I

I shall start the analysis with the conceptions of W. Dilthey. His name was undoubtedly most strongly associated in the methodological consciousness with the antinaturalistic orientation in the humanities.

The protest of the author of "Erlebnis und Dichtung", expressed in his well known opposition: "Erklären — Verstehen", founded, as it is generally accepted, the antipositivistic turning point in the studies of culture against the positivistic thesis about the methodological homogenity of natural sciences and the humanities. This distinction was founded on, common for the whole antinaturalism, as the starting point, opposition between two kinds of experience, namely the sensual ("outer") experience of natural scientists on the one hand and directly-intuitive ("inner") experience of humanities on the other. The essentially distinct character of the humanities against natural sciences is in Dilthey's conceptions connected with "understanding", i.e. a special cognitive procedure considered to be the basic method of the humanities. This claim about understanding is typical not only of those from the times of the antipositivistic turning point but also of those continuing studies on symbolic culture. The difference between the humanities ("Geisteswissenschaften" as he calls the studies of culture) and the natural sciences "is the difference of the tendencies creating their subject in the procedures which determine these groups of disciplines", says the author of *Einleitung in die Geisteswissenschaften*; "there a spiritual object comes into being, here a physical object comes into being in the frame of the study"[3]. "The whole of the socio-historical reality", the study of which Dilthey considers to be the principal task of the humanities, becomes the subject of its studies only "when human states are experienced, when they are manifested in expressions of life and when these expressions are understood".[4] Therefore, if "understanding" consists in the relation of the expression of life to the inner sphere, then applying it "we take up the procedures which in any respect have no analogies to the methods of natural sciences".[5]

Two basic moments describing Dilthey's conception of "understanding" are of crucial significance for the role which the German philosopher ascribes to this way of investigation, preferring its cognitive importance for the humanities against the "intellectualized" explanation used in natural sciences. Therefore, "understanding" is, firstly, a certain kind of intuitive cognition, but a specifically humanistic intuition is meant here, and secondly, this intuition is irrational (aintellectual) and therefore nonconceptional.

The first of the indicated moments, having its antinaturalistic correlatives in such cognitive categories as the phenomenologists' "eidetic insight", Spranger's *a priori* intuition or the Bergsonian type of intuition, is to enable, according to Dilthey and other adherents of this kind of

---

3. W. Dilthey, "Der Aufbau der Geschichtlichen Welt in die Geistwissenschaften" (Polish translation), in: Z. Kuderowicz, *Dilthey*, Warsaw 1967, p. 162.
4. Ibid., p. 163.
5. W. Dilthey, "Das Verstehen anderer Personen und ihrer Lebensäusserungen" (Polish translation), in: Z. Kuderowicz, *Dilthey*, Warsaw 1967, p. 204.

71

cognitive power, a direct, individual contact with the investigated cultural
reality. Such a character of the cognitive act guarantees the scholar that
the results of investigation obtained in this way are adequate and valid to
a degree not requiring any additional justification. Thus, intuition is in
this case a firm basis of humanistic knowledge.

As far as the other moment is concerned, the irrational character of
"understanding", this quality originates from the inner experience which
is the fundament of this intuitive cognitive power, but which however,
should be in principle opposed to the "intellectualized" introspection, i.e.
the one which is the starting point in Fechner's and Wundt's atomizing
psychology practised as a natural science. The latter distinguishes in an
unnatural way the particular elements of the subjective "experiential
wholes" and aiming to them in a form of discursive concepts, thus
intellectualizes them. Contrary to the atomizing psychology, a wholistic
comprehension of a given subjective experience is just the determination
of Dilthey's conception of the inner experience. Thus, the comprehension
is nonconceptional, irrational and as a result

> the whole understanding (...) is irrational (...). Therefore it cannot be represented
> by any formulae of logical procedure. And the final, although quite subjective
> conviction which is inherent in this reproductive experience (one of the mental
> operations which constitute the entire psychic understanding — note by B.K.) does
> not require additional checking of the cognitive value of conclusions presenting the
> reasoning process. These are the borders which the nature of reasoning itself raises
> to the logical treatment of it.[6]

From the two kinds of "understanding", distinguished by Dilthey,
elementary and higher — to the latter he attributes a particular role in art
studies. "Elementary understanding" enables the scholar (thanks to the
sphere of objective spirit) a direct comprehension of these elements of the
spiritual life ("the simplest experiential wholes") of other people which
take the form of "simple manifestations", i.e. activities or their results
such as single gestures, concepts or judgements available to sensual
perception. In turn "higher understanding" allows to comprehend senses
of much more complicated ("complex") forms of spiritual life; they consist
in particular structural "wholes" resulting from the combination of
singular elements whose outer manifestations can be, for example, a work
of art, the personality of an individual, a cultural trend or a historical
period. The process of self constituting of the senses of such "wholes"
within "the higher understanding has three phases and comprises the
following cognitive acts": 1) the transposition of "one's own ego" on a
given "complex" result of the spiritual life (the so-called "insight in the

6. Ibid., p. 203.

72

object"), 2) imitation which means the reproduction in oneself of the "sense" relations combining the particular elements of the experienced "whole", 3) reconstructive experience (Nacherleben), i.e. a repeated wholistic experience.

Let us stress that the process of "higher understanding" expressed in the three indicated phases, possesses *sui generis* features of the inductive procedure. However, it is such an induction in which, according to Dilthey, "a general law is not inferred from an incomplete number of cases" but "a certain structure, an ordered system subordinating the particular cases to the whole is made up of them".[7] An important property of the way in which this structure is constituted consists in that, that it must be given directly to the scholar, it must be experienced by him. Here the different character of Dilthey's irrational induction as opposed to its natural sciences' correlative is clearly seen.

One can easily notice that "understanding" based on direct "inner experience" is the factor determining relationships between particular statements in studies of fine arts, conducted in Dilthey's manner. However, its "higher", "nonelementary" form is taken mainly into consideration because it first allows a reconstruction of the complicated spiritual structures expressed in "complex" manifestations of spiritual life, to which, according to Dilthey belong also works of art. Thus, in this conception, the relationships systematizing all the statements constituting a given discipline of the humanities, and particularly the art studies, can be called the relationships of understanding.[8]

These relationships occur in several versions. One may distinguish here relationships of understanding occurring between statements describing certain "wholes" of spiritual life (e.g. the spiritual structure — "personality" — of an artist) and statements containing descriptions of particular systems of elementary "manifestations" of the spiritual life (e.g. the description of the structure of his work, its sense being characterized by statements describing the structure of the former kind).

One can encounter other kinds of relationships of "higher" understanding dependencies between elements within a given spiritual "whole" come into play. The relationships occurring here combine the statements characterizing the "place" or "function" of a given element in a given structural "whole" with the statements ascertaining the fact of their occurrence. Thus, these relationships can be called "the relationships of

7. Ibid., p. 205.
8. See J. Kmita and L. Nowak, *Studia nad teoretycznymi podstawami humanistyki* (Studies on theoretical foundations of the humanities), Poznań 1968, p. 32.

structural functioning of particular elements within a given spiritual whole".

The third type of relationships, which one can distinguish, occurs between statements determining a given spiritual structure and statements describing its type, e.g. the type of romantic personality. At the same time, it is assumed that the latter statements are inferred from the former ones, although the entailment occurring here does not have, according to Dilthey, an entirely discursive character (because of the concrete way of comprehending the types of spiritual structures in the inner "understanding" experience).

II

Another version of antinaturalistic treatment of the problem of systematizing statements in the art studies is present in those programmes to which a certain "version" of the studies of culture patronizes. This "vision" is representative for methodological antinaturalism in the variant realized by the Baden School of Neo-Kantism but it takes advantages mainly from the achievements of its most prominent representative — H. Rickert.

In order to grasp the specifity of this way of conducting art studies making use (explicitly or implicitly) of certain assumptions of Rickertian type of antinaturalism, let us recall some essential theses of this methodological attitude.

Similarly as for other representatives of this trend, the central point of the programme of humanistic studies postulated by H. Rickert is the problem of method, its confirmity with the studied object and simultaneously adequacy of the cognitive results obtained in this way. Rickert, taking into consideration projects of Windelband who divided all empirical sciences on the basis of the "formal" (methodological) character of their aims of investigations into nomothetic (formulating laws) and idiographic (dealing with singular historical facts), introduces another division, complementary to the previous one, and using a double objective and methodological criterion distinguishes between natural sciences ("Naturwissenschaft") and studies of culture ("Kulturwissenschaft"). The specific features of the disciplines included into the latter of the listed types of sciences is, let us recall it, that they employ a special method of investigations, the usage of which consists in "reference to values" ("Wertbeziehung") of the (potentially cultural) cognitively analysed phenomena. Strictly speaking, these phenomena are "referred to values" through the concepts describing them and their individualizing character is due to this reference. Their content refers only to singular, unique ("happening but once") phenomena because the value ("significance") of a historical phenomenon describing this content is of an unparallel character. This feature distinguishes "historical studies of culture" ("historical", i.e. studying significantly unique phenomena) using these concepts, from the natural sciences ("studies of nature") operating with generalizing concepts ("of classes"). "History (understood as a science — a note by B.K.) considering reality in the aspects of that which is individual, starts — remarks the author of *Die Grenzen der naturwissenschaftlichen Begriffsbildung* – where the natural sciences end, which consider this reality in the aspects of that which is general."[9]

Thus, the fact of "relating" certain values to all these "real" objects is a feature which distinguishes them — a Rickertian scholar makes them the subject of "historical studies of culture" and together they constitute the domain of culture. These values according to him "are respected by everybody (...), or at least by everybody within a given cultural community"[10] (where they function as the "reflected" light of the "second kingdom" of transcendental values).

These values could be explicated as "cultural values" in the following sense: particular states of affairs, indicated by normative judgments expressing them, generally respected in a given cultural community as the aims to be realized, are thus assigned a specific role in the practice of a humanist. They function as a criterion distinguishing cultural phenomena, which are unparallel, the only ones of this kind, because the reason why they are valuable is that they differ from other phenomena and therefore, as stated above, the concepts attributed to them are of individualizing character.

Rickert's "cultural values", as the reference point of the cultural phenomena, decide also about further phases of their cognitive elaboration. Namely, their use allows to establish causal relationships between particular phenomena constructed as "cultural facts". They are to express the "historical" significance, "historical" importance of their particular parts representing the "causes". In this way singular, unique cultural phenomena are arranged into unique series tending towards a higher and higher degree of realization of particular values, to which they are referred and which were assumed by a scholar as the basis of distinguishing them. The causal relationship linking the elements of this series is equally unique, specifically "historical" and singular as those phenomena. This distinguishes it in an essential way from the correlative

9. H. Rickert, *Die Grenzen der naturwissenschaftlichen Begriffsbildung*, Tübingen 1913, p. 273.
10. H. Rickert, *Die Probleme der Geschichtsphilosophie*, Heidelberg 1924, p. 63.

75

relationship in the natural sciences. While the latter one is always a consequence of a general regularity corresponding to a certain law,

the discovery of individual relationships characterizing the first one does not lie in a complete subordination of a cause and an effect to a causal law — Rickert remarks — because then they would lose their individuality and at the same time would no longer be historical events.[11]

Let us add, that being a result of "reference to values", these structurally unique series of cultural phenomena linking the elements of their cause and effect relationships, are the first effect of the cognitive procedure employed, according to Rickert, by a historian to order the available evidence. The latter category consists of, as we could interpret it in the manner of contemporary methodology, all the practically available states of affairs constituted by the source evidence which is treated in the inquiry as the empirical starting point.

Having presented this sketch of Rickert's version of the antinaturalistic method of cognitive consideration of cultural phenomena, we can now pass on to the topic problem of this paper, namely to the way of systematizing statements in the studies of culture as it was assumed by the Baden philosopher.   This way, as it is not difficult to notice, is defined by the cognitive operation described above which, following the author of *Kulturwissenschaft und Naturwissenschaft*, has been called here the principle of "reference to values". In the conception analyzed here, this principle plays a role analogous to that which Dilthey and Spranger attributed to "understanding", i.e. a function of the basic epistemological norm regulating the course of research activities undertaken in the process of studying the phenomena of cultural reality.

Particular phases of elaborating "historical evidence" on the basis of this principle consist in: 1) the construction of the so-called "cultural facts", 2) establishment of causal relationships occurring between them, 3) formulation of historical syntheses ("historical representations"). They lead to the systematization of states of affairs ascertained by appropriate statements always according to a definite value (or a set of values) representing a certain axiologically differentiated state of affairs. It is easy to notice that this moment in an essential way distinguishes Rickert's principle of "reference to values" employed as the factor systematizing statements in particular disciplines of the humanities from its oppositional correlative — explanatory operation used in natural sciences. The order in which the above-mentioned states of affairs ("cultural facts") follow one another expresses the degree in which the differentiated value

11. H. Rickert, *Die Grenzen ...*, op. cit., p. 294.

increases. Thus, it is an order of axiological character which by Rickertian type of antinaturalism is opposed to a nomothetic order based on entailment relationships between statements. Obviously, the latter type of systematizing cannot be taken into consideration in the case of Rickert's principle of "reference to values" as the factor systematizing the investigated statements because, in effect of the realization of a particular value, it is excluded by the "purely" individual character of cultural phenomena and causal interrelationships occurring between them. Therefore, "singularity" and "uniqueness" of "cultural facts" constructed on the basis of Rickert's conception, make them resist generalizations. Instead, they require an idiographic way of investigation; in turn it is known that every idiographism excludes the formulation of any laws.

Passing now to the domain of art studies, the antinaturalistic idea of establishing cultural, particularly artistic, facts in the manner defined by Rickert's principle of "reference to values", can be found in the theoretical reflections on literature of the French sociologist R. Escarpit.

Considering the problem of the "borders of literature" in the work "Le littéraire et le social", the author states first that:

> Selection of various literary facts is the only common feature of the various ways of understanding them. A certain closed system, which is of interest here, gains coherence when it is based not on material subjected to selection but on a selective attitude which is the principal cultural behaviour of every elite society.[12]

Then he refers to the statement of R. van Tieghem characterizing this "attitude" (and method as a matter of fact) which is representative for his own ideas on this subject. And this is the respective quotation, "*Selection* is the first operation: only that which possesses a certain value and this being a literary value, i.e. a certain minimum of art, is worth the name of literature".[13] It is not difficult to notice, that the synthesis of the history of literature constructed on the basis of the systematizing criterion understood in this way, would be an idiographic description of chronologically ordered literary works with reference to the axiological sphere. R. Escarpit explicitly predicts such a situation himself in the conclusions of his considerations devoted to this problem, stating that,

> when one talks about literature, then, whatever way the problem is approached, in the end we are forced either to accept without questioning some prior premises, system of values or ontology, or to resort to an impressionistic subjective evaluating judgement.[14]

---

12. R. Escarpit, "Le littéraire et le social", quoted after: *W kręgu socjologii literatury* (In sphere of the sociology of literature), Warsaw 1980, vol. 1, p. 210.
13. R. van Tieghem, "La littérature comparée", quoted after: *W kręgu ...*, op. cit., p. 10.
14. R. Escarpit, "Le littéraire ...", op. cit., p. 213.

The attitude of R. Wellek and A. Warren, the authors of *Theory of literature*, towards the treatment of historical process (historical synthesis) seems to be Rickertian *in spirit*. Seeking such a method of studying the history of literature, which would allow this discipline to be both "historical and literary", the two authors after criticizing the historically known and most often used methods of systematizing literary works, conclude that,

> The solution lies in relating the historical process to a value or norm. Only then can the apparently meaningless series of events be split into its essential and unessential elements. Only then can we speak of a historical evolution which yet leavs the individuality of the single event unimpaired. By relating an individual reality to a general value, we do not degrade the individual to a mere specimen of a general concept but instead give significance to the individual.[15]

III

M. Weber who refers his "picture" of this sphere of reality to basic ideas of Rickert's conception of culture, proposes within the postulated programme a methodological approach which, however, differs from Rickert's. It is namely the principle of systematizing the evidence which stands in opposition to the positivistic (or more generally — naturalistic) nomothetism.

Thus, Weber similarly to the author of *Kulturwissenschaft und Naturwissenschaft* accepts that the phenomena constituting culture gain their characteristic status only when they are interrelated to definite values, and this is the definitional determination of the concept of culture. One can read in one of the main treaties of this scholar that,

> Empirical reality is culture for us because, and only, when it is considered in reference to the ideas of value (*Wertideen*) it comprises these and only these components which become significant to us because of this reference (...). Culture is, from man's point of view, a finite fragment, endowed with sense and significance, of a senseless infinity of events in the world.[16]

An essential difference between the conceptions of these two authors, the consequences of which are important for the way in which they solve the topic problem of this paper, manifests itself, as it has been mentioned, on the methodological level of their reflections on the studies of culture.

---

15. R. Wellek and A. Warren, *Teoria literatury* (Polish translation of: *Theory of literature*), Warsaw 1970, p. 352.
16. M. Weber, "Die Objektivität sozialwissenschaftlicher und sozialpolitischer Erkenntnis" (in Polish translation), quoted after: *Problemy sociologii wiedzy* (Problems of the sociology of knowledge), Warsaw 1985, p. 72.

Thus, in Rickert's case, the domain which he names "culture" and defines as "all the phenomena to which values are attributed" is itself a certain theoretical construct, the construction of which occurred as a result of "reference to values" of singular phenomena cognitively analyzed with the use of concepts describing them. Therefore, we face here a situation in which the process of the world of culture constitution is at the same time also the process of its knowing.

Weber treats this problem in a different way. In opposition to Rickert, he clearly distinguishes in his conception two "levels" of conceptual articulation of cultural phenomena, two "levels" of studying them. 1) The level of spontaneous self constitution of cultural reality within the frames of — as one could say using the terminology of contemporary reflections on culture — irreflexively occurring acts of participation in culture. According to Weber this consists in "attributing sense and significance" to particular manifestations of culture, i.e. referring them to particular "ideas of value". 2) The level of reflective and scholary analysis, scientific elaboration of the world of culture constituted in this way. In other words — the level of proper reflections on the studies of culture. In this way, in opposition to Rickert's attitude, the process of participation in culture, for Weber does not equal to the process of investigating it in the scholary sense. What for Rickert is the point of "destination" — a cognitive effect of undertaken scholary operations in the form of a description of the sphere of "cultural facts", which are determined by the "reference to values", i.e. the facts constituing culture, in Weber's programme is treated as the "starting point", the proper object of investigations of the "studies of culture". Such an object is built of an empirically given system of facts of culture and next it becomes an aim of investigations. Thus, this is the point at which the problem of method appears for Weber. He solves it in a generally antinaturalistic way, stressing that

> distinguishing and systematizing the constituent parts of reality (tinged by reference to ideas of valuation — B.K.) from the point of view of their cultural significance, is an attitude which is quite different from the analysis of reality according to laws and systematization in general terms. Both types of mental constructions of reality do not remain in any necessary logical relationship.[17]

The method of studying cultural phenomena, postulated by Weber (and consequently used by him in scholary investigations) is known as the conception of "ideal types", and is a development of Rickert's theory of individualizing concepts. What Weber calls "cultural sense" has its

17. Ibid., p. 69.

correlative in Rickert's "cultural value" by reference to which each individualizing concept is constituted.

Let us recall here, that this conception is an effect of Weber's idea of studies of culture which are free of justification. Therefore, besides the role of ideal types as a factor systematizing the investigated material, which is of our interest here, they play also another role — a means for neutralizing scholar's acognitive cultural evaluations.

Returning to the title subject, let us first see what the procedure of constructing ideal types is like in order to show the essence of their systematizing "effect".

The domain of culture, delimited earlier by "reference" of its culture, delimited earlier by "reference" of its particular phenomena to "ideas of evaluation", i.e. constituted in acts of attributing them "senses and significances" which are important from the point of view of these "ideas", is the starting point for a scholar following Weber's methodological directive. The latter category is explicated here in terms of contemporary (socio-regulative) theory of culture, as normative beliefs generally respected within a given society and designating worldview (*Weltanschauung*) senses of activities, i.e. senses usually of an extrapractical character (e.g. religious).[18] Thus, a scholar having to do with thus "created" fragment of cultural reality as an object of his studies, should first reconstruct this set of beliefs — "ideas of evaluation" — which combining "senses and significances" with particular phenomena gave them the status of cultural phenomena. Next he should write down this "content" explicitly in the form of a definite system of judgments characterizing noncontradictorily the phenomena denoted by them. In this way he will obtain an idealizing description of a given set of phenomena, i.e. a description of ideal types; in other words a certain mental ideal-type construction being a form of a descriptively elaborated "idea of evaluation" (or their set). Weber, characterizing this "construction" remarks that

> in its conceptual purity this ideal picture never occurs empirically in reality (...), and thus a historian's task is to find in every *particular* case to what degree reality approximates or departs from this ideal picture.[19]

Thus, Weber's ideal types denoted by concepts and ideal-type statements do not refer to reality in the way in which "varieties", "generalizing" concepts are used in natural sciences, and therefore they cannot

---

18. See A. Pałubicka, *Przedteoretyczne postaci historyzmu* (Pretheoretical forms of historism), Warsaw/Poznań 1984, p. 109.

19. M. Weber, "Die Objektivität ...", op. cit., p. 81.

80

serve — using the author's words — "as a scheme to which reality would be subordinated as a specimen concretization". They are rather "mental means for spiritual subordination of empirical data and nothing else".[20] For Weber the above opposes the humanities to the natural sciences.

Let us see now what is the essence of the subordination by a scholar of an empirically given cultural reality with the help of Weber's method of "ideal types". Strictly speaking, it is a question about the role of the set of ideal-type concepts constructed on the basis of a particular abstract theory (e.g. economics determining the mental "picture" of a potentially real cultural reality in the process of studying its empirically given correlative.

The basic goal of the systematizing activities of scholar-humanist, relating ideal-type construction to the empirical sphere of culture, is the selection of the given material, aiming at determining the causal relationships within its scope. To attain this goal, he should confront an ideal type with an appropriate real system of cultural phenomena. If it turns out, as an effect of this operation, that the "system" shows sufficiently distinct similarity to its "model" — an ideal-type formulation — especially with regard to the causal relationships, then the system may be (hypothetically) regarded as the domain of the discussed type, and next described (conceptually rationalized) in ideal-type terms. The real empirical causal relationships comprehended in this way, are — also hypothetically — a representation of appropriate relationships which occur "inside" an ideal type. Besides, what should be specially stressed, they are always individual in character, which excludes finding out any nomological necessities in reference to them. As Weber says,

reconstruction of a complete causal sequence of any concrete phenomenon in the whole of its reality is not only practically impossible but it is even an absurd undertaking. We choose only these causes to which "essential" components of an event can be *related* in a given sense. The problem of cause — adds the author — where individuality of a phenomenon is concerned, is not a question about laws but about concrete causal relationships.[21]

Summing up this sketchy characteristes of Weber's principle of systematizing statements in the humanities, let us remark that it is possible to consider it in two aspects: from the point of view of: i) content and ii) form.

Thus, on the one hand, when analyzing this principle, one may point to such features of Weber's "systematization" of defined cultural facts, as homogenity, uniqueness or singularity which means that

20. Ibid., p. 85.
21. Ibid., pp. 70-71.

81

the "comprehensed" order is only a "temporal", "momentary" state of affairs of a distinctly idiographic character. In the aspect of its content the method proposed by the author of "Die Objektivität sozialwissenschaftlicher und sozialpolitischer Erkenntnis" is obviously a continuation of Rickert's approach to this problem, or more generally: it is in the methodological sense basically in agreement with the antinaturalistic "vision" of cultural reality.

On the other hand, singularity, uniqueness or idiographism — in a formal aspect — corespond to universality, generality or nomothetic order as features characterizing the ideal-type construction itself. Every essential assignment of this construction to a determined system of real cultural phenomena is always only singular. Particularly, the ideal-type laws functioning here are fulfilled only once in reference to singular situations — their formal "shape" is "obligatory" only "within" the ideal-type system.

The conception of studying cultural reality in the way which takes into consideration the basic idea of Weber's method of ideal types, is quite often employed in scholarly inquires on particular domains of art. H. Wölfflin's theoretical and methodological proposal of studying artistic phenomena within fine arts is one of them.

IV

Antinaturalistic intuition as a kind of direct "inner" experience, opposed to the "outer" experience of natural sciences, is also the basis of these conceptions of systematizing evidence which are characteristic for art studies conducted according to the premises of phenomenology. A short discussion of the systematizing principle of this kind will be presented here in Ingarden's variant of this orientation. In particular it will be referred to the programme of literary studies postulated by the author of *Dispute on the existence of the world*. This programme is an exemplification of his basic philosophical ideas, especially within the scope of our topic subject.

To show the relation between the phenomenological method of direct investigation, known as "eidetic intuition" (in its intellectualistic version differing from Dilthey's irrational intuition) and the methodological principle which is of our interest here — let us first recall some of the basic "ideas" of Ingarden's phenomenology. It seems to be necessary for the clarity of further discussion.

The basic assumption of a philosopher-phenomenologists, which the author of the *Disputes on the existence of the world* shares with other representatives of this orientation, is the statement that "appropriate ideas exist to any objective being", i.e. certain "universals" which "are characterized by a peculiar *duality* of formal structure".[22] Because of this feature, an idea can be considered "from two sides": in the aspect of idea *qua* idea (determined by an appropriate selection of properties) and in the aspect of its content. This content, in which are present "*ideal* concretizations of a certain plurality of (pure) ideal qualities",[23] i.e. a definite system of "constants" and "variables" as well as their mutual relationships should be discovered in order to comprehend the "essence" which is a correlative of the studied object — "a properly qualified individual object". Inquiries of this kind are realized, as it is known, in the already mentioned acts of eidetic intuition.

The above assumption, particularly when referred to studying such an individual object as a literary work (or work of art in general), possesses obviously, specified methodological implications. One of them is, as if appointed "authoritative", the way of systematizing the "material" which consists of particular works more precisely of statements of literary studies referring to them.

So this attitude is, generally, determined within the phenomenological theory of literature (art studies) by a system of appropriate statements obtained earlier as an effect of *a priori* ("essential") analysis of the general idea of a literary work during ontological studies. These statements about the work of art, being of ontological nature and referring to its structure (the basic structure is typical for it because of "the nature of things"), are — according to Ingarden — of a "strictly general" character. Thus, they can be referred to any literary work which is not connected with any concrete literary period (this results from the fact that the ontology of the contents of the general idea of a literary work is the subject of studies, and not particular literary works about the existence of which nothing is assumed here). Therefore, ontological statements, as the primary ones, are for Ingarden a theoretical basis for any statements which are formulated in particular parts of literary studies on a literary work.

Thus, ontological statements about a literary work, as cognitively primary, play directly the role of a factor systematizing the "material" of literary studies (art studies) in Ingarden's methodological programme. All other statements referring to this intentional object are "secondary" in relation to them. However, if it is remembered that these "primary" statements were formulated by the philosopher on the basis of an eidetic

22. R. Igarden, *Spór o istnienie świata* (Dispute on the existence of the world), Warsaw 1962, vol. 1, pp. 45, 51.
23. Ibid., p. 51.

intuition, then one has to accept, that also in this case, similarly as for Dilthey or Spranger, an antinaturalistic intuitive cognitive power is the systematizing factor, although in the variant considered now, the systematization is indirect.

Translated by Stefan Wiertlewski

Andrzej Szahaj

REFLECTION ON THE METHODOLOGY OF SOCIAL SCIENCES IN THE CRITICAL THEORY OF JÜRGEN HABERMAS

According to Habermas, the problem of understanding (*Verstehen*) is the central issue of social sciences. This problem is closely connected with the approach to the category of "sense" (*Sinn*) of social actions. Hence methodological considerations focused on "sense" and "understanding" form an integral whole.

The questions mentioned above are the point of departure for the model oppositions of methodological orientations in social sciences constructed by Habermas. Theories in which the category of "sense" is ignored or treated as a minor one can be labelled as objectivistic-naturalistic. The main feature of these theories is their failure to recognize the fact that social reality is subjectively mediated, i.e. that it is always — as Habermas puts it — "symbolically structured". This ignorance results in elimination of understanding as a procedure giving access to the data, and in the postulate that social research should be based exclusively on the observation of behaviour (behaviourism), or on the models of self-regulating systems taken from biology or cybernetics (functionalism, system theory). In this way the specific subjective (based on conscious-ness) dimension of social life is essentially missed.

Other theories, in turn, do recognize the necessity of the procedure of understanding because they realize how significant "sense" ("meaning") is in the methodology of social sciences. And so they recognize the fact of the subjective creation of social reality, but, at the same time, they overlook the existence of both unintentional mechanisms and structures of social life, and their impact on the subjective processes of interpreta-tion of reality. In this way these theories lead to peculiar idealism.

Another crucial opposition is connected with the nature of pre-theoretical intuitive knowledge to which a social researcher resorts in order to be able to arrive at an understanding interpretation of the field of cognition under investigation. For, as Habermas points out, the researcher cannot avoid resorting to some prior knowledge (*Vorwissen*) which springs from his participation in the structures of the social life-world (*Lebenswelt*) of his own social group. Also the social subjects being studied and the products of their sense-creative activity belong to certain life-worlds of given social groups and, what follows from this, are likewise endowed with some scope of unconscious intuitive "knowledge". The basic problem boils down to the feasibility of grasping the structures and the content of this knowledge. Habermas indicates two possibilities here. One can surmise that this knowledge exists and believe, at the same time, that it has no status of knowledge in the strict sense. Accordingly, one cannot grasp its non-local rules and components which transcend particulars. In this situation a form of phenomenological "insight", imitative projection of oneself into an object of contemplation (empathy) or some other form of intuitive analysis is postulated for the identification of this knowledge. As a result humanistic cognition does not even reach the level of intersubjective explanatory knowledge. One can, on the other hand — most often in response to the difficulties outlined above — ignore the existence of the afore-said knowledge and content oneself — in accordance with the naturalistic assumptions — with mere observation of behaviour. According to the author of *Zur Logik der Sozialwissenschaften,* neither one or the other approach is well-founded. For in the former case we are dealing with subjectivistic distortion, whereas in the latter case — with objectivistic aberration. Habermas is convinced that pre-theoretical knowledge acquired in the process of socialization includes universal components which make possible participation in social communication as such. In this connection he postulates the methodological strategy of "rational reconstruction" of the rules of compentece of social subjects — the rules which are responsible for the existence of the universal core of intuitive pre-theoretical knowledge. However, still before the presentation of the methodological approach postulated by our author, let us reconstruct the main points of Habermas' critique of the methodological orientations dominant in modern social sciences, the crucial elements of his peculiar double fight — against the "objectivistic-naturalistic" approaches and against the "subjectivistic-idealistic" ones.[1] At the beginning, however, we shall present an outline of the argumentation of the author of *Zur Logik der Sozialwissenschaften* against a certain methodological strategy which has been and continues to be expected to

1. This paper is basically concerned with two out of three possible stages of methodological reflection of the author of *Zur Logik der Sozialwissenschaften,* i.e. the stage at which Habermas was working out his own standpoint in the course of making critical analyses of existing methodological-theoretical standpoinds, and the stage at which he articulated his own model of methodology of social sciences on the basis of the paradigm of communication theory. Whereas I omit the first stage marked by the participation of Habermas in the so-called dispute concerning the positivism in West-German sociology (see T.W. Adorno and others, *Der Positivismusstreit in der deutschen Soziologie,* Luchterhand 1970).

help to work out the theoretical foundations of the traditional procedure of understanding. I mean the strategy in which it is assumed that the subjects of action are rational and on this basis their behaviour is being interpreted (explained).

1. The Shortcomings of "Normative-Analytical" Approach

As Habermas observes, the assumption taken from economy that the action of social subjects is of a rational nature has a considerable popularity in social sciences. It refers to the question of the rational choice of the optimum mode of action on the basis of the relation of preference, provided that there are alternative means to accomplish the preconceived aim of action. The approach marked by this assumption is labelled by the author *Zur Logik der Sozialwissenschaften* as "normative-analytical" and qualified as remaining under the influence of the model of goal-rational action. Sciences which make use of this assumption are, in Habermas' opinion, at the service of technical cognitive interest.[2] For, although they themselves contain no information about empirical regularities (hence their "analytical" nature) nor, as Habermas puts it, about "technically utilizable knowledge of the first level", they still to provide information about the goal-rational choice and strategy; information based on the supposition that this knowledge is used. It is for this reason that these sciences constitute technical knowledge of the second level.[3]

According to Habermas, theories of rational choice refer only to a certain extreme variant of action, namely to the goal-rational action. Failing to recognize the variety of possible models they normatively assume that this type of action is a standard one. It is due to this one-sidedness and lack of empirical content — in Habermas' opinion — that these theories are scarcely useful for empirical studies in social sciences.

2.   The Criticism of the Objective-Naturalistic Orientations

Among the theories which postulate to abandon the procedure of understanding, behaviourism, of course, is the most prominent one. In his argument with representatives of this methodological orientation Habermas clearly stresses the fact that human actions cannot be grasped unless the intentions which govern them are taken into account. These

---

2. See J. Habermas, *Erkenntnis und Interesse,* Suhrkamp 1968.

3. J. Habermas, "Ein Literaturbericht" (1967), in: J. Habermas, *Zur Logik der Sozialwissenschaften,* Suhrkamp, Frankfurt/M. 1982, p. 153.

intentions, in turn, can be expressed by linguistic means. In these circumstances the limits of human world are set by the limits of language — Habermas says — and this is what distinguishes *human actions* from *animal behaviour*.[4] The fiasco of behaviouristic strategy becomes immediately apparent when one goes beyond the declarations of its adherents in order to analyze their actual research practice. It turns out then that they actually incorporate some anticipations of intentional connections into the explanatory premises which they rely on presupposing that the behaviour being analyzed is understandable.[5]

Habermas maintains that social sciences are interested in subjective sense and meanings, cultural tradition and systems of values only in so far as they have become institutionalized in a system of social roles. Therefore, theories which study action focused on institutionalized values and socially respected norms cannot be restricted to the analysis of mere internal subjective meanings and senses of these actions. Likewise, they cannot be confined to the study of mere empirical objective context of actions which can be observed without analyzing subjective beliefs. This is, however, what theories relying on functionalistic paradigm and systems theories do. Logical genesis as well as the "rational core" of these theories are seen by Habermas in the fact that they take into account the actually existing objective context of social actions. Although this context is not intended by the acting subjects, it is still an effect of certain intentional actions. The aim of functionalistic analysis is to grasp the relations between objective and subjective (consciousness-based) components of social actions. A definite state of social system is the point of reference here. The functionalistic assumption is applied in order to explain the persistence of this state. Habermas's chief objection to functionalism as well as to system theory[6] refers to the feasibility of both the identification of the states of balance of a social system and the means of this identification actually adopted within these paradigms. In his opinion it is impossible to conceive of an objective state of balance which a social system would "strive" to maintain. Both functionalism and system theory try to conceal this fact, though with little success, by defining parameters of the afore-said state of balance in an *arbitrary* way. Functionalism might become a theoretically fruitful model of explanation if it abandoned its ahistorism; if it thus took into account the fact of the historical changeability of the socially recognized systems of values

4. Ibid., p. 182.
5. Ibid., p. 178.
6. See J. Habermas and N. Luhmann, *Theorie der Gesellschaft oder Sozialtechnologie - Was leistet die Systemforschung?*, Suhrkamp, Frankfurt/M. 1971.

and norms which are the only possible basis for the identification of each state of balance of the system. It is doubtless for Habermas, however, that even in the form in which it has hitherto existed, functionalism has one essential advantage: it follows for the theoretical identification of the role of these social contexts which are of an objective nature, i.e. cannot be reduced to the sum of subjective opinions, senses and values. In this perspective functionalism emerges as a potential antidote against the idealistic aberration in social sciences.[7]

3. The Criticism of the Idealistic-Subjectivistic Orientations

As the German theorist further points out, in order to make theoretical terms operational a stem must be made in the humanities which has no counterpart in natural sciences. What is meant here is the understanding interpretation by means of which the objects of the social reality being examined are transformed into "data". The problem with such an interpretation lies in the fact that it requires taking into consideration each of the visions of this reality produced within the network of subjective interactions on the basis of the commonly respected convictions of a given social group. For, in Habermas's opinion, W.I. Thomas has aptly noticed that: "If one defines situations as real they are real in their consequences"[8] It would thus seem that rules of interpretation should be adjusted each time anew, as it were, to particular symbolically pre-structured objects. In this context Habermas makes a detailed analysis of a number of methodological conceptions which try to cope with this problem by resorting to the phenomenological analysis (Schütz, Garfinkel, Cicouerel, Goffman). The conclusion that follows from these considerations is unequivocal. Phenomenologically oriented sociologists always start with the horizons of their own life-worlds and then, by means of abstraction and generalization, try to get to the essence of sense-creative subjective activity as such. However, what they actually manage to grasp is only a particular fragment of a given life-world identified in the act of phenomenological intuition. In this way, however, the specifically social intersubjective nature of the life-world is being missed. In order to describe this nature it is not enought to simply generalize one's own particular phenomenological experience. One should rather pay attention to the intersubjectivity of the structures of language and communication which ensures both the objectivity of communicationally established structures of *Lebenswelt* and, at the same time, the

---

7. J. Habermas, "Ein Literatubericht ...", op. cit., pp. 185-186.
8. Quoted after J. Habermas, ibid., p. 219.

90

possibility of maintaining the uniqueness of the individual forms of existence.[9]

According to Habermas, none of the variants of phenomenological sociology goes beyond the subjectivistic version of research in social sciences. This means that in each of them the existence of an objective context of action which affects the subjective motives of starting the action is disregarded. This context includes, among others, social institutions, systems of social action (e.g. the system of socially organized labour); binding — embodied in the structures of law and morality — global worldviews (*Weltbilde*). Moreover, phenomenological research is not valid even for the analysis of the subjective context of social actions, nor for the analysis of modes of creating social reality and establishing the intersubjective sphere of social symbolic communication. For one cannot abstract from the fact that the rules of the subjective interpretation of reality are essentially the rules of language, in terms of which acting subjects define each context of action and communicate.

Wittgenstein has noticed what escaped the attention of phenomenologists, namely that there is a close connection between language and life-practice. In this way it has become possible to grasp transcendental rules, according to which social life-worlds are constituted, on the level of linguistic analysis instead of that of phenomenological insight. It has turned out that social actions can be analyzed in the same manner as internal relations between linguistic symbols can. In this way, however, as Habermas points out, linguistic analysis has sublimated society into a conjunction of symbols placing social facts entirely on the level of the systems of signs. It has become especially visible in the theoretical approach of P. Winch who used the late Wittgenstein's ideas to propose a certain vision of research in social sciences.[10] Winch assumed that social actions are so closely combined with forms and structures of linguistic communication that the intersubjectively valid meaning is simply embodied in the observable modes of behaviour. These meanings, in turn, owe their inter-subjectivity to the primary character of linguistically mediated interactions. Hence the norms which govern the actions can be grasped by means of the analysis of linguistic communication. This is what Habermas writes about Winch's approach:

(...) he dissolves sociology in a peculiar linguistic analysis. (...) People act as they speak and therefore social relations are of the same kind as the relations between sentences.[11]

9. Ibid., p. 235.
10. See P. Winch, *The idea of a social science and its relation to philosophy,* London 1958.
11. J. Habermas, "Ein Literaturbericht ...", op. cit., p. 255.

91

The problem that faced Winch was — according to Habermas — how to secure the status of generality for his own theory which transcends the particularism of language games analyzed each time anew. So the point was to construct a theoretical approach within the framework of which the translation of various language games as well as of the results of analyses of these games would be possible. Winch tried to solve this problem in the way that reminds, according to Habermas, of Dilthey's approach:

A language analyst may slide imitatively from the uninvolved position into the grammar of any language game breaking free from the connections with the dogmatics of his own language game which is valid for the analysis of language as such. Winch like Schütz naively relies on the possibility (of the existence — A.S.) of pure theory[12]

— concludes Habermas in order to remark subsequently that:

If we carry on the linguistic analysis which is meant to be descriptive and do away with therapeutic self-limitation, the monadic structure of language games must be overcome and the context in which the pluralism of language games is only being constituted must be clarified. Then, however, the analyst's language cannot simply coincide each time with a given objective language. Both linguistic systems must be mutually translatable, similarly to the very language games being analyzed.[13]

According to Habermas, hermeneutics is the philosophical and methodological conception which has recognized the necessity of this translation. Here, among others, lies one of its greatest merits. It is well known, however, that Habermas's attitude towards Gadamer's hermeneutics is ambivalent. Since the discussion between the author of *Zur Logik der Sozialwissenschaften* and the author of *Wahrheit und Methode* widely resounded in philosophical and methodological literature, it seems

12. Ibid., p. 264.
13. Ibid.
14. See among others: D. Misgeld, "Critical theory and hermeneutics: The debate between Habermas and Gadamer", in: (ed.) J. O'Neill, *On critical theory,* New York 1976; P. Riceour, "Ethics and culture — Habermas and Gadamer in dialogue", *Philosophy Today* 17/1973; T. McCarthy, "Language, hermeneutics, and the critique of ideology", in: T. McCarthy, *The critical theory of Jürgen Habermas,* Cambridge/ Mass. 1978; A.M. Kaniowski, "Krytyczna teoria Jürgena Habermasa a punkt widzenia hermeneutyki" (The critical theory of Jürgen Habermas and the viewpoint of hermeneutics), *Studia Filozoficzne* 11/1980; Z. Krasnodębski, "Rozumienie i emancypacja. Spór pomiędzy teorią krytyczną a hermeneutyką" (Understanding and emancipation. A dispute between critical theory and hermeneutics), *Archiwum Historii Filozofii i Myśli Społecznej* 25/1979; A. Szahaj, "Moc refleksji a siła tradycji, autorytetu i przesądów" (The power of reflection and the force of tradition, authority, and superstitions), *Studia Metodologiczne* (forthcoming).

unnecessary to remind of it even in short. Let us only mention that, according to the former author, the humanities cannot treat language as an absolutely autonomous sphere — which is what hermeneutics seems to be actually doing. For social life is constituted equally by three elements: work, language and domination.[15] The two elements which complement language in this triad have a crucial impact on it which has to be taken into account in humanistic research if one does not want to slide into the idealism of analyzing subjective sense without discovering the objective context in which the sense originates.

4. The Methodological Implications of the Communicative Conditions for Understanding and Interpretation

Let us now proceed to the "positive" standpoint of the theorist in question. The theory of communication (communicative action), which he has been developing since early 1970s, has become the basis of Habermas's vision of research in social sciences. He presented the premises of this theory — gradually modified and evolved — in a series of publications.[16]

And so, the author of *Theorie des kommunikativen Handelns* assumes that linguistic communication, which is one of the elements of establishing social reality, has a claim-structure. The point is that speakers engaged in speech acts have to make four essential kinds of validity claims (*Geltungsanspruche*). These are: the claim to the truth of a proposition which refers to the state of affairs in "objective" reality; the claim to correctness or validity of the normative conviction expressed in a given speech act; the claim to credibility of intention conveyed; and, finally, the claim to comprehensibility of the linguistic phrases used in a given speech act. The necessity of making these claims characterizes *a priori* all com-

15. J. Habermas, "Ein Literaturbericht ...", p. 309.
16. See J. Habermas, "Vorbereitende Bemerkungen zu einer Theorie der kommunikativen Kompetenz", in: J. Habermas and N. Luhmann, *Theorie der Gesellschaft oder Sozialtechnologie – Was leistet die Systemforschung?;* J. Habermas, "Toward a theory of communicative competence", *Recent Sociology* 2/1972; by the same author, "Was heisst Universalpragmatik", in: *Vorstudien und Erganzungen zur Theorie des kommunikativen Handelns,* Suhrkamp, Frankfurt/M. 1984; by the same author, *Theorie des kommunikativen Handelns,* Suhrkamp, Frankfurt/M. 1981.
17. The introduction of the category of *Lebenswelt* as the necessary background of every symbolical communication has become a particularly essential modification. Culture, understood as a scope of intuitive knowledge activated in communication processes, is one of the essential components of a life-world in this conception. See J. Habermas, *Theorie des kommunikativen Handelns,* vol. 2, *Zur Kritik der funktionalistischen Vernunft,* chapt. VI (Zweite zwischenbetrachtung: System und Lebenswelt).

munication in a natural language and all symbolical communication based on it. The fact that it is unavoidably necessary for the participants to assume a "yes" or "no" attitude towards validity claims is also an immanent feature of this communication. Beside it is essential that natural language communication is possible only if there is a tacitly accepted background of common cultural convictions to which the partners in communication resort when they want to reach an agreement on some issue. We shall soon observe how Habermas utilizes these premises of the theory of communication to present a certain original vision of the strategy of understanding in social sciences. Before we present this strategy, however, let us focus for a while on the line of reasoning of Habermas advocating the necessity of employing this strategy:

The principle of subjective meaning — or better — of understanding interpretation refer to the access to social facts, to establishing the data. As controlled observation is replaced by the understanding of symbols, the subjectively intended sense is provided only in combination with symbols. This principle also specifies the basis of experience in sciences concerned with action. Experience is connected here not with private perception of sense, the intersubjectivity of which is guaranteed only in connection with the instrumental action controlled by success, but with linguistic communication.[18]

Hence:

If we do not want to abandon intentional actions as data in social sciences, the system of experience in which these data are accessible is linguistic communication and not observation free from communication.[19]

The following schema shows the differences between the experimental basis of natural sciences and that of social sciences.[20]

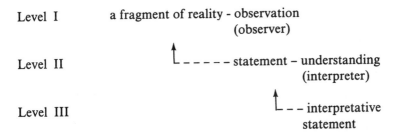

Level I   a fragment of reality - observation
                              (observer)

Level II   statement – understanding
                              (interpreter)

Level III   interpretative statement

The differences between the levels in the schema illustrates the

18. J. Habermas, "Ein Literaturbericht ...", op. cit., p. 158.
19. Ibid., p. 159.
20. J. Habermas, "Ein Fragment (1977): Objektivismus in den Sozialwissenschaften", in: *Zur Logik der Sozialwissenschaften,* p. 595.

differences in access to objective reality. Observation or sensory experience refers directly to this reality, whereas interpretation does so only indirectly — through the understanding of statements about reality. It is even possible — as Habermas claims — to distinguish between two worlds each having a different objective status: the world of states of affairs established independently of symbolical statements (subjective interpretations of reality), and the world of symbolical objects which convey certain meaning and symbolically represent something from the former world. The connection between the objects from the two worlds is contained in the propositional content of every speech act.

As Habermas further says, we can talk about deep structure and surface structure — which are revealed in the course of scientific research — in relation to both the former world (states of affairs) and the latter one (symbolical statements). The structure of the former world consists of the observations of single empirical phenomena or of regularity of their occurrence reflected in observational propositions. Its deep structure, on the other hand, consists of general patterns which underly these phenomena and regularities reflected in theoretical statements. As far as the latter world is concerned, its surface structure consists of symbolical objects, while its deep structure consists of the rules of consciousness according to which these objects have been created; that is to say — the rules of respective subjective competences. The pre-theoretical stage of understanding refers, according to Habermas, to the understanding of the sense of symbolical objects, whereas the theoretical stage includes the reconstruction of the rules which generate these objects. Pre-theoretical understanding is identical with assuming the status of a member of a given life-world in which the meanings attached to given symbolical objects have originated. Thus, it does not go beyond the competence of a layman who "inhabits" this life-world. We are dealing with the theoretical understanding in the case when a social researcher wants not only to employ intuitive knowledge of the social life-world which he finds in the domain of interpretandum, but also to reconstruct it. And so the wish to grasp the rules of competence, which a subject must possess if he generates correct symbolical utterances (objects), is essential in the theoretical approach.

So far it follows from our considerations that Habermas has no doubts that it is not possible to gain access to the objective domain of social sciences unless one uses the procedure of understanding (understanding interpretation). However, in order to recognize correctly the methodological status of this procedure[21] a distinction has to be made first

21. Habermas rejects the — in his opinion — entirely inadequate methodological

between the understanding interpretations applied by researchers and those applied by participants in interactions who coordinate their actions on the basis of the conception of sense used in everyday practice. In the last instance this conception is to lead (and does lead) to the consensual establishment of the socially binding definition of a situation, which includes also the decision about what is to be treated as an "objective" reality, as socially binding normative background, and finally — as the sphere inviolable privacy of an individual. A scientist does not have to strive to come to an agreement of this type. Thus, he does not have to confer with participants of interactions about his interpretation of reality (objective, social and individual). This is because he functions in a different system of action — the system of science. So like an actor he aims at reaching a goal which has to be recognized by taking into account a system of reference different from the one being studied. In this sense a researcher can be treated only as a virtual participant of the structure of interaction (objective domain) under examination. However — as Habermas claims — the acts of interpretation performed by a scientist and those performed by the social subjects under examination differ only with respect to their functions and not to their structure. For the assumption underlying each act of explication of the sense (meaning) of a given symbolical utterance is that one adopts a yes/no attitude towards it. This is inevitably connected with the very essence of all communication. As Habermas observes:

> A social researcher encounters *symbolically pre-structured objects.* They embody the structures of pre-theoretical knowledge which was used by the subjects, capable of speaking and acting, to generate these objects.[22]

In this situation the identification of rules according to which the aforesaid objects are generated must become the essence of research in social sciences. However, if we assume that in principle one has to belong, in a way, to *Lebenswelt* in which the rules are in force if one wants to

---

vision of the procedure of understanding formulated by T. Abel in his notorious text — "The operation called *Verstehen", The American Journal of Sociology* 54/1948. As it is known, Abel suggested that the procedure of understanding should be based on the projection of introspectively established principles of behaviour of the researcher into the behaviour under interpretation. These principles may claim the status of universal statements due to their straightforward nature as the come from the observation of one's self. According to Habermas, the way in which subjects behave is determined by social factors that cannot be grasped by means of any introspection whatsoever. They rather require — what Weber called *Wertinterpretation* - the understanding focused on the meanings and values in their more objective symbolical form.

22. J. Habermas, *Theorie des kommunikativen Handelns,* vol. I, "Handlungs-rationalität und gesellschaftliche Rationalisierung", p. 159.

96

become familiar with them we can do nothing but accept the fact that the understanding of given symbolical structure requires (at least virtually) participation in their generation. This is the very assumption that Habermas adopts. In this way, however, the sharing of pre-reflective, pre-theoretical knowledge, which provides for the generation of correct (in a given life-world) symbolical utterances, with all members of a given life-world is the condition of the cognitive grasping of a given domain of research. The generation of symbolical utterances, however, is never disinterested. On the contrary, it is always directed towards the possibility of reaching an agreement. It clearly follows from this that: "The *understanding* of a symbolical utterance requires on principle the participation in the process of reaching an agreement."[23] On the other hand, the participation in the process of reaching an agreement and of communication is impossible unless one adopts the performative attitude which is connected with positing validity claims concerning the speech acts performed and with particular attitudes towards these claims. Hence, a researcher cannot either limit himself — even if he wanted to — to grasping the mere semantic content of an utterance, he has to adopt a certain attitude towards the validity claims raised by the subjects together with their utterances which are the objects of interpretation.[24] Each adoption of an attitude, in turn, presupposes reference to certain standards of evaluation. The interpreter's standards, which are introduced by him to the research field being interpreted, by their very nature require to be accepted. Hence, even virtual participation in communication processes remains in the bonds of direct participation — an interpreter, like any other partner in communication, adopts a certain standpoint and claims its universal validity. In this case, however, the researcher loses his distinct position as it turns out that he shares the evaluation competence with the actors he studies. At best his competence may be founded on different grounds (standards). Furthermore — together with introducing his own value standards (or with accepting the existing ones) — an interpreter activates pre-theoretical knowledge. In this way he naively, as it were, (unconsciously) co-produces (*Mitgestaltung*) the social reality which he is studied, by mixing his own pre-theoretical knowledge with the knowledge being reconstructed; the one that governs the existing domain of research. In this situation, according to Habermas, if social sciences are to gain the objectivity of scientific cognition the above-mentioned naivety must be overcome. How is this, however, possible? The chance for making

23. J. Habermas, "Ein Fragment: Objektivismus ...", p. 550.
24. J. Habermas, *Theorie des kommunikativen Handelns,* vol. I, pp. 168-170.

understanding interpretation more theoretical lies in the postulate of the reconstruction of communication structures (in Habermas's theory this task is to be fulfilled by the communication theory developed in terms of the so-called universal pragmatics) and of universal components and structures of pre-theoretical knowledge each time activated by those who participate in communication. This knowledge is, in Habermas's opinion, the content of common subjective competences which are indispensable to the generation of symbolical utterances. The theory of socialization, developed within the paradigm of Piaget's developmental psychology,[25] combined with the theory of social evolution,[26] should provide an explanation of the ways in which individual competences are formed and of the ways in which they penetrate into the level of superindividual competences of the whole species.

In the context of "the reconstructive understanding" presented above hermeneutics — reformulated in the spirit of the communication theory — receives a special role. According to Habermas the destination of hermeneutics is to tie the torn threads of agreement. This also, or perhaps first of all, refers to the interpretation of the texts, originated in the past, the sense of which is not fully understood today. One way of grasping this incomprehensibility may be, according to the author in question, to differentiate between the context which the author assumed for this text and the context in which an attempt is made to understand the text.

The task is — he writes — to construct the definitions of situations assumed in the text on the basis of the life-world of its author and its addressees: The life-world (...) shapes the horizon of communication processes whereby the participants (in communication — A.S.) may come to an agreement or consult each other on some issue in the objective world, in the social world shared by them, or in each time subjective world. An interpreter may tacitly assume that he shares the formal references to the world with the author and his contemporaries. He tries to understand *why* the author — convinced that given states of affairs exist, that given values and norms are respected, and that given experiences can be ascribed to particular subjects — advanced certain claims in his text, observed certain conventions, or disregarded them, expressed certain intentions, dispositions, feelings and so on. Only in so far as the interpreter perceives the *grounds* on which the author's utterances emerge as rational ones (*vernünftig*) does he understand what the author's opinion may have been. Within this background one can identify

25. See J. Habermas, *Zur Rekonstruktion des Historischen Materialismus*, Suhrkamp, Frankfurt/M. 1976; by the same author, *Moralbewusstsein und kommunikatives Handeln*, Suhrkamp, Frankfurt/M. 1983; by the same author, "Notizen zur Entwicklung der Interaktionskompetenz", in: J. Habermas, *Vorstudien und Ergänzungen zur Theorie des kommunikativen Handelns.*
26. See J. Habermas, *Zur Rekonstruktion des historischen materialismus,* and by the same author *Theorie des kommunikativen Handelns,* vol. 2, the fragment: "Entkoppelung von System und Lebenswelt" (chapt. VI).

98

single cases of deviation (*Idiosynkrasien*), i.e. such standpoints (*Stellen*) which cannot be comprehended simply on the basis of the very assumptions of the life-world shared by the author with his contemporaries. (...) The sense of the text can be revealed only from the cognitive, moral and expressive components of the cultural scope of knowledge on the basis of which the author and his contemporaries constructed their interpretations.[27]

A question arises, however, what is the procedure whereby the interpreter can identify the assumptions that underly the context in which a given text originated? In accordance with the communication theory there can be only one answer to this — the procedure is to adopt (at least implicitly) some attitude towards the validity claims concerning the text. If the interpreter refused to adopt such an attitude one could suppose that he is not interpreting anything, i.e. he is not striving to eliminate the distortions in communication between the author, his contemporaries and ourselves.[28] If, however, he is doing an interpretation he quite naturally assumes the performative attitude also when he is trying to identify (reconstruct) the presuppositions hidden and at the same time revealed in the text.

5. A Few Comments

Habermas's opinions about the methodology of social sciences doubtlessly deserve an extensive and detailed commentary for which unfortunately there is not enough space here.[29] The problem gets even worse because of the necessity to reveal my own theoretical premises which make the basis of my commentary. This, in turn, would require a separate article. In this situation we shall confine ourselves here to a few very general remarks.

First of all, it is proper to express the essential solidarity with most of the convictions voiced by Habermas which are concerned with the interpretation of the methodological orientations currently dominant in social sciences. In this perspective the wish of the author of *Theorie des kommunikativen Handelns* to make the traditional procedure of understanding more theoretical seems to be particularly noteworthy. For one has to agree with Habermas that this procedure is indispensable to social sciences. This is because these sciences cognitively explore the objective

27. J. Habermas, "Ein Fragment: Objektivismus ...", pp. 593-594.
28. J. Habermas, *Theorie des kommunikativen ...*, vol. I, p. 191.
29. I have expressed my attitude towards the theoretical views of Habermas at length in my doctor's thesis entitled *Kultura a komunikacja. Teoria krytyczna Jürgena Habermasa w świetle społeczno-regulacyjnej teorii kultury* (Culture and communication. The critical theory of Jürgen Habermas in the light of the socio-regulative theory of culture), the typerscript unpublished.

domain which is a specific socio-cultural reality based on beliefs and constituted by the power of sense-creative activity of social subjects. On the other hand it must be pointed out that not only the reality which is the object of interest of social sciences but the whole reality has a cultural status.[30] There are far-reaching consequences that follow from this but it is not possible to discuss them here in short.[31]

It is particularly worthwhile to stress Habermas's postulate to adopt the strategy of rational reconstruction as the procedure whereby the super-individual elements of cultural competence of social subjects — which are the precognitions of the process of cultural communication based on production and mutual understanding of symbolical texts — are revealed. Though, from the point of view adopted here, this competence should be made relative each time in reference to a given social group or a given society and should be treated as a set of commonly respected — within a group or a society — beliefs of normative or directival character which form together the culture of a given society or a given social group. The reconstruction would thus be limited each time to a concrete *Lebenswelt*. It would, in principle, renounce search for the elements of cultural competence common to the whole species. It would not, however, renounce the universality that Habermas sought but would find it in a slightly different way, namely by the reconstruction of the theory of culture which tries to combine certain aspects of the theory of historical materialism with the German philosophy of the humanities.[32]

From the point of view of this conception of the theory of culture the possibility of accounting for human actions, especially the ones aimed at interpretations, is based on the adoption of the assumption about the rational nature of an acting subject. This assumption is the necessary element of the explanation pattern which moreover embraces the description of knowledge used by a social subject to isolate the activities that are acceptable to him and to specify their results. The pattern also includes

---

30. J. Kmita, "A humanistic coefficient of activity and the psychology-humanities relation", in: (ed.) J. Brzeziński, *Consciousness: Methodological and Psychological Approaches, Poznań Studies in the Philosophy of the Sciences and the Humanities,* vol. 8, Rodopi, Amsterdam 1985, p. 87.

31. See J. Kmita, *Kultura i poznanie* (Culture and cognition), Warsaw 1985, chapt. II: "Komunikacyjno-kulturowa interpretacja współczynnika humanistycznego i jej zastosowania" (Communicative-cultural interpretation of the humanistic coefficient and its applications).

32. See J. Kmita, *Szkice z teorii poznania naukowego* (Sketches on the theory of scientific cognition), Warsaw 1976; by the same author, *Z problemów epistemologii historycznej* (Some of the problems of historical epistemology), Warsaw 1980; by the same author, *O kulturze symbolicznej* (On symbolic culture), Warsaw 1982; by the same author, *Kultura i poznanie* (Culture and cognition), Warsaw 1985.

the description of the order of values characteristic of a given subject, presupposing that the result of the activity being explained is the value most favoured by the subject.[33]

At this stage we have to make a certain remark. The point is that we encounter certain incoherence in the approach of Habermas. As we know, originally he criticized all the theoretical standpoints in social sciences which follow the assumption — taken from economy — of the rationality of human actions. On the other hand, in his proposal of explanatory understanding he actually followed this assumption himself. It appears that Habermas first criticized a certain version of the assumption of the rationality of human actions and then followed a different version upon the status of which he did not comment. Let us focus our attention on this question for a while.

The conception of rationality, taken from economy and originally considered by Habermas, is based on the assumption that the goal of rational action and its "scientifically calculable" effect are identical. Habermas is right when he criticizes (following Parsons as it seems) the application of this conception of rationality to the object of humanistic studies, in so far as the focusing of action on a certain value does not coincide with a "scientifically" determined cause-effect relationship. He is not right, however, in forejudging that it is not possible to determine on "scientific" grounds the axiological direction of interpretation-oriented action. So it is true that the chosen value — the sense of rational action which subjectively tends towards the realization of this value — does not need to have the character of a scientifically-empirically articulated state of affairs. These values may be of a "metaphysical" character. But it is also true — what Habermas (at least verbally) denies — that it is possible to articulate them theoretically as the objective semantic references of given propositions. The point is that:

> In order to function effectively the semantics of cultural communication, or the semantics of its different branches, must be preceded by certain forejudgements or assumptions. The point is that each of the semantic rules, be it the one which concerns a certain communicational action or its product, or the one which concerns the element of such an action or its product, relates to a given "meaningful" unit its intersubjective reference in the form of a certain state of affairs or a certain element of it. In other words, it relates to the given unit a certain, so to speak, portion of the world.[34]

While reconstructing this image of the world, we reconstruct at the same time the objective semantic references of the propositions which express intentionally realized values. It is this reconstruction that Habermas otherwise seems to have in mind when he indicates that it is necessary to understand the sense of value-oriented action by means of the reconstruction of the contents of a given life-world which constitutes the context in which the afore-said action is undertaken (comp. note 27). In this way Habermas voices the opinion with which I totally agree: one should look for the key to the explanation ("explanatory understanding") of the sense of a certain interpretation-oriented action in the reconstruction of values and beliefs that are commonly respected in a given social group or society. Habermas also rightly observes that these beliefs and values cannot be treated absolutely autonomously, i.e. that their formation is largely affected by the factors which are beyond the consciousness and have their source in the objective context of social practice. For, as it is assumed within the framework of the theory which I have developed, social practice is a dynamic and hierarchical functional structure due to its property of reproduction and (as a rule) transformation of given objective conditions. This practice includes a number of functionally interrelated subpractices. A distinct position in the system (in the hierarchical structure) is occupied by the "material" practice of production and exchange to which all the remaining practices are directly or indirectly functionally subordinated. The respective sets of values work as socio-subjective regulators of particular practices. The compliance of individual participants of a given practice with these sets of values is a necessary condition for the practice to meet the demands of the whole of social practice. All the above-mentioned sets of beliefs, i.e. all the socio-subjective contexts in which the respective social practices function add up to the social consciousness. As far as the relationship between social consciousness and individual consciousness is concerned the theory which have adopted advocates methodological anti-individualism in its radical form. Thus, the assumption is that social consciousness is explanatory prior to individual consciousness. The latter is usually a psychologically explicable realization of the former. The relation between the two types of consciousness is generally defined by the fact that in their own life-practice, individuals have to comply with particular beliefs, which belong to the sphere of social consciousness, otherwise their actions should not be effective. Let us add that the transformations of social consciousness are explained within our theory in a functional-genetic manner. This means that its preliminary state is explained in reference to: (1) the fact that this state is more highly functional than the previous (or currently existing) ones as far as the objective demand "submitted" by social practice is concerned; (2) the earlier form of social consciousness — "the accumulated intellectual content".

One more remark to end with. It is hard to resist the impression that in his *Theorie des kommunikativen Handelns* Habermas formulated the scheme of the social theory which attempts to achieve a coherent whole by combining two different modes of conceptualization of society: the functional-systemic mode focused on the objective mechanisms of social life; and the mode which is connected with the non-phenomenological understanding of the category of *Lebenswelt* and which stresses the significance of the sphere of socially respected beliefs and values. In spite of this, however, in his studies concerning methodological aspects of social research, and especially the category of understanding, Habermas (despite the verbal declarations) does not fully take into account the earlier-mentioned dependence of socially respected beliefs and values upon unintentional structures of social life (life-practice) which functionally enforce the appropriate sphere of the former ones. One might venture the claim that in his methodological views Habermas does not draw all the conclusions that follow from the critique of "subjectivistic-idealistic" methodological orientations in social sciences, which he has carried out so brilliantly, in spite of the fact that, as it seems, all the premises for the completion of this process are present in his mode of conceptualization of the social theory.

Translated by M. Pawłowska

Ewa Kobylińska

FROM CRITICAL THEORY TO A THEORY OF COMMUNICATIVE ACTION: A CHANGE OF PARADIGM?

Introduction

The names of M. Horkheimer and T.W. Adorno, on the one hand, and J. Habermas, on the other, have usually been associated with one style of thinking — the Frankfurt School. It seems worthwhile to consider whether that standard reception does not conceal a certain real continuity or whether, on the contrary, we are dealing here with a fundamental change in the framework of continuity — the change of paradigm. There is also a third possibility — that of totally different worldview, methodological, and theoretical options, i.e. a supposition that, in fact, there exists no common denominator between Adorno's and Horkheimer's critical theory and Habermas's theory of communicative action.

Habermas, who in his *opus magnum* entitled *A theory of communicative action* (1981)[1] systematically presented his attitude towards the critical theory, defines it as the change of paradigm: from consciousness and historiosophy connected with it to the sociologically grounded theory of intersubjectivity.

I would like to consider whether a certain change of paradigm has taken place and if so, what is the cognitive gain of this change for the research on society. The question is whether the theory of communicative action has been successful in carrying out the common goal, represented for both generations of the Frankfurt School by the formation of a theoretically uniform program of interdisciplinary research on society.

Although it does not seem constructive to begin our analysis with conclusions, an introductory suggestion of the conclusions, indicating the main aspects of my analysis, seems to be necessary. For constructing his theory of communicative action which directly and indirectly expresses its author's attitude to the critical theory, Habermas is using a tremendous conceptual apparatus, constituting the achievement of almost the entire humanist thought (sociology: Parsons, Durkheim, Weber, Mead;

1. J. Habermas, *Theorie des komunikativen Handelns,* Frankfurt/M. 1981.

postempirical philosophy of science, linguistics: from Chomsky to Searl; psychology: Freud, Piaget, and Kohlberg).

In my opinion, besides the above goal, i.e. forming a theoretical basis for an interdisciplinary social research, Habermas shares with Adorno only a very general philosophical worldview of the Enlightenment type, i.e. the attachment to the concept of reason and the faith in the possibility of arranging the social life on a rational basis. A consequence of the belief in the possibility of social emancipation with the help of reason is an attempt of working out criteria for such a rational emancipation. Since emancipation can occur only through a reflection, a specific, self-conscious, two-reflectional theory — which is another commonly shared belief of the Frankfurt School members — working out the criteria of the mind means creating normative bases for a critical theory. The first generation of the Frankfurt School failed, as we shall see, to create such bases because of the paradigm of the philosophy of consciousness which they had adopted. For Habermas, on the other hand, a normative basis for a critical social theory is the theory of communicative action, which is to provide the criteria of criticism.

I believe that a critical theory is not — in its final form — neither a theory nor criticism, but a speculative-normative vision of the dialectically developing reason, which leads to a complete totalization of the society and a civilizational catastrophe. It is not a theory because (1) it does not use any theoretical means known to modern humanities, (2) it is not able to define its research subject, (3) it considers all conceptuality as a deformation and thus it cuts off its own roots, for there is as yet no other way of building a theory than with the use of concepts. Neither is it a criticism because this concept does not indicate who should be the carrier of that criticism and who should organize — on the basis of theoretical knowledge — the emancipational practice, e.g. the political or educational one, if everyone is subjected to the enslaving activity of the instrumental reason. Yet, despite those paradoxical consequences and the denial of the original belief concerning the emancipational power of the mind, a critical theory remains a debtor of the Enlightenment tradition, for it ultimately denies the reason with its own means. It radicalizes its criticism of the reason until the moment of its self-reflexiveness, i.e. until the moment in which it destroys its own basis. It makes an effort to survive in the performative contradiction of *Negative Dialectik*. Only in this way it believes to be able to remain faithful to the lost, non-instrumental reason, whose echo is reflected merely in the wordless *mimesis*.[2]

2. J. Habermas, *Die neue Unübersichtlichkeit,* Frankfurt/M. 1985, p. 219.

Let us examine the question whether a theory of communicative action becomes truly liberated from the paradigm of the philosophy of consciousness. Is this theory the hypothesis of a uniform subject of history creating a framework for empirical research of the society, or a proposal remaining within the utopian perspective of the realization of reason in history? The answer depends on the decision which of Habermas's concepts is considered to be of primary significance. The point is that he offers us implicitly two methodologically and theoretically competing concepts. The key notion of the first one is the "criticism of ideology", while of the other one — "universal pragmatics". Choosing the former, we obtain a possibility of researching real societies, both from the point of view of their development and the socialization of individuals. Choosing the latter, we obtain a certain pattern of universal history, based upon the idea of a two-directional development of the society: the development of the systems of purposive-rational actions and the development of the world of social life. Habermas identifies certain useful analytical distinctions with the actual social structure, a result of which is the normative-empirical hybrid — the concept of the society, whose one sphere is based exclusively upon the co-ordination through agreement, while the other — upon the co-ordination through functional adjustment. At the same time the former concept, the "criticism of ideology", includes a greater emancipational potential than the "universal pragmatics". The latter characterizes the structures of rationality included in language only formally, i.e. defines the general conditions necessary for a rational agreement, but it does not ever determine the subject of the agreement or the subject of the emancipation. Being a theory, it certainly should not be able to afford anything else. Nevertheless, those formal conditions cannot be a normative basis for the criticism of the society. Habermas is trying to solve the growing difficulty in such a way that it interprets the formal conditions as ethical rules, which he later places in the anthropological structures of the species. As a result, it is not known whether they are regulative ideas or empirical regularities.

The theory characterizing the society from the point of view of its communicative structures is based upon dubious assumptions. Adopting them is a result of the belief that a social theory is to be not only a reconstruction and explanation of the existing states of matters, but also an anticipation of the future, desired states. If, however, such a global task cannot be theoretically performed, it does not change the fact that Habermas's partial analyses, the methodological, historical, and theoretical ones, are very revealing and that scientist's cautiousness each time triumphs over the philosopher's vision.

1.   M. Horkheimer's Critical Theory as a Method of Social Emancipation

In 1937 M. Horkheimer published his essay entitled "Traditional and critical theory", in which he tried to present the relation between modern science and practice, as well as to account for the fact of the critical theory's awareness of this relation as a result of its emancipational abilities.[3] The attitude of traditional theory to natural processes or historical events is purely external, claims Horkheimer, which makes it possible for that theory to explain empirical states of matters by means of including them in the structure of theoretical utterances. This kind of analysis of the reality makes it possible for a theory to diagnose, predict, and control natural and social processes. The control function of the traditional theory reveals, however, its background. It belongs to the process of reproduction, thanks to which the human species survives through a groving control over its natural and social environment.[4] Yet, claiming to be a "pure" theory, the traditional theory fails to notice this practical background. Referring to Marx, Horkheimer says that subject and object of cognition are *a priori* defined by the process of social domination over nature. He identifies this process with the history of the human species. In turn, Horkheimer views the creating of history by the human species similarly to the transcendental model of Kant. In its activity the human species is equiped in transcendental, constituting properties, ascribed by Kant to the subject. The only difference is that this time it is the social world that constitutes the transcendental framework within which the species shapes nature not knowing anything about itself. Modern science is unaware of that moment and, therefore, the process of self-preservation is productive, though "blind", at least so far. Thanks to its deep rootedness in the work practice, irrespective of whether it knows about it or not, the traditional theory can be ascribed a positive function: that of rationally conquering nature. The only factor that marks the distance humanity needs to cover in order to fully implement that process is the lack of consciousness of making history.

Horkheimer concludes the critical theory from the traditional theory only *ex negativo*, i.e. as such a theory which is all the time conscious of its practical rootedness. Among its tasks is an analysis of that rootedness: viewing itself as an element of the social development.

Both the traditional and the critical theory are two not unconstrained forms of the same civilizational process of conquering nature. However,

---

3. M. Horkheimer, "Traditionelle und kritische Theorie", *Zeitschrift für Sozialforschung* 6/1937.
    4. Ibid., p. 252.

the critical theory possesses additional knowledge of the immanent developmental potential of the means of production. The traditional theory, one could say, expresses a state of the reason's partial realization, while the critical theory reflects a full realization: a rational organization of human work in the way adjusted to the independent potential of the means of production. It is not clear how a critical theory, which according to Horkheimer constitutes simply a complementation of the traditional theory, can contain the criticism of the existing order. That gap cannot be bridged even by the knowledge of the direction of the development of shaping nature. The point is that even a theory consciously based upon the social process of work, which deals with the internal logic of the development of the process of work rather than diagnozing empirical states of matters and which fictitiously projects that logic into the future, is not able to produce the criteria of social life.[5] That requires the normative philosophy of history. The traditional theory, even properly ammended, can produce only technical knowledge in the broad sense, while it has no grounds for the criticism of the existing social institutions.

Horkheimer is aware of that difficulty and proposes a new version of the critical theory. It no longer constitutes an immanent part of the process of social reproduction through work, but it is a theoretical manifestation of pre-scientific "critical behavior". Thus, besides the category of "work", there appears a category of "critical behavior". The critical theory constitutes an extension and objectivization of that critical behavior and so it internalizes its relation to the analyzed object. Ultimately, however, it is Horkheimer's philosophy of history that predominates — the philosophy which views the history of humanity as a quasi-natural process of a rational conquest of nature and reduces the social practice exclusively to the category of work. There is no place in that historiosophy for "critical behavior": the social practice with which the critical theory could be self-reflexively related. The traditional conquest of nature, self-preservation of species, and social work are three basic categories of Horkheimer's philosophy which make it impossible for him to consistently introduce the critical theory.

The rational process of conquering nature is at first evaluated by Horkheimer positively as a process including an emancipational potential. Since that process cannot continue without conflicts, of which Horkheimer learns from Marx, and since these open class conflicts are not visible in late capitalism, Horkheimer somehow has to explain the latency, the concealment of class conflicts. For that he needs a psycho-

5. A. Honneth, *Kritik der Macht*, Frankfurt/M. 1985, p. 18 ff.

108

logical concept which would be able to explain the "softening" of open class conflicts and the adjustment of individuals (the working class) to the contradictory method of production. In this way the critical theory becomes complemented with psychology, whose elements are taken by Horkheimer from Freud and early works of Fromm.[6] Human internal life is presented as a set of impulses which can be flexibly formed and transformed in a way adjusted to the social requirements. Horkheimer takes from Fromm the idea that the desired structuralization of an impulse takes place in the interaction of a child with its parents. On the other hand, the family institutionalizes in a model way the systemic requirements. From Freud, in turn, Horkheimer takes the interpretation of character as a fixation of one of the stages in the development of child's erotism. Family up-bringing solidifies the psychosexual development of a child on a level adjusted to the requirements of social behavior. What does not fit in this structure will be either sublimed or suppressed in the future, which will also make it socially exclusively as a function of economical processes.[7] In order to prevent this functionalist reduction Horkheimer introduces the third dimension between the sphere of socialization of impulses and the system of social work, namely the sphere of culture. Yet, even that concept undergoes a peculiar evolution in Horkheimer's view's. The dominating philosophy of history pushes it more and more to a marginal position. In Horkheimer's early works culture overlaps the sort of interpretational activities, providing particular social groups with an identity, a common orientation for values. This concept of culture gradually changes into a concept of cultural institutions and organizations mediating in adjusting the processes of behavior to the socially required types of behavior. The point is no longer a co-operative production of models within the framework of symbolic activity, but a socializing function of cultural institutions, which embeds the required types of behavior in individual mentality.

The former concept of culture, correlated with symbolic activity, does not fit within Horkheimer's philosophy of history, reducing the development of civilization to a single process: the development of human ability to work. The latter concept: that of culture as an institution, whose pedagogic and religious "devices" perform an integrative function, perfectly fits in this historiosophy.

---

6. E. Fromm, "Über Methode und Aufgabe einer analytischen Sozialpsychologie", *Zeitschrift für Sozialforschung* 1/1932.

7. E. Fromm, *Studien über Autorität und Familie,* Paris 1936, p. 77 ff.

2. Dialectic of Enlightenment: From a Positive to a Negative Evaluation of Reason

In their *Dialectic of Enlightenment*,[8] Adorno and Horkheimer describe —
with the help of the categories of work — no longer the emancipational
process of conquering nature, but the process of self-destruction of
reason. The technical shaping of external nature and wisely disciplining
the internal one changes into the process of enslaving an individual and
destroying the personality. The socio-cultural evolution, which from the
point of view of a cummulativist development of the means of production
makes an impression of a constant progress, turns into the process of
regression of the species, the process of a "reverse anthropogenesis".[9]
The concept of instrumental rationality, which is a key concept in the
later critical theory of Adorno, appears for the first time here. It is meant
to explain the genesis and dynamics of the process of civilizational
regression. It derives from the Marxist concept of commodity exchange,
interpreted as objectivization. However, in the totalizing approach of
Dialectic of Enlightenment commodity exchange is merely one of historical
figures of instrumental rationality. Commodity exchange performs the
role of a social medium, which changes the technical rationality (towards
the external nature) into the intrasocial rationality.

In the same technical attitude of controlling, in which the instrumentally acting man learns to shape the external nature, he also learns to
independently model his own impulse potential. This is expressed by the
central metaphor of *Dialectic of Enlightenment*: the metaphor of Odysseus
who willingly ties himself to the mast.[10] In the control of impulses the
process of dominating over the external nature is repeated as an
individual and independent imposition of coercion upon the external
nature.

Adorno and Horkheimer assume that in order to become liberated
from the superpower of the external nature which endangers it, the
human species has passed through the limits of passive resistance and
began controlling activity. However, this instrumental objectivization of
nature is accompanied by man's self-objectivization. Thus, the social
process of shaping nature is merely the reverse side of the process of a
constantly greater alienation of man towards his own inside. What relates
the philosophy of history and the theory of social domination is an

8. Th.W. Adorno and M. Horkheimer, *Dialektik der Aufklärung*, Frankfurt/M.
1969.
9. Ibid., p. 44 ff.
10. Ibid., p. 27.

attempt to construct a concept of social domination by way of analogy with the domination over nature. For that reason the social groups forced to perform (manual) work are viewed as representatives of the oppressed nature, an object that totally lacks resistance and can be easily manipulated.

Dialectic of Enlightenment is then limited only to the cases of indirect or direct coercion as the only forms of social domination. Beyond its conceptual abilities are all the forms of executing power which are based not upon subordinating individuals from the point of view of their susceptibility to control (for example, obedience guaranteed by direct sanctions), but upon the processes of creating a consensus. It is then the normative horizons, rather than sanctions, that constitute the basis for power. The cultural norms providing a filter through which all social groups perceive the existing institutions constitute a somewhat fragile, though also efficient consensus, which sufficiently secures a normative recognition of the uneven distribution of social tasks. The social theory then faces a difficult task of recognizing the primarily cultural mechanisms which channel and block the processes of interpretation and production of normative orientations by particular groups in such a way that despite obvious inequalities they may constitute a social consensus. And so the point is to explain theoretically the social situation in which the institutionalized handicap of certain social groups obtains a consensual recognition of all. In sociology (placed in the tradition of the "criticism of ideology"), this problem is referred to as "structural coercion" and it cannot be included in *Dialectic of Enlightenment* at all, for no type of consensually guaranteed domination exist there. Following and generalizing this line of interpretation, we may say that the "old" critical theory leaves no place for the method of social co-ordination of actions which is secured through the processes of interpretation and communication in respect of values by the symbolic culture and that the cultural activity and interpretational abilities of the society, constituting the basis of both integrational and socializational processes, are totally neglected here. According to Adorno and Horkheimer's philosophy of history, interpreting the history of civilization as a spiral of domination over the external and internal nature, individuals (or social groups) should be viewed as lacking intentions — the victims of purposeful techniques of domination.[11]

Both the optimist variation of Horkheimer and the pessimist one of

---

11. I am following here the interpretation of J. Habermas (*Theorie des Kommunikativen Handelns*, vol. II, p. 437 ff) and A. Honneth (*Kritik der Macht*, p. 68 ff).

111

Adorno are based upon one concept from the scope of the theory of action — the category of work. For that reason both variations view social history only from the perspective of the dynamics of human domination over nature. For Horkheimer it is the potential of civilizational liberation, while for Adorno — the cause of the fall of civilizations.

If Adorno allowed to a greater degree these cultural-communicational connections in which the social activity is involved, it would become clear to him that the elements of behavior forced by the sphere of economic reproduction are not directly "reflected" in the models of personality of individuals, but rather they become efficient (from the point of view of socialization) through the mediation of cultural communication.

In his post-war works on cultural criticism,[12] Adorno observes a fact that postliberal capitalism indicates a tendency to concentrate social control in the form of beaurocracy separated from the market. This has some far reaching consequences for the process of socialization. To the same degree to which systemically and administrationally organized capitalism deprives a small entrepreneur of his freedom of decision and economic action, the control of behavior process from the individual rank of conscience to the external rank of planning and managing. It is at this point that mass culture may enter as an effective means of personality control, because the individuals would have already lost their ability to an independent control of impulses. According to Adorno, socialization is a direct influence of mass culture viewed as "cultural industry" upon the individual structure of impulses.

Adorno deeply believes that only administrational means may coordinate the activity of individuals. The macrosubject represented by the centrally governing apparatus behaves towards the society in a similar instrumental way as a single subject towards nature. Adorno's social theory comprises two poles: an individual and organization. He completely neglects the middle sphere: that of social activity and cultural interpretational processes, normatively preserving the institutionalized social inequalities (i.e. ideology).

If this mediation is neglected, we cannot know what should be the subject of criticism of the critical theory. It does not permit the dimension of a social analysis, cultural interaction, but merely the analysis of a system (peculiarly viewed as a set of administrational techniques of governing) and psychoanalysis (also peculiarly viewed as explaining the process of an individual's learning to control its impulses).

---

12 "Resume über Kulturindustrie", in: *Collected Works,* vol. 10, p. 507 ff, Frankfurt/M. 1977, or "Individuum und Organisation", vol. 8, p. 440 ff.

Since Adorno and Horkheimer believe that science as a whole is an instrument of technical or social governing, they are forced to consistently place their considerations beyond this dispositional science. Thus, following the literally historiosophical premises of *Dialectic of Enlightenment,* they place the critical theory beyond the empirical sciences, in the sphere of philosophical activity. Its status, however, is also vague, for every conceptual act is an elementary figure of the instrumental reason. Therefore, the critical theory cannot justify any form of discursive thinking, including its own.

It makes an effort to withdraw from this trap by assuming an exclusively negative function of self-criticism of conceptual thinking, "through the concept of going beyond the concept".[13] The problem remains, however, how the critical theory can formulate utterances concerning the reality, providing that every act of conceptual cognition is at the same time an act of violence in respect of nature and individual. Adorno asks himself a question of how the critical theory can become liberated from the chains of instrumental rationality and still remain a certain form of cognition.

By way of analogy to Freud's "impulse of death" and Caillois "mimetism", Adorno formulates a category of non-instrumental approach to reality.[14] A mimetic attitude towards nature, in which things appear not as objects of manipulation, but preserve their state of "being completely different", opens new possibilities of social emancipation. According to Adorno, art is a substitute form of this mimetic approach to things. A work of art is to be a type of aesthetic compensation of the lost confidence in the potential of the resistance of the oppressed. It is the only cognitive medium, through which one can obtain the information on the situation of a society and not yield, at the same time, to the instrumental reason. However, these works of art are also "mute", for Adorno views them as monads, lacking communicational power.

In the early writings of the scholars from the Frankfurt School, the critical theory was to perform the role of self-consciousness of the revolutionary social movement. After *Dialectic of Enlightenment* it can merely be a reflectional form of a work of art in the form of an aesthetic theory. It is supposed to draw from art its own "logic of cognition" and base upon it the critical theory of a society. More and more helpless, the critical theory wanders between the philosophical reflection and aesthetic experience, striving not to be the former and unable to become the latter.

---

13. Th.W. Adorno, *Negative Dialektik,* Frankfurt/M. 1973, p. 75.
14. M. Horkheimer and Th.W. Adorno, *Dialektik der Aufklärung,* ibid., p. 240.

3. Habermas' Interpretation of the Aporia of the Critical Theory

According to J. Habermas, the program of the early critical theory has failed because it could not be realized in the paradigm of the philosophy of consciousness.[15] The negative dialectic of self-mastering of philosophy leads to difficulties which create an opportunity to ask a question whether this difficulty is not a consequence of the philosophy of consciousness. That philosophy characterizes the subject through the two attitudes that it can assume towards the object: the attitude of cognition, i.e. an objectivizing reference to the world, and the attitude of control, i.e. a theoretical or practical mastering of the subject in order to lead it to a desired state. In other words, two basic attributes of the subject are the *presentation* (of things as they are) and *action* (in order to lead them to the state in which they should be).

As the transcendental (ontological, epistemological) space decreases, these attributes of the spirit (subject), i.e. to cognize and act purposefully, are transformed into functions subordinated to the self-preservation of the species. This self-preservation was viewed in the metaphysical images of the world as a tendency of each being to realize the goal corresponding to its nature according to the natural order. However, in the philosophy of consciousness proclaimed by Marx, Darwin, and the system theory, these attributes of the spirit change into the functions of preserving the system. Cognition and purposeful action are the most effective ways of reproduction and thus of the self-preservation of the species. As long as the relation between the subject and the object limits the self-preservation of the species to those two fundamental modes, the reason can remain an instrumental one. With this kind of conceptual strategy, it is at best possible to indicate that an instrumental reason destroys something in the internal mental and internal social spheres, though it is impossible to show explicitly what this destruction consists of.

It has to be acknowledged that Horkheimer and Adorno do still possess some knowledge of the Mimesis, of which I have spoken before. Yet, since it is totally separated from the cognitive-instrumental relation of the subject to the object, it functions only as a pure opposition of the reason — an impulse. Although Adorno does not negate the cognitive function of that impulse, the rational nucleus — according to Habermas — can be established in the Mimesis only when we change the paradigm of consciousness into a paradigm proposed by the philosophy of lan-

15. I am presenting here the interpretation of J. Habermas included in *Theorie des Kommunikativen Handelns*, vol. 2: *Von Lukacs zu Adorno*, pp. 453-489.

guage, which subordinates the cognitive-instrumental aspect to a broader communicational rationality.

Therefore, a necessary thing here is to pass from subjectivity to intersubjectivity. The subject appears in this approach not as "something" which is defined by the modes of cognition and operating on the object, but as "something" which must communicate in the historical development of the species with other subjects in respect of what is cognition and operating on object. This communication takes place in the medium of the natural language. Individuals make use of the cultural background which makes a basis for the processes of communication and they refer at the same time to something in the objective world, the common social world, and the subjective world, available each time in a privileged way to each of them separately. Communication means here a process of mutual persuasion, which coordinates the activity on the basis of justifying motives.

The concept of communicational rationality refers to "intuition", which stands out as the main motive of the entire work of Habermas. It is based upon religious tradition, protestant and Jewish mysticism. It can be found in the early works of Hegel, Schelling, Böhme, Eichendorff, and also Adorno. It is the motive of reconcilliation in the form of a successful interaction. That situation comes from the area of treating others, the experience of undisturbed intersubjectivity. The mentioned mutuality does not rule out a conflict, but offers hope for finding such forms of social life in which conflicts will be possible to overcome.[16] "The potential of rationality included in the communicationally conceived interaction is something on which we must base ourselves. This is why I am searching for prehistory", says Habermas.[17] The above opinion does not tolerate, however, the statement on the ambivalence of the process of rationalization, in which besides the progress in the area of communication, there is also "something most deeply unsuccessful". Habermas is trying to introduce this fundamental intuition into the theory, though he is not doing it directly, like Adorno.

> If we become oriented towards the questions concerning the truth, we must not, like Adorno and Heidegger, produce those truths outside of science, outside of a scientific discourse, and base them upon some higher respect, the "Andenken des Seins" or "Eingedenken der gequalten Natur".[18]

Habermas introduces the above intuition with the help of two steps: (1) using the conceptual instrumentarium of formal pragmatics, he analyses

16. J. Habermas, *Die neue ...*, op.cit., p. 202
17. Ibid., p. 202.
18. Ibid., p. 203.

the general properties of the activity oriented towards communication and construct the concept of communicational rationality on the basis of it; (2) he investigates the possibility of applying this concept to social relations, institutionalized interactions. The form of social theory changes principally if we assume that human species preserves also thanks to the interactionally coordinated actions. Its reproduction, however, requires a fulfillment of certain conditions of rationality, characteristic of communicational activity. A phenomenon that requires explanation is no longer cognition and control of objective nature, but the intersubjective possibility of communication.

As the normative integration of everyday life becomes more loose, the process of self-preservation of species is more and more dependent upon interpretational achievements of individuals. Naturally, those integrating processes of communication are not unlimited. They encounter a limit not only because of contradictory and opposing interests of individuals and groups, but mostly because of the interference of the "functionalist reason" into the area of communicational practice.

The reception of Weber's theory of rationality by the first generation of the Frankfurt School indicates that social rationalization is always viewed as objectification of consciousness. The paradoxes to which such an approach leads suggest that the problems of objectification cannot be presented satisfactorily in the paradigm of the philosophy of consciousness. For that reason Habermas proposes a new paradigm: that of communication, provided not only by the pragmatic philosophy of language (from Austin to Searle), but also sociological tradition (Mead, Durkheim, Parsons), on the basis of which one can resume Weber's theory of rationalization and become liberated from the problem of the philosophy of consciousness. An assent of Horkheimer and Adorno's theory of objectification is the fact that it stresses the symptoms of deformation of the world of everyday life, not very peculiar for the class theory of society. On the other hand, a liability of that theory is the fact that it reduces the erosion of "Lebenswelt" to a demonized rationality of purpose in the form of an instrumental reason in which knowledge is mixed with power. That seems to be the same mistake which had already been made by M. Weber and which the Frankfurt School has taken over and led to a more radical stage. It consists in confusing the concept of system rationality, or — as we should say today — system functionality, with the rationality of actions. Both concepts appear in the form of a single category: an instrumental reason i.e. totalized rationality of purpose constituting a characteristic of a self-regulating system. The above confusion does not allow the scholars of the Frankfurt School to distinguish between rationalization, orientation of actions within the structurally differentiated "Lebenswelt", and the growth of the ability to control a differentiated social system. For that reason they place the spontaneity not accounted for by the system in the sphere of "the irrational": charismatic leadership, art, love. The weakness of Horkheimer and Adorno's theory lies, above all, in the fact that it is not sufficiently based upon Weber's analysis of rationalization of world images (i.e. upon what he called cultural rationality), but instead — upon Weber's theory of purposive-rational action. For that reason, claims Habermas, they are unable to turn the criticism of an instrumental reason into the criticism of a functionalist reason.

Contrary to Adorno's "monism", a systematic point of reference for the new critical theory is represented by both the communicational and instrumental rationality. Therefore, the growth of instrumental rationality in the area of material reproduction of the society's living conditions can be opposed by the intrasocial and intrahistorical emancipation. As a result of such a re-orientation, the critical theory is renewed as a reflection of a historical-typical process, though one understood as an interactional process of learning. Habermas's critical theory is above all a theory of the structures of social activity and their development. Those structures, on which Habermas's concept of history is based, are viewed by him as intersubjectively constituted and linguistically structuralized social relations. Therefore, the structure of the pragmatically interpreted language is ultimately the fundamental category of the new critical theory — the communicative theory of society.

Translated by Krzysztof Sawala

Zbigniew Gierszewski

TYPES OF COGNITIVE AND MORAL RELATIVISM AND HERSKOVITS' CULTURAL RELATIVISM

An increasing interest in cultural relativism — a stance both theoretical and methodological as well as philosophical (epistemological and ethical) formulated and developed within American cultural anthropology — has already been noted in the philosophy of science for twenty years. The collapse of the cumulativistic conception of the development of science was the circumstance which significantly influenced the growth of this interest. The crucial works of S. Toulmin, Th. Kuhn and P. Feyerabend made many philosophers, historians and sociologists of science, not only within the circle of positivistic ideas, realize the fact that as researchers they are in the position of anthropologists undertaking studies of an alien culture. They began to perceive other theoretical systems, paradigms or conceptual schemas in the same way as anthropologists starting field researches viewed alien cultures half a century ago — they were no longer understandable from outside.

The experience of anthropologists who during direct contacts with non-European (in the cultural, not geographical sense) societies tried to become acquainted with their cultures from inside, to understand their beliefs and actions, resulted both in methodological and theoretical reflections and on a smaller scale also in reflections of an epistemological and ethical character. This reflection was expressed in various forms — as methodological rules, theoretical and philosophical theses and ethical principles. The formulations were most often called relativistic, a very fashionable term then. Relativistic ideas gained a definite form in the works of Edward Sapir and Ruth Benedict in the turn of the 1920's, although some of them appeared earlier in the papers of Franz Boas and other anthropologists from his school. The relativistic trend initiated by Sapir and Benedict was continued in the 1930's and 1940's by American anthropologists, mainly by Dorothy D. Lee, Benjamin L. Whorf and Melville J. Herskovits. Issues formulated by those cultural relativists gained a broader repute outside American cultural anthropology only at the beginning of the 1950's. They were in most cases criticized then by philosophers, including many moral philosophers. This standpoint began to change in the 1960's when the cumulativistic conception of the development of science was questioned within the philosophy of science.

In the discussion on relativism which has been going on for a dozen years or so among British philosophers, the distinction of its forms proposed by Steven Lukes in the essay *Relativism: cognitive and moral* (1977) and in the *Introduction* to the collection *Rationality and relativism* (1982) are accepted presently. (Co-author of the *Introduction* is Martin Hollis, also taking part in the debate on relativism). In both works cultural relativism is thought of as a variant of relativism in its wide aegis.

S. Lukes distinguishes two basic forms of relativism: cognitive and moral, and understands by the former the philosophical thesis that "(...) truth and logic are always relative to particular systems of thought or language" (Lukes 1977, p. 157). Cognitive relativism as the philosophical thesis should be distinguished from an empirical thesis stating the existence of a diversity of world-views, theories, forms of explanation, ways of classification and categorization, etc. According to the philosophical thesis, what is true and the way in which it is determined, and what is a valid or consistent argument, are always internal to a system which is one of many and is relative to a particular society, or context, or a historical period.

In turn, for Lukes, the term "moral relativism" denotes a philosophical thesis stating that,

> (...) there is in principle ultimately no rational way of resolving fundamental conflicts between moral values, beliefs, principles, codes, systems — that there is no warrant (or no warrant not itself internal and relative to a particular moral system) for counting a particular set of moral values, beliefs, etc. as true, valid, correct, objective, etc. (Lukes 1977, p. 161).

This thesis is sometimes referred to as ethical subjectivism, meta-ethical relativism or relativism of values (axiological). Besides, many of other doctrines which the author considers to differ from moral relativism, are included under this label. A doctrine different from moral relativism in philosophical sense is the one constituted by an empirical thesis that, "(...) moral values and principles conflict in a fundamental way, that is, that they are not merely different, but incompatible" (Idem). According to this thesis the conflict between values and moral principles is unresolvable as it cannot by reduced to a resolvable discourse on facts, neither can one of the mutually contradictory principles be included under the other one, nor both of them under a third one. When one considers that such a conflict occurs between moral values (principles) which are accepted in various cultural groups, then this thesis becomes the doctrine of cultural relativism.

Under the label of moral relativism is also included the normative thesis that "(...) an act is, right or wrong, good or bad, or a person, say praise or blame-worthy if and only if he so judges — or, in the cultural form, if his society so judges" (Lukes 1977. p. 161). This thesis demands that moral judgements be made exclusively on the basis of values and principles shared by an actor or his society. It implies — as Lukes notes following B. Williams — three propositions: 1) that the term "right" means "right for a given society", 2) that the formula "right for a given society" should be understood in a functionalist meaning, and 3) that it is not right when members of one society condemn or interfere in the moral values of another society. Proposition 3) which is sometimes called normative relativism, does not follow from propositions 1) and 2). Thus, the doctrine consisting of them is not internally consistent.

The stances outlined above are further distinguished from yet another thesis taken into account by Lukes, which although distant from moral relativism is often identified with it and which J. Ladd called *applicational relativity*. The thesis that moral judgements should take account of context and consequences of moral acts, is its formulation, since a certain moral act may be right in certain circumstances and wrong in the other.

Thus, according to conceptual scheme presented by Lukes, cultural relativism is not a kind of moral or cognitive relativism in the philo-sophical sense, but a peculiar case of an empirical thesis stating diversity of moral principles and values, and noticing conflicts between them.

Cultural relativism was quite differently qualified in the "Introduction" to *Rationality and relativism.* Conceptual scheme presented there specify and order different variants of cognitive relativism, distinguished by Hollis and Lukes on the basis of a traditional convention from merely generally characterized moral relativism. The standpoint of the second kind outlined by them is not however characterized differently than in the earlier essay of Lukes. Taking this into consideration one may state that conceptual scheme proposed by the two authors broaden the classifica-tion given by Lukes previously.

Distinguishing two types of relativism: moral and cognitive, Hollis and Lukes stress simultaneously that they follow in this case tradition negating the cognitive character of moral judgements, although they do not declare themselves for the meta-ethical acognitivism. Their own opinion in this respect is expressed in the following way, "(...) the neat contrast between moral and cognitive relativism, with special arguments relating to each, is dubious in the extreme" (Hollis and Lukes 1982, p. 6).

According to them, cognitive relativism in its most general sense comprises four variants which depending on their force can be ordered into the following sequence: 1) conceptual relativism, 2) perceptual relativism, 3) relativism about truth, and 4) relativism about reason.

Conceptual relativism is a stance in which conceptual schemes of various societies are relative to the situational context in which they are used.

In turn, the position of perceptual relativism is expressed by the famous formula that various groups of people (cultural groups or groups of scientists) "live in different worlds". The best known manifestations of this variant of relativism are: a) its transcultural version in anthropology and b) its transtheoretical version in history, sociology, and the philosophy of science. For Hollis and Lukes, Edward Sapir is an adherent of the transcultural version. In his essay *The status of linguistics as a science* (1929) he wrote:

> (...) the "real world" is to a large extent unconsciously built up on the language habits of the group (...). The worlds in which different societies live are distinct worlds, not merely the same world with different labels attached (...). We see and hear and otherwise experience very largely as we do because the language habits of our community predispose certain choices of interpretation (Sapir 1985, p. 162).

Relativism about truth is a standpoint that there is not a supralocal concept or standard of truth. Favoring the holistic conception of meaning and truth, the adherents of this version of cognitive relativism claim that there is no universal set of non-relativized observable truths and conclude that conceptual schemes are incommensurable.

The last of the distinguished version of cognitive relativism, i.e. relativism about reason, relativizes also that which is called reason or good reason for shared beliefs. This stance is expressed by a thesis that, "(...) what warrants belief depends on canons of reasoning, deductive or non-deductive, that should properly be seen as social norms, relative to culture and period" (Hollis and Lukes 1982, p. 10).

The variants of cognitive relativism outlined above, were ordered, as it was already mentioned, according to their force. Its weakest version is presented by conceptual relativism, the strongest one — by relativism about reason. Every of the versions following conceptual relativism, comprises simultaneously variants weaker than itself. And thus perceptual relativism is also conceptual relativism, whereas relativism about reason shares the theses of the relativism about truth, and perceptual relativism.

Cultural relativism was qualified within the typology of Hollis-Lukes as form of perceptual relativism. When compared with the qualification of cultural relativism assumed earlier by Lukes, this difference gives rise to a question about the reasons of this divergence. Is it caused by different interpretations of the stance of cultural relativism? And if so, which of them is the more adequate interpretation? There exists also a third possibility that does not exclude the previous ones, that both these qualifications do not refer to cultural relativism as a whole but to its various aspects respectively. But these questions cannot be answered without at least a general outline of this anthropological stance.

As I have already mentioned, Melville J. Herskovits was the leading adherent of cultural relativism within American cultural anthropology. His book *Man and his works* (1948) comprises the most comprehensive and systematized treatment of this standpoint. It should be noticed that some of his conceptions criticized then, were elaborated in his later publications. Specifications introduced before *Cultural anthropology* (1956) was published, were entirely included in this work which is not a shortened version of *Man and his works* as its subtitle falsely informs. Later improvements were not incorporated into a comprehensive exposition of the author's standpoint.

For the author of *Man and his works* the starting point for presenting his own stance is the fact generally acknowledged by anthropologists that members of particular societies express evaluations of the different ways of life of other societies. Anthropologists have gradually noticed that these judgements are based on assumptions not valid in every society and — what is more — that the assumptions of different evaluations are in mutual conflict. It is these mutually contradictory principles of various societies which cause differentiation of evaluations articulated by their representatives.

Manifestations of cultural diversity recorded by anthropologists constitute the empirical basis for the principle of cultural relativism. This principle expressed in a concise form states that, "Judgements are based on experience, and experience is interpreted by each individual in terms of his own enculturation" (Herskovits 1948, p. 63).

The above thesis refers to both kinds of judgements held by members of various societies, namely to 1) value-judgements, and 2) fact-judgements. Not only values are expressed by members of a given society in terms of evaluation principles valid in it and acquired by each of them in the process of enculturation. "Even the facts of the physical world are discerned through the enculturative screen, so that the perception of time, distance, weight, size, and other realities is mediated by the conventions of any given group" (Herskovits 1948, p. 64).

The way of perceiving the main directions of the world by Indians from the south-west United States different than in Euro-American culture, is one of the examples which the author quotes to illustrate the cultural conditioning of experiencing the physical reality. These Indians think about the world in terms of six and not only four basic directions. Besides North, South, East, and West they also distinguish "up" and "down" (Idem).

The basic idea for the relativistic point of view is formulated by Herskovits in the following way,

> If, as philosophers tell us, we ourselves can never touch the raw stuff of reality, then it becomes evident that enculturation, which screens our perception and cognition, becomes our essential guide in the effords we make to meet reality in terms meaningful to us, and effective in attaining the ends we desire. To each of us, that is, the reality of the world in which we live is the enculturated reality (Herskovits 1956, pp. 84-85).

The statements quoted above show that enculturation is the key concept in the explication of the relativistic point of view by the author of *Man and his works*. As it is emphasized by D.T. Campbell (1972, p. XVIII), "Herskowits's view of cultural relativism and ethnocentrism is intimately related to his understanding of enculturation".

This concept is based on the assumption generally shared by anthropologists, that "culture is learned" (Herskovits 1984, p. 25). Accepting that "culture is the learned portion of human behavior", Herskovits defines enculturation as "The aspects of the learning experience which mark off man from other creatures, and by means of which, initially, and in later life, he achieves competence in his culture" (Herskovits 1948, p. 25 and p. 39).

It is worth noting that the author of *Man and his works* introduced a new term into the language of cultural anthropology and did not take it from the lexicon then used. This term was coined by E.A. Haggard. Its recommendation was the fact of emphasizing strongly that in the process of environmental adaptation, an individual gains first of all the knowledge of culture in which he or she was born and brought up.

According to Herskovits, enculturation is one of the three aspects of the process of learning (in the broad sense) through which a man adapts himself to his natural and socio-cultural environment. A threefold adaptation to 1) natural environment, 2) other members of the group in which one functions, 3) cultural patterns and norms valid in one's group, is the necessary condition of his development. These three aspects are interrelated in such a way that adaptation to cultural patterns and norms dominates adaptation within a social group and adaptation to the natural environment.

An individual is subjected to enculturation all his life. Therefore, it is a complex phenomenon: it runs differently in childhood and differently in later stages of life.

The process of enculturation comprises both an active enculturation of cultural patterns and norms as well as more subtle, often unconscious learning through observation. In both cases the contents adopted by an individual are culturally defined (Segal, Campbell and Herskovits 1966,

p. 9). In fact, enculturation is a process of conscious or unconscious conditioning, operating however within borders delimited by cultural patterns and norms. "(...) enculturation is the mechanism which orders for each of its members the form extent of accepted modes of conduct and aspiration, and also sets the limits within which variation in individual behavior is sanctioned" (Herskovits 1972, p. 76).

All patterns of thinking and acting valid in a given society are so strongly internalized by its members that their behavior runs mostly automatically beyond the level of consciousness. However, even the most automatized behavior whose sanctions are self-understandable to an individual, does not cease to be a meaningful behavior and thus culturally defined.

The process of enculturation gives man a kind of equipment thanks to which he becomes a fully functioning member of the social group to which he belongs by birth. It equips him with technological knowledge, a system of religious beliefs, a code of moral norms; it channels his creative impulses of artistic character as well as socializes him by a system of rewards and punishments expressed by cultural patterns.

On the other hand, this process imposes limitations on an individual resulting from cultural patterns valid in his (her) society. These patterns, however, do not determine univocally the behavior of an individual but establish to a greated or smaller extent the range of its differentiation. "Culture is not a straitjacket. It is a loose garment, and just as no two societies have identical cultural patterns, so no two members of the same society have identical behavior patterns" (Herskovits 1972, p. 87).

The cultural patterns of each society, regardless of the degree of their acquisition by particular members, do not exclude alternative patterns which could be developed by invention or borrowing. "(...) the force of enculturation does not rule out the possibility of re-enculturation" (Idem). Mutual influence of enculturating and re-enculturating processes is manifested by cultural differentiation, both in the synchronic as well as diachronic dimension.

Patterns and norms internalized during enculturation constitute the framework within which an individual interprets his experiences. Therefore, an accurate definition by the researcher of what is normal or abnormal in human behavior, depends on the cultural framework. The acknowledgement or omission of the framework, decides for example about a different qualification of the phenomenon of possession known to the inhabitants of Africa and to people of the New World originating from that continent. Possession is the highest state of religious experience for them. It is the state during which the personality of an individual experiencing it is replaced by god "coming into his head" (Herskovits

124

1948, p. 66). A person experiencing possession shows often a complete transformation of personality and participants of the ceremony consider him to be a real god.

Scholars who were not anthropologists described this phenomenon in terms of pathology because of its surface similarity to cases noted in psychological and psychiatric literature. Trances of people experiencing possession are similar to hysterie, therefore it was not difficult to equal them with manifestations of neurotic or even psychotic abnormality found in societies of the West. Such a treatment of possession neglects its cultural meaning and passes over its cultural framework. However, when an anthropologist takes into consideration the cultural context of this phenomenon, he cannot think of it as abnormal. It is so because the experience of possession is culturally determined and the way of experiencing it is acquired through learning and practicing. Every act of a person experiencing possession is in such an agreement with the valid cultural pattern that the participants of a ceremony are able to identify the god appearing to them through the mediation of this person on the basis of certain features of his behavior.

Interpretations of possession given in African and Afro-American societies situate it within understandable, predictable and normal human behavior. On the other hand, its descriptions formulated in terms of psychopathology do not reflect in any way its cultural dimension qualifying them as abnormal behavior.

Ethnocentrism is the basis for natural, popular evaluation of cultural phenomena and it is understood by Herskovits (1948, p. 68) as the "point of view that one's own way of life is to be preferred to all others". Such a point of view results from the process of enculturation and particular individuals accept it whether it is verbalized by them or not. It is an evident way verbalized and rationalized within European culture. Among non-Western (illiterate) societies it is generally accepted without distinct verbalization. It is however indirectly expressed in their myths, proverbs and language habits, e.g. their proper names (autoethnonyms) generally equal the term *human beings.*

European ethnocentrism is manifested among others by the Enlightenment idea of progress and by referring to evolutionistic concepts of social and cultural development. Evaluation of cultures in terms civilized — primitive is one of its indicators, clearly noticable in these conceptions. Treating all primitive cultures as similar is its other aspect.

Indicating the evaluative usage of these terms, the author of *Man and his works* notices also their descriptive function. He proposes however to accept other terms, without evaluative connotations, to express ideas constituting their descriptive meaning. He personally takes the term *nonliterate* instead of *primitive,* *"because it is colorless, conveys its meaning unambiguosly, and is readily applicable to data it seeks to delimit"* (Herskovits 1948, p. 75).

Accepting that values are relative to culture, Herskovits does not negate their existence or their psychological validity.

Instead of underscoring differences from absolute norms that, however objectively arrived at, nonetheless the product of a given time and place, the relativistic point of view brings into relief the validity of every set of norms for the people whose lives are guided by them, and the values these represent (Herskovits 1948, p. 76).

Thus, from the relativistic point of view only relative values exist and are of psychological validity. However, there are no absolute values. Herskovits, using the term *absolutes,* does not however call in this way objective, transcendent to every culture values, but only those cultural values which are considered to be absolute by members of a given society and universalized by them in various contacts with other societies of different axiological orientation. "Absolutes are fixed, and, in so far as convention is concerned, are not admitted to have variation, to differ from culture to culture, from epoch to epoch" (Herskovits 1948, p. 76).

Absolute values understood in this way are distinguished by the adherent of cultural relativism from universals which "(...) comprise the least common denominators in the code of all human groups" (Herskovits 1951, p. 162). These values can be discovered inductively by extracting them from a spectrum of differentiation which particular systems of values represent.

Thesis that there are no absolute criteria of values does not however exclude the possibility that such criteria are contained in cultural universals. Certain values can be distinguished in all cultures although the institutional forms present in two cultures are not identical. Morality, predilection for beauty and certain standards of truth are of universal character. The differentiation of forms which these attitudes take, results only from the specific history of particular societies in which they are manifested. In each society "(...) criteria are subject to continuous questioning, continuous change. But the basic conceptions remain, to channel thought and direct conduct, to give purpose of living" (Herskovits 1948, pp. 76-77).

Herskovits distinctly distinguishes his own standpoint from the position of moral relativity (1948, p. 77) or — as he calls it — moral anarchy which negates that man's moral acts are culturally sanctioned. Cultural relativism acknowledges the existence of moral integration in every society. Obedience of moral norms of a group by every individual is necessary for maintaining regularity in social life. These norms are implanted in particular individuals during their enculturation. These enculturations are so similar that the degree of differentiation resulting from them is negligible. In turn, this small differentiation of values recognized by members of a given social group limite the range of individual deviations from common attitudes and accepted moral acts. Cultural relativism admits a relativity of values, also moral, on the cross-cultural level, but not on the intra-cultural one. Therefore, it cannot be considered as moral relativity.

Interpretations of the relativistic point of view as a specific version of moral relativity do not take into consideration its positive axiological aspect. It is

> (...) a philosophy which, in recognizing the values set up by every society to guide its own life, lays stress on the dignity inherent in every body of custom, and on the need for tolerance of conventions though they may differ from one's own (Herskovits 1948, p. 76).

The relativistic point of view comprises also the research activity of an anthropologists; as he is a member of a definite society in which he was enculturated. During his own enculturation he internalized many basic assumptions, patterns and cultural norms of which he makes use to a great degree unconsciously. Undertaking investigations in a strange cultural community he should however — if he intends to grasp the meanings of its members' behavior, their patterns and cultural norms — keep scientific detachment which in turn forces "a rigid exclusion of value-judgements" (Herskovits 1948, pp. 80-81). Thus, acting on the principle of cultural relativism he should try his best "(...) to see the culture in terms of its own evaluative system" (Segall, Campbell and Herskovits 1956, p. 17). An anthropologist's task, consisting in collecting an adequate set of facts may be achieved only to such a degree to which "(...) he frees himself of *a priori* cultural judgements" (Herskovits 1972, p. 91).

The standpoint presented in *Man and his works* has not always been understood in agreement with the author's intentions. Objections raised against it have been in mostly on a different understanding of various statements in which the relativistic point of view was expressed. Answering these unaccurate interpretations and critical arguments resulting from them, Herskovits introduces a differentiation which is essential for understanding his position and for further discussion on cultural relativism. In "Tender- and tough-minded anthropology and the study of values in culture" (1951) he distinguishes three "completely different aspects" of his own standpoint: 1) methodological, 2) philosophical, and 3) practical.

The methodological aspect is constituted by a principle ordering to aim for the highest degree of objectivity (attainable in anthropological studies). A researcher

> (...) seeks to understand the sanctions of behavior in terms of the established relationships within the culture itself, and refrains from making interpretations that arise from a preconceived frame of reference (Herskovits 1951b, p. 24).

The philosophical aspect concerns the essence of cultural values and epistemological implications which result from recognizing the mechanism of enculturation. In turn, the practical aspect is connected with applying philosophical principles in non-scientific activity — particularly in the sphere of relations between members of various cultural groups.

These three aspects are considered by Herskovits to be elements of a logical sequence which in general agrees with the historical development of the idea of cultural relativism. Thus, its methodological aspect from the point of which empirical data are recorded and worked out and which in turn implies certain epistemological theses, is the first one both in the logical and historical sense. Without the earlier collected vast ethnographic documentation showing cross-cultural similarities and differences, one could hardly imagine "a systematic theory of cultural relativism" (Idem).

Data of this kind give rise to the philosophical aspect of this theory from which in turn follow its practical implications.

Problems discussed during the presentation of cultural relativism reflect, according to Herskovits, the experience of enculturation in which absolute values are emphasized. These problems can be observed only within such cultures as the European one. At the same time it is difficult to understand the relativistic point of view within a culture which stresses absolute values.

Finally, I would like to return to questions formulated after the presentation of the typology of various forms of relativism worked out within the British philosophy of social sciences. These questions concerned the reasons of divergence in qualification of cultural relativism which for Lukes is an empirical position not falling even under the category of moral relativism in the metaethical sense, whereas for Hollis and Lukes it is a case of perceptual relativism — one of the versions of cognitive relativism. I suggested then that these two different qualifications might refer to various aspects of cultural relativism and not to it as a whole; in this case no divergence would appear. The third possibility is fully actualized when these qualifications are referred to the three aspects of cultural relativism distinguished by Herskovits. This however gives rise to another question: Are these only seemingly divergent qualifications adequate? At first glance it seems that it is so but this answer is only preliminary one. The detailed answer require however a separate discussion.

Translated by Stefan Wiertlewski

REFERENCES

1. Campbell, D.T. (1972). "Introduction". In M.J. Herskovits (Ed.). *Cultural relativism: perspectives in cultural pluralism.* New York: Random House.
2. Herskovits, M.J. (1948). *Man and his works: the science of cultural anthropology.* New York: A. Knopf.
3. Herskovits, M.J. (1951a). "On cultural and psychological reality". In J.H. Rohrer & M. Sherif (Eds.). *Social psychology at the crossroads.* New York: Harper and Brothers.
4. Herskovits, M.J. (1951b). "Tender- and tough-minded anthropology and the study of values". *Anthropology, 7,* 22-31.
5. Herskovits, M.J. (1972). "Cultural diversity and world peace." In M.J. Herskovits (Ed.). *Cultural relativism: perspectives in cultural pluralism.* New York: Random House.
6. Hollis, M., & Lukes, S. (1982). "Introduction". In M. Hollis & S. Lukes (Eds.). *Rationality and relativism.* Oxford: Basil Blackwell.
7. Lukes, S. (1977). "Relativism: cognitive and moral". In *Essays in social theory.* London: Macmillan Press.
8. Sapir, E. (1985). "The status of linguistics as a science". In D.G. Mandelbaum (Ed.). *Selected writings of Edward Sapir in language, culture, and personality.* Berkeley: University of California Press.
9. Segall, M.H., Campbell, D.T., & Herskovits, M.J. (1966). *The influence of culture on visual perception.* Indianapolis: Bobbs-Merill.

Włodzimierz Ławniczak

THEORETICAL PROBLEMS OF REINTERPRETATION

Certain questions concerning the theory of science cannot be avoided when considering the concept of reinterpretation. Only when they are answered it is possible to put forward hypotheses concerning the objective causes of the historical changeability and variability of reinterpretation. Naturally, each hypothesis of this kind is bound to share the fate of all other interpretations which it concerns: it is replaced with another, possibly more adequate one.

Asking philosophical questions concerning the theory of science in reference to the subject of interest of the historians of science brings about impatience and sometimes even an opposition within their community. They believe that the research over the history of particular disciplines or their groups is autonomous in relation to the theory of science. Acceptance of such standpoint results in false methodological consciousness of the historians of science. The assumptions of the theory of science actually adopted by them look like a jungle of vague intuitions. I am stressing it here because I intend to relate the concept of research progress with the question of why the theory and history of the science of art records such a frequent occurrence of interpretational changes within their scope.

The well known object of interpretation of a researcher of fine arts, literature or music, i.e. such artistic disciplines in which the culturally stabile sense of individual pieces is represented by indicating an individual vision of the world, is the produced individual states of affairs. This state is included either in the syntactic or quasi-syntactic sphere of the piece, or in the sphere constituting the literal (semantic) subject reference of the former (i.e. presented reality), or in the sphere of the aesthetic vision of the world, symbolically communicated by the piece. In its intention, the interpretation of those states of affairs is an answer to the question of why certain types of states of affairs appeared in a given work of art. Providing the answers, scientists indicate the purpose of their occurrence and characterize the less or more culturally "binding", directive knowledge, thanks to which a rationally functioning artist has a right to expect the future recipient to relate a certain property observed in a particular sphere of the piece with the purpose mentioned above.

The logical structure of interpretation which I have suggested becomes similar to a research activity called explanation (with an rationality assumption as a general premiss) and so it can be considered as a case of the latter.

As I have just stated an art researcher refers in a particular practice to the existing knowledge, which can be presented in the form of directives of the following contents: whenever in a given sphere of an art piece there appears a situation which provokes one to approach it in the form of a given state of affairs, it is necessary to relate to it a certain given state of affairs viewed as its sense. An appropriately arranged set of this kind of directives is defined here as a theory which systematizes interpretation. The above indicates that if particular research activities called the interpretations of art pieces are to be viewed as correct and cognitively credible, they cannot violate the directives or interpretational rules representing the style of art in a given period. A theory which systematizes the interpretation of art pieces of a given style possesses in fact a status of a historical hypothesis and can, therefore, be acknowledged to be a kind of a scientific theory, that is if we consider the area of science to incorporate the knowledge which uses pre-axiomatically applied concepts.

A system of historically descriptionally viewed theories which systematize interpretation reconstructs the knowledge which, besides the most general judgements about the world, includes also certain orders of values and linguistic-artistic competence of artists. I call this system the *historical-theoretical* or *interpretational coefficient* of art pieces. It seems reasonable at this point to stress one component of that coefficient, namely the linguistic-artistic competence. The interpretational rules included in it make it necessary to combine certain features, or — as Ingarden calls them — artistic properties (or, to be more precise, the state of affairs in which artistic relations or properties occur), with certain artistic values, which in turn should be related to appropriate aesthetic values. Since the interpretational rules which can be expressed with appropriate directives most often relate aesthetic values with worldview values, the rules concerning the former and the latter are of a semantic character; the respective values are communicated by pieces of art.

Therefore, contrary to what often happens in the interpretational practice of the historians of art and music, one cannot speak of aesthetic or worldview values of art pieces, which are at the same time denied the function of presentation. A work of art which fails to present (in a properly broad sense) is also unable to communicate aesthetic and worldview values. An example of interpreting (explaining) an aesthetic value in terms of a worldview value is a well known statement of Riegel concerning Michaelangelo's *Last Judgement*. It says that Christ's gesture express "condemnation", i.e. a certain worldview value, which makes the terror emanating from Christ's face, the terror indicated by the Holy Virgin's fearful crouching, understandable. Naturally, the set of artistic properties used in the "linguistic" (presenting) sphere finds its explaining value (in the rationalizing sense) in that fear.

Let us notice that the above interpretation is of a historical character and in this aspect it enhances the theory which systematizes the interpretation of works in the style of mannerism, contributing an element of cognitive progress. For that reason the states of affairs in particular presented parts of the fresco *Christ raising a hand, The Holy Virgin is presented crouching* find their explaining values, explicitly unobserved before. They are explained by the presence of such communicated values as "condemnation" and "terror". Those values are not invented *ad hoc*; both occupy an important position in the hierarchies of values adopted in the artistic utterances of the mentioned style. On the other hand, within the theory which systematizes the interpretation of artistic works in the style of mannerism, it would be impossible to find a historical justification for those of its potential components which would legitimize the explanation of the features of the presented figure of the Holy Virgin through the comicality of situation. After the interpretational discoveries of Riegel, this explanation would be similarly unacceptable as an attempt to explain in the modern times the phenomenon of sun rise with the fact of the Sun's revolvement around the axis of the Earth.

The artistic means applied in the exemplary piece of art considered here, meant to achieve an aesthetic value, i.e. an aesthetic communication of an appropriate vision of the world, are at the same time an instrument of enforcing the valorizational function of worldview values, which axiologically arrange this vision of the world. One must not fail to observe that those means respectively limit the scope of the concept of those values, or — in more general terms — historically modify their content. The rules of artistic competence possible to be reconstructed and the system of presented object references connected with them, the aesthetic semantics orienting them, perform in the area of worldview values communicated by the work of art a role similar to the one we currently ascribe to certain forms of linguistic competence in the theories having an axiomatic form. These forms are expressed through explicitly formulated axiomatic assumptions selecting the current conceptual intuition by offering the selected intuitions a status that is revealed through an "imperative" of recognizing appropriate statements (axioms). Thus, if our example can be considered to be a paradigmatic example of the concept of interpretation outlined above, we may already ask a question of what objective conditions must be met in order for an appropriate change of a theory that systematizes the interpretation of a given work of art, style or epoch to be recognized as an expression of cognitive progress. Before we answer the above question, let us ask with what a change of this kind begins. In other words, we shall first consider the context of discovery and then the context of justification of a theory which systematizes interpretation. Naturally we shall deal with questions that belong to the area of interest of the psychology of scientific discoveries. The reason is that a theory answering the question concerning the formal form assumed by the processes occurring in the consciousness of the one who carries out a socially recognized scientific discovery has not been constructed yet and most probably never will be.

All normatively oriented programs of the methodology of scientific research assume that experience is the stimulus for a new scientific theory. The goal of theories is to explain the physical phenomena perceivable by the senses (aided by various instruments), with the use of the knowledge of established regularities, which connect what is experienced with what is not sensually perceived. Theories understood in the above way can be compared to a spot-light which illuminates a piece of reality. It is not until an observer, who moves within the range of the light, accidentally comes across an object invisible in the light that he realizes the limited nature of his theory and the necessity to replace it with another one. The above metaphor seems to be stressing very strongly a common belief, according to which the most important role in the context of a scientific discovery is performed by experience. At, what Kuhn calls a normal stage of science, in the period of "dogmatic sleep", when researchers feel excused by tradition from the duty of revising the theoretical framework of the existing theoretical (interpretational) co-efficient and focus their attention on solving "puzzles", no attention is paid to a question whether those puzzles are not actually "anomalies" brought about by the inherent properties of the theory. Lakatos, who appreciated the importance of that problem, described it in the form of the following rhetorical aphorism: "theories sail across the ocean of anomalies". I do not believe, however, that the formation of "anomalies", in the situation when a given theory that systematizes interpretation was considered to be an accurate reconstruction of the artistic-esthetic consciousness existing in a given historical period, could cause a change in the attitude towards that theory and bring about its revision. As it is indicated by the history of artistic research, each "anomaly" — each state of affairs which is ascertained but does not result from the theory — can be either explained by adding certain theoretical assumptions or re-structuring them, or moved beyond the scope of a given piece or art in which certain features that cannot be interpreted with the rules of a given style have been observed by recognizing that piece. This is what happened with the monuments which had been originally classified as belonging to the Renaissance and were later associated with mannerism. By and large, I would be hesitant to ascribe an important role in the process of the evolution of a theory to "empiricism". I believe that a more important role in that process is performed by "bold" theoretical hypotheses, the origin of which should not be ascribed to the "empirically" observed difficulties of their application. Rather, it must be ascribed to the sphere of changes occurring within the scope of the broadly understood metaphysics, suggesting to researchers particular interpretational ideas and aesthetic values connected with them. The crucial role in this respect always seems to be performed by appropriate worldview values "suggested" to researchers by the epoch in which they live. These values "tinged" such concepts as time, space, mass, force, speed, rhythm, harmony, etc. For that reason no changes in the interpretation of property or quality in both spheres of a work of art (aesthetic and worldview), the syntactic and semantic one, should be expected of art scientists, who are ill-disposed towards all novel concepts in the area of history and the theory of religion, philosophy, aesthetics, science, and — more generally — culture. It is there, rather than in the theory and history of a broadly understood art, that we should expect to find impulses for the construction of new systems of interpretation. History indicates that this source has been drawn from by the great revivers of the history of art such as Riegel, Dvorak, Wölfflin, or Panofsky, to mention only a few. I shall not reconstruct the norms and worldview beliefs determining, according to the authors mentioned above, the artistic activity of the historical epochs or styles investigated by them. I shall merely point to the fact that all of them try to systematize interpretation in a substantial way, by indicating those norms and beliefs as the universal orientational principles of all artistic practice.

The reconstruction of the most important norms and beliefs existing at a given time and determining the artistic (or, more broadly, cultural) activity is always of a hypothetical nature and changes as the time passes. Such a reconstruction is never final. Therefore, the interpretations controlled by it are also not final, even if they are viewed as model or classical ones in a certain period of time.

And so I have ascertained that the sources of changes of a system of explaining, considered here in the form of theories that systematize interpretation, must not be searched for in the circumstance by the principles of which empirical material resists the interpreter and the "anomalies" accumulated in this way leave in the works subjected to interpretation a sphere of undefined spots, but rather in the more and more frequently realized belief that the artistic (cultural) practice of a given time was controlled by a system of norms and — more generally — beliefs, different than the present one.

The approach proposed here, according to which it is not "empiricism" but the dominating "metaphysics" of an epoch that imposes new forms of the theory that systematizes interpretation, can be extended over non-artistic disciplines. This extension makes it possible to avoid certain problems occurring in the theory of science, particularly the question how to avoid charging scientific theories with putting forward *ad hoc*-hypotheses. This question has been considered so important that the methodology of research programs views its main task to lie in establishing the criteria of exclusion from the set of empirical data supporting the theory those which are *ad hoc*. It goes as far as to claim that the facts used in theory construction cannot be used as an empirical basis supporting it. No criteria of exclusion of the data for the explanation of which the theory had been formed has been found so far. It is impossible to determine whether the facts supporting the theory were known to the scientist at the time of constructing the theory or not.

Let us now return to the primary question concerning the context of justification of interpretational research, namely what conditions must be met in order to recognize the change of a theory that systematizes the interpretation of the works of art of a given style or epoch or the works of an individual artist. I shall limit the outline of the answer to the above question to listing some of the criteria of evaluation of the competitive theories that systematize the interpretation of works of fine arts.

The criteria of adopting a competitive paradigm, proposed by Kuhn, have generally been regarded as subjective and psychological, and — for some other reasons — irrational. A person who took a stand in the fight against this subjectivism and irrationalism was I. Lakatos, who adopted Kuhn's belief that the behavior proposed by falsificationalism has not performed any significant role in the development of scientific research.

The question Lakatos asked was how theories should be evaluated. The primary criterion of the evaluation is the degree to which it is supported by the accumulated empirical material. A scientific theory is the more cognitively progressive the more facts it explains. In our case, a more cognitively fruitful historical interpretational coefficient would be the one within the scope of which we could carry out interpretations that would leave less undefined spots in the analyzed works of art of a given style. Such a coefficient would also have to determine in a sufficiently precise way its range of applicability.

However, the degree of support a theory receives from the accumulated empirical material, i.e. the concept of the growth of contents of an empirical theory, is also understood as the ability of the theory to predict more unexpected facts than an alternative theory and thus also its ability to include more empirical contents.

One could conclude that the above criterion does not concern the methodological research program which generates new theories that systematize the interpretation of works of art, new interpretational coefficients. According to a general belief, the humanities do not accumulate prognostic knowledge. However, even a very superficial insight into the interpretational practice of art scientists makes it possible to observe that the values assumed in the new interpretational coefficient are exemplified by a constantly greater number of works of art in the course of research. Certain properties of well known and interpreted works have been totally disregarded or ignored as a cognitive problem because of the previous coefficient, which in this case means that they were irrelevant from the artistic-aesthetic point of view. Yet, even in this case the thesis that all observation is carried out within a theory is confirmed. The fact that on the basis of theories of the humanities that systematize interpretation also successful prognoses can be put forward can be witnessed by anyone who has encountered the problems of reconstruction of lost pieces of texts or lost fragments of art pieces. A coincidence or planned search which succeeds may often serve as a rigid test of a given prognosis. However, these successful programs are by no means suggested by empirically encountered interpretational difficulties, which is in, cated by the fact that new, historically accurate interpretations, new theories that systematize interpretation anticipate artistic "utterances" discovered only much later.

Another criterion of the rational acceptance of the new research program is the heuristic power it possesses. It contains the so-called system of ideas constituting the positive heuristics of a given program. It is characterized by the fact that a heuristically prolific program not only suggests a possibly compete description of the known world, but also implicitly includes a system of ideas assumed by it, a system of its further corrections, precise specifications and consistent development. Moreover, it offers an opportunity to introduce additional assumptions in order to apply them in new disciplines. Besides that, such a heuristics offers indications concerning the way in which the already formulated assumptions can be transformed or changed when interpretational difficulties appear. And so a frequent occurrence of new theories is explained in terms of the presence of positive heuristics in the research program that contains it. A positive and — in certain indicated respects — efective heuristics makes it possible to point to the weaknesses of the existing, alternative theories of the program, indicate the direction of their replacement, quite independently of the encountered empirical difficulties.

The iconological theory put forward by Panofsky can be recognized as such a systematization of interpretation in which the positive heuristics is "embedded". Therefore, at a certain time it began to complete for the role of a dominating historical interpretational coefficient of works of art. It had generated a number of various theories which "specifically" systematize different interpretations. Those theories encompassed the oldest epochs, concerning at the same time the almost modern period. In their interpretational practice, art scientists have commonly used the iconological method. The scope of that theory has made it possible to ascribe to almost all works certain communicational-worldview senses, which subordinated artistic and aesthetic values.

However, not even the most voluminous theory that systematizes interpretation can be considered universal; the same holds for the methodological research program it represents. As a result, a historical interpretational coefficient, implied by even the most perfect theory of that type, cannot be considered to be universal. The reason for it is that this coefficient is viewed as ideal artists' knowledge and norms that cannot be completely updated, the knowledge and norms in the name of which those artists' works were created. It can be imagined as an ideal point of view which the real artists and the interpreters of their works unsuccessfully desire to achieve.

If the current historical coefficient of the interpretation of works of art is viewed as an equivalent of a research program, the criteria of its justified replacement with another coefficient must be recognized as analogous to those accepted for the purpose of a rational replacement of some programs by others. Needless to say, the criteria presented here have been discussed much too briefly, while the analogies have been presented much too superficially, in order to recognize their justificational value. Yet, this superficiality and briefness can quite easily be transformed into appropriate thoroughness. By accepting it, I could assume the role of an adherent of the concept of the theory of science represented by the London School of Economics. (Let me add that some of the above ideas were suggested by discussions included in *Progress and rationality in science,* Dordrecht 1978). My arguments so far have followed its spirit to such an extent to which I meant to point to the fact that the theoretical problems of interpretation in art sciences do not have to and should not be solved in a way completely independent of the one that is indicated by the theoretical reflection on the methodologically more advanced sciences.

However, my balancing of the cognitive status of the theory that systematizes the interpretation of works of art and the theory of mathematized natural sciences is caused not only by the intention to use the research results of Popper's school in order to obtain certain conclusions concerning the former, but also by a reverse intuition, i.e. the modification of those results from the point of view of what is realized as a result of an analysis of theories that systematize interpretation. Such an analysis indicates that the primary factor of changes characterizing the subsequent forms of a theoretical way of interpreting the past, currently created, and possible to be created in the future works of art is the adoption of a new, appropriately changed, general view of the world, i.e. *Weltanschauung*. In the same way in which the adoption of its perspective dictates the way of "reading" the worldview sense of works of art, the way of detecting aesthetic means to communicate it, the artistic means which find their explanatory power in aesthetic senses, the adoption of a certain worldview perspective dominates the form of a mathematical-natural theory predominant in a given epoch. In both cases the mentioned perspective leads to a theoretical idea and in both cases this idea is verified by the scope of its explanatory or prognostic empirical applicability, in particular by the scope of its interpretational applicability, encompassing well known works, works discovered as future masterpieces, currently created or even predicted. In both cases we are dealing with the anticipating function of the mathematical-natural theory and the theory that systematizes the interpretation of works of art.

The above analogy suggests not only the reference of appropriate diagnoses made by the methodology of the natural-mathematical sciences to the artistic activity, but also the reverse situation. It makes us refer the knowledge of evolutional mechanisms governing the changes of theories that systematize the interpretation of works of art to the development of the research practice of mathematized natural sciences. There is no doubt that suggestions of the latter type are disregarded by Popper's philosophy of science. There are at least two reasons for that. First, for an genuine follower of Popper, the great speed of certain changes and their close connection to worldview changes immediately bear distrust in respect of their cognitive meaning. Being a falsificationist, Popper, as well as his followers, does not differ from a positivist significantly enought to let us suppose that the constitution of a new knowledge, qualified by the latter as "true" and by the former as the knowledge of an increased "contents of truth" is conditioned by factors of a cultural nature in the same way as the constitution of "false" knowledge and, respectively, the knowledge of a decreased "contents of truth". It is assumed that the "truth" has the nature of something obvious, that it is given by the "light". As a consequence, it is assumed that only "false" statements require a socio-cultural explanation. Such explanation is at the same time supposed to indicate the obstacles encountered by the activity of the "mind's natural light". Secondly, what is even more important, a follower of Popper has no understanding of the fact that scientific knowledge, which he believes to be embodied by theories of mathematized natural sciences, is as a matter of fact a similar cultural product to particular interpretational contexts of art pieces and, as a consequence, the humanist interpretations which systematize interpretation and which reconstruct these contexts. Their accuracy is not imposed upon "the mind led by the light emanating from it". It seems that an adherent of Popper's concept does not suspect that science — with all its findings — is also a product of culture. He does accept, unwillingly, that those findings must — according to the author of *Objective knowledge* – be placed in the "third world", though he is far from drawing appropriate conclusions from that ascertainment.

And yet, these conclusions seem to be self-evident. Not only do they require that the cognitive status of mathematized natural sciences be viewed in the same way as the subsequent theories that systematize the interpretation of works of art, but also that one search for some formulae common for both cases which would explain generally the changes of both. In the case of the latter, it is the changes reconstructed by non-spontaneous, historical transformations of interpretational coefficients.

We already know that transformations occurring in both cultural disciplines are caused by the appearance of new worldviews on the "social scene". Is it the ultimate explanatory condition? It may be so. Perhaps, however, there is a further reason for the social recognition, social acceptance of those new worldview. The adoption of a concept which would constitute a source of further explanation would seem inviting, for it would also suggest an answer to the question why the growth of explanatory-prognostic, interpretational-anticipational applicability of, respectively, the mathematical-natural theory and the theory that systematizes the interpretation of works of art should provide an argument determining their acceptance on a universal scale. In the former case, we would be dealing with a significant extension of the technological effectiveness of a theory, while in the latter — with the extension of its motivational effectiveness.

Translated by Krzysztof Sawala

Michał Piotrowski

ON TWO "INTRINSIC" MEANINGS OF MUSIC

Modern aesthetics offers two distinct conceptions of value[1] of a musical work — henceforth called *heteronomous* and *autonomous*[2] — based on different answers to the question of "relation between music and extra-musical reality". Those who hold the heteronomous view, believe that musical structures are *manifestations* of extra-musical objects and states of affairs. The proponents of the autonomy theory claim the opposite, i.e. that relations between "music" and the "external world" either do *not* occur at all, or are of marginal significance, and that it is the "internal" structural relations within a musical work which decide about its value.

In what follows, we will be concerned with the autonomy theory, or to be precise, with two of its many specific solutions, both — of a positive character. The aforementioned internal musical relations are conceived in a number of ways, most of them aiming at one of two directions. According to the *substantial* approach, the musical structure is a semantically unmarked object whose meaning is wholly confined to composition of acoustic features; thus, it is seen as "pure form", a construct of "musical thinking", "logic" or "syntax", or else, as a peculiar phenomenon governed by certain "regularities" (mostly, of an "objective nature"). Within the other approach, often called *semantic,* the same structure is dealt with in terms of its symbolic character, but — unlike in heter-

---

1. I assume the concept of value (sense) — in particular of aesthetic value, which is referred to throughout the work — after J. Kmita; see his *Z metodologicznych problemów interpretacji humanistycznej* (From methodology of humanistic interpretation), pp. 28 ff.; also: J. Kmita (Ed.), *Wartość, dzieło, sens. Szkice z filozofii kultury artystycznej* (Value, work of art and sense. Sketches from philosophy of artistic culture), Warsaw 1975, passim; compare: A. Zeidler, "Związki logiki z estetyką. Koncepcje metodologów poznańskich" (Relations between logic and aesthetics. The conceptions of the Poznań methodologists), in: S. Krzemień-Ojak (Ed.), *Studia o współczesnej estetyce polskiej* (Studies in contemporary Polish aesthetic), Warsaw 1977, pp. 125-143.

2. After: F.M. Gatz, *Musik-Ästhetik in ihren Hauptrichtungen. Ein Quellenbuch der deutschen Musik-Ästhetik von Kant und der Frühromantik bis zur Gegenwart,* Stuttgart 1929, pp. 11 ff. It should be added that there are also other terms for those conceptions (aesthetic orientations), e.g. *referential-absolute* (L.B. Meyer); *transcendent-immanent* (H. Goldschmidt); *expressive-immanent* (O. Elschek).

onomous theories — the sign in question will be of a specific musical kind, namely, its referent is also music.

In the paper, I will discuss one variant of the semantic approach which, due to the postulated concept of 'sign', should be better named quasi-semantic or "semantic". Within it, I can see two distinct, albeit closely related — as will be evidenced below — aspects; therefore, talking about the said autonomous conception of the "internal" musical sign and its meaning, I will be using two respective terms, i.e. *grammatical* and *connotational* (borrowing from the linguistic use of the term "connotation").

I

In aesthetic studies, the above concepts of sign and meaning are well familiar, and as far as the semantic intuitions are concerned, they do not reveal any striking differences from one study to another; at the same time, however, one can observe a great many terminological conventions. It is not difficult to find out which of them have gained the greatest popularity. As regards the former, *grammatical* viewpoint, the most frequent terms would be *operational* and *endosemantic* signs. Whatever their names, the "internal" musical signs are, as a rule, contrasted with the objects and semantic properties of the heteronomous type; accordingly, the operational and endosemantic signs are opposed to the *eidetic* and *exosemantic* (or *ectosemantic*) ones, respectively.

For instance, D. Stockmann provides the following characterization of the first pair: *eidetic* – says she — defines the content of the sign, in the sense of extra-systemic (extra-linguistic, extra-musical) reference; the other concept (i.e. operational meaning) stands for the function the sign performs in the relational system. The latter meaning is also called syntactic, formal or functional. Thus, in case of the signs which have an eidetic meaning in a system of signs, it is known what they mean, or at least, that they do mean, that they refer to something; as regards the signs in the operational sense, it is only known how to use them, how to operate them.[3] The distinction is perceived in much the same way by other writers, such as H.P. Reinecke ("The operational meaning is grounded in linguistic syntax, the eidetic one — in semantics.")[4], H.

3. D. Stockmann, "Musik als kommunikatives System", *Deutsches Jahrbuch der Musikwissenschaft* 14 (1969, ed.: 1970), p. 89.

4. H.-P. Reinecke, "'Musikalisches Verstehen' als Aspekt komplementärer Kommunikation", in: *Musik und Verstehen. Aufsätze zur semiotischen Theorie, Ästhetik und Soziologie der musikalischen Rezeption,* Hgb. von P. Faltin und H.-P. Reinecke, Köln 1973, p. 268.

Petri[5], and Ch. Seeger.[6]

Similar definitions are provided for the categories of exosemantic (ectosemantic) and endosemantic meanings. Coined originally for the needs of the information theory by W. Meyer-Eppler,[7] they seem to have been transplanted into musicology by Ch. Seeger, who understood them, respectively, as "extrinsic or outward musical meaning" and "intrinsic or inward musical meaning".[8] Unlike the former authors, W. Bright, who is also concerned with the two concepts, derives their significance for musicology from linguistics. Thus, he observes that the content of a sentence depends, in part, on its extralinguistic associations — the associations with the objects, activities and relations to which the sentence refers. At the same time, however, the sentence content is dependent on its linguistic structure, on the phonological and grammatical relations held between the sentence parts and between the sentence and other sentences. The former type of content is called *exolinguistic,* the latter — *endolinguistic.* As the terms signify the exclusively linguistic "content", Bright proposes to transform them in such a way that they be adjusted to the needs of musicology (or, of all semiotic systems). Thus, he suggests using "-semantic" in place of "-linguistic", ending up with the expressions of the desired degree of generality, i.e. *exosemantic* and *endosemantic.*[9] The terms in question find similar interpretations in H. Petri[10] and J.-J. Nattiez[11] while D. Stockmann assumes rather different conception.[12]

5. H. Petri, *Literatur und Musik. Form- und Strukturparallelen,* Göttingen 1964, p. 82.

6. Ch. Seeger, *Music as a tradition of communication discipline and play",* Part I, *Ethnomusicology* 6/1962(3), p. 156.

7. W. Meyer-Eppler, *Grundlagen und Anwedungen der Informationstheorie,* Berlin/Göttingen/Heidelberg 1959.

8. Ch. Seeger, "On the moods of a music logic", *Journal of the American Musicological Society* 13/1960, pp. 229 ff.

9. W. Bright, "Language and music: areas for cooperation", *Ethnomusicology* 7/1963(1), pp. 28 f.

10. H. Petri, *Literatur ...,* op. cit., pp. 82 f.

11. J.-J-. Nattiez, "Sémiologie musicale: l'état de la question", *Acta Musicologica* 46/1974 (2), p. 157.

12. Namely, she distinguishes two "spheres" of the communication process in music, i.e. *semantic* (or *linguistic*) and *ectosemantic* (or *extralinguistic*). The former is the sphere of all language and music signs, the "sphere of the message and its code". By the *ectosemantic* sphere, she understands the area of phenomena lying outside the message and the code, e.g. all properties which make it possible to recognize the sender of the message, to identify the degree of his "emotional arousal", and so on. In other words, we could say that in the former sphere we have signs, in the latter one — indexes. See: "Musik ...", op. cit., p. 91.

As evidenced from the above, the provided characteristics of the discussed pair of categories support the claim that the authors, in spite of their using different terms, have in mind one and the same basic distinction between two types of meaning. The same applies to many other suggestions, regardless of how unique or exotic their terminology may be.

For instance, G. Haydon speaks of *external* and *internal* meanings: while in the former case sounds signify the states of affairs "existing independently of their musical expression", the latter, internal meaning is, as he says, assigned to particular sounds with respect to their musical contexts. Thus for instance, a given sound, characterized by the quality or meaning which in non-technical terms may be called "stationary" or "static", will be rendered by the musical concept of *tonic*. One and the same sound assumes different internal meanings in different contexts: thus conceived meaning is nothing else but the harmonic function performed by a chord or by its constituent.[13] H. Petri, in turn, identifies, in one of his works, two "spheres of meaning" of a piece of music: ectosemantic and *semantic*; the basic elements of the former are *signals,* of the letter — *signs* (equivalents of language sounds and phonemes, respectively). He claims that not only the semantic status of the signals is unquestionable, but also the signs, due to the rules of a given musical system (e.g. tonal or dodecaphonic) whose elements they are, must be meaningful in their own specific way. Namely, their meanings come from "the musical grammar and syntax", and thus they can be grasped in "intrinsic musical categories". Like in language, the "content" of a performed musical act will be comprehensible as long as motifs, intervals, and the like, follow the grammatical principles of a given system.[14]

The opposition introduced by J.-J. Nattiez, i.e. between *sense* and *meaning,* also reflects the distinction in question. In the author's view, next to accounting for two distinct phenomena, the dichotomy points to an important difference between language utterances and musical structures. Thus, the latter are said to possess sense only, while meaning is believed to be a property of verbal utterances. There is little doubt, however, that Nattiez' *meaning* stands for others' exosemantic meaning, and his *sense* – for endosemantic meaning. This type of sense, writes he, is no longer a language meaning, but it comes from the application rules governing the units within the formal syntax of a given musical system at all its levels, starting with an individual style of a composer.[15]

13. G. Haydon, *On the meaning of music,* Washington 1948, pp. 14 f.
14. H. Petri, "Identität von Sprache und Musik", *Melos* 32/1965(10), p. 346.
15. J.-J. Nattiez, "Quelques problèmes de la sémiologie fonctionelle" *Semiotica* 9/1973(2), p. 185.

There are at least two reasons why the above conception is worthy of note; presently I will mention one of them, namely, its clearly normative character. Assigning to the musical work sense only, and contrasting the latter with meaning, Nattiez expresses his affinity to the autonomous approach. One could expect, therefore, that his stand is essentially distinct from the ones mentioned above, whose authors (as evidenced from their remarks) merely explicate the respective categories, abstaining from any definite commitment as to what kind of meaning they assign to musical structure. If we consider, however, the contexts of the excerpts which were referred to above, the matter looks slightly different. To start with, the authors identify "theoretically" *possible* types of meaning (or of signs), either in general semiotic systems or with reference to music only. Then they proceed to defining conditions for a system to be able to make use of the potential. As a result, it turns out that, due to specific properties of musical systems (first of all, the tonal system), the works of music which are constructed within them, can be assigned (almost exclusively) "intrinsic" (i.e. endosemantic, operational) meaning.[16]

How can this phenomenon be explained? The above general comments are far from sufficient to attempt an exhaustive answer. It does not seem difficult, however, to identify in them some basic intuitions concerning "meaning of a sign in a system of relations", or "meaning derived from language syntax" or "generated by the rules of formal syntax". There is no doubt that the intuitions parallel — *mutatis mutandis* – the ones which are held in linguistics with respect to *grammatical* (*structural*) meaning; likewise, the linguistic opposite concept, i.e. *lexical* (*dictionary*) meaning is equivalent to eidetic and exosemantic meaning. In connection with the linguistic pair, J. Lyons writes:

> The major parts of speech have "lexical" meaning; and this is given in the dictionary associated with the grammar. By contrast, the distinction between the subject and the object of a sentence, oppositions of definiteness, tense and number, and the difference between statements, questions and requests — all these distinctions are described as "structural meanings".[17]

Thus, a linguistic unit, treated as a grammatical sign, signifies a grammatical category — syntactic or morphological — of e.g. the subject, number, case, etc.; in other words, thus conceived meaning is identical with the grammatical function which an element of a language system performs.[18]

---

16. See: D. Stockmann, op. cit., p. 89; H.-P. Reinecke, op. cit., p. 268; H. Petri, *Literatur...*, op. cit., p. 82; Ch. Seeger, "Music ...", op. cit. p. 157; W. Bright, op. cit., p. 29; J.-J. Nattiez, "Semiologie ...", op. cit., pp. 166 f.
17. J. Lyons, *Introduction to linguistics,* Cambridge 1968, p. 435.
18. Z. Gołąb, A. Heinz, K. Polański, *Słownik terminologii językoznawczej* (Dic-

As seen from the above-mentioned authors, musical structure seems to be assigned exactly this kind of meaning, mainly of a syntactic type. For that reason, I opt for the term *grammatical* as the attribute of sign and meaning in the discussed conception since, in my view, such usage is the most adequate account of the observed analogies between musicology and linguistics. It is fair to admit that the conception under discussion is still lacking in precision because of the absence of the exact definition of the "category of the musical grammar and syntax", or in other words, of concrete "grammatical" functions that musical structures perform with respect to a given system. Strictly speaking, the mentioned authors do not seem to be concerned with any subtleties of the problem. It seems, however, that providing of accurate definitions should not present any difficulties; for instance, Haydon's referring "internal" meaning to the harmonic functions of particular chords may serve as indication of a general direction. After all, every formula of "musical language" could be interpreted in that way, such as the concepts related to major-minor system — tonic, subdominant, guide tone, modulation, cadence.

II

We shall turn now to some other intuitions connected with the notion of "intrinsic musical" meaning, namely, to what I named the *connotational* approach, having in mind some suggestions put forward by K. Bühler in his *Sprachtheorie*.[19] In place of connotation, one could also use such terms as valency,[20] or "syntagmatic interdependence, or presupposition".[21] Although they are all linguistic concepts, they seem best suited to provide the uniformed terminology for the categories which, so far, have been rendered by many different names and often have not been explained clearly enough, even though their authors also refer to certain analogies between musical systems and systems of language.

Let us consider, for example, an often quoted statement by G.P. Springer. As he writes, "music is devoid of 'dictionary' meaning" therefore, unlike the verbal language, the system of music cannot be presented as a communicative system. Language utterances, however,

---

tionary of linguistic terminology), Warsaw 1968, p. 213 [entry: *Gramatyczne znaczenie* (Grammatical meaning)].

19. See: A. Heinz, *Dzieje językoznawstwa w zarysie* (An outline history of linguistics), Warsaw 1978, p. 297; Gotab et al., op. cit., p. 296 [entry: *Konotacja* (Connotation)].

20. Compare: G. Helbig, *Dzieje językoznawstwa nowożytnego* (History of modern linguistics), Wrocław/Warsaw/Cracow/Gdańsk 1982, pp. 229 ff.

21. J. Lyons, *Introduction ...*, op. cit., p. 440.

can be assigned, next to his mentioned "lexical" senses, also "purely formal meanings". Hence, the claim that musical structures are not composed of "dictionary" meanings, does not rule out the existence of any analogies between language and music. It is the "purely fo.mal meanings" (in fact, only them) that are characteristic of musical production. This kind of meaning, says Springer, contrasted to "lexical" meaning and called different names (e.g. "grammatical" or "structural"), is directly related to certain musical categories, such as "guide tones", "passing-notes", "dominant" or "tonic". Thus conceived grammar of music defines certain structural relations within the "permissible", i.e. predictable context.[22]

Short of the final part of the above comment, one could think that the author of *Language and music* understands the "grammatical" meaning in the same way as was discussed earlier. In fact, however, he seems to have in mind not so much the categorial function of some specific musical structure (e.g. "guide tone" or "tonic"), as just the "predictable context" which determines such function. As should become evident, the notion of "permissible context" plays a crucial role in the conception of our interest.

Thus for instance, Eco refers to the same question when he mentions "probabilistic relations". In his opinion, music is a typical example of the purely syntactic semiotic system, devoid of semantic *depth*;[23] tones of a scale are figures making up meaningful signs, however, (their meanings being syntactic, not semantic), such as intervals and chords.[24] The syntactic meaning (or the information identified with it) is always based on a "specific probabilistic convention", on specific "rules of probability": intervals, appearing in a work composed according to the rules of a given convention (e.g. following the rules of "tonal grammar"), constitute organic relations within the work. In order to grasp those relations, the listener always chooses the simplest way, using the "indicator of rationality", dependent, first of all, on the accepted language conventions.[25] It is the "organic relations" that determine the said type of meaning: the syntactic meaning of a sign is the following context of that sign, i.e. another "interval or chord", which can be predicted within the given

22. G.P. Springer, "Language and music: parallels and divergencies", in: *For Roman Jakobson,* comp. by M. Halle, The Hague 1956, pp. 508 f.
23. U. Eco, *A theory of semiotics,* Bloomington, London 1976, p. 88.
24. U. Eco, *Pejzaż semiotyczny* (Semiotic landscape), Polish transl. of *La Struttura Assente,* Warsaw 1972, p. 198.
25. U. Eco, *Dzieło otwarte. Forma i nieokreśloność w poetykach współczesnych* (An open work. Form and indeterminacy in contemporary poetics [Opera Aperta]), Polish transl, Warsaw 1973, pp. 177 f.

"musical probabilistic convention" (what is important, the higher ambiguity of a sign, the higher its aesthetic value).

The above outlined proposal is certainly representative of the discussed conception, but there are other, better developed contributions, such as those by W. Coker and, above of all, by L.B. Meyer. They belong to the most interesting theories of modern aesthetics of music, even though they are far from uncontroversial, in particular the one by Meyer.

In W. Coker's view, it is the concept of the iconic sign that is of major significance in music. His argument runs as follows. If we apply to aesthetic the semiotic perspective, a work of art can be approached either as a sign or as a symbolic structure. Of all types of signs, it is the iconic sign that plays the dominant role in a piece of art, even though the other types are not disregarded either. The *iconic sign* (or in short: *icon*) shares a property, or properties, with its referent; in other words, icons are in many respects like the objects they denote.[26] This is of extreme relevance for aesthetics of music because musical works are first of all iconic sign structures whose constituents are *musical gestures*. A *musical gesture* is defined as complex stimulus causing reactions in composers, performers and listeners, and influencing the musical process as well. The musical gesture contains a recognizable formal unit; its essence is selection and organization of melodic and rhythmical features of musical movement; its meaning consists of both musical objects, and nonmusical objects, facts and actions. The musical gestures, adds Coker, the simplest one of which is a single sound, are usually called "figures" or "motifs".[27]

As mentioned above, the gesture-icon may stand for musical and extramusical states of affairs. In this connection, there are two types of meaning identified in Coker's work *Music and meaning,* i.e. *congeneric* and *extrageneric.* In the author's opinion, they are "two major classes of all aesthetic meanings"; in each of them the signs reveal resemblance or correspondence to their referents; in the former class, the signs and their referents belong to the same "genus" while in the latter type, they come from two different "genera".[28] Thus, a *congeneric musical meaning* appears in the iconic sign situation in which a part of a musical work is interpreted as a sign of another fragment, either of the same, or of a different piece of music. Accordingly, an *extrageneric meaning* occurs when a musical gesture is a sign of a nonmusical object.[29] Needless to say,

26. W. Coker, *Music and meaning. A theoretical introduction to musical aesthetics,* New York 1972, p. 30.
27. Ibid., pp. 18 ff.
28. Ibid., p. 60.
29. Ibid., p. 61.

147

Coker's distinction conforms to the ones we discussed earlier, i.e. between "external" and "internal" musical meanings, or between autonomy and heteronomy of meaning of music. Unlike the former authors, however, Coker maintains that both types of meaning belong to the system of music. In his view, on the basis of true or imaginary resemblance, the reference of a musical gesture may constitute either one, or two simultaneous iconic meanings, i.e. (1) a musical gesture may refer to another musical gesture, or (2) musical gesture may denote a non-musical object.

Furthermore, the author identifies several varieties of the *congeneric* relation. First, if the relation occurs within one musical work, we have the "congeneric *intrafluent* meaning" whereas the "congeneric *interfluent* meaning" appears when a musical gesture which is an element of one work signifies a gesture being an element of another work. Coker claims that of the two, the *intrafluent* meaning is far more "important" and more often met. Second, an *extrageneric* sign — depending on its position vis-à-vis its referent — may be either *predictive* (when it precedes its referent), *retrodictive* (when it follows the referent), or *juxtadictive*.[30]

The question arises, however, of how it is possible to interpret adequately one musical structure as a sign of another structure. The problem was also present in Springer and in Eco where, as we remember, the postulated answers referred to "grammatical" and "probabilistic" rules. Apparently, Coker assumes a similar solution when he observes that perceptibility of the relations between musical gestures is largely dependent on the interpreter's beliefs in the very existence of the gesture, in its symbolic character as well as in the adequacy of its meaning. Thus, the perceptibility is eventually decided due to acceptance of the directives of a given musical system which determine the repertory of musical gestures and their meanings. In the author's opinion, the situation is much like in mathematics, where the acceptance of the axioms is also a matter of "faith".[31] However, in another place of his book, this emphasized cultural, conventional status of congeneric signs seems to be questioned when we come across the topic of "tensions and resolutions" which are atributes of "musical movement", and which are determined by the "degree of consonance or dissonance of the chords":[32] thus conceived "tension" indicates that — hypothetically — there should come a "resolution", dissonance is a sign of consonance. Naturally, the relation between "tension" and "resolution" could be understood in the

30. Ibid., pp. 34 ff.
31. Ibid., p. 196.
32. Ibid., p. 46.

above way, namely, its constitution might be said to dependent on the "belief" in certain (i.e. tonal) musical rules. Coker, however, has chosen otherwise. Concluding the discussion, he states that consonance and dissonance phenomena are independent of experience, they affect human senses directly.

Many of Coker's claims can be found in the other mentioned author L.B. Meyer. There is no doubt, however, that the inspiration must have come from Meyer, not the other way round, although Coker need not have been a conscious imitator. To some extent, this holds true of other above presented authors as well, particularly of those who uphold the "connotation" principle. Meyer seems to be the first to have put forward the suggestion in his well known *Emotion and meaning in music.*[33]

At the beginning, Meyer assumes a similar course of presentation of his ideas as others, namely, he makes a distinction between two types of signs and meanings. Thus, the sign (conceived in a behaviouristic manner, after M.R. Cohen and H.H. Mead, as a stimuli) may refer to the "events or sequences of a different kind from its own" or to the "events or sequences of its own kind". The former type of meaning can be called *designative,* the latter and more important one — *embodied.* Keeping this in mind, we can say that the reference of the musical stimuli does not rest with some extra-musical ideas or objects, but is made up of other musical facts which can occur. Thus, a musical event (i.e. a sound, phrase or passage) is meaningful because it refers to another musical event, and makes us anticipate it.[34]

What makes it possible for this conceived meaning to emerge? The author's answer is: our anticipation. If, on the basis of our past *experience,* the present stimulus brings about anticipation of some more or less specific events to follow, we may say that the stimulus carries meaning.[35] We need explain now what is meant in music by "past experience". Generally speaking, it is determined by a set of "habits and

---

33. I am referring to the Polish translation of *Emotion and meaning in music: Emocja i znaczenie w muzyce,* Cracow 1974. It should be added that the basic thesis of the musical semantics present in *Emotion ...,* reappears in Meyer's later works in an unchanged form, albeit in different contexts and from various points of view: from the perspective of information theory ("Meaning in music information theory", *Journal of Aesthetics and Art Criticism* 15/1956-7(4), pp. 412-424); from the point of view of axiology ("Some remarks on value and greatness in music", *Journal of Aesthetics and Art Criticism* 17/1958-9(4), pp. 486-500), and as a methodological problem (*Explaining music. Essays and explorations,* Berkeley/Los Angeles/London 1973).

34. *Emocja ...,* op. cit., pp. 50 f.

35. Ibid., p. 51.

dispositions, learned through exercises in listening and performing",[36] by which we acquire some concrete stylistic norms of the probabilistic character. The acquired norms generate hypothetical sequences of musical signs-stimuli. It is worth noticing, in this connection, that Meyer lays emphasis on the social character of those stylistic systems, as well as on the social nature of the acquisition process of the underlying rules. But in fact, like in Coker, Meyer's theory of *embodied* meaning implies two kinds of assumptions — the musical systems are both cultural and psychological. The stylistic norms differ from culture to culture, and from style to style — they are predetermined "neither by God nor by Nature"; on the other hand, however, what remains unchanged, is the nature of human reactions, the perception principles of systems, and the methods with the help of which the mind, operating within the acquired style, selects and organizes the sense data.[37]

The above cursory review of Meyer's semantics of music does not give credit to the most essential property of his conception, which is a theory of musical *expression*.[38] Thus, if we would raise a question about the tangible value of the musical work, we would not be referred to the meaning constituted in the above explained way, but to the emotional reactions caused by the musical stimuli. From this point of view, the musical structures that have already acquired the symbolic character are, above all, the emotional stimuli, and their *embodied* menanings remain somewhat accidental. The ultimate aim of the composer is not to constitute the sign, but — by operating the stylistic norms — to create such sounds compositions which, in accordance with the "law of emotion", will bring about specific emotional response in the audience.[39]

36. Ibid., p. 82.
37. In my review of Meyer's book *O znaczeniu w muzyce* (On meaning in music), *Studia Filozoficzne* 12/1975, pp. 187- 190, I pointed to some difficulties appearing when one attempts to integrate in one conception two basically distinct approaches, i.e. cultural and psychological (specifically: *Gestalt theory*).
38. The author's use of the term *expression,* however, should be replaced by *impression,* since he is rather concerned with an emotional influence that the musical structures exert, not with presenting of some psychological states, i.e. with their expression. But it has been common practice in musical aesthetics to cover both notions with one term *expression.*
39. Naturally, Meyer's conception of expression (impression) lies beyond our immediate interests in this paper. But as regards his view on semantics, a few additional comments from *Explaining music* are especially worthy of note.
Thus, he claims that understanding of a musical work presupposes understanding of the composer's accepted principles of "flexible strategy", of the "rules of game" that he applies (ibid., p. 14). Special significance is assigned, in this process, to the so-called "implicated relations" which are founded by the composer and decoded by the

Having at our disposal the basic claims concerning the main subject of the present discussion, let us turn back to Bühler's category of connotation. According to a linguistic dictionary, connotation occurs when

(...) certain classes of words not only signify a given event directly, but also, indirectly, co-signify another event which is somehow related to the former one; consequently, when they appear in a text, they in a sense open an "empty slot" for other classes of words which signify the latter event in a direct way. For instance, the adjective not only signifies a property, but simultaneously it "co-signifies", i.e. connotes some object of which the property can be asserted, in other words, when used in a text, it opens the empty slot for a noun.[40]

Next to the above exemplified *categorial-semantic* connotation, the authors of the dictionary mention *formal* connotation which occurs when "(...) one grammatical form (e.g. the indirect case, personal verb form) connotes another form, also — a class of words. For instance, the Polish Accusative (...) connotes its governing transitive verb".[41] Putting aside the distinction between two types of connotation, the very relation can be understood as follows: the appearance of a given language unit in the text "predicts" the occurrence of a certain other unit of a specific class, e.g.

(Adj) *red*: (Noun) *rose, ribbon,* etc;

(Accus) *książkę* (book): (Verb Trans) *read, write,* etc.

There is hardly any doubt that the discussed conception of aesthetics of music follows similar reasoning. Thus, the appearance in a musical composition of a given structure (e.g. "interval" or "chord"), performing

---

listener. They are, in fact, a new name for *embodied* meanings. Within the "implicated relation", a given event (motif, phrase, etc.) has been constituted in such a way that its rational inferences can refer both to its preceding events, and to its continuation. By "rational inferences", the author means such consequences that can be perceived by the competent and experienced listener who possesses sufficient sensitivity and knowledge of the applied style (p. 110). In the author's opinion, we often draw the conclusions of that kind in everyday life, for instance, interpreting a sound of thunder from a distance and gathering clouds as a rain forecast. Similarly in music, a logically composed phrase leads to cadence, and a competent listener is able to predict the coming tonic. It may happen, however, that neither of those implications comes true. The clouds may be blown away, and the cadence can turn to be deceptive. But it does not mean that the predicted consequences were not implicated, only that the implications have not been fulfilled, they have not come true. As the examples show, the objects are implicated *signs* which an experienced observer can interpret in the proper way (p. 111).

As seen from the above, the conception presented in *Explaining* ... resembles the one from *Emotion* ..., but whereas in the latter *embodied* meaning was instrumentally subordinated to the expressive (impressive) value, now, treated as the "implicated sign", it acquires the status of autonomous value.

40. Z. Gołąb et al., *Słownik* ..., op. cit., p. 296.
41. Ibidem.

a specific function (e.g. of the "guide tone" or "dominant"), connotes some predictable — vis-à-vis a given system (e.g. tonal) — consequences (e.g. tonic). In view of the above, it becomes obvious that, as was mentioned at the beginning of the paper, the *connotational* conception is related directly to the *grammatical* one, but there are some important differences between them. Whereas in the latter case the main issue is the structural function of the musical composition, in the *connotational* conception of the structural property of having such function, i.e. of possessing *grammatical* meaning, is but a preliminary condition whose fulfilment brings about musical "connotation". Hence, as was also indicated above, the *connotational* conception should be treated as a developed variant of the *grammatical* approach.

Translated by Nina Nowakowska

PART TWO: SCIENCE AS A DOMAIN OF CULTURE

Jerzy Kmita

THE LEGACY OF MAGIC IN SCIENCE

The idea of comparing magic thinking with scientific one has already quite a long tradition in two disciplines of the humanities in particular: in ethnology, also known as cultural, or social anthropology and in philosophy. In ethnology, however, already in the period when it was dominated by positivistically oriented classical evolutionism, certain similarities between the two ways of thinking are generally more stressed than in philosophy which reveals rather the differences. It is true in both situations: when it tries to present scientistically the essential advantages of science over magic, or when an opposite, anti-scientistic tendency prevails. For a few reasons I will refer here principally to some of the results of ethnological thought devoted to the "logic" of magic thinking which, by the way, I identify — accepting in this respect E. Leach's point of view — with the "logic" of myth.

Firstly, ethnologists, or rather a quite numerous group of them which acknowledges the cognitive significance of treating magic as a separate way of viewing the world, a way, comparable with religion, because of its social function, as well as with art or science — provide information on the subject which, quite understandably, is more professional and precise from that supplied by philosophers. Secondly, they present it in the form of a certain "holistic" system. This was a common practice already before structuralism made this approach a matter-of-course for an ethnologist examining any branch of culture. This circumstance is understandable, too, if one bears in mind that they deal, in the first place, with magic which is called primitive, i.e. with a way of thinking which organized a developed image of the world within the culture of the earliest — in the historical-theoretical sense — traditional societies. A philosopher, unless he is also an ethnologist, like for instance E. Gellner or M. Godelier, can encounter "directly" only some fragments isolated already from their original context which therefore do not form a clear system. Finally, an ethnologist, even so congenial to positivistic scientism as the representatives of classical evolutionism, compare magic with science more "calmly", so to speak, than a philosopher and that is why he is able to pay more attention to sometimes important similarities between these two ways of building the image of the world.

In the remaining part of this paper we are not going to discuss any results of the ethnological comparisons of magic and science which can be found in E.B. Taylor, J.G. Frazer and, especially later, in M. Mauss and H. Hubert, as well as in L. Lévy-Brühl, and finally in some functionalists and structuralists. The present author is not interested, as far as this matter is concerned, in the question to what extent magic knowledge about the world is based — as scientific knowledge is said to be — on "inductive reasoning", or to what extent in both cases we deal with the prediction of observable facts on the grounds of the so-called "intermediate variables", theoretic and scientific on the one hand and magic on the other; the present author is interested, however, in a certain feature of scientific thinking which will be presented below, and which seems to be genetically related to the "logic" of magic thinking. Ethnologists did not heed this phenomenon at all, it is a philosopher who points it out in a very general way: E. Cassirer — if one recognizes his characteristics of myth, as one of the symbolical forms considered by him, which I believe to be justified, to be an attempt to reconstruct the primitively magic image of the world. Cassirer, in relation to the mentioned symbolical form, which, by the way, he tries to reconstruct on the basis of the results of ethnological research, says: There is in us, when we create our own reality with the use of extra-mythical symbolic forms, a residue of mythical thinking which cannot be easily removed;

> (...) we must look at the greatest works of human culture with greater modesty. They are neither eternal, nor immune. Our science, poetry, art and religion are only an upper leyer of a much older stratum which reaches very deep. We should always be prepared for violent upheavals which can shake our cultural world and social order to their very foundations.[1]

Thus, I am talking about this Cassirerean "older stratum", magical or mythical in its origin, which is hidden in science and other areas of modern culture and whose presence in them would supposedly explain, in particular, common features of magic and science revealed by ethnologists.

1. The Legacy of Magic in Religion and Philosophy

The just mentioned trait of scientific thinking, having its origin, I believe, in magic, manifests itself more freely, is less stifled, in other than science disciplines of culture: in religion, philosophy and in art. This state of affairs would be in perfect agreement with the Cassirerean intuition quoted here, as well as with a presupposition about the theoretical-

1. E. Cassirer, *The myth of the state,* Garden City 1955, p. 374.

historical precedence of religion and philosophy over science. Religion and philosophy transfer to science the substance of their legacy of primitive magic. In order to define the character of this legacy let's take a closer look at ethnological views concerning magic.

Frazer's concept of the magic viewing of the world, reinterpreted and clarified by the structuralism of C. Lévi-Strauss, who, by the way, uses also certain assumptions of R. Jakobson in respect to poetry, indirectly suggests a model of magic which — for reasons which will be clear shortly — on my part, I would call primitively syncretic. Let's take a closer look at the concept of J.G. Frazer first.

As it is known, according to this concept the phenomena which make up the universe of the magically thought world are joined together causally within its sphere, according to the principles of analogy and contiguity. The first of them can be expressed briefly by the formula: similar generates similar; the second by another formula: phenomena or things which come in contact with each other even momentarily establish and maintain a causal nexus with each other. Parenthetically speaking, a somewhat later supplement by M. Mauss who proposes a third principle: "opposite fights opposite" seems to be only a consequence of adopting the principle of analogy, understood in a sufficiently wide way, as one of the basic tenets of magic thinking. It can also be added that M. Mauss criticizes — from the viewpoint of a follower of Durkheim's ideas — the J.G. Frazer's concept as it reconstructs correctly rather the ways along which the magic thinking develops, its "form", but does not explain its "compulsive" character, its "force" with which it influences individual minds as a specific form of collective consciousness.

Ethnological structuralism, on the contrary, sides with Frazer's "formalism" proposing, however, to expand and modify it in the following way. There are two basic types of relationships with the help of which the human mind structures the reality. These are: (1) the analogy relationship, a similarity conceptualized by the mind which enables to regard a phenomenon as a metaphor, or a symbol of another phenomenon and therefore it may be also called a *symbolic,* or a *metaphorical* relationship; (2) the contiguity relationship, often in the form of a mereological relationship of a part to the whole, hence Frazerean contiguity, which entails a permanent relationship of a causal character. A specific feature of magic, or mythical "logic" ("mytho-logic") is the transformation of the metaphorical relationship into the contiguity one, entailing causal nexus and a reverse transformation metaphorizing a contiguity relationship. The latter one is also called a *metonymic* relationship due to the terminological tradition of poetics which calls a phenomenon being a mereological "part" of a complex a possible metonymy of that complex.

Thus a symbolic relationship is transformed in magic thinking into a metonymic relationship, implicitly causal, and a metonymic relationship into a symbolic one which, in turn, may be a basis of another metonymic relationship. For instance, a piece of a person's clothing symbolizes this person — a metonymic relationship is transformed in this case into a symbolic one; on the other hand a metonymic action upon this piece of clothing, let's say destroying it, transforms into a symbol of destruction of that person, in turn, this symbolic relationship: between destroying a piece of clothing and exterminating a person — transforms into an implicitly causal, metonymic relationship. It can be easily seen that both structuralistic principles of a reverse transformation imply two corresponding Frazerean principles. The first ones are applied by C. Lévi-Strauss to the analysis of the text of a mythical story: contiguity between the segments of the text of this story and parallelly — between successive episodes presented in it, is treated as a key to finding symbolic relationships (metaphoric relationships), that is manifested in the statement that this story is a kind of a palimpsest in which onto the original order of symbolizing an external metonymic order of the story is superimposed.

This otherwise valuable result of the structuralistic analysis of magic thinking gives rise, however, to at least two critical observations. In the first place, it assumes the Hjelmslevean idea of isomorphism between metonymic and — respectedly — symbolic order of a text and between the same orders of the reality of a mythical story presented in it. This assumption, based on intuition that human mind structuralizes the world and the speech describing it in an isomorphic way seems to be rather arbitrary, however it is not in any way necessary for accepting these results of the structuralistic analysis which can be referred exclusively to the world viewed by the magic thought. Secondly, what is more important, the concept of the "logic" of transformation, of which the mind subject to this logic is, of course, not aware, gives way to doubts. The point is, that the transformation from symbolizing to metonymy, or vice versa, may be unconscious, however if we are to speak about even unconscious transformation of this kind, we must assume that symbolizing and metonymy as such are consciously distinguished by this mind: if it were not like this any "transformation" from one to the other would not be feasible. But exactly this seems to be doubtful: the possibility of primitive distinguishing between a symbol and metonymy. It appears clearly to be historically later than primitive magic thinking[2]

2. This observation is one of the basic points of departure of the article by A. Pałubicka, "O trzech historycznych odmianach waloryzacji światopoglądowej" (On three historical versions of the "Weltanschauung" valorization), *Studia Metodologiczne,* 24.

and is falsely moved back by structuralism onto that thinking. I would like to call it primitively syncretic magic thinking because it views the world as a universe of interrelated phenomena. Each of these relationships is at the same time symbolic and metonymic. The formula: primitive magic syncretism — is supposed not only to show that primitive magic is involved, but, in the first place, that syncretism is stressed which does not mean (as it is generally understood) combining already distinguished elements, but — on the contrary — the combined appearance of elements which only from a later point of view are considered to be different. I believe that the diversion of this primitive magic syncretism within thinking that distinguishes two types of relationships between phenomena: metonymic and symbolic — is a historically later phenomenon.

One of the more instructional examples of the primitive magic syncretism seems to be the mental context of an action called after M. Mauss the exchange of gifts. This exchange, when taken outside of this context, from the point of view of the modern, European cultural equipment of an ethnologist, appears to be a phenomenon called by K. Marx a simple exchange, coming under the formula: "commodity-commodity". Under this formula — from this point of view — apparently comes also a more complicated, Melanesian form of gift exchange, called "kula". Basically it means that a gift given by tribal group A to a tribal group B, usually by the chiefs, passes, in the same or another form, to group C, etc. until finally it returns to tribal group A. There is also a similar case which is called "potlatch", known on the both sides of the Pacific, which is a kind of a condensed (in terms of time — lasting a few days, and in terms of place which is fixed) — "kula". When we take into account the original mental and cultural context of that exchange of gifts, credit for this pioneering idea goes to M. Mauss, we realize that we do not have to do here at all with a simple exchange of commodities in modern, European meaning of this term. Because even in the most simple form of a gift exchange apparently, it must be admitted, we face two appropriate metonymic relationships: a thing being at the disposal of A passes to B, and then a thing which is a property of B passes to A, however these relationships are symbolic in the syncretic way at the same time: the fact that B receives a gift from A symbolizes parallelly another fact, i.e. the former falls into dependence from the latter. This state is changed only by the act of reciprocation. The sense of giving or reciprocating a gift is not only practical, economic, of course this exchange has some economic functions, but at the same time it has magic and symbolic functions. Both these senses form a certain primitive syncretic whole which is hard and maybe even impossible to be comprehended by the modern, European mind; maybe some of it has remained in our contemporary feeling of obligation to reciprocate a gift.

Without going into details of further examples of primitive magic syncretism, such as only apparently purely symbolic participation of Dyak women in war by carrying imitations of weapons during male expeditions, or preparation of a good hunt by the Mbuti by only apparently a purely symbolic ceremony of disposing a forest to share its supplies with the people, called "molimoo", let's turn to the second model of magic thinking. I shall call it — in contrast to primitively syncretic — dualistic magic, because in contrast to the previous case, the relationships between phenomena, primarily between certain actions and their effects, are understood here as being composed of two differentiated components: metonymic and magically symbolic. Configurations, in which these components co-appear, may be different: they may follow one another, they may accompany one another parallelly — always, however, the presence of the second of them, the magically symbolic one, assumes the intervention of special knowledge, as a principle accessible only to individuals selected in a socio-cultural way: wizards or wizard-chiefs. For this last reason dualistic magic can be also called professional magic because only professionally initiated individuals are able to activate by appropriate actions those magically symbolic relationships; the profane must be satisfied by the knowledge of "ordinary" metonymic relationships.

The former name is, however, more important for us because it stresses the specific division of primitively syncretic magic relationships. Their symbolic-magic component belongs already to a peculiar sphere of magic — expanded gradually in various beliefs in different ways, either in a personal direction (demons, ghosts, gods) or impersonal. In the latter case we have to do with a certain supersensory, supermetonymic, but "pervading" metonymy, order of relationships, in the form, on the other hand, of relatively primitive "mana", but on the other of the more and more sophisticated, already religious or philosophical cosmic order.

Many ethnologists have frequently observed that magic thinking, contrary to religious thinking, is always practically oriented, i.e. it is interested only in such relationships between phenomena, knowledge about which is useful in obtaining desired, practically advantageous effects. Far less frequently, however, this difference is used as a criterion distinguishing magic from religion. It seems that the latter state of affairs can be explained by a circumstance that magic thinking is frequently perceived, also in philosophy, or sociology, exclusively in its dualistic professional form when, especially this thinking co-exists with parallelly prevailing religious beliefs, another opposition of it becomes conspicuous in relation to the last mentioned ones: the knowledge of relationships and magical-symbolical senses is limited to small fractions of given communities. It often is "unofficial", prohibited, especially applications are prohibited — by parallelly prevailing religion, or even law, on the other hand, meanings and relationships of a religious type are "official" and known (in the prevailing manner) to all the members of a given community of believers. This is the viewpoint of E. Durkheim, or M. Mauss, among others — adjusted by them, with certain difficulties, to their own concept of collective consciousness whose special form is supposed to be magic thinking. It is obvious that his point of view does not take into consideration the phenomenon of completely "lay", non-professional, primitive magic syncretism, and — that in order to include this phenomenon within the framework of assumption that magic viewing of the world is different from the religious one — only that practical disposition of magic is left as a basic delineating criterion. If we do not appeal to it we must consequently give up the attempts to distinguish magic from religion.

As a matter of fact, such resignation can be seen in ethnology. At the same time two of its theoretical orientations are capable of justifying it: structuralism and scientism, especially scientism citing ideas of K. Marx. Structuralism is not interested in the question of varieties of the symbolic relationship capable of being distinguished substantially, of metaphoric relationship, especially in the question of practically "self-interested" variety and "disinterested" variety; thus magical on the one hand and religious on the other. Most probably this is a result of the fact that structuralism ahistorically, implicitly assumes that symbolizing is a relationship always of the same type, formally based on a subjectively projected analogy — making in the way the modern, European meaning of this relationship an absolute one. The source of scientistic ignoring of the fact that magic symbolizing is one thing and religious is another, is similar; in both cases the same cognitive "error" is committed — it is believed from this point of view: subjective illusions are held to be objective, ideological, in Marxian sense, viewing of the world. Symbolizing understood so generally and ahistorically — irrespectfully of the fact whether it is treated as a way of thinking leading to an "error" from the scientistic point of view, or as a certain universal, historically constant component of human thinking about the world — contributes decisively to the negligence of the difference counterposing magic to religion.

This difference, however, is valid and essential, and — as it was said — is related to the opposition: magic thinking practically oriented — religious thinking axiologically oriented. This opposition can be expressed, by referring to the different position of the symbolized instance in magic thinking and in religious thinking, in the following way: in the primitively syncretic, magic viewing of the world the symbolized instance has not been completely isolated yet, in the dualistic-magic thinking it is already present, but it is only a kind of a bridge used practically to join human activities with practically palpable, desired effects of them, however, on the grounds of religious viewing of the world the symbolized instance is not as much a bridge as it sanctifies, gives ultimate values to human actions, it gives them superpractical additional sense, a sacred one. In the first case the symbolic relationship, if it appears separately at all (as it is the case in dualistic magic), is used exclusively by individuals "initiated" to exert certain pressure on the symbolized instance, on the sacred magical sphere, to make them give higher practical efficiency to human actions; in the second case we have to do with an additional, sense-adding, axiological valorization on behalf of the values included in the religious sacred sphere which is not only more or less inaccessible to human manipulation, but — quite to the contrary — that whole our reality of metonymic relationships, perceptible to the senses and capable of being manipulated is subject to the higher order of the sacred sphere. In the first case, the practical sense of human actions or life is at the same time its sacred sense, also in dualistic magic which still inherits this aspect of primitively syncretic magic. In the second case, the already clearly isolated practical effect of actions is not sufficient to add sense to them; the support of axiologically valorizing symbolic relationship referring to the sacred religious sphere is indispensable for them. It is accompanied by, as M. Weber puts it,

> (...) a feeling that in the real world is something "senseless", as well as a demand that the whole order of the world become in some way a sensible "cosmos", or a conviction that "it can or should be like this" — being a product of proper religious rationalism.[3]

The just quoted author of *Protestant ethic* contrasts religious, but also philosophical thinking with magic, making use of the notion of "intellectuallism":

> The more intellectualism supersedes the belief in magic — causing world processes to become "disenchanted", to lose their magic sensible essence, they only "are" and "take place", but they do not "mean" anything — the more grows the need to order the world and the "way of life" as a whole in a meaningful and "sensible" way.[4]

---

3. M. Weber, *Szkice z socjologii religii* (Polish translation of Weber's selected writings on religion), Warsaw 1984, p. 12.
4. Ibid., p. 195.
I would like only to mention here that I omit — in order not to complicate my discussion — the three following questions; otherwise fundamental for any philosopher: (1) the question of the difference between religion, or its intellectualized theological

161

It can be easily observed, in fact, that a philosophical doctrine like platonism satisfies probably in the highest degree these tendencies of religious thinking which contrast it with magic. Complete dependence of the world of sensory "illusion" on the world of imperfectly incarnated, axiologically symbolized by that "illusion" — ideas, and absolute inaccessibility of the latter to sensory examination, a perspective characteristic for practically oriented human actions. Historically known religious realize the above tendencies in various degrees. Undoubtedly, e.g. the catholic religion, with its concept of the possibility of divine interference, brought about by prayers, in our wordly lives and "interests", with its cult of sensory perceptible symbols, like images or lithurgical ornaments, which when practically manipulated give us grounds to expect gaining some influence on divine decisions manifested "in this world" — is closer to magic thinking than protestant religion which abandons more or less radically, depending on its particular version, possibilities of this kind. It is thinkable, that it would be possible to define philosophical thinking as a most radical embodiment of antimagical tendencies of religion.

---

form and philosophy, (2) the question of fundamental reorientation of philosophical thinking documented by Kant's intellectual works which is to be discussed later, (3) the question of the "scientific nature" of the academic studies in the humanities.

As far as the question (1) is concerned it poses a very difficult problem to solve until philosophy accepts the assumptions of Kant's "Copernican shift"; for until this moment the said difference has rather a quantitative character — since important here is the extent to which ontologically oriented pre-Kantian philosophy, let's say "metaphysical" (in the phenomenological sense of this qualification) takes into account theological decisions. So when I speak: "religious thinking, but also philosophical" I want to include in this formula "metaphysical" ontology which takes the metonymic order of the world to be determined by "the word of God" (theology), or to an appropriate degree independent from it (philosophy). Theology differs from pre-Kantian philosophy as much as it conditions that order on still magic understanding of "the word of God" (a word which is magical syncretically, symbolizes something and at the same time causes that which it symbolizes). Kantian thinking can be easily distinguished — as philosophical thinking — from theological one because it is purely epistemologically oriented, i.e. it answers only the question according to what principles the human mind constructs the metonymic order and, independently accompanying it, the symbolic-axiological order — without going into the ontological questions of these orders. When I speak a little later about the philosophical-epistemological plane of differentiating these two orders I mean then philosophy separated from "metaphysics". That much about question (2).

About question (3) I want to say only that academic studies of the humanities would be a science in the sense assumed by me — as much as it would meet Weber's postulate about "independence of evaluating judgements". This statement does not have to be explained here, I believe, neither can it be developed.

What has religion and philosophy inherited from magic? What is the essence of the religious-philosophical continuation of the tradition of magic thinking?

The primitive magic syncretism, dualistically-magic syncretism of the sense of practical actions, of human life in its practical dimension — finally destroyed by more or less radical religious-philosophical dualism — is continued on this ground in the form of a powerful tendency to supplement the metonymic order of the sensory world, capable of being practically manipulated, by symbolic-axiological order. That which has been originally a syncretic unity transforms now into a tendency only to unify two opposing components of it, each of them — taken separately — is not sufficient. It is not sufficient — not simply for human intellect formed in a religious-philosophical way (through a historical accident), as Weber has it, but it is not sufficient, I would claim, to cause human individuals to feel obliged to undertake actions "required" of them by unconsciously created by their hitherto practice, new conditions of the continuation of social existence. These actions which are now "required" are defined and regulated by a new, post-magically oriented culture. This last term means, according to me, a system of normative-directival convictions capable of universal motivation of actions which in their "mass" are able to produce the present continuations of further social existence. This capability is dependent, however, among others, on the question whether individual people, equipped with the tradition of magic thinking are able to "design" and assimilate the culture "required" at the moment, making it in this way a real, universally respected regulator of their actions. I would claim that the passage from the magically-oriented culture to the culture oriented in a religious-philosophical way was possible only thanks to the fact that the latter one offered to substitute constant unity of metonymic order with symbolic-axiological one for the primitive syncretic unity which I would identify with Cassirerean "older stratum" of our culture. Moreover, I believe that culture can fulfil its socio-regulatory function as long as it maintains that unity. The latter one, the necessity to maintain it to support the socio-regulatory function of culture is the legacy of magic we are interested in here — clearly present in religious-philosophical thinking.

2. The Paradox of Science

The modern-European culture is characterized by a property which Weber called — the second — "disenchantment of the world", believing also that it was prepared by Protestant religion. This property is manifested by further loosening of the unity of metonymic and symbolic-axiological orders in the next stage of departing from the primitive magic syncretism — in the process started "for good" by the culture of religious-philosophical thinking.[5]

The second "disenchantment of the world" means that practical effects of human actions, which are distinguished in the culture of religious-philosophical thinking from superpractical values symbolized axiologically by them, are made dependent solely on "sensory" perceptible, extra-sacred metonymic order. In this context the religious-philosophical sacred sphere does not determine the metonymic order, but is used exclusively for axiological valorization of practically oriented actions, existing within this order. Presently, this is the only form of continuation of the legacy of magic. The metonymic order itself is revealed independently, in respect to logic, from religion or philosophy through everyday experience, and through modern scientific knowledge deepening this experience whose cultural status perfectly expresses the essence of the second "disenchantment of the world".

Scientific knowledge is perceived in the modern-European culture as an adequate, or gradually approaching the future adequacy, description of the metonymic order of the world. This order has been made

---

5. Thus, social appearance of religion as a way of viewing the world, sketched above, which valorize axiologically the practical sense of human life and activity, already clearly separated from its sacred dimension, starts the process of the gradual decline of the socio-regulatory pressure of culture. For, this pressure, i.e. the degree of peremptoriness with which culture imposes on individuals goals and manner of their actions — is the greater, the more closely in the given by it image of the world, the metonymic order is bound to the symbolic-axiological one. The primitive magic syncretism does not distinguish them at all, it "melts" them into a unity; the modern-European culture, however, not only does assume this differentiation, but also gradually makes the symbolic-axiological order more and more subjective, arbitrarily put at the end, maintaining traits of objectivity, only for the metonymic order.

From this point of view one should question L. Kołakowski's concept of religion as a generator of the "power" of culture. The situation seems to be quite opposite: it is religion, with the dualism *sacrum-profanum* that initiates the process of the gradual destruction of the peremptory power inherent in culture, at the same time being a decisive moment in the "suicidal" development of the latter, developing in the proper direction a tendency visible already in dualistic magic. The peculiarity of religious thinking (and generally — the so-called by him "mythical" one) pointed out to by L. Kołakowski supposed to consist in special unity of normative (evaluating) judgements and descriptive ones within the religious experience manifested in appropriately syncretic mental units ["In peculiarly religious perception there is no difference between 'descriptive' and 'normative' contents of that which is perceived: the act of faith in God involves indistinguishably at the same time the act of acceptance of his moral instructions as valid (...)" — L. Kołakowski, *Czy diabeł może być zbawiony i 27 innych kazań* (Can the devil be saved and 27 other sermons), London 1982, p. 115], is in fact a feature of the primitive magic syncretism, to which mystic religious experience tries to return in opposition to theological intellectualism peculiar to religion.

independent in respect to its essence from symbolic-axiological senses of actions calculated on the basis of its knowledge. This mutual independence of the metonymic order and symbolic-axiological one, in respect to their essence was particularly clearly expressed by Kant on the epistemological plane: getting to know the first of them is the task of "theoretical reason", and constitution of the second is the task of "practical reason", between the two "reasons" there is a fundamental difference: the "theoretical reason" cannot say anything about the values to the realization of which we should devote our practical actions because the metonymic order of the world comprehended by it does not determine these values, but the "practical reason" does indicate these values, or rather proposes them, without being able, however, to refer, when arguing from them, to cognitive patterns valid within the "theoretical reason". If we refer to these patterns while remaining in the sphere regulated by the "practical reason" we fall into internally antinomic "metaphysics".

The philosophy of Kant is inasmuch a telling example of the cultural, modern-European status of science as on the one hand it reduces its cognitive competence to the possibility of (gradual) revealing by it exclusively the metonymic order of the world, on the other hand it tries within so reduced limits of competence to make them fully valid. This first image of science — as an instrument of learning only about the metonymic order of the world, learning much improved in comparison to opinions based on everyday experience — would suggest an opinion that it represents — as an area of modern-European culture — a complete break with the principle inherited from the primitive magic syncretism, of joining this metonymic order with the symbolic-axiological one.[6] As a matter of fact, the results of cognizance regulated by modern-European science destroy to a higher and higher degree the foundations of the said principle revealing more and more clearly the "objective" self-sufficiency of the metonymic order of the world. To be sure, science functioning in this way is an effect of the demands of the modern-European, capitalist manner of production which "requires" a purely metonymic calculation, paying no heed — in this calculation — to symbolic-axiological senses of planned actions. Moreover, that manner of production, requiring from

---

6. E. Cassirer describes this situation in the following way: "In the ethical sense man is a free subject of action, (...) motivations depend on his own judgement and his own conviction what is a moral obligation. (...) It does not mean 'indeterminism', but rather a special kind of determination. It means that law we are subject to in our actions is not imposed from outside, but that moral subject imposes that law on himself". (E. Cassirer, *The myth ...*, op. cit., pp. 361-362).

its subjects individual ingenuity in the field of technology, and consequently in the practical application of successive scientific discoveries in the commercial-production sphere, creates a proper functional "pressure" — aimed at the community professionally producing such discoveries.

At the same time, however, the said community, continues in so far the tradition, inherited from magic, of unity of metonymic thinking with symbolic-axiological one, as it by no means accepts the idea that the goal of its professional activity is the same as the result of this activity appearing in the metonymic order, i.e. it boils down to supplying data for technologically efficient commercial-production practice. Science "does not want" to think scientifically about itself. Science universally accepts the Kantian idea that the manner in which the metonymic order of the world is revealed by scientific proceedings is cognitively reliable, moreover, exclusively reliable one, because behind this manner stands the "theoretical reason" giving to it reliability. It can be said that the post-Kantian philosophy to a large extent thrives on the exploitation of that supermetonymic ambition of the theoretical scientific reason. Giving it up scientific practice "would feel" axiologically degraded, deprived of proper legitimacy, would probably loss much of its development impetus. Philosophy therefore, answering this need of scientific practice, tries in different ways to supply science with the evidence it needs, confirming that it is not only technologically useful, which can be seen in the scientific manner, i.e. exclusively within the purely metonymic order; but — independently from that — reliably comprehends the world. The self-consciousness of science, still maintaining the unity, inherited from magic, of the metonymic thinking with the symbolic-axiological one which is being destroyed by the very scientific image of the world and scientific methods of its construction, demands from philosophy to ensure this unity for itself.

Thus, science finds itself in a paradoxical situation: on the one hand it creates an image of the world which is subject to the metonymic order only, which is believed in advance to be the only object of cognition subject to scientific methods; on the other hand it needs an axiological-epistemological support which assumes the supplementing of this order by the symbolic-axiological order, imperceptible for the metonymic thinking. In that second respect it continues the legacy of magic, i.e. the tradition of joining the two orders; breaking away from it, to repead it, threatens with the loss of socio-regulatory "power" by the methodological consciousness of scientific practice.

Remaining is the question of the truly schizophrenic placement of these trends of modern philosophy whose range of problems has not only been dominated by the fact of the institutional constitution of scientific practice together with the methodological consciousness by which it is regulated,[7] but — moreover — by the task of epistemological justification of the said practice and consciousness. For, within our trends, an epistemological-axiological apology of such a manner of thinking is striven for which beforehand repudiates the argumentative structure of any apology of this kind.

Particularly striking is the unusual persistence with which the discussed trends of scientism, led by the various versions of the classical 19th-century positivism, do not see their internal incongruity, do not try to ask whether the manner in which the scientific construction of the image of the world is cognitively sanctioned within their framework fits itself within the methods of construction of the said image. Spontaneously, always a positive answer is given to this question. To be sure, to the prevalence of such attitude contributed greatly unawareness of the symbolic-axiological, that is also evaluating status of such notions like: truth, cognitive adequacy, etc., which was powerfully stressed by F. Nietzsche who showed generally that all hitherto philosophy had been basically an activity sanctioning, or proposing values in a more or less veiled and arbitrary manner. It is arbitrary not in the sense of Hume's thesis about evaluating judgements, which is "disarmed" in positivism with the help of psychologism. A deeper sense is at stake here: values are not to be met in "life", it means that they cannot sanction also a proper justification of anything on the basis of even purely "descriptive" premisses (concerning the world subject to metonymy). Please notice, that even without accepting the category of "life" — one can agree with the fact that in the first place one has to positively or negatively evaluate axiologically the appropriate justification procedures, in order to be able

7. This circumstance seems to concern almost all the trends of modern philosophy. One has to agree here with the opinion of S. Sarnowski who says: "The phenomenon of science (...) is undoubtedly the main historiogenous factor of modern times, the main product of the civilization developing in those times. This civilization continues in its most fundamental design until today, therefore modern times also continue until today. (...) Therefore one should speak about continuous existence of modern civilization, about its basic unity, which is created by science. One could also speak about continuous existence of modern philosophy. Contemporary philosophy is not anything else, but a continuation of that which appeared already in the 17th century. Then its specific character manifested itself in its co-existence with science. This characterizes it also today" [S. Sarnowski, Świadomość i czas. O początkach filozofii współczesnej (Consciousness and time. On the origins of contemporary philosophy), Warsaw 1985, pp. 10-11].

A conclusion drawn from the above opinion is the following: "Philosophy of science is cultivated not only by those who consider themselves to be the representatives (...) of Philosophy of the sciences, but it is cultivated by whole modern philosophy (...)" (ibid., p. 12).

to consider them — respectedly — as valid, or invalid.

Only neopositivism has scrutinized the methods of its philosophizing, comparing them to methods believed by it to be scientific. In order to avoid the internal incongruity discussed here it programmed philosophizing consistent with a procedure ascribed by it to logical-mathematical sciences. It was supposed to be based on the formulation of the so-called analytical statements concerning the syntax of the language of science, the language being understood as an axiomatically characterized logical-mathematical construct. If this program had been realized by the neopositivists they would surely have avoided — as it was the case with those who were working in logic which was entirely incorporated into the field of mathematics — the schizophrenic situation of the scientistic philosophy of science; however, they would have ceased to be philosophers. Nonetheless, they are declared not to be philosophers any more by their opponents who identify their program with their real practice. This practice, however, is not determined by the said program. That which neopositivists constructed in various versions, as a language of science, is not at all a philosophically neutral, capable exclusively of purely formal analysis, logical-mathematical structure. Firstly, this structure by its appropriate formal features manifests empirical, epistemological intuitions of positivism. Let's recall neopositivistic notions derived from this tradition, e.g. terms like: "observation sentences", "perception sentences", "confirmation" etc. Secondly, it is used in an evaluating-epistemological way as it is treated as a peculiar normative standard in the light of which the "cognitive sensibility", "cognitive advancement", etc., of the notional apparatus used by particular disciplines of real scientific practice, are evaluated. Thus, neopositivism does not cease in its practice to be philosophy hence it continues in its peculiar way the legacy of magic introducing into the metonymically constructed image of the world the symbolic-axiological order meeting in this way the still living demand of science creating this picture.

Parenthetically speaking, starting form the end of the 19th century, science has many times mocked its own scientistic apologists declaring through its own direct representatives that these apologists are too strongly bound to epistemological normativism which results in their incorrect perception of the nature of the axiological direction of science. The conventionalists were the first to react to this autoscepticism, being frequently at the same time these direct representatives of science, especially of mathematicized natural science. However, greatly they have soothed the conflict between the proposed ideal of the cognitively valid scientific procedure and the mode of self-reflection — by, on the one hand, stressing rather the historical analysis of scientific practice, on the other persuading that achieving the truth is not that much a goal of it after all — they did not give up the project of epistemological legitimization of this practice to such a degree as it was done by these trends of contemporary philosophy of science which are less and less distinguishable from sociology of knowledge.

It would seem, to observe finally, that the simplest way of relieving oneself from troubles resulting from the schizophrenic situation of the scientistic philosophy of science would be a complete abandonment of the above-mentioned project. True, it is a fact that this situation is avoided in this way. It does not mean, however, that equally significant troubles are avoided then as well — if only one still wants to cultivate philosophy, i.e. an intellectual activity striving to meet the need, indirectly inherited from magic, for supplementing the metonymic order by the symbolic-axiological one. These troubles are avoided neither by e.g. Hegelian historism, nor the so-called Nietzschean nihilism, nor — let's say — Heidegger's "fundamental ontology". In the first case we face the problem of the basis of sanctioning of the historiogenous effects of the reflexive transformation of the past; it could be created only by the absolute, in fact assumed here, point of view of finished history. In the second case there is no solution of the antinomy consisting in the fact that axiological improvisation, peculiar to "life" pervaded by the will of power is to be considered as a value, as an exception, not improvised. Finally, in the third case is questioned the philosophical character of the result of the abandonment plan of the way of thinking correctly believed to be the source of philosophical troubles: religious-philosophical dualism. However, it is the source of philosophy in general. A return to primitive syncretism, appearing from the perspective of modern-European culture as a liquidation of the subject-object opposition, represented by the category of "being", memory about which is supposed to be a guarantee of "authentic existence" — would not it be an act of resignation from cultivating philosophy? Generally: a tendency clearly visible in contemporary philosophy, manifested especially by the concept of "fundamental ontology", which consists basically in searching for something primitive in respect to opposition: subject-object, practical reason-theoretical reason, metaphore-metonymy — is it not simply an autoliquidatory tendence of philosophy? What would be left of its essence consisting in modern times in projecting the symbolic-axiological order onto the scientific, metonymic one, if the thing left to it was the reflection on how that primitive reality: "being", "structure", Marxian social practice — from themselves metonymic and symbolic-axiological thinking? The interpretation of poetry as a way of thinking still closest — in comparison to religion and philosophy — to the primitive magic syncretism[8] (Heidegger, structuralism after C. Lévi-Strauss), or the interpretation of science (Marxism as a theory of theoretical practice) have little in common with the continuation of the range of problems constituting the essence of modern philosophy.

Translated by Zbigniew Nadstoga

8. E. Cassirer very convincingly has shown the closest kinship of poetry, and generally of art as a separate symbolic form, to symbolic form of myth (primitively syncretic magic thinking); in both cases we have to do with "expressive perception", taking that which is perceived as an expression uniting the perceiving one with him who is being perceived (common to both these sides): "(...) physical becomes psychic" when "(...) the process of perception is reversed to the point when it is pure expressive perception, and not perception of things, and when as a result of it, it is simply and entirely internal and external" (E. Cassirer, *La philosophie des formes symboliques,* T. III, Paris 1972, p. 102). For this subject-matter see J. Sójka, *O koncepcji form symbolicruych Ernsta Cassirera* (On Ernst Cassirer's conception of symbolic forms), Warsaw 1988, pp. 83-110.

Jacek Sójka

CASSIRER'S THEORY OF SCIENCE IN THE LIGHT OF RECENT METHODOLOGICAL DISCUSSIONS

I

Let us assume that a consistent epistemological reflection must ultimately propose a certain method of obtaining scientifically legitimate research effects. A consequence of such considerations on knowledge has usually been normativism. On the other hand, the theory of science could be viewed as "non-normative epistemology". It most often assumes a positive valorization of science, though it does not valorize any specific scientific methodology.

The theory of science in the above sense does not have to be a minor offshoot of epistemology. We can see nowadays how the development of science and certain humanistic disciplines remains significantly ahead of the philosophical propositions concerning their methods. Therefore, epistemology is unable to influence the development of science. If the positivist norms of legitimacy of scientific statements were faithfully followed, such great progress in the research of the natural sciences would be impossible. This also holds true for anti-positivist epistemology. A characteristic example is the failure of Husserl in his work on the philosophical basis of sciences (which does not question the fundamental significance of phenomenology for the 20th century philosophy). One should also remember that this pre-scientific — in its assumption — reflection was, in spite of all, dependent upon science in such a key issue as the operations of consciousness. Moreover, psychology has made such a great progress in the meantime that it has significantly outdistanced phenomenological analyses of consciousness.[1]

Stimulating the development of contemporary science has ceased to be the domain of internal, conceptual, philosophical factors. Instead, the determining factors are the external ones, such as the organization and

---

1. Comp. J. Piaget, "The place of the sciences of man in the system of sciences", in: *Main trends of research in the social and human sciences,* part one: *Social sciences,* Mouton/Unesco, Paris/The Hague 1970, p. 38.

172

the financing of the science, the industrial demand, and the non-state unions of researchers.[2]

In this context, the non-valuating, theoretical-descriptive standpoint of Cassirer is worthy of special attention. It deserves such attention also in other contexts. I am thinking here about the frequently proclaimed need of viewing science from the point of view of the theory of culture,[3] the discussion on the post-Kuhnian, evolutionist concept of the development of science, and the thesis of the end of the domination of epistemology in philosophy.

II

Cassirer has presented his views on science in the most complete way in his work *Substanzbegriff und Funktionsbegriff. Untersuchungen über die Grundfragen der Erkenntniskritik,* Berlin 1910. He repeated his conclusions in his most important work entitled *Philosophie der symbolischen Formen,* vol. 1-3, Berlin 1923, 1925, 1929. The concepts included in these works must be viewed in the context of the revolution originated by Frege and Russell in the area of logical foundations of mathematics. What Cassirer aimed at was a description of the principles of concept formation, already prevailing in science which could not be understood without taking into account the achievements of modern logic. In particular, this could not be achieved by positivist epistemology, based upon the logic of Aristotle.

The principles of which I am speaking here are the rules of the developing of concepts, i.e. the principles of scientific abstraction. Mathematics and modern natural sciences proposed concepts, whose rules of construction could not be expressed in the language of traditional logic. Cassirer points to the so-called serial concepts and border concepts, as well as to the scope of logical-mathematical knowledge implicated by the theory of multitude.[4]

The abstraction of Aristotle seems to be serving the practice perfectly well. We perceive objects and group them into classes on the basis of their common properties. The only thing taken for granted here is the multitude of beings and mind's ability to perceive the relevant properties. The procedure of creating such classes can be repeated almost indefinitely on a

2. Comp. G. Holton, "Do scientists need a philosophy?", *The Times Literary Supplement* 4/1984, p. 1231. X:

3. J. Kmita, "Epistemologia w oczach kulturoznawcy" (Epistemology in the eyes of a cultural scientist.) *Studia Filozoficzne* 4/1984.

4. E. Cassirer, *Substance et function. Eléments pour une théorie du concept* (transl. by P. Caussat), Les Editions de Minuit, Paris 1970, p. 7.

constantly higher level of abstraction. In a sense, the concept is already embedded in reality itself because what makes objects similar and what makes them different remains in those objects. The same is supposed to concern mathematical concepts. Constructing a concept of a tree, we extract from the multitude of varieties all properties that are common, while when constructing a concept of a quadrangle, we extract what is common for all quadrilateral figures. A characteristic feature of the pyramid obtained in this way is that the more general a concept, the less specific features it includes. On the top of that pyramid we would find "anything at all".

However, says Cassirer, we expect something different of science: exact and unambiguous definitions. Those unfortunately disappear as the abstraction of this kind proceeds.[5] The entire metaphysics of Aristotle is present here. What was common was at the same time a creative force, thanks to which things exist. Biological species determined the goals pursued by life and the entire development of nature. Hence constructing concepts by indicating the essence of a general object reflected the self-development of the substance. In this way, writes Cassirer, the ways of logic determined by the concept of substance and logic based on the concept of relation had to part. For Aristotle, relation was something secondary to a single thing.

The argument between nominalism and realism, reminds us Cassirer, concerned the metaphysical reality of concepts. Yet, nobody questioned the very theory of constructing concepts.

Positivist psychologism uses this Aristotelian model for describing the mental sphere. Instead of a series of similar objects, we have a series of representations. In turn, the mechanism of association distinguishes what is identical. Thus, a concept may be defined as something that remains in memory as a result of the sedimentation of subsequent perceptions.

According to the author of *The Philosophy of Symbolic Forms*, all that, however, has nothing in common with constructing concepts in modern science. The concepts of which Aristotle wrote are characteristic of a descriptive and classifying science, while mathematical and geometrical concepts are quite different. They define ideal "objects", which cannot be experienced by senses and whose existence is purely relational. Multitude perceived through senses is replaced with theoretical multitude.

This concerns not only the exact sciences, but also the common experience of the world, on which the classical doctrine of abstraction is based. When perceiving objects, we construct concepts as long as we

5. Ibid., p. 17.

perceive the similarities and abstract from the differences. Therefore, the basis of abstraction is identification, the recognition of an object as the same or similar to that once perceived. That synthesis of the mind no longer possesses a sensory equivalent. Abstraction cannot be pursued, claims Cassirer, without arranging our perceptions in a series compatible with a certain pattern of its generation.[6] It is the identity of relations between the elements of the series (against the background of changing properties of the elements of the series) that constitutes the specific form of a concept. Whether this procedure will additionally produce a general mental picture is a secondary question, one more psychological than logical.

Thus, the point is to find a certain general formula, the realization of which would be the particular elements of the series. The generic character of such a formula could not be opposed to particular elements of the series which are the variations of this general pattern. The formula itself could not exist without the generated series. If we agree that a mathematical function is an example of such a formula, it appears that a concept based on such a mathematical relationship opposes a typological concept determined by substantial metaphysics. Developing that formula is, then, developing the concept, although objects denoted by it (e.g. energy) are not the "things" constructing the common image of the world. The concept of function, according to Cassirer, gives sense to the modern concept of nature and the model of its development from simple to complex forms, providing the most general principles of the functioning of living organisms are preserved. The concept of an animal would not be worth much, if the facts of reproduction, breathing, and movement were eliminated from it only because various animals perform these functions differently. A concept is a result of discovery, rather than classification. In this case, it is a result of a "code of an organism", operating behind the versatility of living organisms.[7]

Such a theory of constructing concepts required a new psychological basis. Here Cassirer points to Husserl's *Logical investigations* as a source of a new conception of consciousness. In this approach, a certain autonomy of acts of consciousness is recognized and syntheses characteristic of this are, which cannot be a direct result of what is sensory, are analyzed. Empiricism assumed that all contents of consciousness are somehow equivalent. However, Husserl's conclusions indicate that it would be impossible without pointing consciousness in a specific direction. Re-

6. Ibid., p. 27.
7. Ibid., p. 34.

presentations can be equivalent only in a certain respect.[8]

Within the framework of Cassirer's theory of concept, formation common perceptions lose their validity. Constructing the concepts of science, which at the same time means discovering them, is not based on these perceptions. Similarly, these concepts are not simply "purified" concepts of the common language; their home ground is mathematics. This means that the theory of the 20th century science, believes Cassirer, does not speak of representations, but rather of judgements. The point is the logic of judgements, rather than the logic of representations. The more general a representation, a mental picture is, the less contents it possesses. It is quite the opposite with judgements: they define more and more precisely the area of comparisons and relations in which what is particular exists. A universal validity of a judgement does not mean the scope of the object of a judgement, but rather a certain quality characteristic of the relations between objects, so that even a judgement of a single object can possess a universal validity.[9]

Cassirer does not deny the fact that the concepts of science are not reflected in the sensory experience. However, he does believe that it concerns not only concepts such as "atom" or "ether", but also those "purely" empirical ones like "matter" or "movement". The concept of sensory experience is not treated here as something absolute. It is assumed that it is above all a theory that creates new possible experiences.

Particularly important are Cassirer's remarks concerning the semantics of the language of science. The relation between sign and object is not viewed here as the relation between replica and object previously known and experienced. We are dealing here with a symbol and an "object" as a place in the system of relations. What is signified exists only within the framework of knowledge as a whole or, to say it more individualistically, in the system of previous perceptions. Those problems would later become the basis of Cassirer's philosophy of symbolic forms.

Cassirer believes that in this way the philosophical problem of reality or of what is real (in science) is connected with the problem of truth.[10] Cognition means establishing the validity of a number of predicates. Such a definition of cognition positively revokes the traditional philosophical dilemma resulting from the fact of an object's transcendence in relation to our representations. A concept does not reflect the reality of objects (since it has not been known yet, before the cognitive act), but rather it discovers the relations between things and "creates" them for man. It transforms the

8. Ibid., p. 38.
9. Ibid., p. 261.
10. Ibid., pp. 323-324.

176

subjective impressions into a manifestation of permanent objects. Thinking is not an obstacle in reaching the reality, but makes being available to us.

The opposition between subject and object loses its significance for the defining what is subjective and what is objective. The latter terms can no longer mean, respectively, what is dependent upon consciousness (the implied risk of illusion) and what is independent of it, i.e. real (though in what way cognized?). It was a characteristic feature of metaphysical thinking that it changed the logical correlation (subjective-objective) into an opposition between two "object" spheres, two rows of being. However, the question of credibility of concrete, individual impressions, which entails the above opposition, is not the problem of science. The problem of science is to establish the scope of validity of those individual impressions. Possessing ready assumptions at its disposal, science coordinates particular acts of perception, subjecting them to experimental verification, if the latter is possible. The statements which have the most general scope are objective, contrary to those which can be applied only to narrow, specific conditions. What is objective exists in a constant opposition to what does not posses such a qualification, i.e. to what is subjective. It never exists absolutely.

For every currently objective content, a correction can be found which transforms it into a merely "partial expression of being". Thus, Cassirer views the development of science as a constant change of objective contents into subjective ones, a constant reduction of the scope of validity of judgements and searching for more general judgements to replace them. The only constant element is that act of correction, the criticism. Cassirer stresses that in the case of reducing the scope of validity of elements of knowledge,

the point is not a certain substantial change occurring while these elements pass into the sphere of subjectivity; it is only a critical evaluation of knowledge. "Things" do not become degraded to the rank of ordinary "representations". Simply, the judgement which could initially pass for a general one, now appears to be restricted to a specific situation and specific conditions.[11]

Cassirer's criticism of positivist empiricism, included in his polemics with the traditional theory of conceptualization, does not mean, however, any kind of anti-empiricism, but — on the contrary — empiricism *sensu stricto*. The whole knowledge is made dependent upon experience, which — however — is defined in a different way than that of positivists.

Modern physics, and not only it, has given up its pursuit to penetrate nature, if it is understood as the first and absolute cause from which empirical phenomena can be

11. Ibid., p. 310.

concluded. The only problem is (according to Kant — J.S.) the necessity to "syllabize phenomena in order to be able to read them as experiences".[12]

Therefore, the point is not the rejection of empiricism, but the rejection of metaphysics, and the belief that an assumptions-free and pre-scientific description of reality is possible. According to Neo-Kantians, questions concerning being can be asked only within a certain conceptual structure. The answer, on the other hand, will always be determined by culture. Thus, Cassirer's rejection of ontology is identical with — as he calls it — translocation of reflection from the realm of being into the realm of sense. By way of analogy, this new empiricism is also a new, non-metaphysical realism. The fact of incompatibility of theoretical concepts with the common experience cannot mean that

> a modern physics would have to renounce, contrary to the classical theory, a realistic status of physical concepts, but that it defines this requirement in a different way than its predecessor and that it must support this requirement in a complex way. The knowledge of the symbolic character of these concepts, far from denying their objective validity, creates the basis of this validity and its theoretical fundamentals.[13]

We are dealing here with a kind of naive realism of classical physics and with critical realism of 20th century physics. The methodological consciousness of the latter originates, according to Cassirer, from the critical work revealing its basic assumptions. This explains, to a certain point, the domination of the traditional theory of concept formation in the 19th century, despite a significant development of science itself. Within knowledge, wrote Cassirer,

> the use of hypotheses and assumptions precedes the knowledge of their unique function as assumptions. As long as it does not develop this knowledge, science can consider and express its own principles only in a substantial form, i.e. a semimythical one.[14]

III

It is not possible, however, to say that Aristotle's theory of concept formation still remains, at least to a certain degree, valid? Is the mathematical formula expressing a common rule of empirical series and not the common factor of various phenomena, obtained through abstraction?

Aristotle's "common factor" was substantially understood, however, as something embedded in a thing and remaining that thing's significant —

12. E. Cassirer, *La philosophie des formes symboliques*, vol. 3: *La phénoménologie de la connaissance* (transl. by C. Fronty), Les Editions de Minuit, Paris 1972, p. 479.
13. Ibid., p. 35.
14. E. Cassirer, *La philosophie des formes symboliques*, vol. 2: *La pensée mythique* (transl. by J. Lacoste), Les Editions de Minuit, Paris 1972, p. 44.

from the metaphysical point of view — part. It assumes the existence of an obvious *consensus* concerning the essence of things. It is possible only in the sphere of everyday life, the sphere of commonness, having complete confidence in sensory evidence. The world's "objectivity" appears only within the framework of "Lebenswelt". One cannot deny the fact that all trees have something in common, though the concept of tree implies this primitive division of the world of nature (nowadays considered to be commonplace). Searching for a real and necessary community, we find it in the processes of growth of cells governed by the genetic code. It is this common, abstract order that Cassirer had in mind. The abstract nature of modern science leaves the metaphysics of common perception far behind. Also the traditional divisions within science lose their validity. Genetics uses the achievements of biology, chemistry, and physics, without being either of them.

Aristotle's science was determined by his metaphysics. Contemporary science, lacking metaphysical support, is sort of suspended in vacuum: we analyze "something" the nature of which we do not know yet and the essence of which we will never know (according to the so-called anti-essentialist view of science discussed by Popper). The philosophers of the Marburg School (Cohen, Natorp, Cassirer) were right in their claim that this object is "the X in the equation of cognition". At the same time, however, a research is always based upon a certain language and even a pure experiment requires theoretical assumptions. To put it in the language of philosophy, it is thought that makes being available to us; nature will not reveal anything to us by itself, without the mediation of consciousness.

This double, as it would seem, fatalism is not "fatal", however. There exists an extraconceptual technological efficiency, the growth of which indicates that one is going in the right direction. On the other hand, there exists a constantly greater universality of scientific formulae, thanks to which the old ideal of unity of knowledge seems to be fulfilled. A humanist (more than a natural scientist) preserves the consciousness that science is part of man's cultural efforts. For that reason Cassirer has placed science on an equal level with other symbolic forms.

This does not mean that science is handicapped; neither does it imply any subjective "impurities". The theory of "impurities" was a result of a metaphysical belief that one already possesses a definition of what is real and so the only thing left is to reflect it in an unfalsified way. However, we do not posses that metaphysical insight into the essence of things and the only tool of that quasi-reflection is a theoretical model, a purely human and cultural mirror, which can be, at best, made independent of the commonsense assumptions. A thought does not stand in opposition against being. That symbolic thesis can also be expressed in the language of hermeneutics: "prejudices" open the way for us to what we are examining. We can add that in the past it also concerned the commonsense's ones.

The above problems are reflected in the history of epistemology. For positivists, the primary unit of cognition was perception and the so-called observation sentence based upon it. Empiricist metaphysics implied the possiblity of such isolated insights into reality. If, however, a theory is viewed as a set of judgements in the logical sense, rather than mental processes of judging, there will appear a dependence of judgements upon the language in which the predicate of the judgement is formulated. This language is the language of the entire theory. The independence of a single, perceptional insight into reality disappears. A theory becomes the primary unit of antipositivistic epistemology. It soon turned out, however, that the problem of the methodological accuracy of a theory and the legitimacy of its statements cannot be solved once and for all,[15] despite the fact that the rationality of science itself was an ideal here. As a matter of fact, we are dealing with a never-ending discussion between scientists and with a system of particular non-absolute agreements, rather than with the final agreement. Yet, in order not to lose the very idea of rationality of science, those principles of obtaining a certain consensus in time and space also had to be classified in a certain system. The rules of epistemological discourse of the scientists form what Lakatos called a research program. Thus, the methodology of scientific research programmes implies not a specific metaphysics, but rather pragmatics. The functioning of science within culture means at the same time that the thought of which Cassirer spoke is viewed dynamically here. Culture is viewed here as a form or the framework of discourse.

IV

A result of viewing science as a cultural discipline seems to be historical-cultural relativism. The norms of legitimacy of scientific statements and the ontological assumptions of the language in which they are formulated (both norms and statements) are culturally determined and historically changing. Therefore, particular stages of the development of science should propose incommensurable images of reality. In fact, it can be indicated that the same terms used in different theories often denote different "objects".[16] On the other hand, however, the image of the

15. J. Kmita, "Epistemology ...", op. cit., p. 26.
16. Comp. J. Kmita, *Szkice z teorii poznania naukowego* (Studies in the theory of scientific cognition), Warsaw 1976, p. 134.

development of science presented by Cassirer assumed the continuity of that development. Thus, to indicate that the standpoint of this type can be coherent means to point out that the approach to science from the point of view of the theory of culture does not have to entail extreme relativism.

Positivism assumed a cummulative nature of the development of science, a constant growth of knowledge within the framework of an unchanged, though constantly extended conceptual apparatus. The anti-positivistic reaction pointed out that scientific knowledge depends upon a number of assumptions, which vary historically. Therefore, the development of science proposes a number of visions uncomparable with one another.

More recently, however, a more moderate belief has become predominant. It is a synthesis of empiricist gradualism and antipositivistic catastrophism, called evolutionism.[17] It emphasized the existence of certain superior philosophical assumptions, common for different stages of the development of science. They are not absolutely timeless assumptions, but rather they are characteristic for longer periods of time, much longer than the time in which a given theory is accepted. The development of science consists in "adding and cancelling data, techniques, hypotheses, and theories". There are also revolutions in science, which lead to the origination of quite new theoretical languages. However, the theses of catastrophism are rejected here by putting forward six countertheses:[18]

(1) The development of science takes place mainly through adding, rather than replacing.

(2) Not every revolution in science is an answer to the crisis taking place in a given discipline. This is particularly visible in mathematics.

(3) Scientific revolutions do not revoke all previous achievements. Neither do they ever encompass the entire system of knowledge. The analogy to a political revolution is unjustified.

To the above argument, put forward by M. Bunge, we may add that speaking of revolutions in science, we should refer rather to the primitive meaning of that word. The point is not a destruction of what is old, not an "overthrow", but a turn, the result of which is a return to the established natural order.[19] This order in science is a relatively coherent image of the world, only slightly enhanced by the revolution.

17. Comp. M. Bunge, "A change in science: is it gradual or catastrophic?" (Polish transl.), *Studia Filozoficzne* 9/1984; G. Holton, "Do scientists ...", op. cit.

18. M. Bunge, "A change in ...", op. cit., pp. 51-54.

19. Comp. J. Garewicz, "Inaczej o rewolucji kopernikańskiej w filozofii" (A different view of Copernican revolution in philosophy), *Studia Filozoficzne* 2/1984, p. 118.

(4) Bunge considers as the most mistaken and dangerous thesis of catastrophism the statement that competitive theories are incommensurable and do not have a common semantic root, while "their senses and referential classes are totally separate".

It is enough to notice here that if two theories are considered to be competitive, it happens so because they share meanings and even make it possible to put forward certain common problems. E.g. the theory, according to which certain mutations are neutral, competes with standard genetics, according to which each mutation is either favorable or — most often — unfavorable. On the other hand, no linguistic theory could in any way compete with any geological theory, since they deal with different disciplines.[20]

Bunge does not stand alone in this belief. K.D. Apel also speaks against Feyerabend's total rejection of Popper's methodology. It is impossible to think of a competition between theories (thus also verification and falsification) without assumed measurements of comparison.[21]

(5) The conceptual structure is not a mental prison from which we can be liberated only by mysticism or a completely irrational, revolutionary overthrow. A modern scientist is always self-critical, i.e. he is also a researcher of his own theory. (Comp. critical realism discussed by Cassirer).

(6) It is not true that there exist no objective measurements of comparison of competitive theories. E.g. the principle of correspondence says that a new theory must preserve the old one within the scope of its practical applicability for small volumes or small speeds. Anticipatory abilities are also a form of a measurement of comparison. The compatibility with the theories from the "neighbouring fields" also counts here. "E.g. a new chemical theory is not even considered if it directly contradicts the principal part of physics and even a psychological theory is not worth considering if it contradicts neurology."[22]

That last argument is quoted today by many philosophers of science. There is no general consent any more to O. Neurath's image of science as a construction of a ship on an open sea. H. Putnam views science as an entire fleet. On each of its ships the crew proceeds with repairs, but not to such a degree as to risk sinking, as Neurath believed. However, the crews do also receive help and words of encouragement from the crews of other ships. Those who are discouraged may change ships. It sometimes happens that a

---

20. M. Bunge, "A change in ...", op cit., p. 52.

21. K.-O. Apel, "Limits of the ethics of discourse" (a typescript of a paper presented at the conference on "Morality and customs", J.W. Goethe Universität, Frankfurt/M. 1985.

22. M. Bunge, "A change in ...", op. cit., p. 53.

ship sinks, but it never does so alone or without help. Nobody, says Putnam, is imprisoned in a solipsistic hell of theory.[23]

The undertaking known as science cannot be identified with an isolated theory. It places the problem of discontinuity or incommensurability in a different perspective. I believe that the standpoint of E. Cassirer in the question of the development of science implies such an evolutionist approach. Science is a symbolic approach. Science as a symbolic form does not have to imply an extreme historical-cultural relativism.

V

The second half of the 20th century ended the great epistemological debates between researchers. Philosophical inspiration was replaced with the "organization" of science. And so, the question arises whether the norms of rationality, which traditionally govern the behavior of scientists, constitute a "degenerating research programme"? H. Harris believes that "rationality helps, but it is not a prescription for making discoveries". On the other hand, what scientists do has little in common with "the logic of a scientific discovery".[24]

The above can be understood in the following way. Epistemology has secured its primary position within modern philosophy together with the origin of science, which in turn means: together with the triumph of empiricism. However, nowadays we are experiencing a peculiar "disenchantment of science", which is connected with the loss of validity of empiricist epistemology. Empiricism has always implied individualism, for it has always been addressed to an individual. Confidence in sensory perception has been connected with assigning a great role to individual judgements and decisions. Historically, an equivalent of that epistemological principle was liberalism in the sphere of practical philosophy. The individualism and empiricism of Locke and Bacon was aimed against the Church's monopoly of the interpretation of the Universe.[25]

If the philosophical inspiration the end of which is observed by Holton was not a directly empiricist one, it certainly preserved one very importat feature of empiricism: the turn towards an individual. It is only an

23. H. Putnam, "Philosophers and human understanding" in: (Ed.) A.F. Heath, *Scientific explanations,* Boston 1981, quoted after G. Holton, "Do scientists ...", op. cit., p. 1234.

24. H. Harris, "Rationality and science", in: (Ed.) A.F. Heath, *Scientific explanations,* op. cit., quoted afte G. Holton, "Do scientists ...", op. cit., p. 1232.

25. K. Mannheim, "Ideology and utopia" (Polish transl.), in: (Eds.) A. Chmielecki et al., *Problemy socjologii wiedzy* (The problems of the sociology of knowledge), Warsaw 1985, p. 323.

183

individual researcher that can be "inspired". Yet, modern science is identified with a team effort rather than an individual option. In this sense, the most rational thing is not to use the norm of rationality as a restriction. The researcher's individual choice is replaced here with the "silent" rationality of the research programme.

In this situation one often hears a thesis of the end of domination of epistemological philosophy. Similar to metaphysics, which had once lost support (although this fact was realized only later), epistemology is losing its support nowadays. "All epistemological speculation remains within the scope of the opposition between an object and the subject", says a sociologist of knowledge.[26] Since, as I have already said, the 20th century philosophy, including the philosophy of symbolic forms, invalidates the epistemological question, traditional epistemology (and also the opposition between metaphysics and the theory of knowledge) loses ground. What remains seems to be practical philosophy connected with "acting", rather than "cognition" and "being".

Is there anything, then, that protects science against anarchy? There must be some principles, at least in the question of the introductory acceptance of hypotheses. At least this is what every adherent of rational criticism believes. Yet, even in this respect he becomes disillusioned. Also incoherent hypotheses are accepted — like, that of S. Glashow (winner of Noble prize in physics for 1979) — basing on their simplicity as a sufficient condition. Let us add that the point is no longer a condition sufficient for the confirmation of a given hypothesis, but merely for taking the risk of its acceptance.[27] Considering Hume's distinction between what is rational and what is reasonable, I think the activity of researchers tends to be merely reasonable. In other words, it tends to be pragmatic, based upon intuition only when there are chances of making a discovery. Such a philosophy, not always consciously respected, is pragmatism. One of its founders, Ch.S. Peirce, proclaimed a thesis of the relation between the rationality of knowledge and the rationality of action. According to Holton, the logic of Peirce's discovery is not a book product, an *a priori* project resembling those of Descartes or Bacon, but "an applied logic". It assumes a constant, self-correcting research discourse. On the other hand, the guarantees of making discoveries are not found in the *a priori* sphere of methodological assumptions, but "in the future". The rationality of "cognitive activity" consists in its double orientation: "towards the community of researchers" and "towards the future".[28] What is implicitly

26. Ibidem., p. 322.
27. G. Holton, "Do scientists ...", op. cit., p. 1232.
28. Ibid., p. 1234.

184

present in the research practice is not the classical epistemological norms, but rather the ethical ones, i.e. the practical norms of scientific discourse.

However, that discourse not only respects these pragmatic principles. Researchers' *consensus* is also conditioned by certain descriptive beliefs. Cassirer indicated all the time that a thought makes being available to us and that there is no pure, non-cultural cognition. Holton adds that it concerns not only logic and mathematics, but also certain long-lasting "themata" which influence the way in which researchers apply analytic tools and empirical findings available to them. The influence of these beliefs is also indicated by the fact that a researcher often has to accept or refute a hypothesis, for which no empirical test exists yet. What is more, theories are accepted despite serious doubts. In the case of Glashow's theory, it was not only the elegance of style, but also the old concept of the unity of nature. Despite that, the course of the research process, not involved in epistemological arguments, reflects the continuity of certain primary questions of an often ancient background.

> The modern philosophers' apparatus of strict demarcation criteria, of the logic of justification, of the supposed incommensurability of successive stages of science, has not been able to deal with the persistent thematic side of the scientific imagination.[29]

However, that aspect was reflected, I believe, by the symbolistic approach to science. E. Cassirer's theory of science, being later (at the end of the 1920's) part of his philosophy of culture, still preserves its validity. Naturally, it does so not as a description of the state of research, but as a description of a cultural entanglement of the method of modern science. The appreciation of his concept becomes possible not only thanks to the anti-empiricist turn of the reflection on the theory of science, but also thanks to the evolutionist synthesis of gradualism and catastrophism. One has to remember that in the period of forming of the 20th century methodological reflection, Cassirer's (more generally, that of the Marburg school) description of science exerted no influence upon that process. The reason is that this methodology originated from the spirit of empiricism.[30]

Translated by Krzysztof Sawala

---

29. Ibidem.
30. W. Stegmüller, *The structure and dynamic of theories* (transl. by W. Wohlueter), Springer Verlag, New York/Heidelberg/Berlin 1976, p. 217.

Wojciech Burszta

THE EPISTEMOLOGICAL ASPECT OF THE CONTROVERSY OVER CULTURAL RELATIVISM

The present paper, which is a preliminary presentation of an extremely extensive subject matter, will make an attempt at identifying the domain which the ethnologists call "cultural relativism". There are various variants of the latter distinguished by ethnology. On the other hand, contemporary philosophy of science elaborates widely on the issue of "relativism versus objectivism of cognition" which, from many points of view, overlaps the controversy over cultural relativism. Thus, various relevant approaches will be ordered. In conclusion, we shall present an approach which makes it possible, at least partially, to present the essence of the controversy between "relativists" and "objectivists" from the viewpoint of assumptions adopted in this paper.

As the title suggests, we shall be interested in the epistemological aspect of cultural relativism. Hence, let us initially assume, following M. Herskovits, that within the framework of this concept three planes of discussion can be distinguished: (1) philosophical, (2) methodological and (3) practical.[1] If we adhere to the above division it will appear that a consistent limitation of plane (1) will not be possible. This is so due to the obscurity of the discussion on relativism. The available literature on the issue is sufficient evidence that planes of considerations have been characteristically "mixed" by research workers. Hence, it is not easy to adopt a clear approach to fundamental epistemological settlements, if they exist at all.

In view of the above it seems indispensable to distinguish two aspects of the controversy in question. They are contained in the following questions which are often answered as if they were identical: (1) what is the "world of culture" (what is the cognitive status of claims made about it) and (2) what can we say about it in the framework of scholarly research. With regard to the latter question it should be pointed out that it is of special interest to ethnology, a science which studies cultures that are often extremely

---

1. See M. Herskovits, *Man and his works. The science of cultural anthropology,* New York 1856; cf. also his *Cultural relativism,* New York 1972.

different from the culture of the researcher.

Since the idea of cultural relativism was born in the framework of the ethnological reflection on culture, it seems apt to consider the manner in which the science developed its theoretical and methodological assumptions which derived directly from the idea of relativism.

The first fifty years of ethnological research were characterized, as is commonly known, by the dominance of historical-comparative orientations in their broadest sense. Among the features distinguishing this type of research one finds the research of culture which objectivized, recorded and accepted. And because it objectivized ("naturalized") the cultural competence of such researchers as Tylor, Lubbock, Graebner, or Schmidt, the cultural systems which differed from modern-European ones (especially Anglo-Saxon) did not pose any problems of the interpretative nature. Together with the respect for the positivist "philosophy of progress", this restricted the framework of quasi-historical "laws of evolutionary development" or the theory of "cultural circles". Historical-comparative ethnology was not able to distinguish two kinds of conditionings in which representatives of cultural sciences were involved. This concerns distinguishing (1) the researcher's own cultural context from that of activities and products which constitute the cultures under study and (2) axiological neutralization of one's own cultural context. The latter is a logical consequence of the former and describes the refrainment from attributing one's own cultural valuations to historical subjects of respective activities and products.[2]

In the case of representatives of historical and comparative directions the objectivization has no double character: the recognition of the researcher's own cultural beliefs as "objective" ("natural") deprives the cultures under analysis of "humanistic coefficients" characteristic of it; they are treated as an expression of "false consciousness" which the researcher reveals (J. Frazer's concept of magic, cognitively fertile for many reasons, which has been used and documented by structuralists, serves as a classic example here).[3] The "mixing" of judgements of common cultural experience with beliefs of the philosophical nature, characteristic of researchers-ethnologists who were positivistically oriented (e.g the idea of progress treated as an expression of an absolutely "objective" fact) was

2. Cf. A. Pałubicka, *Przedteoretyczne postaci historyzmu* (Pre-theoretic versions of historicism), Warsaw 1984; W. Burszta, *Język a kultura w myśli etnologicznej* (Language and culture in the ethnological thought), Wrocław 1986.

3. It suffices to have a look at E. Leach *Culture and communication,* Cambridge 1976; Frazer's genuine theses which are basic to indicating the metaphorical-metonimic character of cultural communication have been re-interpreted there.

depicted in the conceptions of ethnological cognition. Naive realism was their expression — cultural activities and products were seen as "objective" data which were valorized from the philosophical point of view in accordance with the order of the researcher's cultural preferences. Thus, there could emerge typological-developmental schemes, so characteristic of evolutionism, in the field of technical innovations (Morgan's "ethnic epochs"), families (also Morgan's), religion, law, etc.

The recognition of the intentional, specifically humanistic character of cultural phenomena was the main consequence of the conceptual-structuralist breakthrough in ethnology, the consequence most significant for our purposes. The idea of cultural relativism was one of the effects of the recognition of the (1) contextual character of activities and objects which make up the culture, (2) their ethnic locality and (3) systematization. From that time the idea has been always present in different variants of the theory and research practice in world ethnology. Obviously, and it should be strongly emphasized, the idea was not merely (perhaps in the first place) an answer to the practical-cognitive directives of ethnology; reasons of the normative nature and those related to the philosophy of life played a big role. For example, D. Sperber says that anthropologists have a tendency to treat superficial and irregular differences as a "bottomless precipice" between different cultures. This view is adopted especially willingly as it requires that those who adhere to it declare themselves in favour of liberalism in their approach to different philosophical systems.[4] In order not to complicate our considerations, let us skip the problem of the formation (and justification) of relativizing research tenets; the latter problem should be carefully analysed in its historical-theoretical aspects and thoroughly researched. This is justified by the assumption, widely adopted by the philosophy of science, that norms cannot be considered the logical components of the system of claims that a given science makes.

Thus, let us see what anthropologists imagine that they claim when they advance the thesis of the said cultural relativism. The issue, formulated in this way, separates the question of how relativism is seen by ethnology from that of what is the objective reference of the cultural relativism thesis on the basis of assumptions advanced in this paper.

The doctrine itself has an extremely great number of meanings, it is often imprecisely verbalized or treated as a kind of "key-word" which does not require definitions or connotations of that which it denotes. Researchers who were first to adhere to this thesis and who respected it as a research directive claimed that cultures as such are incomparable as each of them

4. Cf. D. Sperberg, *On anthropological knowledge,* Cambridge 1985, chapter III.

creates a specific "reference system" for its subjects. The acculturation process is a moment which decides on the unique separateness of a given cultural system. As M. Herskovits, one of the adherents of the cultural relativism said "beliefs are based on experience and experience is interpreted by each individual in the categories of its acculturation".[5] Hence, for Herskovits there is no other experience but cultural; reality then is always cultural reality. Each kind of beliefs is determined by the local character of a specific culture and can only be explained within its context. It is also significant for such cultural relativists as Herskovits to distinguish between so-called cultural absolutes and cultural universals. In the formal sense universals denote as much as common types of institutions (e.g. the family, the moral system, the law, etc.) found in all kinds of societies. The contents of each of the systems are conditioned by the cultural experience of a given society. For a relativist who thinks this way there are no concrete and universal norms or values because there are no objective absolute values. We must assume then that there are only abstract and formal cultural universals which differ with respect to the manner of realization (the manner of filling a local culture with their contents), both in the temporal and spatial aspects.[6]

Materials collected by ethnologists seemed to a greater and greater extent to confirm the thesis with proofs that the possibilities of solving "the same" problems which members of different cultures face, are practically unlimited. And it was no longer surprising and "rationally" explicable that there are six quarters of the globe or only two; one can have only two names for colours, or say about them that they are "wet" or "dry", that there are cultural norms, kinds of institutions, customs and rituals between which common points can hardly be found. Different cultures as functioning entities (or groups of "patterns" according to configurationalists) from different worlds, different kinds of reality, fully comprehensible to those only who were acculturated in them. And, according to Herskovits, one can be acculturated only once.

Research practice of relativistically-oriented ethnologists was to lead to attempts at making the varied material-descriptive inventory more precise and arranging it in different thematic blocks, which would constitute individual scopes of the overall meaning of the term "cultural relativism". The following aspects of the doctrine can be distinguished: ethical (moral) relativism (with E. Westermarck[7] as the forerunner in ethnology), the

5. M. Herskovits, *Man and his works ...,* op. cit., p. 63.
6. Ibidem. See also D. Bidney, "The concept of value in modern anthropology", in: (Ed.) A.L. Kroeber, *Anthropology today,* Chicago 1953, pp. 689-690.
7. E. Westermarck, *Ethical relativity,* London and S. Lukes, *Rationality and relativism,* Oxford 1983; W.V. Quine, *Word and object,* New York 1960.

relativism of truth (there are no universal categories which would permit saying that a given vision of the world, a type of thinking or systems of beliefs are true or false), the relativism of reason (there is no universal logic, system of inference, etc.), the relativism of perception (what we experience in the world does not stem from the nature of the object being experienced), the conceptual relativism (different ways of world conceptualization) and the linguistic relativism (a specific variant of the relativism of perception, if, following E. Sapir, we assume that the experience of the world is always mediated through language).[8]

Before we discuss in greater detail the principles according to which the thesis of relativism is constructed and the consequences resulting from our adherence to one of its variants, let us devote some time to two issues. Let us notice that the six aspects of the overall conceptual scope of this concept can be reduced to one of them, namely to the conceptual relativism or, speaking more broadly, to the *cognitive* relativism. I. Jarvie is only partly right when he claims that cognitive relativism refers to a range of phenomena other than those which he distinguished as second — the ethical relativism.[9] Cognitive relativism is not so much a generalization of the moral relativism (as the said author wished it were the case) but constitutes the *basis* of the cultural relativism. In order to wonder at all whether the thesis of relativism is true or false, what it means, etc. we should adopt a concept of culture within which such a problem can appear. If we want to explain why such and not any other activities and cultural products (e.g. a kind of ethical norms permitting a "seasonal" killing of children and the old) appear in this particular culture we must first reconstruct the mental "background" of the culture which decides on such kinds of activities and/or products. Only if the cultures in question are treated as certain "mental", cognitive "entities", systems of knowledge, judgements, etc. can we explain the phenomena of the appearance and interpretation of facts related to culture (explain behaviour and its effects). If we adopt this line of reasoning (*nota bene,* generally accepted by cultural anthropology in various verbalizations), then, when we want to consider the validity (or falsity) of the cultural relativism, we should focus on the cognitive (conceptual) relativism. In this sense all decisions related to the relative character of the beliefs shared by subjects of different cultures are at the same time decisions of the cultural relativism. In other words: when we speak of a given state of affairs which is in a way a confirmation of any

9. It is I. Jarvie, *Rationality and relativism. In search of the philosophy and history of anthropology,* London 1984.

of the denotations of the term "relativism" possible, we must point to systems of beliefs which are primary in relation to it. Obviously, the adoption of this perspective is not yet a sufficient premise that would motivate the adherence to relativism or its negation; however, it permits to specify the range of problems likely to be considered.

A thesis of the linguistic relativism, often identified with the Sapir-Whorf hypothesis, is treated as a variant of the conceptual relativity understood as above. Within its framework it is maintained that all natural and social reality experienced by man is "encoded" in communicative units of language of the appropriate culture (mainly in its grammatical structure). In this case the existing conceptual scheme is identical with language; if, then, languages are different, then the conceptual schemes are different as well. In turn, we could consider the way in which the relativism of perception can be logically reduced to the conceptual relativism and the latter, again after the adoption of appropriate premises, to the linguistic relativism.[10] However, let us leave this aspect of the problem aside for the time being.

It is characteristic that the thesis of relativism discussed in this paper is taken up mainly by the researchers who deal with the mental-persuasive aspect of culture. Representatives of contemporary ecological neo-evolutionary orientations or sociobiologists pass these problems round, to speak metaphorically. They often think that the controversy over relativism is of purely verbal character. There are two reasons for this. First, they do not usually take into account the "humanistic coefficient" of each culture;[11] they do not attempt to reconstruct conceptual forms characteristic of it and hence they do not wish to relativise their judgements. On the contrary — they assign them an overcultural dimension which destroys determination barriers between phenomena of appropriately different cultures. C. Lévi-Strauss's position with respect to the problem is different: although he does not negate directly the relativist anthropology he opposes the results of its findings. He calls the theory of culture he practises "metaempirical objectivism" and the "superficial" controversy over the interpretation of the obvious diversity of the world of culture is of no interest to him.

The other reason for which the problems we are interested in are neglected by the directions mentioned seems to stem from the fact that the epistemological aspect of culture cognition is not noticed. When speaking

10. Cf. at least D. Davidson, "On the very idea of a conceptual scheme", in: (Eds.) J.W. Meiland and M. Krausz, *Relativism, cognitive and moral,* Notre Dame 1982, pp. 66-80.
11. I am using this concept in the sense designated by J. Kmita; see at least *Kultura i poznanie* (Culture and cognition), Warsaw 1985.

about relativism they take into account only its methodological and practical aspects. They limit its applicational range to the elimination of its own cultural resources in order to arrive at the "objectivity" of the culture under study. Solutions at both levels are considered sufficient to be adopted so that eventually ethnological cognition has an objective character.

Before we confront the two ways of looking at cultural reality, the relativist and objectivist (absolutist), let us ask about the consequences which the thesis of cultural relativism is to bring about.

The consequences of this type of optics are at least twofold. It was initially believed that due to, as we thought, facts stated unquestionably, which confirmed the relativism, cultures cannot be evaluated. When living in different cultures we live in different realities and whatever we say within each of them is true. Critics immediately noticed a paradox concealed in this reasoning: while supporting the relativity of e.g. moral principles, at the same time we condemn absolutely any outside interference into other societies. The other consequence, much more significant from the cognitive point of view, is the inability of comparison, legally valid description and explanation of any cultures. They can be quite different conceptually and there are no objective ways and criteria that would permit an "insight" into their structure (even the analysis of the language of a given culture or, speaking more broadly, the use of linguistic data as such if we are to adopt the obligatory linguistic relativity, ceases to be such a way). Thus the possibility of conducting any scientific research on culture is questioned. The consequence of the second kind embraces the initial thesis about the inability to evaluate cultures — as we are unable to explain, describe or compare them, what criteria should we adopt for their evaluation? — Researchers-relativists cannot claim two things simultaneously: (1) the validity of opinions on attested facts depends on their cultural background (cultural relativism in the sense of the cognitive relativism) and think that (2) cultural anthropology conducts objective research and arrives at such claims (it is a semantic nonsense to say that "relativism exists objectively"). Hence, a consistent relativism means being antinomic (the situation was discussed in detail by A. Tarski at one time). If we adhere to the statements made by Herskovits, whom we have already quoted a number of times, we can say that each opinion expressed by the researcher is always a projection (unintentional) of his/her own acculturation patterns which are incomparable (by virtue of the consequence of relativism) with any other patterns in different cultures. This was the road that considerations on relativism and most of its critics (philosophers and advocates of the theory of scientific cognition) followed. The idea of cultural relativism (especially cognitive relativism) is treated as a peculiar kind of neo-Kantianism. Such researchers as Herskovits or Rorty reject these fragments of Kant's philosophy which have him treated as a cultural absolutist and only adopt the supreme thesis that the human mind imposes basic concepts and categories on the basis of which sensory data are organized and experience interpreted. They added, however, that these notions do not have a universal character but are subjected to changes in time or that different individuals in different cultures can use different, incomparable in the extreme case, sets of these concepts and categories when experiencing the world.[12] Hence, each culture uses its own "schemes of cognition" each of which provides a completely different, yet entirely legally valid, way of interpreting experience. Societies live in "the same" physical world but their "cognitive world" is always different.

Thus, it seems that we can point to a distinct structural similarity between different versions of relativism. The similarity is concealed in the inability to answer the question in what way the conceptual, moral or linguistic relativity can be explained if the possibility of referring to some coordinate system, within whose framework it is possible to determine the limits between respective cultures, is negated. Let us repeat: relativists assume that there is no higher standard of objective knowledge in this respect. However, when we say that all methods of cognition are relative we simultaneously support that one's own doctrine of relativism is absolute, which decides on the inner contradiction of the assumption. A consistent spokesman for cognitive relativity entangles himself in the so-called vicious circle of proving; as was the case with, for example, linguistic relativism. W.V. Quine said:

> The view of the world which we attribute to aborigines depends on the way in which we interpret their words and grammar of the aborigines depends on the view of the world we attribute to them.[13]

And thus, says Quine in conclusion, the impressive (and most significant for the relativists) question of whether the aborigines see the world differently than we do cannot be answered. The final conclusion is rather shattering — relativism destroys its own foundations and what remains for the orthodox advocate of this doctrine is to fall into extreme subjectivism.[14] At this moment, however, the entire problem is in a way doubled. We are dealing with two overlapping relativisms: subjective and objective

12. See Davidson's considerations in *Relativism ...*, op. cit.

13. W.V. Quine, "Philosophical progress in the theory of language" (Polish translation), in: (Ed.) B. Stanosz, *Lingwistyka a filozofia* (Linguistics and philosophy), Warsaw 1977, p. 515.

14. This formulation is that of R. Trigg in his *Rozum a zaangażowanie* (Reason and the committment), Warsaw 1977.

(M. Mandelbaum's terminology).[15] By virtue of the former it is said that each judgement should be treated in reference to the individual who makes the claim; moreover, by virtue of the objective relativism, claims must be relative to the overall context of the culture to which they pertain.[16] It seems that the ideal of anthropology as "cultural critique" or the contemporary "semantic anthropology" of M. Crick's are attempts to realize this model of anthropology which is confronted with the double cognitive entanglement of the researcher.[17]

The reasonings of ethnologists have gone in a slightly different direction than those of philosophers. From the very beginning of this science the view of the fundamental psychic unity of the human kind has been accepted; it is one of the fundamental assumptions of historical-comparative anthropology though even today it has a few variants. For some anthropologists psychic unity is related to the results of mental activities in the form of specific, universal practices, artifacts and especially beliefs — the concept is then related on many sides to the problem of cultural universals. Let us mention here A. Bastian's concept of *Elementargedenken* and *Völkergedanken*. Referring to these two terms Herskovits would probably say that the former do not exist (there are no cultural absolutes) and as regard the latter one can say that as abstract universals they are realized in concrete cultural conditions. The psychic unity was also proven in the context of the development of specific cultural parallels as indications of a uniform activity of the human mind. This is a possible understanding of Lévi-Strauss's concept of the universality of the incest taboo and its structural inversion — exogamy. The human mind goes beyond the frames of nature when determining the incest taboo, which is universal only because in the human mind always three basic structures of thinking are apparent: the requirement of norm as norm, the principle of mutuality and the synthesizing character of gift. Still another group looked for universal logical principles; it is indispensable to ascertain their occurrence if one wants to pursue science, especially for the empirical phases of the activity which provides data used in all kinds of inter-cultural generalizations. In fact, at least at the present stage of the development of science, these are kinds of forejudgements indispensable to undertake research, e.g. an *a priori* acceptance of the existence of logic or the ability to

15. M. Mandelbaum, "Subjective, objective, and conceptual relativism", in: *Relativism...*, pp. 34-61.

16. Ibid., pp. 30-36.

17. G.E. Marcus and M.J. Fischer, *Anthropology as cultural critique,* Chicago 1986; M. Crick, *Explorations in language and meaning,* London 1978.

18. C. Lévi-Strauss, *The elementary structures of kinship,* Boston 1969.

194

perform set-theoretic operations by the subjects of the cultures under study.

The research activity of the adherents of relativism "broke" the individual types of universal features of human cultures to a different degree. For example, Whorf stated that there is no logic as such and that logic is isomorphic with the grammar of a given language. T. Gladwin, who researched the methods of navigation used by one of the tribal groups, stated that they do not use induction and deduction at all.[19] Arguments of the advocates of objectivism were thus directed at the "breaking" of relativist truths (we can mention an entire range of works of this type; for example *Basic color terms* by Berlin and Kay is a classic work undermining the linguistic relativism).[20]

Since the present paper does not aim to illustrate the controversy over relativism and its variants completely, let us now have a look at where the core of the controversy between advocates of relativism and "objectivists" is. At this point we must return to the double dimension of the problem mentioned before: on the one hand it is the forejudgements pertaining to the world studied by ethnologists and on the other it is the possibility of its valid description. The "fusion" of both problems is the basic cause of the obscureness of the controversy between relativists and "objectivists".

Let our departure point be a claim that consistent relativism strikes its own research practice by forejudging that the "world" or "reality" do not exist independently of the conceptual schemes which refer to them (there is no experience other than cultural). Thus we cannot assume that what the subjects of different cultures perceive as a world is similar in some way. A problem arises of how to achieve the understanding of other conceptual systems if the existence of any reality independent of beliefs is negated? If we assume that systems of beliefs of members of a given culture refer only to this culture and the world of the researcher's cultural beliefs is an entirely different world, completely external and incomparable with the former, then how is it possible to reconstruct the former? For these reasons an anthropologist (and any other researcher of culture) has no choice but to proclaim himself, often intuitively, in favour of the objectively-realistic assumption that different cultures organize mentally the same external world in principle but conceptualize and describe it differently (e.g. because they use languages structurally different). Not always is it known

19. B.L. Whorf, *Język, myśl i rzeczywistość* (Polish translation of *Language, thought, and reality*), Warsaw 1982; T. Gladwin, "Culture and logical process", in: (Ed.) W. Goodenough, *Explorations in cultural anthropology,* New York 1964, pp. 167-177.

20. B. Berlin and P. Kay, *Basic color terms: Their universality and evolution,* Berkeley 1969, and numerous other works.

what the situation with those alternative ways of looking at the world (which are reflected in the conceptual scheme of a given culture) is. If we relate the possession of a conceptual scheme with the possession of a specific language a question arises whether more than one language is able to express the same scheme? A positive answer implies the existence of something like a set of mutually translatable languages. However, another question arises: do two specific cultures have different conceptual schemes only when they use languages which are not mutually translatable? Anthropologists reject this question and claim that there is always some translatability possible between any two types of languages since the "world" about which the languages speak is basically the same.

It seems that an assumption of a certain kind of metaphysical relativism is written in the framework of sciences which research different cultures in different aspects. The assumption states that phenomena seen by the subjects of most different historical and contemporary cultures are in a way similar (and even: must be similar). Otherwise it would not be possible to "grasp" these phenomena, describe and explain the way of their conceptualization by the participants of given cultures and, eventually to "translate" them into the conceptual system of the researcher. Eventually, we shall always mean a linguistic translation, which has its own epistemological consequences (which we shall not consider in this paper).

The assumption of the metaphysical realism is, it seems, the indispensable condition for undertaking scientific practice as such. This is clearly seen in the case of ethnology. A researcher who represents a given system of scientific knowledge cannot make a specific claim without having assumed that its objective reference is real. For logical reasons one cannot make a specific claim and simultaneously put it in epistemological bracket — ponder over it critically. Hence, also cultural relativism cannot state anything about the culture under consideration and claim at the same time that it is "impermeable". B.L. Whorf's works are somewhat similar in this respect. He describes precisely and in detail the structural complexities of the language of Hopi Indians and suggests at the same time that practically the vision of the world contained in this language is absolutely incomprehensible for an European. The problem does not lie, however, in the researcher's attempt to prove that the semantic objective reference of his claims is the "objective reality". The adoption of the assumption of metaphysical reality is not univocal with its inclusion into the scope of essential premises of ethnology's findings (a researcher does not have to justify his value choices, and especially epistemological values). It appears, however, that ethnologists act just this way, including, which may seem paradoxical, representatives of directions regarded as relativist. This is confirmed at least by the discussion on the opposition between research of the emic and etic types. According to this conception the emic research is to be equivalent to what may be called a reconstruction of culture characterized objectively without attributing judgements which derive from the culture and language of the researcher; the etic analyses mean research which makes use of such attributions by virtue of the assumption. "The emic point of view" would then correspond to the relativist programme of research while the "etic point of view" would aim at obtaining objective classifications of phenomena without considering their particular-subjective conditionings. Contemporary ethno-science treats itself as a strictly "emic" trend, which reconstructs phenomena of the cultures under study in their genuine context, discovers cultural senses relativized to specific cultures and not having universal denotations. However, if we look more closely at the claims made by representatives of the said orientation we find out that they simultaneously claim that (1) the emic research pertains to the subjective formulation alien to a given culture, *of the same* phenomena which (2) are given in their etical description (only in a different way). The two forejudgements stem from the assumption which abolishes the validity of the "emic-etic" dychotomy and which says that individual "external" phenomena with respect to two random cultures (e.g. one under study and that of the anthropologist) are in a way given in the same way to the researcher and the participants of the cultures under analysis. The inconsistency emerging here stems from the premise of the metaphysical realism mentioned above, which is "set of motion" by the researchers who do not realize that in this way they do not relativize the phenomena they study to their genuine humanistic coefficient but *de facto* reduce them to the assumptions of their own semantics. It is worth emphasizing here that on the basis of the assumptions adopted in this paper what is "etical" is not any "objective" reality but this which is given as a phenomenon objectivized on the grounds of the researcher's culture. The question whether so-called pure emic descriptions are possible at all should also be answered negatively. It is not possible to learn a culture without using any attributions or, using W.V. Quine's terminology, analytic hypotheses.

The core of the controversy of relativists with "objectivists" seems to lie precisely in epistemological decisions on the cognitive status of claims pertaining to the "world of culture". Here, however, the controversy is, at least today, practically insolvable since it is reduced to subjective axiological decisions. The only thing that remains is to focus on the problem: what can be said practically in science about the world of culture, what kind of claims can be regarded as legally valid. This is at the same time a reduction of the controversy "relativism-objectivism" to methodological and practical (or practical-cognitive) aspects.

In conclusion, while outlining future research in this respect, I would like suggest a research perspective which in my opionion might make possible effective congnitive decisions. As our point of departure we must adopt a view that science can be conceived of as one of the domains of culture, as a system of judgements which form social methodological consciousness of scientific practice. Thus, if we assume that scientific cognition is a set of judgements "produced" in the framework of scientific practice in a culturally regulated way, then we should be consistent and begin our reflection over recognition with the adoption of settlements general in character and belonging to the theory of culture. A theory of culture called socio-regulational is the departure point of the theory of the scientific cognition which I have adopted here. The theory of cognition which assumes the concept of culture mentioned above is, in turn, historical epistemology. Considering that the latter deals with, among other things, research on the history of science and especially on the history of the scientific reflection over culture, it provides (may provide) e.g. ethnology with many directives which will make the expansion of the "state of possession" of this discipline possible. It should be, however, remembered that it is not so that these directives or the research results achieved are a simple consequence of the general cultural claims adopted before (within the socio-regulational theory of culture). Hence, the relation of historical epistemology to the theory of culture assumed within its framework consists in a continual mutual influence of both levels of knowledge. Such an approach permits analysing numerous phenomena from the circle of science in the context of the theory of culture and, more importantly, reflecting over culture itself. In the future considerations of the cultural relativism, the perspective outlined here should prove especially useful, mainly because the pursuance of the relativity of human cultures is closely linked with the pursuance of the cognitive possibilities of humanistic sciences. The feedback between historical epistemology and the socio-regulational theory of culture permits considering both aspects of the problem with the application of uniform assumptions and ter minology.

Translated by Zbigniew Nadstoga

Michał Buchowski

ETHNOCENTRISM, EUROCENTRISM, SCIENTOCENTRISM

All animals are equal, but some animals are more equal than others
George Orwell

When one paraphrases the above motto in the spirit of its alegorical sense, namely that "all people are equal, but some are more equal than others", he deals with a formula which can be believed to have underlain the anthropological sciences (ethnology). The consciousness of the difference between individuals and their statuses, groups, or races, rooted in everyday experience, seems to be immediately included in the cultural heritage of all communities. It was that kind of sense of group distinction (identification may take place on various levels) that constituted the reason for the occurrence of anthropology and that defined the scope of its issues.

Group identification, which usually pejoratively implies the treatment of other groups (the "locals" are always "better" than "strangers"), constitutes a parallel equivalent of the image of an ethnic society. It seems to be for that reason that — among the title concepts — the concept of ethnocentrism is considered to be the most general one. Its specific case is Eurocentrism, characteristic of our cultural environment, while one of the local attributes of the latter is scientocentrism.[1] It is easy to notice that when establishing the range of the above categories, I am referring to their intuitively defined connotations and — let us add — only to a degree which makes it possible to accept a certain structure for the present argumentation. I consider to be the most important definition of each of those "-centrisms" the fact of perception, description, and interpretation of cultural phenomena, distinct from the perspective of a particular culture — in a way, "measuring somebody else's field with one's own measuring device". Thus, ethno-, Euro-, and scientocentrism not only mean (1) considering one's own worldview and thus also oneself to be superior than others, which is mainly connected with the ethical plane of the problem;

---

1. I am certainly aware of the degree of inaccuracy and conventionality of the terms quoted here. It may sound paradoxically to quote, e.g. an appropriate conceptual cluster, indicating that an American (or, say, Japanese) anthropologist of culture is Eurocentric!

but also (2) depriving other cultures of their peculiar humanist coefficient by imputing them their own cultural experience, considered at the same time to be objective and adequately describing the world, which — in turn — is connected with the evaluative-cognitive aspect of the respective "-centrism".

The above statement that the consciousness of the distinction of other cultures is constitutive for anthropology is supported by the fact that it formed not only this scientific discipline, but also its most vital problem of epistemological nature: how it is possible, despite an often striking difference between the analyzed cultures and the researcher's culture, to learn about the former in an adequate way.[2] The history of our science can be viewed as a process of passing from a common, folk experience of this cultural distinction, its codification and systematization, to a gradually acquired consciousness if its nature and significance and putting forward solutions to cognitive difficulties manifested in this way. That history is at the same time a picture of a struggle with particular variations of ethnocentrism, efforts aimed at becoming liberated from its domination. Let us, then, outline its most important episodes in order to be able, ultimately, to suggest a global diagnosis and initial conclusions.

A good place to start out reflection is the pre-history of anthropology. A reflection on human cognition resulting — to a large extend — from folk images was characteristic of already the modern travellers, missionaries, and philosophers. The ancient division into civilized and barbaric peoples has survived until the beginings of our era, in which it has been constantly reinterpreted.[3]

Besides other, verified information, almost all descriptions of other peoples from ancient and Renaissance times included various stories of wild cyclops, monsters and cannibals. Caliban from Shakespere's *The tempest* remained a dominating image of human-like creatures inhabiting foreign countries. A characteristics of the savages as wearing animal skins, eating raw meat, and speaking a strange language, provided by S. Cabot (Hodgen 1964, p. 112), was something quite natural and, at the same time, rather moderate.

Geographical discoveries and contacts with conquered peoples have soon created a theological problem. Are other "people" human at all: do they possess a soul? The argument that took place in 1550-51 between a scientist, J.G. de Sepulveda and a Dominican priest, B. de las Casas became a reflection of that problem. The former sanctioned colonization

2. An exceptionally synthetic and well-aimed characteristics of the formation of beliefs on this matter can be found in the chapter entitled "The unity of man" in E. Leach's book (1982), which was the source of many observations quoted in the present work.

depriving Indians of the benefits of law and culture, while the latter maintained that they are also God's children and may become part of the Christian community. The pope and history acknowledged las Casas to have been right, though many years had to pass before this principle was generally recognized and effectively sanctioned. That problem was also incorporated into the complex interpretations of the Bible, its chronology, and versions of man's creation. If we all are the descendants of Adam, then what is the origin of racial differences and how did the Indians originate in America? In his book *Man before Adam,* I. de la Preyere put forward a real heresy: the Bible concerns the Jews and Christians, while other peoples were created before Adam. His work was burnt at stake, while the author himself escaped a similar fate by a hairbreadth (Jarvie 1984, pp. 39-42). Yet, the study did manage to break the biblical monopoly of interpreting Man's history and from a question concerning the monogamous and poligamous origin of human kind.

In that period two contradictory ideas opposed one another. The author of one of them was Montaigne, whose followers were Rousseau, Vico, and Lord Monboddo. The 16th century French philosopher wondered whether being different had to mean being inferior. Comparing the cruel practices of Europeans and the simple nature of Brasilian Indians, he reached a conclusion that the latter are governed by natural law and are far from the decay characteristic of certain European norms. And so a myth was created of a "noble savage" inhabiting the Gardens of Paradise, whose later story was that of Decline. However, more popular was the other image, referring to Hobbes's concept of a sinister natural man, according to which the story of humanity is a constant progress. J. Locke complemented it with his own observation that morality may be a matter of convention; he had no doubt, however, where his own position was and to what degree it was more privileged that that of others.

Let us add that even in the 18th century, an anatomist, W. Tyson, performed a thorough research on the basis of which he considered the Pygmies to be the missing link between apes and man. Linnaeus's standpoint was similar. He divided the human species into "fair, sanguine, brawny; covered with close vestments; governed by laws Europeans" and "black, phlegmatic, relaxed, anoints himself with greace, governed by caprice" Africans (Leach 1982, p. 83). This should be of no surprise to us, for similar criteria are used in zoology even today to give characteristics of animals. Besides, the opinion of the contemporary "man from the street" seems to be quite similar to the one above.

Let us stop at this point for a moment and point out several facts most significant in this context and appearing from those pre-anthropological reflections. First, let us note that most problems of independent ethnology was formed already in the period preceding the institutional birth of the scientific discipline. Its propositions are not speculative constructs drawn in the workshop of a scientist, but rather the effect of century-long considerations determined by the changing socio-historical context and inevitably referring to common images on this problem. Secondly, the relation with the folk vision was co-responsible for mixing several levels separated later: the political, theological, and moral one. Thirdly, many problems of the 19th century anthropology were already put directly in this moralizing-philosophizing climate. An example is the concept of progress, unity *vs.* the multitude of the genesis of *homo sapiens,* the ethical relativism. Fourthly, the cognitive aspect was almost absent from those mediations, which seems quite obvious from the modern perspective.

Evolutionist anthropology appeared against that intellectual background, enriched with the past century achievements of other humanistic sciences and the aroused faith in the unlimited possibilities of science being developed in European societies and clearly indicating the superiority of our civilization over the peoples inhabiting the colonies of the great empires. Already at this point, we may assume that all those phenomena had to determine the ideas put forward by evolutionist anthropology. The unity of the linearly developed human kind was ultimately recognized, but racism was still preserved. The ideology of progress tangled up with Darwinism led to the domination of the belief concerning the stage development of societies. In the light of triumphant positivism, science was openly defined as an ideal of rational thinking, accurately interpreting the objective laws of nature. Cognition of this type was thus becoming the embodiment of all objective cognition.

However, it was necessary to explain why other societies do not think scientifically (*ergo*: rationally) and remain, therefore, on a lower stage of development. Here, a thesis of the childish character of primitive peoples appeared very helpful. According to it, they make attempts to think rationally, but "are somehow unsuccessful". There appears a mistake in the chain of associations which combines their mental processes: certain effects are illusively ascribed to inappropriately identified reasons (Tylor 1871). The laws of continuity and similarity governing the ways of associating natural phenomena appear to be the basis of descriptive reasoning, while the magic they regulate — ineffective (Frazer 1890). The methodological individualism of Tylor and Frazer, two prominent researchers of primitive human thinking, limited the problem of rationality to the purely individual level.

The generation of early anthropologists also pioneered the articulation of the problem discussed here. The question of rationality *vs.* irrationality of thinking has been viewed similarly in the literature ever since. From our point of view, it is possible to ascertain that those anthropologists solved the question from spontaneous positions of exponents of common cultural experience of the enlighted spheres of Victorian England. In these categories they verbalized the problem of variety of cultures and thinking, using a scientific terminology that systematized it. They were still unable, however, to observe its cognitive significance; their own vision of the world appeared naturally obvious and objective for them, while the methods of exploration which is assumed — perfectly reliable when learning about the types of reasoning of the representatives of primitive cultures. They identified the cognitive aspect of their studies with the "truth" of the worldview expressed and recorded in them. If the essence of the previous stage were included in the formula: "even if all people are human, we are still more equal than others", it would have to be acknowledged that evolutionists only concretized quite clearly the notion of "we".

Once formulated, the problem began to live its own — naturally, to a certain extend — life. The attitude towards it represented by each subsequent orientation can be followed both in open declarations and in the contents implicitly assumed by hypotheses. The next hypotheses worthy of our special attention are those of Levy-Bruhl. His general hypothesis was a sort of an inversion of the statements of evolutionism, at least in a double sense. Firstly, adopting the basic assumption of Durkheim, he claimed that man's way of thinking is ultimately determined not by individual mental processes, but by the social structure overlapping collective beliefs. The latter have become his actual subject of interest. Secondly, English scientists believed that the primitive man "strived" to be a rational creature, while French philosophers maintain that the primitive man "does not want" to be a rational creature at all. The constitution of the society in which he lives makes him spontaneously obedient to the prelogical conceptual mechanisms. The rational principles of Aristotle's logic, so common among Europeans, are replaced here with the logic of sentiment and the law of participation. The laws of "inclusion and exclusion" cannot be applied in this context, for the vision that matters here is the one of the world in which distinct phenomena and things can be identical, undergo transformations, feel and think like man and solidarily with him (Levy-Bruhl 1951; 1960).

The above theory was totally rejected by Malinowski and his followers. According to them, the alleged mysticism of primitive peoples is a false idea. The thesis of inborn rationality of all people has become the dogma of functionalism. Members of tribal communities distinguish between facts and fiction perfectly well and they use criteria corresponding to the most severe rules of logic. Malinowski even acknowledged that in the cases in which he was not able to determine unambiguously the borderlines between particular spheres of life, the Trobrianders were perfectly successful (Malinowski 1935, p. 460). There is a clear "dividing line between primitive science and magic" (Malinowski 1931, p. 636). According to Leach, he was right in his stressing equality of the degree of rationality of civilized and primitive societies. Yet, he was false in his assumption that a civilized man consistently perceives the difference between what is magic and what is not.

> He would have had a much better case if he had insisted that Europeans are ordinarily just as incapable as Trobrianders of distinguishing the two categories. In seeking to prove that Trobriand savages are not really savages after all, he endeavours to impose upon them a precision of mental classification such as is ordinarily demanded of professional logicians (Leach 1957, p. 129).

Subsequent generations of functionalists have taken up this subjects, though they did it in a way significantly different from the approach of their forerunner. Those scientists, at least as far as scientific circles are concerned, did not have to oppose any more the belief concerning the total inferiority of the human subjects they were investigating. Particularly important is the standpoint of Evans-Pritchard. His conclusions can be presented in several fundamental statements.

(1) The tribes he was investigating make no distinction between mystic and empirical beliefs; the way of acting of the respective two types of forceses identical in their belief.

(2) Despite the above, an analysis must be carried out with preserving both categories, assuming in advance their objective accuracy.

(3) There still remains an epistemological question, for the first time formulated explicitly:

> Is Zande so different from ours that we can only describe their speach and actions without comprehending them, or is it essentially like our own thought expressed in an idiom to which we are unaccustomed? (Evans-Pritchard 1937, p. 4).

This problem has implicitly appeared in the works of Levy-Bruhl and Malinowski (e.g. when he was considering the methods of exploration), but it had never before been formulated so clearly. Evans-Pritchard pointed out that even though they hold magic beliefs, the human individuals he analized are capable — contrary to that apparent obstacle — of logical thinking, although it is governed by principles other than that of the Europeans. The dichotomy of "mystic" and "objective" forces, which he applied "externally", served the purpose of indicating that state of affairs (Kuper 1983, p. 83). A dozen or so years later Linehardt (1954) considered primitive people to be totally rational, although arranging the world according to other principles. Almost fifty years later Leach went as far as to say that actually, the essence of humanity is irrationalism, because people constantly interrupt the natural order which they themselves assume (Leach 1982, pp. 97-99), while the mythical and poetical nature of human thinking could be expressed in terms of metaphorical and metonimical transformations (Leach 1976).

Functionalism implicitly suggested also an alternative view of rationality. If Malinowski was followed in his belief that culture is a functional whole, his followers thus acknowledged the *sensibility* (in contrast to *rationality*) of all beliefs included in it and institutions connected with them. Even if someone questions the literally viewed rationality of magic, he must still acknowledge its functional usefulness which represents a differently viewed rationality. Magic responds to human needs, above all the psychological ones, and this role — according to Malinowski — is recognized perfectly well by both the researcher and the objects of his research. The view of rationality introduces a certain chaos, however, which excludes any reasonable discussion concerning it. A peculiar type of a vicious circle originates: culture functions and so everything within its scope is rational, which is why culture functions. This vicious circle originates from the equivocation which confuses, as a matter of fact, two separate levels of analysis: functioning the whole socio-cultural system and the contents and structure of the system of culturally functioning beliefs. Now we know that not all elements of culture serve the purpose of preserving the social equilibrium. What is more as far as the latter aspect is concerned, it has been pointed out that even assuming the distinctiveness of the idiom used within the analyzed culture, conceptual elements and plots which are not in harmony with the remaining ones exist (Gellner 1970, pp. 43-47). Orthodox functionalists simply found what they were searching for: the image of a conceptual context in which a given idea occurs is assumed *a priori*; thus, the interpretation neglects the facts which can be alternatively understood.

In spite of the above, the main achievements of different varieties of functionalism seem unimpairable. Particularly significant seem to be the ascertainments concerning the equivalence of the cognitive strategies of various types of societies, strategies which are expressed both in Malinowski's variation, determining the identity of logical forms of thinking of the primitive and civilized societies, and in Evans-Pritchard's variation, later developed by his followers, assuming the mystical-rational syncretism constituting a coherent whole governed by homogeneous "principles of causality". Levy-Bruhl still seemed to believe that "all people are equal, but some are less equal than others", while Malinowski — that "all people are equal because they are equal to the more equal ones", and Evans-Pritchard — simply that "all people are equal (basically)". A common denominator of different versions of the research behavior of functionalists is still represented by the constant, open or concealed,

206

absolutization of the rationalism and objectivism of logic and cognition represented by the scientist. At the same time an important methodological question appeared concerning the ability to understand or subjectively adequately interpret the aboriginal systems.

In order to close the period preparing the modern discussion on epistemological limits of anthropological cognition, it is still necessary to say a few words about the standpoint of Lévi-Strauss (1962). His vision undoubtedly equals the modern European thinking and primitive one. According to him, the brain structures of individuals constituting all communities, all "people", are equal. Thus, there is no basis to assume that the cognitive product of these structures is worse in the case of primitive societies than in the case of the civilized ones. Both methods of arranging reality is equally effective. Therefore, the French ethnologist is indebted with his predecessors to a much larger degree than it is generally acknowledged. For example, similarly to Frazer, Lévi-Strauss is searching for rational relations that make any sense. According to him, in the case of primitive logic, these relations occur on the perceptional level in terms closely connected with what they describe. Savage thought is, then, different from the "domesticated" one in respect of the former's preference in relation to the logic of the concrete. Let us notice, however, this direct inference of concepts from usually experienced realities is a perfect form of realizing the positivist postulate, expressed, e.g. in Mach's propositions. It is, however, at the same time an inversion of the evolutionist treatment of primitive thought as one indicating tendencies towards transcendentalism (Gellner 1973, pp. 173-174; 1974, pp. 152-154). Lévi-Strauss differs from Frazer not in his view of the nature of primitive thought, but in his opinion on science. Frazer searches for the uniqueness of science in the fact that it takes into account — in a very precise way — the data provided by experience, while Lévi-Strauss — in the fact that it abstracts from that data. Lévi-Strauss believes that experimentation is almost the most favourable occupation of primitive people. In this last respect one cannot overlook references to the findings of Mauss, Hubert, and Durkheim (1950), while as far as the question of the coherence of conceptual systems is concerned — those of Levy-Bruhl, so often criticized by him.

The evolution of the anthropological epistemological problem, manifested in the question concerning the essence and possibility of penetration and understanding of culturally strange systems of beliefs, has a long tradition. In the course of its history, the significance of epistemological barriers appearing in the attempts of a scientific penetration of non-European cultures has been observed and appreciated to a constantly growing degree. Most of the representatives of the stages discussed so far seem to have shared several features. They were oriented ethnocentrically, for they measured other cultures with categories taken from their own; they were oriented Eurocentrically, for they spontaneously considered their categories to be most effective cognitively; finally, they were oriented scientocentrically, for modern European science remained for them the ideal of rationality and objectivity, the only possible basis of reflecting the real laws of nature — any nature. It is possible to eliminate or at least minimize the doubts which accompany the epistemological considerations of the consequences of each of these orientations in relation to the cognitive value of the results of ethnological research? I shall try to find the answer to this question in the selected findings of contemporary arguments concerning this matter, particularly within British social anthropology, philosophy of science, and sociology of knowledge.

Modern anthropologists still seem to believe that treating societies ethnocentrically, either submerged in a permanent error or presenting consciousness similar to that of drunk man, is a matter of past. The method of intensive research carried on location and complex explanations made it possible to become liberated from this false supposition (Gellner 1970, pp. 28-29). Meanwhile, the author of *Culture and communication* is right in his observation that:

> The majority of contemporary social anthropologists regards the distinction between "primitive" man and man in general as anachronistic and untenable, yet to the newcomer it must seem that their methods of research and the themes to which they devote most of their attention take this distinction for granted (Leach 1982, p. 55).

In fact, such a division results from specific conceptual categories of anthropology as a scientific discipline. This is also the source of apparent naturality of that division. The accepted criteria and categories, however, are often different: savage/civilized, prelogical/logical, mystic/rational, closed/open (Horton 1967; 1973; 1982), pre-literary/literary (Goody 1978), using pre-operational/operational/formal ways of thinking (Hallpike 1979). All that indirectly indicates one thing — the problem still remains current and unsolved.

Solving it appears to be extremely complicated, for it has far-reaching ethical and political implications. This, in turn, causes that many researchers are not able to become liberated from this non-cognitive burden. For example, Lévi-Strauss in *Race and history* (1952) rejects any divisions and considers as barbarous all those who believe in barbarity. However, this definition contains a paradox. We know that there exist barbarians who believe in "barbarity" and thus we are among them, as well as those after us who report on the fact of our "barbarity". That attitude is not a result of any uncautiousness, but rather of "tolerant, understanding liberalism, of which sophisticated anthropology is a part" (Gellner 1970, p. 31).

208

Getting involved in non-cognitive problems is, then, dangerous, while attempt to reconciliate ethical relativism with cognitive rationalism pose always many difficulties (cf. Jarvie 1984). Thus, very significant for anthropology is a certain epistemological syndrome which appears somewhere on the borderline between the problems connected with opposing objectivism and subjectivism of cognition, rationalism and relativism, naturalism and antinaturalism of social sciences, realism and instrumentalism, or — finally — nomothetism and idiographism. Therefore, mutual penetration of various concepts originating within different sciences is not surprising. Let us also note that attempts to delimitate primitive thinking help, on the principle of contrast, to define scientific thinking. The methodological anthropological problem is at the same time a general methodological problem; more than that — it is even an epistemological one.

Let us turn, however, to anthropological aspects of our considerations. As far as the possibilities of intercultural comparisons and evaluations and the possibilities of conducting them are concerned, modern anthropological discussion can be limited to two opposing standpoints: the relativist and rationalist one. Needless to say, a number of variations can be distinguished within each of them. Yet, the fundamental subject of discussion remains to be the question concerning the degree of cognitive "penetration" of primitive cultures and the possibilities of their interpretation.

Inspired by the concepts of P. Winch (1958; 1970), relativists claim that we have no right to any objectivization of cognition and the knowledge characteristic of scientific European culture. There are no universal standards predisposed to constitute a criterion of truth and sensibility. Only hermeneutic methods can be helpful in understanding and translating other systems. Nevertheless, according to M. Hesse (1980, p. 45), explanation ends where it is not questioned by "local *consensus*". In the opinion of Barnes and Bloor, even the criteria of accuracy of explanation are relative and relativized to a given system. Nothing authorizes us to usurp the right to alleged cultureless objectivism.

Relativists can, then, be said to support a form of peculiar equality of rights when speaking of any culturally argumented beliefs. They charge rationalists with following Lakatos, Laudan, and Mannheim (e.g. Hollis 1982, p. 75) in their proclaming the form of dualism, dividing beliefs into rational (true) and irrational (false), each of which requires a different type of explanation. According to relativists, a sociologists of science should view all beliefs in the same way and — with the help of empirical methods — should search for causes of their appearance and gaining credibility. The question of truth and falseness of beliefs is neglected (Barnes and Bloor 1982, pp. 23-25).

They also try to impair the main arguments of rationalists supporting the existence of certain general-human cognitive universals. In this way they negate the existence of "materially true" knowledge based on pure experience, which is embedded in common experience and simply absolutizes it. The recorded facts evoke various impressions and associations. If they were to be identical for all, then — acknowledging at the same time the versatility of human cultures — we would be entrapped in a contradiction impossible to solved. That universal empiricism fails to notice in its naivette the opposition between the psychophysiological and sociological aspect of the experienced contents. Similar charges can also be raised in the case of the stem — usually proposed *a priori* – of common beliefs based on primary perceptual situations, irrespective of the context and supposedly enabling an inter-group communication. Also the third concept seems to be invalid, a concept according to which the principles of inference (noncontradiction, identicality and negation (Lukes 1973, pp. 238-239)) are universal because — in the opinion of relativists they constitute culturally determined factors. Brain structures can determine conceptual mechanisms and abilities, but not the contents of the accepted beliefs. Rationalists adopt their assumptions *a priori* and are not able to indicate credible arguments supporting them.

We posses no rationality criteria which universally constrain the operation of human reason, and which also discriminate existing belief systems or their components, into rational or irrational groups. Variability in institutionalized beliefs cannot be explained by a conception of external causes producing deviations from rationality. Likewise, the culture of neutral science cannot be distinctive because of its rationality, in a universal rather than a conventional sense (Barnes 1974, p. 41).

By and large, the dream of rationalism (in the sense considered here) about legitimizing universal knowledge independent of the social context cannot be realized. Its ultimate consequence is dogmatism.

But if at this point the relativist must retire defeated, to gaze from some far hilltop on the celebratory rites of the Cult of Rationalism, he can nevertheless quietly ask himself: what local, contingent causes might account for the remarkable intensity of the Faith in Reason particular to the Cult (Barnes and Bloor 1982, p. 47).

The opponents of relativists carry out their criticism on various levels. On a philosophical plane, they are charged with the fact that the acceptance of their extreme ideas practically excludes practising anthropology. It is impossible to totally neglect one's own conceptual network (Jarvie 1984, pp. 77-78). On the other hand, it is difficult to negate any form of communication with others, interpretation of separate cultures, and their translation into the cultural categories represented by the researcher. It is also possible to ask how is one to fully accept the theses of relativism if relativism is the truth. There is also another problem: if everything is relative, one also has to accept the ethnocentric vision

(Gellner 1979, pp. 2-3). Therefore, relativism disenables any scientific criticism, for each theory has its own, basically unquestionable, reasons (Sperber 1982, p. 153).

Yet, it is not that line of polemics that is significant for us here. The most important argument of rationalists can be presented in the following way: if we want to speak of comparatist research of systems of beliefs, it is of vital importance that there should exist a common core of (universal) observations, judgements, beliefs, and principles of reasoning, sharing which may become the starting point for the processes of conceptual agreement and translation (e.g. Horton 1982; Lukes 1982; Hollis 1970). The differentiation of concepts and systems does not rule out non-relativist explanations. On the primary level, it is not indispensable. Hypotheses of the sort put forward by Sapir-Whorf have been impaired by such studies as those of Berlin and Kay (1969) or Malotki (1983). Researches of this type acknowledge the universality of certain psychological laws, perception of colors, time, facial mimicry, or knowledge of geometric figures. Therefore, as Cole and Scribner put it (1974), "we have no evidence for a 'primitive logic'" (p. 170). The above conclusions are supported by suggestions resulting from neurophysiology and concerning the unity of cognitive structures of all people, as well as the thesis of the inborn nature of many skills, e.g. the acquisition of language.

Around the common core placed in the above way is centered a group of universally shared base ideas. Horton calls them primary theories (Horton 1982). We describe them in the terms of a descriptive language and they can be defined as the universals of common social experience. The universal participation in it is determined not by the circumstances indicated by philosophers, but by the natural ones. If it were to be different, "we would have been destroyed by mammoths". These generalities enable inter-cultural communication. Combined with the thesis of rationality of behavior of every acting human subject, aiming at the most effective explanation and prediction of phenomena, as well as controlling the environment, they allow for speaking of less or more effective systems, i.e. less or more rational ones.

Cultural differentiation is manifested first of all in the range of the so-called secondary theories, which refer to the universal stem, but constitute merely its "theoretical" explanation. They include a number of beliefs defined by Sperber as "apparently irrational" (Sperber 1982). It is possible to point out several methods of interpreting them, and thus — indirectly — attempts of neutralizing their incommensurability in relation to the cannons used by science (Lukes 1982, pp. 276-280). Those are: (1) the intellectualist one in the version of (a) Frazer, who considers them to be unsuccessful attempts of explanation and (b) Horton, who point to the co-existence of accurate and inaccurate concepts in all types of system; (2) the symbolist one, making it necessary to view social beliefs which cannot be directly criticized in a rational way, but which possess their own instrumental functions (Beattie, Turner, Leach); (3) the fideistic one, referring to the necessity of the researcher's sharing a given religious experience and thus ruling out the application of "external" cognitive criteria; (4) the cognitive one, represented by Sperber (1976; 1982). "Apparently irrational beliefs" are only partly judgements which cannot be subjected to tests of falsification. They expand, however, human imaginative and conceptual abilities.

Concepts of this kind serve the rationalists the purpose of defending the principle of unchangeability of objective principles of critical thinking while acknowledging, at the same time, the arguments of ethical-worldview relativism. The measurement of the degree of rationality is carried out with the help of the evaluation of the existence of alternative theories and their competitiveness (clear inspirations originating in Kuhn) and then also the openness of society (Popperian inspirations), like e.g. in the case of Horton. It can also be represented by the ability to draw conclusions from experience. Jarvie (1984) makes an institution of it: science as a social product secures the realization of the above ideals and the efficiency of actions in the best way so far. For Gellner (1979), a scientific vision which controls the actions of a constantly greater number of societies (probably because of its effectiveness) is simply "our" vision and, irrespective of the degree of its accuracy, we cannot escape from it. Again, "all people are equal (ethically), but some are more equal (cognitively) than others".

Supporting either side seems to be impossible to be argumented convincingly, if such an argumentation were to consist in indicating the falseness of the premisses of the opposing standpoint. Generally speaking, this dispute concerns certain philosophical and worldview "pre-judgements". In many aspects it resembles a verbal dispute in the sense that particular statements differ not only axiologically. When parenthesized epistemologically, the assumptions with which a researcher begins to solve substantial problems lose their meaning if we do not try to evaluate the results of his research in the categories of direct perception of embedded in various cultures various worldview systems. These assumptions also determine, to a probably insignificant degree, the growth of practical technological effectiveness of the results of the research practice. They significantly determine, however, the style of presentation and interpretation of data (e.g. whether this is a sociological description of unconscious social processes or an attempt at a hermeneutic analysis). Ultimately, it is necessary to acknowledge that, irrespective of the adopted assumptions of the considered type, the researcher facing the facts (no matter how perceived) is forced to use categories which offer the minimum of communication. It is also necessary to assume that even a cultural system extremely different than the one represented by the researcher can be arranged according to formal-logical assumptions applied by him spontaneously. Therefore, the phenomenon of imputing appropriate assumptions to the analyzed cultures will, to a certain degree, always take place, of which one has to be aware. Otherwise, one has to assume the standpoint of Heideggerian mystical identification of interpreted senses with the interpretational ones, an identification which neglects the semantic antinomy indicated by A. Tarski.

Let us now summarize the above considerations following the process of historical formation of our epistemological problem of anthropological cognition.

(1) The history of ethnocentrism goes back to the images of "alien" societies prior to the period of the formation of anthropology as a separate scientific discipline.

(2) This ethnocentrism still influences anthropological research consciousness, making the results of the analyses it regulates function as a manifestation and persuasion of modern European worldview, the compatibility with which is viewed as a certificate of cognitive legitimacy.

(3) The following stages can be distinguished in the process of formation of the epistemological anthropological problem:

(a)   the pre-anthropological period closely connected with folk images and ethnocentric attitudes, gradually enriched with philosophical considerations;

(b)   the evolutionist-positivist period, in which anthropologists spontaneously expressed their Eurocentric ideas being a combination of ethnocentric-scientistic beliefs; two varieties of it can be distinguished: the classical-evolutionist one and the one of Levy-Bruhl;

(c)   the period of classical functionalism, acknowledging the rationality of all societies according to the principles of European categories;

(d)   the period which is a sort of a combination of the conceptions of Levy-Bruhl and Malinowski, in which systems were considered as coherent and rational according to different principles;

(e)   the modern period characterized by a constantly greater domination of a tendency to a clear articulation of the epistemological problems, connected with the unsolvable dispute between relativists and rationalists.

(4) The considered history is clearly characterized by two features:

(a)   a gradual conquest of normative rationalism by an axiological neutralization of the researcher's cultural equipment, aimed at an objectivising approach;

213

(b) a gradual achievement of the belief concerning the necessity to account for the humanistic coefficient — unknown to the researcher — of the examined cultural phenomena and the growth of the consciousness of its significance in the interpretation of those phenomena.

(5) The observed autonomization of the cognitive aspect of ethnological research, culminating at the moment of formation of their epistemological problem, goes together with the development of "technological" applications of the results of anthropology. It also becomes more independent of common experience. Therefore, it could be considered as a certain indicator of a growing theoretical character of that discipline, a process which is still in progress.

The question is whether an anthropologist represents a certain variety of ethnocentrism. The answer is that he inevitably and unquestionably does so, though it cannot be a reason for neutralizing its research practice. It must adopt certain "scientocentric" pre-judgements mentioned before. They create certain impassable epistemological barriers of a semantic-conceptual nature. The point is, however, to minimize within these limits the influences of these factors of ethnocentric origin which are by no means necessary to obtain an indispensable minimum of scientific intersubjectivity when solving the problems of cultural sciences. Any progress in that discipline, achieved with great difficulty, will never end in a complete success, however. Anthropology will always resemble the famous paradox of poor Achilles constantly pursuing his tortoise.

Translated by Krzysztof Sawala

REFERENCES

1. Barnes, B. (1974). *Scientific knowledge and sociological theory.* London.
2. Barnes, B., & Bloor, D. (1982). "Relativism, rationalism and the sociology of knowledge." In M. Hollis, & S. Lukes (Eds.). *Rationality and relativism* (pp. 21-47). Oxford.
3. Berlin, B. & Kay, P. (1969). *Basic color terms.* Berkeley.
4. Cole, M., & Scribner, S. (1974). *Culture and thought: A psychological introduction.* New York.
5. Evans-Pritchard, E.E. (1937). *Witchcraft, oracles and magic among the Azande.* Oxford.
6. Frazer, J.G. (1890). *The Golden bough.* London.
7. Gellner, E. (1970). Concepts and society. In B. Wilson (Ed.). *Rationality* (pp. 18-49). Oxford.
8. Gellner, E. (1973). "The savage and the modern mind". In R. Horton, & R. Finnegan (Eds.). *Modes of thought. Essays on thinking in* (pp. 162-181). London.
9. Gellner, E. (1974). *Legitimation of belief.* Cambridge.
10. Gellner, E. (1981). "General introduction: Relativism and universals". In B. Lloyd, & J. Gay (Eds.). *Universals of human thought* (pp. 1-20). Cambridge.

11. Gellner, E. (1982). "Relativism and universals". In M. Hollis, & S. Lukes (Eds.). *Rationality and relativism* (pp. 181-200). Oxford (a repr. from Gellner, E. (1981)).
12. Goody, J. (1977). *The domestication of the savage mind.* Cambridge.
13. Hallpike, C.R. (1979). *The foundations of primitive thought.* Oxford.
14. Hesse, M. (1980). *Revolutions and reconstructions in the philosophy of science.* Hassocks.
15. Hodgen, M. (1964). *Early anthropology in 16th and 17th centuries.* Philadelphia.
16. Hollis, M. (1982). "The social destruction of reality". In M. Hollis, & S. Lukes (Eds.). *Rationality and relativism* (pp. 67-86). Oxford.
17. Hollis, M., & Lukes, S. (Eds.). *Rationality and relativism.* Oxford.
18. Horton, R. (1967). "African traditional thought and western science". *Africa, 37,* 50-71, 155-187.
19. Horton, R. (1973). "Paradox and explanation: A reply to Mr. Skorupski" (part I and II). *Philosophy of the social sciences, 3,* 231-256, 289-312.
20. Horton, R. (1982). "Tradition and modernity revisited". In M. Hollis, & S. Lukes (Eds.). *Rationality and relativism* (pp. 201-260). Oxford.
21. Horton, R., & Finnegan, R. (Eds.) (1982). *Modes of thought. Essays on thinking in western and non-western societies.* London.
22. Jarvie, I.C. (1984). *Rationality and relativism.* London.
23. Kuper, A. (1983). *Anthropology and anthropologists. The modern British School.* London.
24. Leach, E. (1957). "The epistemological background to Malinowski's empiricism". In R. Firth (Ed.). *Man and culture. An evaluation of the work of Malinowski* (pp. 119-137). London.
25. Leach, E. (1976). *Culture and communication. The logic by which symbols are connected.* Cambridge.
26. Leach, E. (1982). *Social anthropology.* Fontana Paperbacks.
27. Lévi-Strauss, C. (1952). *Race and history.* Paris.
28. Lévi-Strauss, C. (1962). *La pansée sauvage.* Paris.
29. Levy-Bruhl, L. (1951). *Les fonctions mentales dans les societes inferieures.* Paris.
30. Levy-Bruhl, L. (1960). *La mentalite primitive.* Paris.
31. Linehardt, G. (1954). "Modes of thought". In E.E. Evans-Pritchard et al. (Eds.). *The institutions of primitive society* (pp. 95-107).
32. Lukes, S. (1973). "On the social determination of truth". In R. Horton, & R. Finnegan (Eds.). *Modes of thought* (pp. 230-248). London.
33. Lukes, S. (1982). "Relativism in its place". In M. Hollis, & S. Lukes (Eds.). *Rationality and relativism* (pp. 261-305). Oxford.
34. Malinowski, B. (1931). "Culture". In *Encyclopaedia of the social sciences,* vol. 4 (pp. 621-646). New York.
35. Malinowski, B. (1935). *Coral gardens and their magic.* London.
36. Malotki, E. (1983). *Hopi time.* The Hague.
37. Mauss, M. (1950). *Sociologie et antropologie.* Paris.
38. Sperber, D. (1976). *Rethinking symbolism.* Cambridge.
39. Sperber, D. (1982). "Apparently irrational beliefs". In M. Hollis, & S. Lukes (Eds.). *Rationality and relativism* (pp. 149-180). Oxford.
40. Tylor, E. (1871). *Primitive culture.* London.
41. Wilson, B. (1970). *Rationality.* Oxford.
42. Winch, P. (1958). *The idea of a social science and its relation to philosophy.* London.
43. Winch, P. (1970). "The idea of social science". In B. Wilson (Ed.). *Rationality* (pp. 1-17). London (a repr. from Winch, P. (1958)).

Anna Pałubicka

STRUCTURALIST OVERDETERMINATION AND
HISTORICAL MATERIALISM

1. Historical Materialism and the Concept of Explanation

Various interpretative versions of Marxism or its fragments which have
emerged every now and again are undoubtedly formulated in the "spirit of
the epoch". They are connected with what may be called the prevailing
thoughts of respective epochs or, more precisely, its intellectual trends
which have appeared socially. In the present paper we are going to focus on
the attempt at assimilating the intellectual trend, undertaken by the
Marxist philosophy, yet without its inspiration, namely the trend of
structuralist thinking. This attempt is a special case of the phenomenon
signalled a moment ago, the reverse of which is, in fact, its opposition: the
influence of Marxist ideas on the intellectual trends of the epoch, formed at
a specific time. I think that the two kinds of influence are usually parallel.

It seems to me that the fact that Marxism is able of a creative
assimilation of the concurrent mental orientations is one of its intellectual
charms and at the same time one of the sources of its acceptance by
intellectuals. Owing to this a dialogue between Marxism and non-Marxist
orientations is possible. If it is required that Marxism remain "sensitive" to
the modern times then its ability shown continually to reformulate
creatively, yet "after its fashion", ideas which are genetically alien to it, is
one of the obvious manifestations of the said sensitivity. The ideas then
constitute an integral component of social reality to the extent to which
they are generally accepted that by no means can be restricted to the sphere
of economic practice and its "objective" conditions, as some Marxists have
postulated.

I am aware that the view that Marxism, and especially its basic
component, i.e., historical materialism, is continually subject to various
interpretations and thus changes its form, which leads to the collision of
different versions of Marxism, more or less related to the intellectual trends
of the epoch, is "debatable". This view is always opposed by the adherents
of the "authentic", "true" Marxism. They represent a position that a
reconstruction of the assumptions of Marxian theory which gets down to
the crux of the intentions of Marx himself is the only reconstruction

possible, the only reconstruction that corresponds to the spirit and latter of respective statements made by the creator of the theory of social development relevant here. All other interpretations of this theory which do not correspond to this reconstruction are inappropriate, revisionist. Opponents to this position think that one "true" reconstruction of the theory in question does not exist. Marxian texts are subject to the mechanisms that are appropriate to this sphere of culture since they are symbolic-cultural products which "demand" the reconstruction. The mechanisms, in turn, the interpretative mechanisms are objective enough, owing to culture, that no individual consciousness is able to change or revoke them. They act irrespective of the will and consciousness of particular subjects but at the same time they are applied alternatively and hence results obtained "to their dictation" assume the form of various versions of Marxism; some of them become socially significant in the epoch in which they appear. However, no researcher has at this disposal some "miraculous" supernatural insight into the mental structure under interpretation so as to reconstruct it "adequately". It is obvious that the multiplication of quotations from a given text by Marx does not decide on the "adequacy" of the reconstruction of the mental structure being recognized. In the situation when univocal criteria for an effective arrival at the intentions of Marx "concealed" in the recording of his mental output are lacking we must accept only their sense defined most generally: one which can be coordinated with the whole of this recording with the ideas he is referring to and, at the same time, with the ideas which function presently. The problem does not lie only in obtaining interpretative coherence of the reading of texts by the author of *Capital* and texts to which he refers in them but it is also important that socially "influential" concepts created later were a means through which certain invariants of the formerly interpreted, reconstructed sense can be accessed so that the latter were a general formula of the former (which they exemplify) or, as an explanation of the fact that these concepts appeared in the role of the subject of social acceptance by a community interested in unveiling the conditions of the formation and elapsing of historical system formations. The latter agrees more with that most general sense.

I adhere to the latter position which opposes the concept of the obvious sense of Marxian texts and consequently of the idea that that sense would be a discovery of the "absolute truth". Hence, I do not think that the passing of judgements of the type "truly (genuinely) Marxian position", "distorted Marxism" are intersubjectively testable (leaving out evaluations which are openly incompatible with the most general sense of Marxism, its invariants), nor do I think that even if evaluations of this kind could be justified intersubjectively they would automatically guarantee the validity of judgements qualified positively by them. I prefer to treat each significant interpretation of historical materialism which gives evidence of appropriate social acceptance as Marxist if its creators (or creator) explicite identify themselves in this spirit.

The problem lies not only in the fact that the concept of the only obvious sense of Marxian texts leads practically to scholastic, insolvable disputes or, more precisely, ones which are solved extraintellectually but mainly in the fact that this concept is a barrier for the process of an appropriate critical use of new, inspiring ideas and at the same time cuts Marxism off the influence of the contemporary thought. If, generally, this is not the case, if the persistent, apparent presence of Marxism in that thought is noticed, this is evidence that different, practical realizations of this conception are not able to dominate Marxist thinking. Perhaps this is so because they are different.

The concept of explanation, formed in so-called analytical orientation in contemporary philosophy of science undoubtedly originated outside the influence of the Marxist trend. Explanation is understood in this framework as a certain type of a formal relationship between respective statements of empirical sciences. A relationship, which introduces a specific system ordering to the respective sets of statements (corresponding to research domains and especially individual theories). This relationship, if we omit "probabilistic explanation" proposed by C.G. Hempel, supplementing the former "model of explanation" constructed by him (and by P. Oppenheim), has a deductive character (in a fully developed form it is logical inference). Because, as was said, it introduces the basic systematizing order to the set of claims made by a given research domain (or theory) it is usually thought that it is the "aim" of empirical research to determine it (K.R. Popper) or that the basic structure of those domains (theories) is their explanatory structure (E. Nagel).

It should be noticed here that the concept of explanation defined in the most general way differs from its 19th century counterpart advanced by J.S. Mill in that its character is formal-logical and hence (1) it does not forejudge that its premises (so-called explanans) represent "ultimately true" settlements, usually interpreted in the spirit of metaphysical realism, (2) it does not forejudge that its main premise is to be the so-called "causal law", hence that the relationship of explaining is a formal expression of the counterpart of the overall causal-consecutive nexus. When P. Duhem claimed in his *Physical theory* that science does not explain but classifies (orders) he obviously meant explanation in the 19th century sense. He would probably not object to the thesis that science explains provided he knew the sense of the later philosophy of science. It is worth noticing, however, that that 19th century concept of explanation has remained until today. And therefore when thinkers who are not particularly interested in the results of contemporary, analytical philosophy of science, speak about explanation they still mean the causal explaining, often conceived in the spirit of metaphysical realism. This is so for example in the case of the structuralist reflection over science which, being faithful to the traditions of the French thought of the turn of the 19th and 20th centuries does not use the new concept of explanation. The fact that explanation as meant in the contemporary analytic philosophy of science may contain in its premises laws of different kinds, that causal explanation is only its certain, secondary variant (as E. Nagel accounts for this in his *The structure of science*) is entirely neglected here.

I am of the opinion that the concept of explanation — in the form in which it is used in modern philosophy of science — can be used as a useful tool for the interpretation of historical materialism and also as a useful tool for the interpretation of various other concepts which attest the determination of specific phenomena of a given type by phenomena of a certain other type. For there is no difference between claiming such and such determination of the phenomena tested, and postulating a specific type of explanation, i.e. claim that these phenomena should be explained (in the framework of a given research domain, research discipline or theory) by means of a specific type of law as fundamental explanatory premise. Two reservations are indispensable here. First, the use of the concept of explanation, in the sense of contemporary analytic philosophy of science, does not have to correspond to the adoption of an assumption that the explanation is, as the philosophy in question wishes, the supreme research task; postulating a specific form of explanation, a specific kind of explanatory laws can only serve as for example initial assumption of the respective research and its aim should be seen in the mere determination of respective laws, not so much for explanation as for forecasting and projecting effective (from the viewpoint of these laws) future activities. Second, the use of the concept of explanation, to interpret particular theoretical concepts is relevant only when the interpretation aims at their reconstruction as certain scientific theories and not philosophical or ideological systems. If we mean the reconstruction of a given concept in its philosophical or ideological sense, the concept of explanation is of little use in this context.

I do not wish to claim that the Marxist concept, and in fact the Marxian theory of historical materialism, as it is the latter which I consider to be the focal point of the Marxist concept, can be exclusively interpreted as scientific theory which would assume especially or determine specific relations of explaining. It can be equally well interpreted philosophically or ideologically. Since, however, I am also interested in the structuralist idea of overdetermination in its Althusserian version (representing the "theoretistic deviation", condemned later by the author of *Reading Capital*) which aims to be a methodological assumption of a respective scientific theory, the concept of explanation seems to me to be the most convenient comparative plane in relation to the applied theses of historical materialism and that idea of overdetermination.

The structuralist (Althusserian) overdetermination seems to be a conceptual base for the interpretation of primarily this thesis of historical materialism which claims that social consciousness is determined by the socio-economic structure to which the consciousness "corresponds". On the basis of the assumption adopted here about the appropriacy of the concepts of explanation and determination, historical materialism would claim that respective features of social consciousness are explanable by respective features of the "base", i.e. the socio-economic structure. How is this determining relation, understood in this way, interpreted by the structuralist-Althusserian idea of overdetermination?

2. The Structuralist-Althusserian Overdetermination

L. Althusser identifies the Marxian "living concrete whole", i.e. the totality of historically located social life with the "structure, dominant-oriented one". In L. Althusser's terminology the latter concept denoted a structure whose character is hierarchical. This hierarchy is made up of levels which can be identified in this structure; the levels also assume the form of structures and one of such levels is characterized by a distinguished position in the context of the "global" whole. This subordination is expressed with a statement that the basic structure overdetermines the other. To a structuralist this means that relations which constitute it are in a way divided by all other levels. Each of them repeats in itself these relations of the opposition (paradigmatic) and dependencies (L. Hjelms-lev's "functions") which occur within the basic structure in the con-stituting role. As a Marxist L. Althusser identifies these oppositions with dialectic contradictions. The Marxian dialectic contradiction is "reflected", in Althusser's opinion, at different levels of the "dominant-oriented" structure — from the basic level.

In order to understand the essence of these considerations it is necessary to take into account these structuralist concepts which do not connect the overdetermination idea with Marxist inspirations. According to A.J. Greimas there exists especially something like a structure whose "filling" subordinated to it, the "statement" ("énoncé") is identical with the architectural shape of the town — this shape marks, say, the opposition: the centre — suburbie, main streets — side streets, etc. It is "started" by this structure which does not represent anybody's consciousness, any subjective manner of seeing the world and yet governs particular activities of people who cooperate in the creation of the respective shape and even "starts to dominate" in their reflection over what they created involuntarily. In this reflection this structure "duplicates itself", strengthens itself — through its manifestations, consciously created, e.g. when crossroads created spontaneously "at the dictation" of the town structure is announced by crossroads sign, placed consciously. This crossroads sign is overdetermined: duplicates with its "significant" and "signifié" what has been spontaneously created, "stated" by the town structure. Thus it serves to consciously consolidate or strengthen the structure. It is not so that the initial "statement" of the structure or the structure itself causally necessitated the allocation of crossroad signs, that what is overdeterminated by the basic structure (by its basic "statement") is a conscious consequence of its occurrence or its direct manifestation in a specific basic form; it is rather so that the overdetermined phenomenon is a conscious choice functioning in the role of the conscious strengthening of the structure, which in "the first stage" in a "basic manner", "states itself" directly and in a non-reflexive manner.

Now, if the unconscious, extra-subjective, anonymous (also in the sense of the group-social anonimity) structure is identified with the structure which "states itself" spontaneously through the social-economic base, the conscious duplication of the structure "stated" in this way, taking place in the sphere of social consciousness, will only be a "mechanism" which consolidates this structure but not the effect of its existence. Respective contents of social consciousness cannot be causally explained by making references to that basic "statement" of our structure. Causal nexuses, "linear" determinations, are relevant, yet only within the limits of respective levels. Hence, each of them has a peculiar "transitoriness" (a temporal order of consecutive segments).

There is no doubt that Althusser who interpreted the relation of social consciousness to the socio-economic base as that of structuralist overdetermination intended to avoid the mechanistic, causal-consecutive understanding of this relation, the "linear" level-internal relation.

All interpretations of historical materialism occurring in scientism (i.e. treating the Marxian concept of social development as a scientific theory which assumed or determined explanatory relations) which appeared until the time of Althusserian Marxism assumed that the concern is within this materialism about causal explanation, about causal-consecutive determination. The basic theses of historical materialism were treated as causal laws. In these interpretations, attacked somehow by the anti-scientist trends of Marxism ("young" Lukács, Gramsci, Korsch) socio-economic base causally determined social consciousness and, still "earlier" the productive forces determined in an analogous way the production relations etc. Thus, from the point of view of idea of determination, scientistic interpretations of historical materialism do not differ from common sense, from causal thinking. This phenomenon is related to the extremely important significance of Marxism as ideology. Only under the condition of referring to the causal-consecutive reasoning, rooted in the common experience, can this ideology be motivationally effective.

Let us return to the structuralist-Althuserian interpretation of historical materialism. It is structuralist also in that it assumes the Hjelmslevian separation of the "denotative" scientific articulation of the structuralized system (in L. Hjelmslev — always "semiotic") from its "connotative" articulation. The former reconstructs the structure in a "straightforward way" — it is not induced by its conscious, overdetermined judgements, on the contrary, it sees in them only the effect of the overdetermination. The latter is always "connotative", i.e. it treats the "connotative" conscious effects of overdetermination as direct testimony of the reality. Hence, structuralists, far even from Marxist, speak in the first case of science and in the second case about "ideology". While maintaining this structuralist position, L. Althusser expands his own concept of ideology and "empiricism" which is to be the theoretic equivalent of ideology.

Science, he says, treats of an extra-subjective structure, one which is not relativized to any consciousness and which "selfexpress" first in the basic level system and later in overdetermined systems which duplicate them. Ideology, in turn, that is consciousness which creates systems — overdetermined levels, extra-scientific cultural consciousness, as it could be defined, is a kind of knowledge about itself which places it in opposition with its objective (or rather objectifying) contents as "reality"; hence its character is anthropological-humanistic: it "sees" the world as a system of objective phenomena or ones which determine the human image about it or which are determined by these images. "Empiricism" sanctifies ideology. It is a theory which shows the cognition of the world as a result of the clash of the human subjectivity with a sphere of "ideologically"-objective phenomena, a result which treats this cognition as human mental assimilation of the objective world, external in relation to the humanistic subject of this cognition. As a result science is always "anti-empirical"; it does not "worry" about what ideology says about the world since it understands perfectly well that this ideology is only overdetermined, hence it only absolutizes mental figures which appear to it (the overdetermined manner of thinking) as "objective reality". As a consequence, science is not capable of explaining itself. However, it can explain extra-scientific culture as overdeterminated ideology.

Although the Althusserian concept of science (and extra-scientific culture) is naive in that it excludes science from the scope of ideology, i.e. from the scope of (extra-scientific) domains of culture and thus makes the science a kind of cognitive absolute, yet at least it draws attention to an understanding of (extra-scientific) culture which makes of it not a simple effect of a specific state of the socio-economic base but an overdetermined phenomenon, i.e. a phenomenon whose right of existence means the consolidation of a structure "stated" at the basic level, hence at the level of the socio-economic structure.

Let us then ask a fundamental question: what kind of explanation does the evaluation of a given cultural phenomenon understood as an overdetermined phenomenon represent?

This question can only be answered reasonably and at the same time in accordance with L. Althusser's intentions when overdetermination is not interpreted as a kind of causal determination. Another possible interpretation should also be excluded, namely that that the overdetermined phenomenon is nothing else but the Hegelian concrete; a contribution to the self-development of the absolute, hence a kind of thinking which — unintentionally — serves the developmental purposes of the absolute, i.e. contributes, in its own way, to the objective spirit which understands itself better and better approaching gradually the "viewpoint" of the teleologically assumed absolute.

The latter interpretation would make a spokesman of idealistic teleology out of an adherent of the overdetermination idea: the structure which initially "stated itself" spontaneously at the basic (socio-economic) level is equipped with an aim: its consolidation in the consciousness and later its revolutionary transformation following a consistent development by the consciousness of the basic dialectic considerations which it duplicates. Ideology only consolidates unconsciously a structure which exists independently and which it positively reproduces in a misstaked form. However, the science freed from overdetermination, "knows" that its task is to objectively diagnose the structure passively reproduced and consolidated by overdetermined ideology but also to design the transformed structure which, owing to science, gets the chance of being transformed into the designed shape, which is the solution of its existing contradictions.

It is clear that this is not what L. Althusser meant; the philosopher would undoubtedly include this idealistic-teleological formulation of the role of science into the framework of a theoretical justification of ideology: within the framework of "empiricism" which treats the object of scientific cognition as an ideological "objective reality" — subordinate to (1) cognition and (2) manipulation of the object of cognition based on the latter.

Is, however, the concept of overdetermination which abandons the teleological-Hegelian assumptions free of any teleologism? This would be the case only if we simultaneously reject the view that it is the duplication of the same structure which according to L. Althusser "stated itself" spontaneously at the basic, socio-economic level that is the destiny and task of ideology and hence the destiny and task of all domains of culture different from science. Then the thesis that these domains consolidate the said structure in the sphere of consciousness ceases to be a simple consequence of this view on ideology, teleological in principle, on its "task" and becomes a source of the problem: why and under what circumstances do extra-scientific domains of culture function in a "consolidating" manner with respect to the socio-economic base? The problem is in principle expressed in the question about the type of the non-causal determination (non-causal explanation) which historical materialism assumes when it "takes" ideology "out of" the characterization of the currently existing socio-economic base.

3.   *A Type of Explanation Suggested by the Concept of Overdetermination*

When we abandon the teleological idea that the duplication of the structure which initially "stated itself" is socio-economic relations is the destiny ("task") of ideology, i.e. that of extra-scientific domains of culture, there remains a question whether in the concept of overdetermination freed from that idea there is not such a project of interpreting the thesis of historical materialism about the conditioning of social consciousness (ideology, culture) by socio-economic base which would be fully appropriate for the articulation in terms of explanation conceived of in the spirit of contemporary, analytical philosophy of science and which at the same time would be compatible with the obvious interpretative invariants of the said thesis. I think that this question can be answered positively. The following premises would justify this position.

Firstly, the judgement that such and such contents of the ideology consolidate the existing socio-economic structure should be treated as a judgement which forms an element of the explanans accounting for the fact that these contents constitute either an object of its general, social acceptance or an acceptance restricted to particular classes. Secondly, it has to be shown, though only partially within the framework of this judgement, that individual types of activities subjectively motivated by the said contents lead "in their mass", in the causal-consecutive mode, to effects owing to which the existing socio-economic base is either reproduced, i.e. consolidates itself truly, or is transformed in accordance with the interests of a respective social class. And thirdly, with respect to the second premise, the judgement which is mentioned in the first premise, should be treated as a certain special case of a more general judgement: the ideological contents in question either consolidate the given socio-economic base or transform it. Thus, the structuralist overdetermination as conceived by Althusser would correspond to the explanation of the fact of general or class universality of such ideological contents which would motivate activities that consolidate the socio-economic base (but not activities which would transform it).

Having assumed the above limitation are we in a position to say that Althusserian overdetermination is in principle a design of a certain version of explanation — general or class-limited acceptance of these or other ideological contents? We mean here these ideological contents which can be understood as a "mechanism" which consolidates the existing condition of the socio-economic base.

There is no doubt that what L. Althusser defines as (overdetermined) ideology, identified as it were with the contents of extra-scientific domains of culture (in our terminology) constitutes one of the most significant objects of interest to historical materialism. The latter assumes that the phenomenon which forms this object represents a means with whose aid the class in power maintains the existing state of its possession. For the author of *Reading "Capital"* this phenomenon is not causally conditioned by that state. Yet, in the case of both Marx and Althusser we are dealing with the mental construction which cannot be directly expressed in the form of a specific scheme of explanation: it does not follow from the fact that specific judgements motivate activities leading (in the causal-consecutive model) to the reproduction of the existing socio-economic base, hence to the consolidation of the existing production relations that these judgements will be accepted either by all society or by the interested class.

Instead of speaking about the effects of activities socially motivated by specific judgements, or, shortly, about the effects of social acceptance of these judgements, we can also speak about the social, objective function (as it occurs irrespectively of the intentions of an individual or a group of which they are aware). Hence, a question arises: under what condition can the indication of a socially-objective function of specific beliefs (judgements) explain the fact of their universal acceptance by all society or by a few classes only?

This question is usually neglected — not only by Marxists but also in the framework of all such intellectual orientations which use the concepts of function or "interest"; if it appears that a given manner of thinking is in some sense "favourable", functional, compatible with the "interest" of a given individual, social group, society, it is believed then that the acceptance of this manner of thinking by a given individual, social group, society is explained: it is "obvious". However, in these cases we are not dealing with explanation in the sense adopted here.

In order for this explanation to take place the premise about the indispensability of the overall respect, within the framework of a given community, to a relevant type of beliefs for the reproduction of the existing system of socio-economic conditions or their respective subsystems, should be supplemented by an additional premise, an assumption: a community in question is characterized (at the time in question) by some such general properties guaranteeing that in this period the process of reproducing that aspect of the socio-economic conditions of social existence which is of interest to us takes place permanently. The reasoning goes then in accordance with the following scheme:

(A) At time t community C reproduces permanently a global property P of its socio-economic context;
(B) in order to maintain property P a universal respect for type T beliefs is indispensable in C (at least at period t);
   A respect for type T beliefs (in period t) prevails.

Following J. Kmita, I call the above reasoning functional explanation.[1] It can be easily seen that the omission of premise (A) and the acceptance of premise (B) — about the functionality, "beneficialness" for C etc. of type T beliefs — is typical of teleological thinking and the claim that premise (B) makes a sufficient justification of the conclusion (explanandum) (community C accepts type T *beliefs because the maintenance of property P* is "favourable" to it, it is a value for it, for the human kind, for progress, for the "Reason" arriving at an appropriate goal, etc.).

Hence the Althusserian structuralist overdetermination can be elucidated as an intuition of a certain kind of functional explanation, a valuable intuition as it destroys the stereotype of the causal connection between the socio-economic base and the state of social consciousness. This stereotype not only makes the defence of the viewpoint held by historical materialism extremely difficult but, moreover, inspires its numerous psychological, individualist interpretations. But there seems to be no doubt that these kinds of interpretation are not contained in the range of permissible "readings" of the position taken by the author of *Capital*. The fact that he was not a psychological interpreter should be considered as one of the assumptions which define a group of the interpretative invariants which we mentioned at the beginning of this paper.

It should be also stressed that premise (A) of the functional explanation

---

1. This explanation is discussed for example in J. Kmita, *O kulturze symbolicznej* (On symbolic culture), Warsaw 1982.

of the kind of interest to us does not restrict the domain of its applications exclusively to cases of the maintenance of beliefs of specific type. It can be formulated in various versions. For example, when taking account of the idea of (functional) adjustment of production relations to the increase of production forces (A) can be modified as follows: At time t community C reproduces "material" conditions of its further existence, and this is only possible (under relevant conditions) when the production relations are exchanged for more functional ones with respect to the existing level of production forces. A parallel, relevant modification of premise (B) would help obtain a scheme of explanation of (functionally) "forced" change in the consciousness of a given social group. The acceptance of this scheme does not exclude the recognition of the possibility of the occurrence of change meant by Gramsci who called the October Revolution a "revolution against *Capital*". This would be the case only if the disfunctionality of production relations were treated with respect to the state of production forces as the only *cause* of all revolutional change. The October Revolution in such a traditionally-scientistic perspective must appear as a revolution which cannot be explained in the categories of historical materialism.

While interpreting structuralist overdetermination as a kind of functional determination we will admit that we are dealing with a special case of this determination; the type of beliefs being explained is determined within the framework of the structural properties of their system or (which has been the same for a structuralists since Hjelmslev's times) — their "plan of contents" (an image of the world corresponding to them). The problem concerns paradigmatic and "functional" relations in this system (or image of the world). This would be a significant impoverishment of the explanatory capabilities of historical materialism. Therefore M. Godelier, a contemporary French philosopher and anthropologist who bases his Marxism on the structuralist-Althusserian "reading of *Capital*" introduces at this point an appropriate correction of the notion of overdetermination and defines his corrected version "structural causality".

While defining structuralism with all due respect in its version put forward by Lévi-Strauss as a "gigantic theoretical exercise" M. Godelier draws attention to the fact that within the framework of this orientation the attempt "at keeping an object of thought outside thought itself" which requires an "analysis of forms and fundamentals in the 'fetishization' of social relations" has been aborted. On the results of this analysis which only "few Marxists have attempted" "(...) depends not only a scientific explanation of political and religious elements in general, but also and foremost an explanation of the circumstances and stages of development of rank, caste or class societies, and even an explanation for the

227

disappearance from history of former classless societies."[2] It is the
"internal requirements (...) with respect to the mode of production" which
are "the object of the thought" that cannot be noticed in the "thought
itself", in the structure it adopted overdeterminationally; they are "(...)
channels by which the mode of production determines, in the final
analysis, the nature of the different instances of (...) society and, since the
effects of these constraints are simultaneously active on all instances, by
the action of the system of constraints, the mode of production determines
the relation and articulation of all the instances among them and in
relation to itself, that is, determines the general structure of the society as it
is, the specific form and function of each of these instances which go to
compose it."[3]

Thus, in the terminology adopted here it is the functional reasons in the
form of objective requirements of society reproduction which are the
Godelierian "object of thought" that form social consciousness, explain it.
The objective requirements determine the way of thinking and mental-
regulated types of social institutions — to the accuracy of the condition of
their compatibility with these requirements. This condition cannot be
expressed exclusively in the categories of a specific formal structuring of
relevant ways of thinking and institutions:

> To search and find the system of constraints determined by a social process of
> production, is to proceed epistemologically in such a way that one can show the
> structural causality of the economy on society and, at the same time, the general
> specific structure of this society, its logical ensemble, even though this economic
> causality, this general structure of society and this specific logical ensemble are never
> directly observable phenomena as such, but facts which have to be reconstructed by
> thought and scientific practice.[4]

The Godelierian "structural causality" continues the Althusserian-
structuralist idea of overdetermination as much as it assigns the function of
consolidating economic structure and "overall structure" of society
specific of a given society to the mental-institutional overdetermined
phenomena. However, at the same time it does not make the topicalization
of this function dependent exclusively on the formal-structural features of
the said phenomena. In Godelier's opinion we are particularly unable to
investigate the structure which is separately "stated spontaneously" by the

2. M. Godelier, *Perspectives in Marxist anthropology*, Cambridge 1977, p. 50.
3. Ibid., p. 53. Let us add that the "observability" in the context of the stated citation
does not mean the potential presence (understood phenomenalistically) of a phenomenon in the researcher's perception but the culturally forejudged possibility of
recording the given state of affairs by the consciousness of a historical witness to this
state of affairs.
4. Ibid., p. 53.

socio-economic base of the societies of hunters and gatherers in order to look for the duplication of this structure in the system of beliefs of these societies: "(...) we can no longer analyse the relations and systems of economics as if they were one fetishised and autonomous domain."[5]
Translated by Zbigniew Nadstoga

---

5. Ibid., p. 61.

PART THREE: ON CULTURE AND CULTURAL PARTICIPATION

Krystyna Zamiara

PSYCHOLOGICAL *VERSUS* CULTURAL APPROACHES TO PARTICIPATION IN CULTURE

In most general terms "the cultural approach to participation in culture" refers to the concept of cultural participation formulated by various culture studies while the phrase "the psychological approach to participation in culture" — to concepts originating in the sphere of psychology. Such a broad understanding of the above terms results in their poor cognitive efficiency, insufficient differentiation between the psychological and cultural approach, impediment of the specification of differences as following definite epistemological assumptions both within psychology itself and without, i.e. in culture studies or on the "common ground" of psychological sciences and humanities. The latter case concerns the opposing pair of psychologism and antipsychologism in particular; the first, assumed not only in psychology but also in the humanities — the second, restricted to the latter. Evidently enought the above terms, in their broad sense, render difficult the definition of the influence of epistemological positions on concepts concerning cultural participation. At the same time this influence appears more important than it can be inferred from the difference between the cognitive interests of psychology and humanities respectively.

Psychologism treats all socio-cultural phenomena investigated by the humanities as essentially psychological. Thus it suggests their reduction to psychological phenomena. Antipsychologism, on the contrary, considering the peculiarity of humanistic phenomena, their irreducability to psychological phenomena, recognizes the attempts of psychologism as groundless. An appropriate methodological thesis, specifying both "reducibility" and the procedure leading to the realization of this task, always becomes a component of the above statements. Within the context of the psychologistic approach there merge two conceptions of reducibility. The first defines reducibility as a form of explanation: the psychological laws provide "final" explanatory premises concerning socio-cultural phenomena: thus all the statements of the humanities should be reduced (in the course of intertheoretical explanation) to psychological laws (theories). The second was established within a variant of antinaturalism in the humanities. It rejects explanation as a legitimate scientific procedure in the humanities (early psychologistic version of W. Dilthey's epistemology). Here reducibility occurs *via* the "fact" registering notional apparatus of this science: psychological notions — referentially defined by peculiar psychological experiences — should become the final conceptualization of socio-cultural phenomena and reveal their psychological nature. Explanatory psychologism, related to methodological naturalism, was sometime more popular than the notional psychologism formed within methodological antinaturalism. The following remarks will concentrate on the former.

Considering the epistemological perspectives established by psychologism in particular, individual participation in culture is conceived as an essentially psychological phenomenon, i.e. its features and determining factors can be adequately described only on the grounds of psychological knowledge. Although humanistic knowledge is not completely devoid of cognitive value it "masks" the real character of the phenomena. Sometimes the adherents of this view do not accepts "academic" psychology as directly useful for the description or explanation of cultural participation. Consequently, they construct an adequate "humanistic psychology". The Diltheyan attempt at establishing "humanistic psychology" as central among the humanities provides an example — at the same time — opposing the "academic" school of Wundt.

Antipsychologism, in turn, maintains the irreducibility of cultural participation phenomena to psychological ones, and may accept, or not, referrences to psychological knowledge in the description and explanation of some features. The variety of assumable positions depends on the version of methodological anti-individualism coexisting with antipsychologism: a moderate version assuming that "only some non-biological phenomena have partly their final determinants among social phenomena"; a radical version assuming that "all non-biological individual phenomena have at least partly their final determinants among social phenomena"; or an extremely radical version assuming that "all non-biological individual phenomena have all their final determinants among social phenomena".[1]

It can be noticed that the coexistence of antipsychologism and a moderate or relatively radical version of methodological anti-individualism allows for the investigation of individual participation in culture both by psychology and culture studies. This viewpoint implies a subdivision of cognitive interests, depending on various qualities and

1. On variants of methodological anti-individualism see: J. Kmita, *O kulturze symbolicznej* (On symbolic culture), Warsaw 1982, p. 55.

aspects of cultural participation, into objects of psychological and humanistic investigation respectively. The realization of such a programme would finally lead to a co-operation of psychology and culture studies in forming mutually supplementing "images" of cultural participation.

This co-operation of psychology and culture studies is basically excluded by the cognitive paths of psychologism related to methodological individualism as well as by antipsychologism accompanied by an extremely radical version of methodological anti-individualism. The former accepts the investigation of individual participation in culture only in psychological terms — the latter in exclusively cultural. Both must be considered as inadequate. Their inadequacy derives mainly from the absolutism within the given epistemological perspectives concerning either psychological or cultural elements of the cultural participation process. An impartial, possibly complete image of this process should contain both the subjective and the objective aspect. The former aspect includes the features of participating subjects together with their determinants which guarantee the proper qualities of the cultural participation process itself. The latter aspect, in turn, comprises those features of culture in general, or its certain field, plus the determinants of those features which guarantee the (other than in the former) qualities of the participation process. The above distinguished aspects imply that certain features of the cultural participation process depend on the characteristics of the participating subjects while other features of this process — by the qualities of the objects of participation. The first aspect may be, initially, defined as "psychological" while the latter as "cultural".

A consequent differentiation of the above aspects becomes possible only within the epistemological perspective of antipsychologism as related either to the moderate or relatively radical version of methodological anti-individualism. And this seems to be the optimum viewpoint for the investigation of cultural participation. On its basis it is possible to differentiate between culture as such — and its particular fields — and individual participation. Consequently, it implies that both the features and the determinants of phenomena belonging to the two spheres, or levels, do not overlap completely. Thus, not all features of culture (or its given field) are simultaneously the features of individual participation process, and vice versa. Analogically, though the determinants of phenomena belonging to the first sphere appear among the factors determining phenomena from the latter one, there is no identity but a one-sided inclusion of adequate classes of determining factors. The phenomena from the sphere of cultural participation are partially determined by (extra-cultural) psychological (psycho-biological) factors. Hence, considering the assumed epistemological viewpoint it is incorrect both to reduce cultural participation to the sphere of psychological phenomena and to ignore the psychological aspect of phenomena constituting the process.

The psychologistic-individualistic epistemological approach tends to "narrow" the image of participation by omitting the aspect exposed by the cultural studies. It does not take into account those features which are determined by the characteristics of culture as the object of participation. This is the effect of reducing culture as such to the sphere of phenomena constituting cultural participation and their, in turn, consideration as essentially psychological. Such reductive manipulations occur within various psychological trends (especially in introspectionism, behaviourism, psychoneurophysiology) mainly when concerned with such cultural spheres as language, art, religion and science. Phenomena deriving from these fields are reduced to individual participation (in the first and second case — of a sender-receiver character) and then defined in terms of psychological categories. And so language, as a supra-individual communicational system, defined by its specific rules, obligatory both for the sender and the receiver of linguistic messages, emerges as a set of physical-verbal reactions learnt in the course of conditioning adequate reactions to stimuli (behaviouristic concept). Both the verbal reactions and the verbal stimuli are considered as physical and immediately observable. Hence it is impossible to grasp what is essential for the particular linguistic actions, sending and interpreting, i.e. their importance as means of communication. The relation between a linguistic activity and a definite message is mental and not physical. This relation is constituted and based on social consciousness.[2] Thus a particular linguistic activities conveying different messages, cannot be properly distinguished from one another. Their differentiation relies on causal, misleading "physical" features. A given activity may have various physical representations and physically identical behaviours may represent different actions.[3]

The problem with discerning the varying cultural activities (i.e. activities with different ascribed meanings — on the grounds of social consciousness) refers not only to the psychologistic reduction in behaviourism. They are inseparably related to psychologistic reduction irrespective of whether socio-cultural activities are reduced to behavioural or psychical phenomena (including individual consciousness). The above problems result

2. Argumentation in favour of this thesis appears mainly in: the works of J. Kmita: *O kulturze symbolicznej*, op. cit., *Kultura i poznanie* (Culture and cognition), Warsaw 1985.

3. J. Kmita and L. Nowak, "O racjonalizującym charakterze badań humanistycznych" (On rationalizing character of humanistic studies), *Studia Filozoficzne* 5/1969.

from the fact that the relation of particular socio-cultural activities to their meanings is constituted on the grounds of social consciousnessWhat is more, it is totally independent of the "natural" cause-effect nexus accepted as the psychological conceptualization of this nexus (their products) within any reduction of humanistic statements to psychology. The omission of social consciousness, i.e. of the supra-individual mental reality, and its forms — various fields of culture, parallelled by a simultaneous treatment of cultural consciousness interrelations as "natural regularities" (psychological), leads to such descriptions of cultural participation process which do not differentiate among those participants — neither in regard of the varieties of cultural fields nor considering the individuals' relation to a given field. A consequent behaviouristic reduction of linguistic communication phenomena, such as language, art, customs etc. (statements describing these phenomena) to regularities (principles) of the S-R type standardizes both the elements of the various cultural fields and the related participation activities by considering them in terms of a physically stimulated reaction of organism. The above situation hinders the distinction between participation forms in a given cultural field — active and passive, of the sender and receiver etc. The phenomena of cultural participation, expressed in terms of individual experiences (and not external behaviour) — as in Maslow's theory representing the so-called humanistic psychology — assume a uniform character. Here, active participation is discussed in terms of a generally conceived creative process, equally manifested in the contexts of various cultural fields and sections of social life. Basically, the characterization of this process ignores all socio-cultural determinants (criteria) of creativity: "creative" means "novel" in the context of individual achievements and not within a socio-cultural context. It also turns out that participation in such various cultural fields as art, science, religion etc., can be defined in terms of a single psychological experience called by Maslow "top experience". Thus from a psychological angle, the aesthetic experience, a mystic experience, the experiences of discovering or solving scientific problems, are all equal and reduced to the "top experience".[4]

The epistemological approach pointed out both by antipsychologism and the radical version of methodological anti-individualism produced, admittedly, a specifically "narrowed" image of cultural participation. On the other hand, it also differs from the psychologistic individualistic

---

4. Stencel E., "Koncepcja człowieka w tak zwanej psychologii humanistycznej na przykładzie poglądów A.M. Maslowa i C. Rogersa" (The concept of man in the so-called humanistic psychology on the basis of A.M. Maslov's and C. Rogers' views), *Studia metodologiczne* 24/1985, p. 91.

prospects. It totally disregards the subjective aspect, i.e. the relation of participation to some features of the participating subjects — assuming that the image of particiption is delimited by the features of culture being the object of participation. This results from the reduction of psycho-logically determined phenomena of individual participation in culture to the sphere of culture and cultural participation conceived as a set of supra-individual phenomena. An example is provided by the Althusserian theory of cognition, totally abstracting from the subject of cognition.

The term: "psychological approach to cultural participation" and "cultural approach to cultural participation" will be applied to concepts formed within the epistemological prospects comprising the thesis of antipsychologism and of moderate, or relatively radical, methodological anti-individualism. The former term, in this context, refers to the description of the psychological aspect of cultural participation con-centrating on such features of this process which are affected by the psychologically determined characteristics of the participating subjects. The latter term refers to the cultural aspect of participation in culture. It concentrates on features determined by either their qualities or the context of objects, i.e. culture as such or its particular fields. Evidently, from this epistemological viewpoint both the approaches of psychology and culture studies are mutually complementary and not exclusive. Thus it proves this viewpoint as optimum for the investigation of cultural participation phenomena.

Evidently, the investigation of the psychological aspect belongs to psychology while that of the cultural is in charge of various culture studies. It implies, particularly, the difference of apparatus meeting the require-ments of the problems. The psychological apparatus aims at the in-vestigation of the functioning of an individual against the context of environment, at the analysis of his consciousness, self etc. In culture studies, disregarding the often considerable differences among scientific procedures (resulting from e.g. synchronic vs. diachronic approaches to investigated phenomena) all of them were developed to facilitate a penetrating analysis of fields or spheres of culture and their qualities. The place of cultural participation studies, considering our epistemological viewpoint, becomes a purely pragmatic question. They can be arranged as sections, on the one hand, of psychology and of culture studies on the other; or as a new interdisciplinary study concentrating on this problem exclusively. In the former case the psychological section would produce knowledge on the subjective aspect of cultural participation compatible with the knowledge concerning the objective aspect of participation, produced by the specific sections of culture studies. In the latter case the compatibility would result directly from observing the requirements of logical coherence in the specific theories of cultural participation. Independently of the accepted practical solution, the investigation of cultural participation requires an efficient co-operation of psychology and culture studies. Thus drawing upon the methodological achievements (scientific procedures) or knowledge of any discipline implies neither a violation of their autonomy nor a depreciation of the cognitive results.

The assumed descriptive terms: "psychological approach to participation in culture", "cultural approach to participation in culture" are narrower from the ones initially introduced. They are referred only to psychological and culture concepts formulated in the context of anti-psychologistic and moderate, or radically anti-individual epistemological propositions respectively. Besides, considering the choice of the epistemological viewpoint, the above terms have a normative character.

The relative autonomy of psychological (assuming methodological anti-individualism) studies on cultural participation is rarely viewed as reasonable. This leads to unnecessary controversies, imputation of psychologism when it is non-existent, as well as to supplementation of psychological knowledge by *ad hoc* common sense statements when the cultural approach to participation process requires a psychological supplementation. This situation furthers psychological attitudes both among psychologists and representatives of cultural studies who consider the anti-individualistic programmes favouring exclusively cultural aspects of cultural participation. They assume that it hinders studies on the subjects of this process limiting the problems to those of minor importance. All such misunderstandings are rooted, firstly, in not noticing the varieties of anti-individualism and their consequences for cultural participation studies. Secondly, it is the rigid classification of all the psychological investigations of cultural participation as psychologism unless they contain an explicit declaration concerning their understanding of culture. The absence of definite referrences to cultural theories in psychological concepts concerning, e.g. artistic creativity, scholarship, sociallyoriented activities etc., need not be symptomatic of psychologism. They frequently imply referrences to culturally defined standards as conceived on the grounds of common knowledge, thus representing the cultural approach.

The one-sidedness of the cultural approach to individual participation in culture, i.e. the necessity of a proper psychological supplementation, can be illustrated by the socio-regulatory theory developed by the Poznań culture studies.[5] This theory concentrates, primarily, on a characteristics

5. An exposition of the basic statements of this theory is to be found in the works of J. Kmita, see: note 2.

of culture as supra-individual mental reality containing two types of statements: normative and directive, providing a socio-subjective regulation of the social practice. The particular fields of culture are differentiated on the basis of those regulatory functions, referring to specific types of social practice. Both social practice and culture are approached diachronically and described in terms of a functional-genetic mechanism. This is not the place for a detailed presentation of this theory. However, its basic statements refer to culture as such, to specific fields and spheres, emphasizing its various qualities and aspects. Thus the subjective, supra-individual (the genetic component of the developmental mechanism — the historically earlier state of culture) factors are pointed out as conditioning these qualities and aspects. Analogically — the objective social factors (a functional component of the evolutionary mechanism comprising the actual objective needs addressed to the given cultural realm by the various types of social practice).

The above theory also contains a definite characteristics of individual participation in culture — general and specific (referred to the particular cultural fields). It is derived from the content and function aspects of culture as such, or of its fields. Thus it represents a cultural approach toward individual participation emphasizing features determined by the qualities of the objects. Participation is defined in terms of subjection or conscious acceptance of cultural norms and directives. In referrence to participation phenomena, functional relations between cultural fields and types of social practice they supervise are reflected as the relation of participation in a given cultural field to a respective social practice. Hence, this theory excludes participation in culture as unrelated to social practice. Participation in a definite cultural realm coincides with a respective participation in social practice of an individual (or a group). The latter is rather univocally defined. Cultural participation assumes a specific, subjective rational participation in a proper type of social practice. As the fundamentally hierarchical types of social practice represent the whole of social life, at a given stage of historical development, there are no individuals participating in no cultural field together with its respective social practice. As regards participation in specific cultural fields the above theory formulates a general functional requirement imposed upon cultural participation as related to the regulatory function of culture. It demands, on a large scale, either subjection or at least conscious acceptance of the applied normative or directive statements, constituting the content of a given cultural realm (the final efficiency of a given social practice, regulated by these statements, depends on this requirement).

Considering the all-important character of functional dependencies, there follows the conclusion that detailed characteristics of the participation process, referred to the particular cultural fields (and the functionally related types of social practice) are not subjectively universal by assumption, i.e. applicable to any individual. Contrarily, they reveal a normative rather than descriptive character in relation to any subject. A transformation into description occurs only in relation to those who fulfil the included normative requirement — the requirement of participation in a given cultural realm (plus respective social practice). Here the difference between a cultural and psychological approach is distinctly elucidated — the latter being always subjectively universal, comprising any subject. The above theory contains a general characterization of the cultural sphere which implies a model characteristic of individual cultural participation and which in relation to real persons has an originally normative character. It appears as descriptive-idealizational in relation to those who approximately enough fulfil its requirements. The basically descriptive character of those model characteristics derives from their statement of cultural participation conditions by culture as such; the subjective aspect of participation process is omitted (otherwise: as they represent the approach of cultural studies to participation).

Although a characterization of participation provided by cultural studies omits the aspects of the process (psychological) depending on participating subjects, it is impossible to abstract entirely from the subjective aspect. As cultural participation is defined by the requirement concerning the participating subjects it implies its fulfilment at least by some persons. It relies, similarily, on an implicitly accepted psychological statement based either on common psychological experience or on scientific psychological knowledge (the above theory refers to the former type).[6] Stating that participation in a certain social practice equals the realization of some of its subjective-rational activities, this theory assumes that some people are capable of it, i.e. that they both acquired and are

---

6. This statement is based on the results of an analysis of psychological knowledge produced by particular trends in psychology. It shows that this science always depreciated the common approach to human activity as determined by subjective factors — such as conscious intention or convictions concerning its realization — and thus considered it as non-scientific. This negative attitude is gradually modified by cognitive psychology. See: K. Zamiara, *Metodologiczne znaczenie sporu o status poznawczy teorii* (The methodological sense of the controversy about the cognitive status of theories), Warsaw 1974, and "Pavlov's theory and Marx's directive of the functional-genetic explanation in humanities", in: *Poznań Studies in the Philosophy of the Sciences and the Humanities,* vol. 1, no. 3, B.R. Grüner Publishing Co., Amsterdam 1975, pp. 1-22, and K. Zamiara, "Problem metodologicznej specyfiki psychologii kognitywistycznej" (On the methodological peculiarity of the cognitive psychology), in: K. Zamiara (Ed.), *O kulturze i jej badaniu. Studia z filozofii kultury* (On culture and its investigation. Studies in the philosophy of culture), Warsaw 1985, p. 190.

directed by some normative-directive statements belonging to this cultural field. And so theory seems to assume some definite statements concerning the object of the learning process in ontogenesis though it characterizes neither the process nor its conditioning factors (psychological). Anyhow, the object of cognition certainly consists of the normative and directive statements constituting various cultural fields as well as the socio-subjectively regulated activities belonging to specific types of social practice. Symptomatically, the theory claims this for the object of the learning process in ontogenesis, though not a sole one.

The above analysis, I believe, reveals the one-sidedness of cultural approaches and indicates the necessity of supplementing them by the subjective, psychological aspect. The latter would contribute to a complete image of cultural participation by including the characteristic features of participating subjects — contrary to objects — and "attesting" the implicitly assumed elements of common psychological knowledge under-lying the cultural characteristic features. The socio-regulatory theory has no means of evaluating the empirical correctness of the components constituting subjective characterizations of participation although it is self-sufficient in evaluating the empirical correctness as referred to culture or cultural characterization of participation. This thesis cannot be affected by the present state of academic psychology and its verdicts — especially the negative ones proving the incorrectness of psychological statements, implicitly assumed by the above theory. The dominating behaviourism, in particular, which qualifies as non-scientific all subjective-rational ap-proaches to human activities, should not provide grounds for the rejection of a cultural characterization of participation to the extent to which it assumes a subjective-rational character of participation in a given social practice and its regulating cultural domain.[7] The above is an address, abstracting from actual realization, of this theory to the psychology of cognitive tasks.

Such a main task is the accurate definition of a participation process as related to its subjective, psychological aspect and supplementing the cultural one. Assuming the latter there emerge questions which can be competently resolved by psychology. The most general ones concern, firstly, the psychological understanding of cultural approaches to par-ticipation in terms of respect and conscious acceptance of cultural normative and directive statements. Secondly, they refer to psychological mechanisms conditioning the participation process of an individual: its course under normal conditions, the process of learning participation.

---

7. K. Zamiara, *Metodologiczne znaczenie sporu ...*, op. cit., part III, chapt. IV, V.

Assuming the idea of permanent individual development in ontogenesis (an idea nowadays popularized by developmental psychology) the process of learning cultural participation should be conceived as continuous, though of varying intensity, during an individual life. The following are exemplary questions.

What is — from the psychological point of view — respect or conscious acceptance of normative and directive statements belonging to culture? What psychological factors govern the phenomena of respect or acceptance of cultural statements by any individual? What is the process of learning those two forms of cultural participation like? What psychological determinants of this process are there? On what psychological factors does the intra-individual changeability of cultural participation forms depend (i.e. the passage from mere respect to fully conscious acceptance of definite cultural beliefs)? The latter question refers to the psychological conditions of the "depth" of individual participation in a given field (sphere) of culture — regard (respect) would thus denote a superficial participation while the other form — "deep", "full", participation. How does the (practical) activity of the subject influence the process of acquiring normative and directive beliefs? Are all activities of individuals, within an external context, of a subjective-rational type? Otherwise, are subjective-rational activities a psychological reality or are they products of humanistic scholars who applied rationalization to a definite individual behaviour? What is the relation between the scholarly procedure of humanities and "rationalization" in the psychoanalytic sense? To what extent do some activities (assuming their subjective, rational character) fulfil certain cultural demands due to which they acquire social status as elements of social practice? What psychological factors determine the degree of uniformity of individual activities and cultural pattern, i.e. decide either about close uniformity or only about a homology of the pattern, and individually accomplished action? The same problem of compatibility with cultural pattern can be referred to the content of particular cultural spheres and thus analyzed individual consciousness. What psychological factors determine the degree of compatibility of, on the one hand, individual beliefs and, on the other, of cultural statements (normative and directive) and those derived from social consciousness (e.g. constituting social experience or products of scientific social practice)?

Apart from those general problems concerning the psychological conditioning of cultural participation, there are more specific ones referring to participation in particular cultural fields (types of social practice) or concerning — from the viewpoint of cultural studies — types of participation in a given field. Respective statements of the socio-regulatory theory should provide starting points for formulating questions related to the latter group, i.e. statements differentiating particular fields and spheres, imposing varying requirements upon the participating individuals, characterizing — from the angle of cultural studies — the varieties of participation as related to a definite cultural sphere. One of such weighty statements distinguishes some cultural fields (science, art) as requiring functionally active, contrary to passive, participation, i.e. this participation transforms (modifies) the previously given normative and directive statements representing the historically defined form of a cultural field. This active participation is not functional in relation to such spheres of cultural communication as language and custom. They require passive participation devoid of individual modifications (affecting cultural beliefs). Conscious acceptance of content is an indispensable condition of active participation in any cultural field. Thus, while in some cultural fields participation relies on respect for beliefs only (language, customs) in other (science, art) it requires a deeper form, i.e. conscious acceptance of pertinent beliefs. The following are the exemplary questions.

What psychological factors enable the participation of individuals in particular spheres? The question contains the problem of the inter-individual differences as referred to participation: certain psychological factors decide about inter-individual differences predisposing to participation in definite cultural spheres (the statement that not everyone can participate in science but everyone can in "material culture" illustrates the idea). Analogical statements can be posed considering the varieties of participation in culture:

What psychological factors guarantee an active or a passive participation in a definite cultural field? What psychological factors are in charge of sender- or receiver-participation in communicational realms of culture? This question becomes vital in referrence to art and science where some psychological factors, not only socio-cultural, predispose individuals either to sender- (e.g. artists, scientists) or receiver-participation (interpretation of art, assimilation of the given scientific knowledge). What does — from the psychological point of view — sender-active, sender-passive, receiver-active and receiver-passive participations mean? What are the psychological determinants of these phenomena? What psychological mechanisms underlie the process of learning various types of cultural participation in different fields? Is it possible to affect usefully the course and effects of the processes of learning participation in a certain field?

Is the contemporary psychological knowledge in charge of ready answers to such questions? Generally, not. The so far accepted epistemo-logical perspective — constituted by ontological naturalism (its softer or harder versions), methodological individualism and psychologism is

241

responsible for this situation (the above enumerated assumptions contribute to the shared methodological consciousness of various paradigms in psychology).[8] This epistemological perspective hinders a positive consideration of the three elements — constituting the indispensable part of the co-ordination of the psychological and cultural aspects of this process — of the cultural approach to individual participation in culture:

(1)　individual consciousness in terms of beliefs and logical dependencies between them;
(2)　individual activities as subjectively-rationally determined;
(3)　consciousness and individual activity within the context of the objective conditions of social practice and forms of social consciousness.[9]

Thus, there are only two possibilities till a certain "humanistic psychology" is constituted on the ground of different epistemological assumptions and capable of co-operating with cultural studies in the investigation of participation process. The first consists of a referrence to the non-literary meaning of psychological statements; an essentially corrective referrence in terms of correspondence.[10] The second consists of a heuristic use of the existing psychological solutions in formulating hypotheses concerning the psychological aspect of cultural participation process.

The former encounters an essential obstacle. To refer to certain psychological statements (theories), in the course of an essentially corrective correspondence, one needs a theory capable of defining the (relative) historical legitimacy of the corresponded knowledge, which is measured by the range of its efficient applicability. Doubt arise whether the socio-regulatory culture theory — omitting the subjective aspect of cultural participation and including elements from the common psychological experience which should be, as stated above, confirmed by psychological studies beforehand — is suitable for this purpose. This

8. This problem was analyzed in the following works: K. Zamiara, "Znaczenie badań psychologicznych dla poznawania kultury" (The importance of psychological investigations for the study of culture), in: S. Pietraszko (Ed.), *Przedmiot i funkcje teorii kultury* (The subject and functions of culture theories), Wrocław 1982, p. 89; K. Zamiara, "Czy istnieje szansa korzystania z teorii psychologicznej w badaniach nad kulturą" (Is there a chance of applying a psychological theory in the investigations of culture, in: T. Kostyrko (Ed.), *Teoria kultury a badania nad zjawiskami artystycznymi* (Culture theory and the investigations of artistic phenomena), Warsaw 1983, p. 171.
9. K. Zamiara, "Czy istnieje szansa korzystania ...", op. cit., p. 179.
10. For a characterization of the notion of an essentially corrective (strict) correspondence, see: J. Kmita, *Szkice z teorii poznania naukowego* (Essays in the theory of scientific cognition), Warsaw 1976, p. 157.

theory may only correct the silently assumed, in psychological knowledge, elements of common experience concerning the cultural aspect of participation. Otherwise, this theory allows for a critical evaluation of these elements of psychological concepts concerning individual participation, which contributed to a faulty recognition of the object of this participation as well as of some features of the process. To this extent these attempts at defining the essentially corrective relation of correspondences appears as sensible. However, it is groundless to consider this theory as capable of corresponding all psychological concepts of individual participation in culture; also due to the subjective aspect of this process. This task could be fulfilled by a future theory of cultural participation formulated "on the verge of" psychology and culture studies, defined by the socio-regulative cultural theory — on the grounds of an epistemological position, previously accepted as optimum for the investigation of cultural participation (including antipsychologism together with the moderate or radical version of methodological anti-individualism). Thus we are left with the problem of designing such theories: accompanied by the heuristic use of psychological knowledge, compatible with the cultural approach to participation, contained in the socio-regulatory theory and considering the partial results of the attempts at corresponding psychological knowledge to the latter theory.

Translated by Ewa Kębłowska-Ławniczak

Andrzej Pluta

ON APPLICATION OF THE NOTION OF PEDAGOGICAL CULTURE

Introductory Remarks

The conception of the so-called pedagogical culture has not always met
with an appreciative response on the part of pedagogical studies, but
recently it seems to be gaining in popularity and becoming one of the
crucial issues to be discussed in the years to come. Presenting the subject
matter of the conception, and some epistemological principles underlying
specific suggestions of how "pedagogical culture" should be defined and
applied, I will also touch upon general problems concerning methodology
of pedagogical studies.

My assumed point of view is that of the social-regulative theory of
culture.

The paper is divided into several parts, each being an attempt to answer
one of the following questions:

1. What are possible applications of the notion of culture in pedagogical studies?
2. How do pedagogues approach the question of the relationship
   between culture (in general) and pedagogical culture?
3. What are the fundamentals of the conception of pedagogical culture
   that have been worked out so far?
4. What are the methodological implications of the available solutions?
5. What conditions should be fulfilled so that the notion of pedagogical
   culture could acquire the practical and cognitive status in scientific
   pedagogical studies?

1. Pedagogical Concern with Culture and Pedagogical Culture

As regards application of the notion of culture, following the tradition of
the Poznań school for cultural research, we may distinguish between: the
practical-cognitive function, i.e. description of the adopted (by a given
community) values-aims of the educational institutions, as well as of the
means by which the aims are achieved; and, the direct educational
function, i.e. propagating of "true" culture (educational propagating of
"true" values), including propagation of "true" pedagogical culture (i.e.

244

"true" values which determine educational activities and/or "truly" valuable (for instance, effective) methods leading to their achievement.

1.1. A Restricted Notion of General Culture in Pedagogy

Pedagogues usually refer to the approaches prevailing in general socio-logy, sociology of culture and cultural anthropology, which can be found in such authors as S. Czarnowski, J. Szczepański, A. Kłoskowska, K. Żygulski. Although the verbal expressions of the encountered ideas may differ from person to person, the ideas themselves reveal a high degree of resemblance. For illustration, consider the following definitions:

a) culture is the entirely of the products of human activities, both material and immaterial, of the values and accepted manners of conduct which have been objectivated and adopted by some communities, and which are passes on the other communities as well as to the next generations,[1]

b) culture is a relatively integrated whole comprising human actions which follow the patterns common in a given social community, the patterns that have been developed and acquired in the course of interaction, as well as their results,[2]

c) culture consists of the bulk of the objectivated components of the social output, shared by a number of social groups, which due to their objective character are fixed and ready to spread in space,[3]

d) culture is the totality of material goods producted by people and accepted by some community, and of the scientific, moral, social, artistic and technological values, as well as the processes in which the goods and values are obtained, acquired and passed on to other communities.[4]

In pedagogical studies, the presentations of the senses of the term "culture" are usually followed by the authors' own conceptions of the notion, which are, as a rule, selective and evaluative. A. Kamiński, who is commonly quoted by the scholars interested in the concept of pedagogical culture, is a good example of such an approach. Thus, he writes:

A pedagogue would be reluctant to classify within cultural phenomena all values and manners of conduct "adopted by some community" (for instance, by a group of

1. *Pedagogika. Prodęcznik akademicki* (Pedagogy. An academic textbook), Warsaw 1978, p. 39. The quoted definition comes from J. Szczepański.
2. M. Grochociński, "Kultura pedagogiczna rodziców" (Parents' pedagogical culture), in: (ed.) M. Ziemska, *Rodzina i dziecko* (Family and the child), Warsaw 1979, p. 300. The quoted meaning of the term comes from A. Kłoskowska.
3. *Pedagogika ...*, op. cit., p. 39; Grochociński, op. cit., p. 299. This meaning of the term is used by S. Czarnowski.
4. W. Okoń, "O kulturze pedagogicznej" (On pedagogical culture), *Rocznik Pedagogiczny* 9/1984, p. 236.

alcoholic); appreciating the needs of a sociologist, as far as pedagogy is concerned, we would rather reserve for such facts and actions as drinking habits a different attribute, i.e. "subcultural", not "cultural". Such confinement of the notion of culture to the values approved by the social elite is absolutely necessary in pedagogy because we are not satisfied with claiming the integral relationships between an individual and culture — we wish to influence these relationships.[5]

Accordingly,

from the point of view of a pedagogue, culture is a set of values (intellectual, aesthetic, social, economic, etc.), norms (moral, legal, etc.) and patterns (behavioural, institutional, etc) which we wish to propagate, and with which individuals and social groups should be accustomed in order to develop appropriate needs and interests.[6]

As seen from the above, the notion of pedagogical culture is construed in the context of the existing senses of the term "culture".

1.2. Culture as Property of the Small Group – in an Educational Theory
A rather restricted conception of the discussed notion appears in K. Konarzewski's work, which is due to many reasons, but mainly because of the author's rejecting of the priority of theoretical-historical studies over psychological knowledge in cultural research.

By culture of the group, Konarzewski understands social memory of the group, the shared ideas of its identity which include answers to such questions as: Who are we? Where do we come from? Where are we going to? What do we admire? What do we disapprove of? which all have been recorded in the acknowledged language texts, such as codes (e.g. of technological rules or of moral norms), or in customs and habits (e.g. rituals and games), and which, therefore, can be passed on to the next generations. Thus conceived culture is, at the same time, a certain property of the group characterizing its most advanced stage of development. The author mentions three such stages: of the community, of the social organization and of the group. In the latter one, the group is perceived by its members as a supraindividual totality organizing their lives. One of a pedagogue's aims is to introduce into culture such elements which would form a new centre of integration, or which would inspire the group's inventiveness by creating new texts (i.e. codes, myths, stories and tales), as well as rituals and games.[7]

5. A. Kamiński, *Funkcje pedagogiki społecznej* (Functions of social pedagogy), Warsaw 1982, p. 54 f.
6. A. Kamiński, *Funkcje ...*, op. cit., p. 55.
7. K. Konarzewski, *Podstawy teorii oddziaływań wychowawczych* (Fundamentals of the theory of pedagogical activities), Warsaw 1982, pp. 209 f., 262, 271 ff. Konarzewski thinks it worth emphasizing that similar stages of the group development were identified

2. Types of Values Propagated by the Notion of Pedagogical Culture

As was mentioned above, the general notion of culture is borrowed by pedagogues from sociology and social anthropology, and then it is intentionally narrowed down in order to uphold the evaluative and persuasive character. Generally speaking, the situation consists in identifying and describing the values shared by professional and non-professional educators, i.e. the values-aims of educational interaction, as well as the means by which those aims-values are achieved, together with the justifying persuasion and with the propagation of the values. Such situation is typical of a pre-theoretical stage of the humanities.

I will attend now to the types of values postulated by the conception of pedagogical culture. As a result, we will gain better understanding of what it is, of its components and of areas of its dissemination.

As it seems, the conception of pedagogical culture propagates three types of pedagogical values, i.e.

A) the first value is acceptance of the personality of a pupil. Emphasizing importance of the properly formed personality, pedagogues apply evaluation procedures, pointing to its "normalcy", i.e. lack of deviations from the educational norm, and treating the "normalcy" as a positive indicator of the level of pedagogical culture. At the same time, they use the concept of "normal" personality to stress the importance of the pupil's personality being formed in a certain way.[8] Thus formed personality is often identified with the idea of individual pedagogical culture.[9]

Referring to the ideological notion of a "versatile individual", they emphasize the integrity of a pupil (i.e. of his biological, psychological and spiritual features), as well as the dynamics of those characteristics and their constant development during the life time.

The dissemination of pedagogical culture remains in a close relation with our care of the all-round development of children, youths and adults, the more so that the initial milieu conditions not always favoured such development.[10]

---

by A. Makarenko, i.e. of the group anarchy, of its discipline and of its culture. Makarenko's terminology only too clearly indicates the author's axiological evaluation. Konarzewski's terms are apparently descriptive, axiologically neutral.

8. W. Okoń, "O kulturze ...", op. cit., p. 241.

9. J. Szczepański, "Rola kultury pedagogicznej w kształtowaniu społeczeństwa socjalistycznego" (The role of pedagogical culture in forming the socialist society), in: *Rola kultury pedagogicznej w kształtowaniu socjalistycznych stosunków międzyludzkich i postaw moralnych* (The role of pedagogical culture in forming of the socialist human relations and moral attitudes), Warsaw 1979, p. 13 ff.; J. Maciaszkowa, "Kultura pedagogiczna rodziców (Parents pedagogical culture) in: *Pedagogika opiekuńcza* (Protective pedagogy), Warsaw 1977, pp. 162-175.

10. W. Okoń, "O kulturze ...", op. cit., p. 241.

The theme of the non-instrumental personality values is occasionally related to Marxist ideology.[11]

B) the values which ought to be respected by a pupil. Observing, and rightly so, the expansion, because of the new social needs, of the objective function of pedagogical culture, i.e. of the process of updating, of permanent cultural initiation (permanent education, learning without limit, whole life education), the pedagogues, when speaking of their pupils, have in mind children, youths and adults. As for an adult learner, the values he is supposed to respect usually refer to the postulated acceptance attitudes toward current achievements of science and technology, as well as to the encouraged active participation in various fields of culture. At the same time, however, he is persuaded to gain such a position in life which will express his readiness to articulate, develop and revise his accepted philosophy of life.

The propagated "true" values, directing human actions, cover the following domains which should be respected by a pupil:

(a) the acknowledged cultural standard of the personality, and the values presupposed by the standard which should be felt,

(b) the moral and common law values,

(c) the values of certain directive beliefs, accounting for the instrumental relations between the palpable values and the elusive, final values,

(d) the aesthetic values, understood as communicative images of the world and evaluative assessments of "life",

(e) the values belonging to applied technology and to symbolic culture (in the narrower sense of the word).

Presently, I will briefly discuss the above types of values.

In the first instance, we have to do with axiologically defined *Weltanschauung* values and values reaching other areas of culture (the conception of trust in the so-called educational ideal and its achievement). The former values are, first of all, those which are believed to be associated with universal and fundamental ontological features of human beings (i.e. acquisition of awareness, authenticity and creative abilities; respect for the rights of an individual as the supreme value; emancipation), and those which show what kind of person a pupil, who is in the process of permanent education, should become.

In the second class of values, attention is drawn to the states of affairs indispensable for establishing interpersonal relations (relations of the following types: pupil-teacher, pupil-pupil, pupil-other individuals); the pupil's ability to enter interactions with other persons acquires positive

11. J. Szczepański, "Rola kultury ...", op. cit.

evaluation. In accordance with the theory of the "versatile individual", the pupil's manners and morals define axiological attitudes towards others and toward his own self (i.e. self-consciousness, self-confidence, optimism). Emphasis is laid on such actions, expressing personal manners and morals, which in everyday pedagogical practice have not been sufficiently exposed, or are endangered, albeit still functional (e.g. acts of self-sacrifice, lack of selfishness, tolerance, expressions of personal culture of emotions). Hence, as it seems, comes negative evaluation of certain *Weltanschauung* beliefs which threaten school life and contribute to the educational crisis. This concerns, above all, consumers' attitudes that have been exerting a destructive influence upon cultural education in Poland since 70's, the result of which has been an increase in mental diseases, alcoholism, drug addiction, broken families, and a decrease in acts extending beyond basic moral obligations uniting all members of society. In connection with this, W. Okoń writes:

> (...) the rate of juvenile delinquency has become evidence, as negative, of this (i.e. pedagogical — A.P.) culture. Its absence is the cause that in the whole world we observe an increasing number of young and very young people taking to cigarette smoking, alcoholic beverages, drugs, and crime. The rates of these pathological phenomena define the level of pedagogical culture, i.e. its failure.[12]

At the same time, tribute is paid to the community norms and to the norms of tradition which promote the sense of group identity and group membership (e.g. with reference to school, family), introducing an axiological hierarchy into a pupil's life. For instance,

> various aspects of social life in a family give rise to the situations which provide evaluation conditions of the pupil's experience, deciding about his getting acquainted with reality and living in it.[13]

A special position in the discussed group is occupied by the values of the "pedagogical attitude" which are mainly conveyed to the students who are candidates for future professional pedagogues. They are the personality values and ways of their forming, viewed and "evaluated" in different historical variants, and compared with the contemporarily accepted, or rejected, values of various personality types and methods of their formation. We can quote, in this connection, E. Durkheim, the acknowledged author of the concept of pedagogical culture:

> History of schooling or, at least, of national education is the preliminary to pedagogical culture. (...) Everyday pedagogy, which is needed by the teacher for his enlightenment and for his daily practice, requires (...) better understanding of reality

12. W. Okoń, "O kulturze ...", op. cit., p. 241; see: M. Grochociński, "Kultura pedagogiczna ...", op. cit., p. 329.
13. M. Grochociński, "Kultura pedagogiczna ...", op. cit., p. 332.

and of various difficulties which ought to be faced. Such understanding may obviously by reached owing to historical culture.[14]

Also, a contemporary historian of education writes:

History of education enables us to understand the relation between pedagogical phenomena and the social and cultural background of the country and epoch; it develops the sense of historical perspective (...) respect for progressive traditions in education. (...) At the same time, the above elements are the crucial aspects of our conception of pedagogical culture. The true pedagogical culture, which should be possessed by all educated teachers, must be founded on an extensive historical basis.[15]

As regards the third group of values, we can also say that the conception of pedagogical culture contains a number of "instructions" leading to achievement of "true" values; they say how the pupil should live, how he ought to get ready for his own independent and successful life, how he should express his attitude toward the respected values, to other people and to his own self.[16]

Proceeding to the next set of values, let us first notice that for the so-called pedagogical meaning of art or, in other words, for the role that artistic communication plays in formation of the social awareness of the relations between "life" values and the respective *Weltanschauung* values, and for the persuasive meaning of the conveyed message (e.g. of literary works), the most important thing is

what it written down with the writers' pens (...) or what comes from other men of culture. In particular, works of great and well known authors may, due to their suggestive character, exert a considerable influence upon pedagogical culture of society. We will not be mistaken to assume that Bolesław Prus contributed more to pedagogical culture in Poland as an outstanding novelist and author of chronicles, than as a writer of pedagogical articles, perhaps even more than the whole bunch of his contemporary pedagoues-positivists.[17]

We face the great impact of mass culture, related to expansion of the consumers' attitudes, which brings about reduction of "spiritual" values and their being "pushed" down in the hierarchy of value systems functioning in society. In addition, the semantic principles of artistic communication, derived from a given philosophy of life, have been losing social relevance, they are no longer respected. In other words, artistic

14. E. Durkheim, "O kulturze pedagogicznej" (On pedagogical culture), in: (ed.) S. Kot, *Źródła do historii wychowania* (Sources to the history of education), part II, Warsaw 1930, pp. 400, 402.

15. S. Wołoszyn, *Dzieje wychowania i myśli pedagogicznej w zarysie* (An outline history of education and pedagogical thought), Warsaw 1964, p. 29.

16. Cf. J. Maciaszkowa, "Kultura pedagogiczna ...", "O kulturze ...", op. cit., p. 239.

communication of highly conventionalized semantics has almost ceased functioning in the evaluation system of life attitudes; this makes it impossible for the pupil to respect the pedagogically desired values, as far as his *Weltanschauung* is concerned. The above is a critical reconstruction of some common sense arguments, put forward by the pedagogues who draw attention to the dangers of passive participation in mass culture.[18]

The values pertaining to culture of applied technology and to symbolic culture (in the narrow sense), have already been referred to, whenever I raised the question of the *Weltanschauung* evaluation. In this place, it should be added that the pedagogues list a number of values falling in the area of culture of applied technology, as well as a great many values defining exercises of physical fitness and games, within non-professional physical culture.[18]

C) the values which are connected with educational methods; by education, I mean its two variants, i.e. directive and normative ones.

In directive education, the pedagogues move forward the activities governed by elements of the so-called intellectual culture, which comprises theories of pedagogy, psychology, sociology, as well as didactic directives and theories, historical knowledge and the teacher's accumulated practical experience.[20] The education should consist, using J. Szczepański's words, in pedagogical school culture penetrating whole society. Non-professional educational activities, particularly in the family variant, are to resemble professional school practice, with respect to the bulk of knowledge determining values-aims. The importance of thus conceived education is additionally upgraded by various evaluative formulas, referring to its desired "scientific" and "professional" character (only an educated person can be a good educator; parentage is also a profession, etc.).

Within the values related to methods of normative education, one should mention two types, i.e. the effective ones, and the ones that take care to "violate pupils' integrity", which are "discursive" in nature (the two sets are by no means mutually exclusive; the "discursive" methods are historically open).

The pedagogues' activities leading to pupils' acquiring and respecting of the normative beliefs can be characterized as follows:

18. M. Grochociński, "Kultura pedagogiczna ...", op. cit., p. 313 f.

19. Comp., W. Kot, *Podstawy marksistowsko-leninowskiej filozofii* (Fundamentals of Marxist-Leninist philosophy), part I, Poznań 1978, p. 46; see: M. Grochociński, "Kultura pedagogiczna ...", op. cit., p. 311; J. Maciaszkowa, *Rola szkoły w przygotowaniu młodzieży do życia w rodzinie* (How school prepares children for family life), Warsaw 1977.

20. J. Szczepański, "Rola kultury ...", op. cit., p. 7 f.; E. Durkheim, "O kulturze ...", op. cit., p. 400 ff; S. Wołoszyn, *Dzieje wychowania ...*, op. cit., p. 29.

(a) persuasion which communicates the desired norms; as the pedagogues are well aware, it will be effective if the teacher — its author has
enough authority over his pupils, in other words, if he has adequately
identified pedagogical cultural competence, i.e. a system of rules of
cultural interpretation necessary for pedagogical activities;

(b) axiological justification which is a type of persuasion, related to
various aspects of the procedure called by such names as "identifying",
"understanding", "expressing one's experience". Axiological justification
upholds the view that for the pupil to achieve the persuasive values (often
of a non-instrumental, final character), it is advisable and necessary that he
should follow certain persuaded values; the view is often strengthened by
the teacher's referring to his personal experience or to examples from
literature. Consider, for instance, the following axiological justification:

> if you learn, get better understanding and are able to form your own judgment on
> such issues as human development, you will certainly have a good chance to become
> a versatile person, make a happy family, and live a worthy and happy life.

The above can be additionally strengthened by such comments as:

> believe me, it is largely thanks to my psychological and pedagogical knowledge that
> my marriage has been such a success, if Barbara and Bogumił, from M. Dąbrowska's
> novel, had had more time for each other, had they been willing to know each other
> better, their marriage in failure;[21]

(c) the normative education which makes use of the teacher's personal
manners;[22] it seems that in order to influence his pupils, the teacher is likely
to make use of his personal manners and habits, attempting to make his
competence "less professional", by reference to certain specific persuasive
values which are present in non-professional practice of family life; thus
activated values will be as follows: protectiveness, immediate reaction to
the child's needs in accordance with his system of values, unexceptional
acceptance of all pupils, unselfishness, and even love;

(d) supplementing all the above methods with a "discursively" negotia-
ted choice of values. In the social structure of pedagogical influence, the
pupil is said to be the subject of education, by which I understand the
persuasion that, having become aware of his identity and individuality, he
should acquire pedagogical culture. Some latest pedagogical studies —
extending beyond the issue of pedagogical culture — go even further.

21. The example could also serve as a reconstruction of the subject "propedeutics to
family life". See also: J. Kmita, "Rozumienie w procesie odbioru dzieła literackiego"
(Understanding in the process of reception of a literary work), in: *Problemy teorii
literatury (Problems of literary theory), series 2, Wrocław 1976.*
22. I use the concept of "Practice of personal manners and habits" after P.
Ozdowski's *Teoria kultury wobec hermeneutyki Ricoeura* (Theory of culture and
Ricoeur's Hermeneutics), Warsaw/Poznań 1984.

252

Namely, they postulate a subjective unity between a theoretician (scholar), education and a practitioner (pedagogue), which together make an educator, and a pupil. Thereby, they show how to arrive at an educational dialogue through hermeneutics;[23]

(e) the "discursive" choice of values by the pupil is to be promoted by the teacher's insistence on an extended and modified notion of "normalcy", as compared to some still obligatory cultural norms and directives constituting the cultural standard of the pupil's personality and its acceptance. The teacher is assigned a role of a psychotherapist who is encouraged to treat various deviations from the cultural standard of personality as variants of "normalcy", sometimes valuable ones, who should, moreover, persuade the pupil and his environment (his peers, parents and other teachers) to accept the "modified normalcy". Detailed projects of thus conceived axiological education, referring to the principles of the so-called humanistic psychology, are contained in psychological-pedagogical studies whose number is increasing every day.[24]

Concluding the present survey of the values postulated by the conception of pedagogical culture, let me remark that from my assumed point of view of culture, the pedagogues' endeavours to disseminate pedagogical culture should be defined as an attempt to outline the practical and administrative basis of an optimal level of people's participation in culture which has been theoretically conceptualized.

2. *On the Principles of Epistemology and Extra-Cognitive Axiology of the Notion of Pedagogical Culture*

The context of the epistemological assumptions of the notion of peda-

23. See: J. Rutkowiak, "Stosowanie teorii pedagogicznej w praktyce a dialog edukacyjny" (Pedagogical theory in practice and educational dialogue), *Kwartalnik Pedagogiczny* 1/1986; also by the same author: "Dialog bez arbitra jako koncepcja relacji pomiędzy nauczycielem a uczniem" (A dialogue without a mediator as a conception of the teacher — pupil relation), *Ruch Pedagogiczny* 5-6/1984; A. Folkierska, "Dialog i wychowanie" (Dialogue and education), *Kwartalnik Pedagogiczny* 1/1986; S. Ruciński, Wychowanie jako wprowadzenie w *życie wartościowe* (Education as an introduction to life of value), Warsaw 1981; S. Górski, *Psychoterapia w wychowaniu* (Psychotherapy in education), Warsaw 1986.
24. See, for instance, R. Miller, *Socjalizacja – wychowanie – psychoterapia* (Socialization — education — psychotherapy), Warsaw 1981; H. Rylke, G. Klimowicz, *Szkoła dla ucznia. Jak uczyć życia z ludźmi* (The school for a pupil. How to teach living with people), Warsaw 1982; comp. also J. Kmita's comments on the evaluative-persuasive reaction of humanistic psychology to the current needs of pedagogical practice: J. Kmita, *Aktualność marksistowskiej koncepcji poznania naukowego* (Actuality of the Marxian conception of scientific epistemology), Poznań 1986.

gogical culture is not specifically pedagogical, but is borrowed by pedagogues from sociology and anthropology, together with the general concept of culture which in the latter disciplines is treated as a subject matter of study, not as an object of axiological persuasion (axiology is implicitly present in those studies as well, but unlike sociologists and anthropologists, pedagogues almost exclusively focus on evaluation of culture).

2.1. The Epistemological Assumptions Underlying the Sociological and Anthropological Concept of Culture

In order to "understand" a scientific conception, or one that pretends to be of a scientific character, i.e. in order to grasp its meaning, it is necessary to approach it from the viewpoint of a certain theoretical and methodological humanistic factor. Taking such a factor into account, it is possible to relate a given set of statements to their so-called literal reference which is a specific transformation of the practical and objective reference.

A thorough analysis of the epistemological assumptions of the sociological and anthropological conceptions of global culture reveals their positivistic philosophical and methodological orientation. The perspective applied in those conceptions is of the phenomenalistic (though not all sociologists are consistent in following the principles of phenomenalism, which is seen in their using such terms as patterns, norms and values), naturalistic and individualistic character. I will not go into details since the problems have been interestingly reviewed elsewhere.[25] For illustration, I will only refer to the phenomenalistic manner of conceiving culture, and to certain consequences that such methodology brings about for a pedagogue.

Thus, the principles of phenomenalism do not distinguish between pupils' participation in culture and manifestations of such participation (i.e. specific actions), between culture as an independent "entity" and acts of participation in it, which additionally makes it impossible to distinguish between natural and cultural conformity of such actions. Consider a few simple examples. A pupil unexpectedly raises from his desk. Is it a reaction to some physical stimulus, such as a sudden pain, or an expression of respect for an entering adult? Within the conception of culture adopted by pedagogues from sociology, there is not way to solve the problem, and the blame for this rests with phenomenalism which does not provide any grounds for posing questions about the observed conformity. Let us modify the above example as follows: the headmaster enters the classroom

25. W. Śliwczyński, "O tzw. empirycznej socjologii kultury" (On so-called empiricist sociology of culture), *Studia metodologiczne* 24/1985, pp. 263-289.

and all pupils raise from their seats. Such a collective reaction could be interpreted by many teachers as their pedagogical success, evidence of "correct" manners (a result of the applied educational methods), whereas others may treat it as pupils' "normal" behaviour. If our pedagogues and pupils were approached as informants, questioned about the motives of their actions on the headmaster's entering the room, the answers we would probably get, would roughly fall in two groups: (1) "because it is done", "because every pupil at school does it" — that way the pupils's behaviour would be recognized as belonging to the sphere of habits; (ii) "the pupil should show respect for adults, his superiors, teachers, headmaster, etc.", "the pupil is meant to ..." — and here would follow a list of actions steered by the respective norms. As evidenced, one cannot identify the pupils' participation in the culture of habits and beliefs with the material phenomena, i.e. their actions on the headmaster's coming into the classroom; one should rather talk about their accepting (respecting) of certain beliefs, on the basis of which they undertake certain actions, i.e. raising from their seats. The action involved is, both, nonreflexive (according to a rule of the conventionalized semantics: "it is done"). and semantically unconventional — as a habitual action, it reveals a given *Weltanschauung* value (in the discussed case: a moral one, i.e. respect for adults, superiors, teachers, etc.).

Returning now to K. Konarzewski's narrow notion of culture, it must be admitted that in the opening of his *Podstawy teorii oddziaływań wychowawczych* (Fundamentals of the theory of pedagogical activities) the author declares his reluctance to include axiological considerations in the theory of education, unlike many other pedagogues who explicitly assume axiological evaluation. In my opinion, however, axiology is implicitly present in his definition of culture as the currently most advanced stage of the development of the educational group. What, in fact, should the said development consist in: (i) increase is a number of elements, increasing integrity ("stronger" relations among the elements); (ii) changes approaching a desired state of affairs — certain ideal (changes "for better"); (iii) a sequence of regular changes?

The author does no seem to be sure himself, jumping from one of the above senses to another. Moreover, he seems unaware that both individual, and the educational group (or any other group, for that matter) are "doomed" to culture. In his theory, only such group is representative of culture that respects the norms and rules accepted by the author in his introduced notion of culture as the most advanced stage in the group development. From the point of view of the nonnormative conception of culture, culture is reflected in any group, regardless of the fact whether it has managed to produce written records, customs and habits, or whether such "elements of culture" are missing in its history.

The origin of culture is conceived by Konarzewski in an individualistic way. This approach becomes obvious when claims that culture is the product of the individuals living within one social structure. By no means does he imply a process which would reveal the functional character of determinacy. The progress of the group development is presented by him by reference to certain regularities of everyday psychological and pedagogical experience. At the same time, however, since the social psychological-pedagogical experience treats the relations between actions and their meanings as objective, the cultural senses must be (from the perspective of this experience) objectively "inherent" in those actions, and in the products. Accordingly, for the author, who does not go beyond the cognitive horizon of positivistic methodology of science, only such a group possesses culture that has managed to produce it and have it "objectively" recorded. Besides, although the author speaks of moral and habitual norms, in fact, he does not discuss the values which are devoid of practical tangibility, but only manifestations of their realization (in the form — as he claims — of rituals, games and written codes) which are, in his view, practically ascertainable; neither does he distinguish between the actions of the group which are ruled by the axiologically desired beliefs, and the habitual ones which are communicative actions.[26]

2.2. Pedagogues' Extra-Cognitive Contribution to the Concept of Pedagogical Culture

In view of the fact that the conceptions of pedagogical culture are mainly of an evaluative and persuasive character, we should rather expect the context of beliefs than practical and cognitive reflection. Strictly speaking, the pedagogues describe and promote certain types of values, using scientific, as they claim, methods. Thus, the cognitive value is assigned by

26. For lack of space, I cannot elaborate on the author's concepts of habits, rituals and games. It seems that pedagogues would profit a lot of those terms, and a few others related to them, could acquire some scientific rigour. A number of works by J. Grad, making use of the social-regulative theory of culture, might be of great assistance while putting the terminology in order. Thus, see his: "Obyczaj — system komunikacji symboliczno-kulturowej" (Customs — a communicative system of symbolic culture), *Lud* 67/1983; "Święto — światopogląd — obyczaj" (Festivities — worldview — customs), *Studia Metodologiczne* 23/1984; "Obyczaj a moralność" (Customs and morality), in: (ed.) J. Kmita, *Studia z teorii kultury i metodologii badań nad kulturą* (Studies in theory and methodology of culture), Warsaw/Poznań 1982; "Moralność — dziedzina światopoglądu" (Morality — a domain of a social system of beliefs), in: (ed.) K. Zamiara, *O kulturze i jej badaniu* (On culture and cultural research), Warsaw 1985.

256

them to the belief (*Weltanschauung*) statements, while the evaluation — as a methodological instrument of influencing teachers— concerns the pupil's personality, the values he should respect and methods of education.

Telling the truth, the conceptions of pedagogical culture are not scholarly projects of pedagogical study, but rather programmes for educators (mainly, in normative education). They promote a concrete system of *Weltanschauung* values, and the relevant (e.g. discursive, uncontroversial) manners of participation in various areas of culture. Possible social appeal of those conceptions can be related to the objectively appearing demand for such school and extracurricular pedagogical activities that will introduce pupils (also adults) to a given way of participation in: (a) the belief sphere of culture (in the "true" *Weltanschauung* values), mainly, of the secular ideological philosophy, strongly opposed to the consumers' attitude; (b) other fields of culture in which the participation, albeit itself non-ideological, requires the pupil's acceptance of certain scientific beliefs (i.e. secular and anti-consumption). The attitudes propagated by the authors refer to the much argued philosophical dichotomy between "to have" and "to be", the respective life aspirations and educational aims.[27] Thereby, they express their annoyance with the "true" values being absent from daily life practice, with the "whole" culture being in danger of degradation (because of spread of negative pedagogical culture). Putting together evaluative propositions and descriptive statements, the pedagogues are able to articulate their own axiological belief attitudes towards the educational reality.

The pedagogical analyses supply the positivistic conceptions of experience with some extra elements pertaining to "understanding" and "emancipation". The latter is applied to entire culture and to pupils' personality. In this sense, the conceptions of pedagogical culture, viewed from the "external" perspective, are descriptions of the pupil's experience of his introduction to culture, of his participation in social life and in a system of beliefs; the descriptions are further supplemented by inducing the pupil to adopt certain methods of culture acquisition. More specifically, the pedagogues' considerations fulfil the educational and cultural function because it is the "true" pedagogical culture and "true" manners of its realization that are persuaded, as well as, the function of the *Weltanschauung* evaluation (the "true" pedagogical culture, being a superior ideological value, is identified with the *Weltanschauung* message of "the versatile individual"; we can observe here the pedagogues'

27. See: B. Suchodolski, "Wychowanie między 'być' a 'mieć'" (Education between "to be" and "to have"), in: (ed.) Cz. Kupisiewicz, *Nowoczesność w kształceniu i wychowaniu* (Modern education and upbringing), Warsaw 1982.

attempts to form the social belief that certain tangible actions and values serve the realization of *Weltanschauung* values, and are upgraded by the latter).

Thus, the pedagogues' assumed relations between the adopted epistemological principles and variants of cultural evaluation are fairly easy to deduce. The sociological approach to culture, expressed in the categories devoid of axiological meaning (of course — inconsistently), is opposed (despite the pedagogues' making use of the implicit axiology) to the approach to evaluation which, however, also falls in the domain of positivistic methodology, and which upholds involvement in propositions of cultural evaluation. Favouring the ideological functions of reflections on pedagogical culture, the authors place those reflections directly in the sphere of pedagogical practice.

3. Pedagogical Culture as a Topic of the Scientific Study

The function of *Weltanschauung* evaluation in reflections on pedagogical culture, specifically, the direct cultural and educational functions, requires using the methods which make it difficult to advance practical-cognitive aims. The practical-cognitive function of reflections on pedagogical culture should provide (depending whether the reflections are of a pre-theoretical or theoretical character) either the statements reproducing directly pedagogical and psychological experience, or the theoretical statements explaining the social facts of acceptance of the beliefs that govern actions undertaken in pedagogical practice. For that reason, it seems necessary, for a pedagogue pursuing scholarly research, to keep his direct cultural-educational activities apart. Athough a pedagogue cannot escape axiological evaluation (participation in reproduction and construction of the belief systems), there exists a fundamental difference between his providing of pedagogical statements with the help of which the cultural and educational initiatives will be put to practice at school, and providing of the "statements" immediately introducing individuals to the participation in culture. It is worth noticing, in this connection, that the process of ideological isolation of the pedagogues' research study lest it should not evaluate the domains in which the evaluation would contrast too sharply with the evaluation that the ruling class ideology would try to impose, that such isolation conserves — as was the case in Poland in the 70's — realization of the cultural-educational function, in particular, the results reporting fulfilment of the desired *Weltanschauung* values ("true", i.e. the already achieved "socialist" pedagogical culture).

The existing social demand for the theoretical results of the pedagogical study covering the entire pedagogical reality could be observed in the

258

social function performed by pedagogical studies; the function that would be liable to immediate verification because a theory of pedagogical culture would not only explain the facts covered by the conceptions of pedagogical culture proposed so far, but it would also point to the superiority of certain predicted effects of the practical pedagogical actions motivated by those facts.

Thus, the change of pedagogues' approach to the question of pedagogical culture will bring about increase in "technical" effectiveness of pedagogical knowledge. This will be achieved when a theoretical conception of culture can influence the notion of pedagogical culture.

Recently, a number of valuable suggestions leading to a theoretical conception of culture have been put forward by T. Parsons, W.H. Goodenough and other authors of cognitive anthropology. They are all against identifying culture with material, phenomenalistic facts (biological, products, actions); culture is a certain "whole" which must be acquired by members of a community. The first of the above authors writes as follows:

> In case of human interaction, the mediating and stabilizing factor is *common culture*, i.e. commonly acknowledged systems of symbols whose meanings are understood by both participants in more or less the same way. The existence of such systems, in particular, of the language systems, is encountered in each community.[28]

W.H. Goodenough, in turn, says:

> Culture is not a material phenomenon, it does not consist of things, people, actions or feelings. It is rather an organization of all those constituents. It is a form of what people have stored in their minds, of their models of perception, cognition and interpretation of the world. Culture of a society comprises everything a person should know, everything he ought to believe, in order to undertake such social actions that are acceptable for the community members; it behaves like this in any role the society will assign to its member.[29]

To "understand" the culture conceived as the whole which cannot be directly observed (in Goodenough's words — to access its ideational order), we should postulate a research programme which would rule out the restrictions of positivistic epistemology, and which would indicate methods of adequate descriptions of the "mental" reality. Already in this place, it can be suggested that this kind of reflection on culture and on scientific methodology should point out their mutual relationships. The ideas I have in mind (expressed, for instance, by F. Znaniecki and E.

28. T. Parsons, *Social structure and personality* (Polish translation), Warsaw 1969, p. 46.
29. The quotation after: W. Burszta, *Język a kultura w myśli etnologicznej* (Language and culture in ethnological thought), Wrocław 1986, p. 100 f.; see also: J. Kmita, *Kultura i poznanie* (Culture and knowledge), Warsaw 1985, p. 72 ff.

Cassirer) emphasize the necessity of referring in a scientific study to the logically prior findings pertaining to culture. Accordingly, it seems tenable to treat studies in scientific methodology (including pedagogy) as a branch of the broadly understood study of cultural research, in accordance with J. Kmita's conception. Consequently, if we assume that reflections on pedagogical practice and on its underlying social competence, i.e. pedagogical culture, should refer to the theory of culture in order to escape the domain of ideological arguments, then the adopted point of view will no longer be based on the normative assumptions. It must be added, however, that by postulating the confinement of the pedagogical study to the practical-cognitive function, I do not claim any absolute superiority of thus obtained scientific results over the persuasive-ideological initiatives in pedagogical practice which were described above in the paper.

Nonetheless, following the assumed theory of culture, I would like to maintain that: (1) culture, as a set of commonly respected mental "principles", underlies people's actions (social practice); (2) science is a branch of culture, therefore, studies in scientific methodology are a special type of cultural research; (3) pedagogy, with its own studies which make it an independent discipline of culture, and with its concurrent ideological reflection, remains in a specific relationship with pedagogical culture, i.e. with certain flexible "sets of mental principles" underlying, in a directive-normative way, the pedagogical practice of historically rooted communities. In pedagogy, the "principles" can be verbalized, so to say — passively, either in their directive part (as a branch of science), or in the normative part (then we have ideological, axiological reflections; needless to say, there may be a third possibility, when a scientific study and ideology are not kept apart); or the "principles" can become the subject of a critical reflection which tries to explain their universal character; (4) the subject of the pedagogical scientific study is different in each of the above types. Only in the latter type can it acquire some complexity. It is composed, then, of both, the directive pedagogical statements, historically inherited by a given community and respected by its members, and of some new theoretical ideas about pedagogical practice from the point of view of which the social fact of general acceptance of those statements can undergo explanatory procedures and critical reviews. Accordingly, the heading of the present section of the paper is slightly misleading. It is not pedagogical culture which can acquire the status of a topic of scientific studies, but the acceptance of the subjectively reconstructed pedagogical culture, and an objectivated description providing grounds for explanation of the acceptance.

Translated by Nina Nowakowska

Paweł Ozdowski

LOGICAL SEMANTICS AND PSYCHOLOGY OF
COGNITIVE PROCESSES

The paper is an attempt to apply J. Kmita's logical semantics (see Kmita 1985) to a preliminary explication of several elementary concepts from psychology of cognitive processes. For some time now, the conceptual framework of the semantics has been used by the authors from the Poznań Centre for Cultural Research in their works on the theory of culture, i.e. in their investigation of culture in its many aspects. The method has shown its feasibility and one may only hope that it will turn out equally useful in the field of psychology. Our aim, however, is far-reaching. The paper is an opening chapter of a larger work in which the adopted point of view is extended to cover motivation processes of an individual. In this way, we hope to arrive at a conceptually unified method of dealing with psychological processes, and at a coherent theory of personality. That would be a good starting point to consider an integrated theory of psychology and social science within a common set of assumptions.

1. Psychology and Psychological Processes

Following J. Kmita's semantics of culture, I assume that knowledge is a set of logical propositions. Each time a proposition is expressed by a sentence, the former is the meaning of the latter. It is also assumed, however, that propositions (human judgments) need not be put into sentences in order to determine human behaviour. Each proposition consists of concepts. At the level of linguistic verbalization, concepts are expressed in language terms (e.g. individual terms, predicates and functors) whose meanings they constitute.

Each concept is identical with a given system of propositions which is a potential (not necessarily verbal) definiens of that concept. Such system is the contents of the concept (its connotation) and, at the same time, it determines its scope and semantic reference (denotation). It follows that each proposition is identical with some system of other propositions, like in arithmetics where numbers are identical with systems of other numbers (e.g. $2 = 8/4$). Hence comes an essential property of knowledge in which each concept and each proposition are linked with the other elements in an "avalanche" way. The system of propositions which are identical with a given proposition or with a given concept, forms the assumptions of the semantics of that proposition or of that concept.

There are two basic types of propositions, i.e. descriptive (e.g. "It's raining today") and evaluative (e.g. "It's fine weather today"). While reference of a descriptive proposition is a certain state of affairs, evaluative propositions assign values to the states of affairs. Values are either aims of human behaviour or states of affairs which are connected with the aims and which serve as the means and conditions of their achievement within the available human knowledge.

Propositions are either quantified or unquantified (e.g. "All people are envious"; "Some people are envious"; "John is envious").

A major difference between the present approach and many others is that semantic reference is not assumed to be a representation, a mirror image or an approximation of the objective reality, though I do not claim that such assumptions are false either. I believe, instead, that no hypothesis as to the relation between human knowledge and the objective world can be proved on empirical grounds,[1] and that scientific theories do not require the acceptance of such hypotheses. A choice of one hypothesis over another may be essential for human motivation, in a similar way as, for instance, believing in external life. But like in the latter question, science does not support any possible interpretation of epistemological status of knowledge. The principle of explaining empirical facts without referring to epistemological realism, but without negating it either, will be called the methodological norm of epistemological or in short, the assumption of epistemological neutralism.

The classical theory of truth, i.e. epistemological realism, implies useful criteria of typology of propositions. Thus there are propositions which are false, true, doubtful, plausible, etc. They form a degree scale of assertion of human judgements.[2] It seems that the continuum can also be upheld within epistemological neutralism. The classification would depend on the infallibility criterion (infallibility in a pragmatic not deductive sense), from the point of view of the effective application of the accepted values, as they are conceived by the subject on the basis of his knowledge. The criterion seems to be the explication of the empirically accessible contents of the common sense concept of truth. Thus "Dwarfs live in forests" is considered false by most adults, which means that anyone applying the

1. It was J. Kmita who noticed that assumptions of empirical realism cannot be proved empirically.

2. For an interesting discussion of the problem from the point of view of sociology of knowledge, see (Ziółkowski 1986).

given set of values disregards the conditions referred to by the above proposition. "There is after life" is considered true if the subject acknowledges the state of affairs denoted by the proposition and takes it into account in his endeavours. Doubts which may accompany the acceptance of the latter proposition will involve uncertainty as to the desired effectiveness of achieving one's aims.

I assume that a certain amount of changes that every human being brings about to the world, is dependent on his knowledge. The changes which concern the physical world can be called acts of behaviour, those which involve the state of knowledge of the individual who causes them are psychological actions and processes. All changes dependent on the subject's knowledge are actions. In this sense digestion, for instance, is not an action, but turning a key in a lock, is. Accordingly, I will call all psychological processes of an individual his psyche, and his knowledge — his personality.

Psychological processes consist in forming by the subject new propositions which may be modifications or refutations of the older ones. When descriptive propositions are involved, we shall call them cognitive processes, while evaluative propositions will be referred to — motivation processes.

An essential feature of the present hypothesis is the assumption of psychophysical dualism,[3] which finds support in J. Kmita (1985) where the author argues that an attempt to identify propositions with states of affairs, leads to semantic antinomy and logical contradiction. Upholding the identity inevitably involves mixing the object language with the metalanguage. It follows that there is no neurophysiological theory which would be capable of defining knowledge (even more so — psychological processes) within its conceptual framework. Accordingly, psychology as well as any other branch of humanities, must be relatively independent of neurophysiology.

The present approach differs significantly from a common practice prevailing in modern theories of cognition and motivation in which both neurophysiological and non-neurophysiological concepts are used on a par (in particular, concepts which characterize individual knowledge). Such theories tacitly assume that future developments of neurophysiology will eventually allow to define the latter concepts within a neurophysio-

---

3. Kmita's approach to the mind-body problem and its dualistic consequences, were discussed in (Zamiara 1983). The hypothesis of dualism is by no means unpopular today. Among its proponents are, for instance, J. Piaget (1953, p. 145) as well as K.R. Popper and E.C. Eccless (1977).

logical framework.[4] Such an approach prevails in theories of perception, memory, and motivation. As was mentioned above, it involves logical contradiction.

It goes without saying that my hypothesis by no means discards obvious interdependencies between psychological and neurophysiological processes. The inborn human nervous system, biological processes of maturation and ageing, physiological transformations (e.g. pathological) which affect the nervous system, they all exert an influence on psychological processes, and the influence should be carefully studied. On the other hand, the psychological processes affect various physiological processes, among them the neurophysiological ones. Some of the relevant interdependencies will be mentioned further in the paper.

2. First Order Cognitive Processes

The basic cognitive process — henceforth called first order cognitive process — consists in forming by the subject unquantified propositions which fulfil the following conditions:

First, they denote situations of which the subject, as far as he can judge, is or was a participant.

Second, they are usually accepted with the highest degree of assertion.

They are judgments referring the subject's present or to his past situations. The former will be called perceptual propositions, the latter — remembrance or memory propositions (remembrances). The cognitive processes and acts whose result is a perceptual proposition is perception (perceptual acts), and the cognitive processes and acts which bring about remembrances are memory processes (memory acts).

A necessary condition of perceptual propositions which refer to the outside world (within the assumed semantics) is that the subject perceives some concrete physical stimuli. It turns out that, when the stimuli or their parts are recorded and/or transmitted (by means of technical devices), the unquantified propositions which are formed on their basis can be quite similar to the propositions formed on the basis of the immediate stimuli. Often however, forming such a proposition requires an additional quantum of knowledge which is unnecessary in acts of immediate

4. This is the view held not only by psychologists. Thus, C. Lévi-Strauss expects that binary structures of mind which he studies, will be described by neurophysiology. The list of psychologists who are adherents to this conception, would certainly be long. One can mention here Z. Freud (1975, p. 159) and many contemporary scholars, e.g. J.S. Bruner (1978, pp. 64-69), who is usually taken to be a leading cognitivist. On this and other questions of cognitivism, in particular on its heterogeneous character, see (Zamiara 1985).

perception. This is a way of the subject's acquiring of information about the events in which he, in his opinion, does not take part. It should be added that the propositions referring to the situations in which the subject does not participate in person, are normally accepted with a lesser degree of assertion than propositions of immediate perception. I will return to the problem while discussing inferences as cognitive processes.

It is worth noticing that stimulus reception, which is indispensable in some acts of perception, is commonly interpreted in a different manner. Namely, it is assumed that stimuli "transmit" information about the objective world. It is an erroneous view since it implies the antinomous assumption of the identity between a certain event and a proposition (a piece of information about the world). Another view that physical stimuli determine specific images of the world is also implausible. Studies in history of science (in particular, Kuhn 1968; Feyerabend 1975) confirm that acts of perceiving the world by many generations, may stop being what they used to be, due to scientific reinterpretation. What in fact undergoes change, are semantic assumptions of those perceptual propositions. Thus, it is not physical stimuli that determine semantic reference of the subject's perception, but his acknowledged semantic assumptions. To pursue the point further, I should comment on the relation between perceptual propositions and their semantic assumptions.

As mentioned above, propositions consist of concepts. There are two types of concepts which play a major part, individual and predicative. The semantic reference of an individual concept is an individual object. From the syntactic point of view, it is either proper name (e.g. Poland) or a definite description (e.g. the capital of Poland). A predicative concept of first degree denotes either a set of individual objects or a relation (at least binary) between individual objects; higher order predicative concepts denote sets and relations of higher order (sets of sets, set relations, relations of relations). Predicative concepts are expressed by terms which belong to the syntactic category of predicate, (e.g. x is swimming, x is taller than y). As was mentioned above, such perceptual propositions are unquantified. It means that their constituents are always individual concepts and first order predicative concepts. Unlike quantified propositions, they do not contain higher order predicates.

We should note that the assumptions of the semantics of individual concepts will be unquantified propositions, whereas the semantics of predicative concepts of both first and higher degrees, will always entail the assumptions that are quantified propositions. A definition of any individual term or predicate will prove the point.

Let us call — following a common practice — the set of unquantified propositions which are accepted by the subject — his concrete or specific knowledge, and the set of quantified propositions — his abstract or general knowledge.

It is evident that concrete knowledge is always related to general knowledge by means of its semantic assumptions. The relation is two-fold: first, it is direct, since general knowledge comprises the assumptions of the semantics of predicative concepts which belong to concrete knowledge; second, it is indirect, because the semantic assumptions of individual concepts involve predicative concepts whose semantic assumptions belong to general knowledge.

As follows from the above, perceptual propositions are closely related to general knowledge which is a necessary condition for them to occur. Moreover, they add to concrete knowledge, becoming its new elements. They refer to new individual objects which become elements of new sets, or are assigned the previously existed relations. In the latter case, their novelty depends on the fact that relevant classifications have not been recognized earlier by the subject.

In each case a perceptual proposition is innovative with respect to the subject's concrete knowledge, and conservative vis-à-vis his general knowledge. In everyday life, in which common sense knowledge plays a major role, this is an exceptional situation and it is usually received as something out of the ordinary, as for instance, a miracle or an ex-traterrestial surprise visit. I cannot go deeper into the question, but it is worth mentioning that such situations are of great significance for scientific perception and knowledge. I mean here, first of all, results of laboratory experiments which are conducted with an intention to control empirically the assumed knowledge. Empirical verification is meant to show either consistency or inconsistency between the general knowledge and perceptual propositions. The inconsistency takes place when an individual object becomes an element of a set to which it cannot belong on the basis of the assumed general knowledge, because it is an element of some other set. It may also occur due to such relation assignment which contradicts one's general knowledge. Consider the following example: If a physician recorded a patient's death and then saw the decreased rise from bed, that would be an instance of perception contradictory with the doctors' general knowledge. The semantics of the predicative concept "has died" entails that if x is died, then among other things, all x's muscules and his motor processes have ceased functioning, which would make him unable to move, therefore it cannot be the case that for the individual object x both, x has died and x is moving, are true. One cannot belong to the set of the dead and to the set of those who are rising from bed, at the same time. As the example shows, even those perceptual propositions which contradict one's general knowledge, are very much dependent on it.

This is because only some of one's semantic assumptions can be violated by a given perceptual proposition, others must be sustained. Otherwise, as was already mentioned above, perception would not be possible at all. Total independence from semantic assumptions is a fiction, of which even philosophers seem to be nowadays aware.

Everything that has been said about the relations between perceptual propositions and their semantic assumptions, applies to the relations between remembrance propositions and their semantics.

3. Second Order Cognitive Processes

The outlined theory of perception and memory leads to one more conclusion. If the doctor has recorded the patient's death, he is able to predict, in agreement with his general knowledge, a number of other events, such as, that after some time the body's temperature will fall, and that physiological processes will bring about death of brain cells. He may also hope that the autopsy will enable to perceive the results of the anomalies.

General knowledge, by defining relations between various types of phenomena (sets of sets, relations of relations, etc.), together with concrete knowledge which comes from perceptual acts and/or remembrances, provide premises for inferences. By inferences I mean here only those propositions which belong to concrete knowledge and are neither perceptual propositions nor remembrances.

For the inferences referring to the future, we shall use the commonly accepted term predictions. Many of the subject's predictions are likely to find confirmation in his future acts of perception.

The subject's forming of the inferences which fulfil the above conditions, will be called second order cognitive process.

Perceptual propositions and remembrances differ from concrete inferences, first of all, in a degree of subjective assertion.

In the light of the subject's beliefs, inferring is a way of acquiring knowledge in one of the following situations: 1) which takes place at present but the subject is not a direct participant, 2) which will occur in the future, 3) which took place in the past but the subject was not personally involved.

4. Third Order Cognitive Processes

I will discuss now cognitive processes of the third order. I mean by them acts of forming by the subject general propositions which sometimes can imply constructing of new semantic assumptions. They are either assumptions of the semantics of perception and memory, or they are premises of inferences (not necessarily the influences which are confirmed by an act of perception or remembrance). Like the above discussed perceptual propositions, the new general propositions may be related to other general statements in one of two ways. First, most often, they are logically consistent with the remaining statements. Second, they may logically contradict (exclude) the previous judgements. In either case we shall concentrate on agreement/disagreement of a proposition with its semantic assumptions. Thus, when it was first formed, the quoted below proposition refuted some of the assumptions of its underlying semantics. "The velocity of light in vacuum is constant, i.e. independent of its source." The statement was in disagreement with the semantic assumptions of "light", according to which the term denoted a kind of wave of a substance called "ether". It has come to be consistent only with the new semantic assumptions underlying the special relativity theory which falsified the hypothesis of ether.

It often happens that the general propositions which contradict certain semantic assumptions, become assumptions of the semantics underlying the perceptual propositions which have also been in disagreement with certain elements of general knowledge. As seen from the above, forming new semantic assumptions on the basis of their inconsistency with some of the old ones, may accompany the process of refuting the latter. Thanks to such modifications, it is possible to obtain a higher degree of logical consistency, which is extremely important if we aim at a psychological analysis of scientific research. It can be easily proved that the described procedure is undertaken in order to achieve logical consistence within the knowledge which would enable effective predications, i.e. such predications which will be confirmed by future acts of perception. In this light, such scientific activities as defining, classifying and explaining, are various manners of reconstructing of the accepted knowledge, and possibly of constructing new knowledge which comes from modifications of the old one. The latter case takes place when deductive logic does not allow to bridge the gap between the newly modified knowledge and the previously accepted one, which seems to be a major topic in modern philosophy of science.

Entirely different motivation will underlie such third order cognitive processes as reflections of philosophical, theological and religious character, on which, however, I shall not elaborate here.

5. Fiction

The cognitive processes which have been studied so far, have all a common feature, namely, the propositions which are their output are treated by the subject with a positive degree of assertion. As was mentioned, this fact should be interpreted as the subject's acceptance of such propositions as effective means (of a higher or lesser degree) to achieve his intended aims. However, the subject can also construe propositions which do not serve the purpose of effective actions but fulfil other aims. Without going deeper into the contents of the latter aims, we may note that artistic fiction and entertainment literature have this property. In the worlds of artistic fiction, in story-telling as well as in jokes spread from mouth to mouth, characters and events are usually fictitious. Fiction is a function of one of the following properties.

(1) Fictitious propositions contradict some of semiotic assumptions underlying non-fictitious statements, or

(2) Fictitious propositions, though they are consistent with the semantics of the non-fictitious ones, are neither perceptual propositions nor remembrances nor inferences nor premises for inference.

We can make use of (2) while discussing the so-called realistic fiction, the concept which comes from theoretical literary studies. A separate issue is constituted by metaphoric propositions, which are normally expressed by sentences of type (1), though they are not fictitious statements. Metaphorization, as a relatively independent type of psychological processing, deserves an extensive study of its own, but for lack of space I shall not deal with it in the present paper. (For more information, see Ozdowski 1984, where semantic and pragmatic analyses of metaphor are presented in connection with P. Ricoeur's theory of symbols).

Thus, fiction is construing fictitious propositions of both, general and concrete character. But fiction can also consist of perceptual illusions and hallucinations, i.e. either of propositions whose fictitious character is confirmed by the subject's later psychological processes, or of propositions which are considered fictitious in the eyes of others. The former comprise dreams and hallucinations caused by hunger or sensory deprivation, while the hallucinations which are the result of illness belong rather to the latter group.

6. Introspection, Extraspection, Understanding

From the semantic point of view, one can distinguish two types of knowledge. Knowledge of the first type refers to the subject's psychological states and processes, his internal world unavailable to anyone else except him. This is introspective knowledge. Knowledge of the second type refers to the outer world which is shared by other subjects. We shall call it extraspective knowledge. Following our earlier claims, we should apply the principle of epistemological neutralism to all types of knowledge. Accordingly, we must state that there are no empirical grounds to hold the view that extraspective knowledge mirrors properties of the objective world. Similarly, there are no empirical arguments supporting the theory of correspondence between the scope of reference of introspective knowledge and the respective psychological processes. Moreover, it seems possible to compare a system of knowledge construed within the limits of a given psychological theory, with the introspective knowledge of a subject, or even, with the introspective knowledge shared by members of a social community. However, there are no evaluative criteria to measure a degree of distortion that the objective psychological reality undergoes when being articulated within either common knowledge, or within various psychological theories. This does not mean, of course, that there are no other criteria to evaluate those theories. But greater explanatory or predictive adequacy of a given system of knowledge can be treated as better approximation to the objective reality solely from the realistic point of view.

The reason I pay so much attention to the problem is that from the times of the classical psychology of introspection, or rather its philosophical implications, through the psychoanalytic criticism of introspection, up to the present-day (one can mention J. Piaget in this connection),[5] introspective cognition has invariably been interpreted in terms of realism, i.e. in terms of the distorted or true images of human psyche.

Following the traditional terminology, I will use the term consciousness for all psychological processes which lead to introspective knowledge. We have here, first of all, introspective perception, though due to psychoanalysis, we can also speak of introspective inference. Unconsciousness, in turn, will be used to stand for those psychic phenomena which are postulates of psychological theories but have no semantic referents in introspective knowledge.

It also seems plausible to assume that whenever a subject performs an act of perception, extraspection (or understanding) and introspection are simultaneously involved, though depending on his current aims, they are not of equal significance for him. In other words, his attention is drawn each time to one of these actions only. One can imagine that the subject is capable of developing metaintrospective knowledge as well. But keeping in mind the principle of epistemological neutralism, we should not claim in

5. Piaget's remarks on introspective cognition can be found in the work which he co-authored with E.W. Beth (Beth and Piaget 1966, pp. 199-202). See also K. Zamiara's discusion of Piaget in (Zamiara 1979, pp. 33-35).

scientific studies that our aim is to represent the essence of introspective knowledge at a higher semantic level.

Introspection is closely related to such subject's knowledge that is directed at understanding. Its propositions denote other people's psychological states and processes. At least some predicative concepts of these propositions belong to introspective knowledge as well. A major difference lies in that the specific judgements about other people's psychic states, are rather inferred than perceived. Hence they have a lower degree of assertion.

Understanding of inference draws from both, extraspective and introspective premises. The former may be, for instance, people's behaviour or various physiological symptoms, such as blushes, trembling voice, etc. In the latter case, we infer by analogy with our own and other familiar experiences. Next to the above psychic acts, a basis of the understanding knowledge is intersubjective communication, which is the topic of discussion in section 7 below.

7. Intersubjectivity

Epistemological neutralism rejects the opinion that in the ontogenetic development, the child's descriptive-evaluative knowledge is "inferred" from the objective reality. In other words, we claim that it cannot be learned. Therefore, it either must be inborn or is developed in the process of ontogenesis from a genetic code common to the human species. Many experiments conducted by J. Piaget and his school (see Piaget 1955) seem to confirm the latter hypothesis. They have shown that elementary concepts of the object, of ego, of time and space, of causal relation, and some others, develop in the process of ontogenesis and are absent from the child's mind in its first months. We cannot, however, rule out the possibility that some concepts are innate. Some ground for the hypothesis of the innate concepts is provided by the observed "visual preferences" in babies who are only a few days old (see Schaffer 1981). Hypotheses well grounded in further experimental studies, will certainly throw more light on these matters.[6] In addition, however, there emerges a question of intersubjectivity.

6. The following description may serve as an illustration of how cautious one must be in his judgements. Trying to prove his point, Piaget observed that a child of 5-6 months could not recover a small toy, for instance a box, with which he had earlier played. That was an argument for the psychologist that the child did not posses a concept of the object and that its existence for him was each time relativized to a concrete perceptual image. However, T. Bower proved that if we did not hide the toy, but switched off the lights instead, the child would immediately find the toy in the dark room, which could be

Only few elements of knowledge are universal for the human species. It is rather the case that the knowledge held by individuals living within one and the same community, is composed of components which do not differ very much from person to person. We shall call it intersubjective knowledge. It seems possible to construe an ideal model of such knowledge which is shared by a community.

In order to explain intersubjectivity of knowledge, we need not refer to the objective reality, which finds similar representation in each member of a community.

Suffice it to assume that each of the persons who have similar knowledge, will undertake similar psychological actions, provided circumstances be also similar for everybody. That is, that each of them construes propositions much like the ones formed by other members of his community.

The origin of knowledge in children is of much the same character thanks to the inborn equipment of the species. Any further unique developments of individual knowledge, depend on unique configurations of circumstances which every child encounters. To the extent that the circumstances are common, the individual systems of knowledge are similar to one another.

It is worth stressing, that though the circumstances have an influence upon propositions formed by a subject, the propositions themselves do not have to reveal any similarity to the respective circumstances.

Intersubjectivity in communication processes is of a special and very important character. In agreement with the principle of epistemological neutralism, I see it as follows. The participants of communication — in a simple act, individuals — undertake communicative actions whose results are communicative meta-propositions i.e. "x believes that he communicates p to y" and "y believes that x communicates r to him". The communication is effective if the proposition *that p* is identical or very much similar to *that r*. We may say then, that the scope or degree of intersubjective knowledge becomes larger. To be more exact, the results of the subject's psychological processes become intersubjective.

In conclusion, I would like to repeat the leading idea of the paper in a condensed form, adding to it a touch of exactness which seems expedient.

My intention was to present basic concepts of psychology of cognitive processes which would accord with the principle of epistemological

---

easily recorded with the help of ultrared rays. From this Bower concludes that the child is aware of the object existing outside his field of perception, but probably he does not know yet that one object can be placed inside another (see Bower 1977).

273

neutralism. The result is a conception of human being whose behaviour is determined by descriptive-evaluative knowledge. Unlike in other psychological theories, the outside objective situations are not treated as determinants of the subject's actions. They are considered, however, as referents of the subject's knowledge. Thus, they are objective vis-à-vis his knowledge. But their objectivity in the absolute, unrelativized sense cannot be provided. Hence, it does not make sense for psychology to treat them as objective. They influence the subject as long as they are components of his knowledge.

The S-R model, prevailing in psychology since its birth, as well as its variants in which all kinds of intermediate variables are introduced,[7] are thereby definitely rejected.

The defended view may be called radical cognitivism, where "radical" accounts for the rigorously observed principle of epistemological neutralism. Unlike many theories of cognitive psychology (e.g. Kelly 1955), however, I assign major significance to evaluative knowledge. Though motivation processes have not been covered in the present paper, I hope to have made it clear that no activity, including psychological acts, can be undertaken unless it is motivated by some evaluative proposition.

Translated by Nina Nowakowska

7. For lack of space, I cannot discuss the problem at length, but I want to emphasize that the model has dominated not only those branches of psychology of whose main, or even exclusive, interest are cognitive processes (introspectionism, cognitivism), but also those which concentrate on motivation processes (psychoanalysis, humanistic psychology).

REFERENCES

1. Beth, E., & Piaget, J. (1966). *Mathematical epistemology and psychology.* Dordrecht.
2. Bower, T.G.R. (1977). *A primer of infant development.* San Francisco.
3. Bruner, J.S. (1978). *Beyond the information given* (Polish translation). Warsaw.
4. Feyerabend, P.K. (1975). *Against method. Outline of anarchistic theory of knowledge.* London.
5. Freud, Z. (1975). "An outline of psychoanalysis". In Z. Freud. *Beyond the pleasure principle* (Polish translation). Warsaw.
6. Kelly, G.A. (1955). *The psychology of personal constructs.* New York.
7. Kmita, J. (1985). *Kultura i poznanie* [Culture and cognition]. Warsaw.
8. Kmita, J. (1986). "Scientism and anti-scientism". In P. Buczkowski & A. Klawiter (Eds.). *Theories of ideology and ideology of theories, Poznań Studies in the Philosophy of the Sciences and the Humanities* (pp. 69-105), vol. 9. Amsterdam: Rodopi.

9. Kuhn, T. (1968). *The structure of scientific revolution* (Polish translation). Warsaw.
10. Lévi-Strauss, C. (1962). *La pensée sauvage.* Paris.
11. Ozdowski, P. (1984). *Teoria kultury wobec hermeneutyki Ricoeura* [Theory of culture versus Ricoeur's hermeneutics]. Warsaw/Poznań.
12. Piaget, J. (1955). *The child's construction of reality.* London.
13. Piaget, J. (1953). *The problem of consciousness.* Princeton/New York.
14. Popper, K.R., & Eccles, J.C. (1977). *The self and its brain.* London/New York/Heidelberg.
15. Schaffer, H.R. (1981). *The growth of sociability* (Polish translation). Warsaw.
16. Zamiara, K. (1979). *Epistemologia genetyczna Piageta a społeczny rozwój nauki* [The genetic epistemology of J. Piaget and the social development of science]. Warsaw/Poznań.
17. Zamiara, K. (1985). "Problem metodologicznej specyfiki psychologii kognityvistycznej" [The problem of methodological specificity of cognitive psychology]. In K. Zamiara (Ed.). *Kultura i jej badanie. Studia z filozofii kultury* [On culture and culture research. Studies in philosophy of culture]. Warsaw.
18. Zamiara, K. (198). "In support of psycho-physical parallelism". In J. Brzeziński (Ed.). *Consciousness: methodological and psychological approaches, Poznań Studies in the Philosophy of the Sciences and the Humanities* (p. 94-108), vol. 8. Amsterdam: Rodopi.

Tadeusz Zgółka

STUDY OF LANGUAGE AS A FORM OF SYMBOLIC CULTURE: METHODOLOGICAL FOUNDATIONS

The present humanistic thought states at least several approaches to natural language study. Linguistic phenomena can be conceived in psychological terms (language viewed as a symptom of an individual's psychological activity), in sociological terms (language as a tool integrating or disintegrating social structures), logical (language as capable of expressing both true and false statements — referring to reality), philosophical, ethnographic or pedagogic terms etc. However language can be also viewed as one of the cultural phenomena characteristic of a given community. Thus language appears among other phenomena constituting "(...) the set of all forms of social consciousness present in the practice of this community".[1] Hence language becomes a form of social consciousness including instructions, norms and ideas supervising the social language practice.

Language, as a form of social consciousness, belongs to a specific group of cultural phenomena, i.e. to symbolic culture. In order to elucidate the classification of language as a part of symbolic culture, it is necessary to characterize the notion of the forms of social consciousness constituting the sphere of culture. Thus

(...) each of them — because it functions as a socio-subjective regulator of a given social practice — contains two types of presumptions: (1) normative presumptions, defining values — aims to be realized, (2) instructive presumptions stating that for the realization of a certain aim it is enought, it is necessary or both enought and necessary to proceed — considering the conditions — accordingly.[2]

So much for the forms of social consciousness in general, and now as far as the specific features of symbolic culture are concerned, they are described as follows:

A jar of jam or a pair of shoes can be consumed without any of the normative-instructive presumptions indispensable for their production; greeting gestures, linguistic utterances, theatrical performances and religious rituals — or their effects — cannot be consumed without respecting proper normative-instructive presumptions, even if attributed to their subjects by the consumers.[3]

1. J. Kmita, *O kulturze symbolicznej* (On symbolic culture), Warsaw 1982, p. 72.
2. J. Kmita, *Kultura i poznanie* (Culture and cognition), Warsaw 1985, p. 11.
3. Ibid., p. 31.

These assumptions require a comment. Characterizations of the essence of natural language — at least some of them — introduce a differentiation between the plane of linguistic competence and performance. The latter can be interpreted, especially by philosophers of culture, as special practice — here, as the social linguistic practice. The practice is functionally subordinated and supervised by the presumptions constituting the social linguistic consciousness (i.e. linguistic competence). Thus linguistic competence includes presumptions (social, more than individual; generally accepted) supervising social language practice (linguistic performance). The regulation of linguistic practice takes place within linguistic competence which decides whether, e.g. a sequence of sounds forms an utterance in a given language or not. It can be, in particular, the question of whether it is an interrogative sentence.

On the level of competence, communication messages (not exclusively — as it will be explained below) are ascribed to particular linguistic utterances. Finally, competence consists of rules (instructive presumptions) able to appoint the proper linguistic means for the realization of definite communication tasks (e.g. how to construct an interrogative sentence within a given language). The latter are, among others, grammatical rules.

For a student of symbolic culture language provides a very convenient illustration as, on this example, all the properties — common to all other phenomena — can be easily and convincingly demonstrated. However, in many respects, language is a peculiar manifestation of symbolic culture. It is often believed that it occupies a privilidged position among such other forms as magic, religion, customs, art or science.

> The content of each culture — claims E. Sapir — can be expressed by its language and there is no linguistic material — considering both content and form — which for the users of this language would not symbolize real meaning, independently of the opinions expressed by the representatives of other cultures.[4]

Hence, language becomes a cultural form capable of concentrating all other components, using each of them, used by the majority either as an instrument (e.g. when linguistic expressions are formed into magic incantations) or material (e.g. in literature conceived as a certain form of art, i.e. artistic culture). This provides the grounds for ascribing language a specific cultural function. Its knowledge and use may determine participation in many other cultural forms. One cannot participate in most forms without conforming to the rules of the language they require. As a rule,

---

4. E. Sapir, *Kultura, język, osobowość* (Polish translation of E. Sapir, *Selected writtings in language, culture and personality*), Warsaw 1978, pp. 37-38.

even a passive, purely receptive participation in the above-mentioned extralinguistic cultural forms is impossible.

The non-professional character emerges as a second specific feature differing language from other cultural forms. It refers to the classification of language according to the two varieties proposed by the philosophy of culture: professional and non-professional. Simply, the non-professional character of linguistic communication consists in the fact that, in its process, no specialist and disjunctive sets, categories of senders or receivers can be differentiated.

In principle, this subdivision is possible within artistic culture as it implies a specialist group of artists-creators (treated as senders) of literary works and works of art, and their receivers — "consumers". This subdivision — as already mentioned — is not valid for the sphere of social linguistic practice for the parts of senders and receivers of particular utterances are played, interchangeably, by all individuals — members of a definite linguistic community.

Evidently, the difference between common linguistic communication and artistic culture is partly based on passive/active participation in social practice as present in both cultural forms. So far as participation in artistic culture is concerned (for the purpose of clarity folk culture must be excluded from the present study; it would demand a separate treatment), for the majority, it is limited to passive reception while a user of language becomes — *promiscue* — now a creator of utterances, now a receiver-interpreter.

Full participation of particular individuals in the social linguistic practice is evidently conditioned by the degree of knowledge and command of language varieties, forms and types. It may happen that the command of only some models of linguistic utterance limits, beforehand, the individual's participation in linguistic communication.

Let us refer to the rather illuminating example concerning the two fundamental models of language functioning in the majority of contemporary natural languages, i.e. the spoken and the written mode, differentiated by the method of constructing and the channel of transmitting language utterances. Historically, the vocal form usually precedes the graphic one. Similarly, in ontogenetic terms, the spoken form is naturally mastered by its users. Consequently, it implies that a natural nonpathological individual development of the *homo sapiens* representatives includes also the ability to use the spoken variety language. On the other hand, the graphic representation of linguistic utterances is learn later, often laboriously in a more or less organized, systematic manner.

However, there was a time (in some societies even nowadays) that the ability to write and read was an elitist skill, and only the privileged could master it. There were even professional *scribes,* i.e. clerks specialized in the use of written language. Evidently, when considered in this context, the non-professional character of social language practice, immediately provokes doubts. Although a *scribe* does not monopolize language use in general, his role is similar to that of a writter or, sometimes, of a linguist. A writer using a certain mode of language, called the artistic mode (sometimes poetic), becomes a non-professional sender of specific language messages. A linguist, apart from other tasks, functions as a codifier of certain rules controlling language use. Analogically, a *scribe* is a specialist in the use and codification of the written variety of language. Thus he also becomes a professional.

It seems that within this context there appear the sources of a certain type of written language magic. The belief in the magic power of writting is reflected in the Latin saying *verba volant, scripta manent.* Writting is considered as a dangerously durable form of linguistic utterance. Here, let us recall the biblical scene when Jesus saves a harlot from being stoned. Her would-be murderers are dispersed by Jesus' simple act of writing thir foul deeds (sins — in religious terms) on sand. Their sins were not only revealed but, what is worse and more dangerous, preserved in writing. Another analogous literary scene appears in *Konopielka* by E. Redliński:

> I can see the boy is afraid that he appeared poorly in my writing. Well, all right, all right — I comfort him. Let's write: Ziutek is a good boy, obedient, hardworking ... but gready! He'd eat everything! — Oh, no, no! I'm not gready, I'm not! — I can see he is afraid. Let him fear a bit, it will make him good. But he is nearly crying. Well, well how much afraid he is of the written.[5]

Magic beliefs and fears concerning language are certainly rooted in illiteracy, i.e. a rather common situation of language used in its spoken form exclusively. The written version, limited to professional, connected with either political or spiritual power (magi, wizards, wise men, priests, etc.) was automatically related to sanctions on the part of either earthly power or its supernatural principals. Hence, both the fear and belief in the magic power of writting.

The latter occurs even nowadays and in societies hardly defined as primitive. It is also reflected in opinions and certain ways of reasoning: "This is certain (was or will be) because it was written (in a book, newspaper, etc.)". Another example: "It cannot be a fantasy; I saw it written in a book". This type of reasoning emphasizes the distance between what was heard and what was written or read. This distance is motivated by a conviction depreciating the value of what is said (as anybody can say

---

5. E. Redliński, *Konopielka* (in Polish), Warsaw 1973, pp. 111-112.

anything) as opposed to what is written (the ability to write, genetically, being ascribed to the privileged, chosen professionals).

The non-professional character of social language practice, emerges as less clear and evident than it might appear at first sight. There are ways of using language, analogous to the above quoted example of the written variety, especially, the artistic one, which — particularly in historical terms — can be considered as skills mastered only by professionals.

At present let us resume the problem of the generally available uses of language, i.e. those having a seemingly unquestionable non-professional character. Simultaneously, attention should be focused on the mode of functioning of language, especially, on the position of utterances formulated in culture. B. Malinowski, one of the outstanding researchers of culture provides a proper opening:

> (...) the primary and authentic function of language is its basically pragmatic character, (...) it is a behaviour, an indispensable element of harmonious human activity. On the contrary: to consider language as a means of forming or expressing thoughts equals the assumption of a most one-sided viewpoint, choosing a more detached and specific function.[6]

Apparently, this statement contains a reversed perspective in viewing language. The most widely acknowledged opinion, propagated mainly by linguists, relies mainly on the belief that the essence of language is to communicate thoughts, opinions, statements, etc. The frequently occurring aphorism states that language — to be more specific — a linguistic utterance provides the guise for those thoughts. Due to this verbal guise, exchange of information, thoughts and ideas between various individuals using the same language is rendered possible.

However, as it was also observed by B. Malinowski, for a long time, other pragmatic aspects of linguistic communication have been recognized. Firstly, it was observed that linguistic communication does not occur as isolated from its external circumstances. If communication is realized during the so-called speech act, it is usually accompanied by a mimic, gestural context and situational arrangement consisting of all the objects present during the act of speech. The extra-communicational aspects of the speech act proved the importance of these conditions.

Let us refer to a simple example. A speaker formulates a linguistic utterance in the form of a question. The interrogative character of the statement is signalled by purely linguistic means. It can be the presence of an interrogative particle, a reversed word order (as opposed to the indicative mood) or the interrogative intonation of the question. However, let us assume that the sender intends to formulate the so-called rhetorical

6. A.K. Paluch, *Malinowski* (in Polish), Warsaw 1983, p. 269.

question — flavoured with pathos, irony, etc. These qualities cannot be expressed by purely linguistic means. Nevertheless a linguistic utterance can be supplemented by appropriate mimicry (e.g. a wink) or gestures (tapping one's forehead). From the point of view of the sender's intentions information passed due to mimic — gestural means (to impose a rhetorical character) can be equally, or even more, important than information passed *via* linguistic channels. It is also an opportunity to notice the subjection of particular gestural-mimic arrangements to definite cultural conventions which, analogically to linguistic rules, are non-professional.

Thus the above example illustrates a quality of speech acts, its multi-channel character. Communication during speech acts, as already suggested, has a multi-channel character, i.e. apart from the articulatory-auditory channel there is the visual one (connected with gestures and mimicry) and, perhaps, other elements.

A further feature of speech acts is their multi-functional character, i.e. the multifunctional quality of the transmitted linguistic utterances. As already mentioned, the sole function of most (though not of all) linguistic utterances is communication. However, it has been known, for long, that not the only one. There are such functions as the poetic or the expressive one. The recent twenty five years have revealed the existence of a whole variety:

> Functions of speech acts vary depending on their effects: they can annoy, flatter, excite, persuade, entertain, offend, embarrass, etc. For example, the staement: "I like your dress very much" may flatter an elegant lady to whom it is addressed, may embarrass a naked girl met on a remote beach, offend or annoy the receiver dressed — in her opinion — is something improper.[7]

Hence the theory of speech acts distinguishes among three basic aspects called locution, illocution and perlocution. The first refers, essentially, to the content of linguistic utterance. Such a content is simply expressed by means of words. Whether the words are arranged to inform somebody, to give orders, to ask for something, etc., is considered within illocution. It is worth adding that illocution varies (e.g. from a polite "would you mind my interrupting you?" — which, contrary to linguistic illusions — is not a real question — to a rude "Shut up!"). Perlocution takes care of what the sender — sometimes consciously, sometimes *nolens volens* – achieves *via* a speech act, due to the realized linguistic utterance. The effect can be the

7. R.A. Kneblewski, "Komunikacja werbalna i niewerbalna w aspekcie filozoficz-nym. Rozważania metodologiczne w kierunku teorii aktów komunikowania" (The philosophical aspects of the verbal and non-verbal communication. Methodological considerations toward communication theory), in: (Ed.) A. Schaff, *Zagadnienia socjo- i psycholingwistyki* (The problems of socio- and psycholinguistics), Wrocław 1980, pp. 243-244.

embarrassment of a politely interrupted interlocutor or offence on the part of somebody told to shut up.

As it is easily observed the problem of locution, illocution, and perlocution is far removed from pure linguistics in the traditional sense of the term. It rather enters the realm of customs. Evidently, it can be stated that traditional linguistics concentrates on locutionary aspects of linguistic utterances which would result in a limited reflection on language in society, and especially, as related to culture. Emphasis on the functioning of language as related to speech acts points to its presence in non-professional culture, i.e. in its forms and varieties characterized by a continuous exchange of sender-receiver positions, of the asking and the asked, offending and offended.

The investigation of speech acts gave rise both to the problem of linguistic utterances, which are not addressed to any receiver, and to the fascinating though not new idea of creating things by means of words. The latter suggestion appears in the fundamental, for the above problem, monography by J.L. Austin: *How to do things with words*.[8] "Doing" things with words, creating through the power of language is not a new idea. It is one of the dreams cherished by humanity and as old as human language itself or even older than humanity if one considers St. John's Gospel in which the act of creation originates in the word: "Before the world was created, the Word already existed; (...) Through him God made all things; not one thing in all creation was made without him". Thus the becoming of the world requires the word. To create means to name. Let us still quote from *Genesis*: "Then said God: Let the light be. And the light was created". It is a classical example of a religious belief in the creative power of word. Analogous views on the creative power of word can be found in the sphere of magic.

However, these cases are not relevant to the authors of performative theories (performative utterances). "Things" created by the causative power of a word are not physical beings. They are "social facts" rather, intentional "things" existing in the consciousness — either individual or intra-individual. It is easy to notice that the utterance "I give you the name of John" is not directed to the baptized one. What is more, it does not address an inanimate object, such as a newly launched and christened ship. More doubts arise around the formulation: "I take you for my wife". This formulation is not so much a message, addressed to *ad hoc tempore* wife, as a public declaration in the presence of definite people or — in terms of religious ritual — "in the presence of God". A "private" utterance of these words, not in the presence of witnesses and clerks, need not contribute to the creation of "anything", i.e. marriage as a religious or lawful institution. A similarily performative character have sentences beginning with: "I promise", "I challenge you", etc. "Things" created by these phrases are

282

contracts, obligations, social institutions, etc.

However, it is necessary to observe a difference between performative utterances and their previously considered illocutional and perlocutional aspects. A peculiar feature of performatives is the minimal function of a receiver of these language formulae. In extreme cases the receiver is redundant. In the above cases we mentioned the role of a "witness" watching the speech act. Nevertheless, it is as difficult to accept the newly launched ship as a "receiver" as to identify the roles of receiver and "witness". Sometimes, however, a receiver is indispensable; marriage provides the example. Neither the consciousness nor the psychological state of a receiver is important. Even if the partner is not very enthusiastic about marriage vows — what is more — even if she feels disgust or is terrified, the marriage will be contracted. The speech act accompanied by the proper rituals is treated as "Rise!", i.e. a peculiar creation through language.

Thus the aim of uttering formulae containing performative phrases is not to evoke particular states of consciousness or to form ideas in the receiver's psyche. Their function is to create definite facts in other spheres of culture, such as customs, religion, political and legal culture, morality, etc.

The above quoted examples, derived from the theory of speech acts and reflections on performative utterances, mainly emphasized the use of linguistic utterances which aim is not communication. Consequently, the commonly accepted view that linguistic utterances are to convey information describing a somehow represented extralinguistic reality only, have to be verified. Performative utterances do not represent, but create reality.

However, it is not this single viewpoint that reveals this creative aspect of language, its causative-creative power. Let us consider the three following examples of language utterances as illustrating their primary feature, the creative power. Though each of the examples would suffice for the subject of a separate and detailed study, our analysis will be limited to the main points in order to follow the lines of the main problem in the present study.

The first of the examples is the developing concept, i.e. the Sapir-Whorf hypothesis, otherwise called the hypothesis of linguistic relativism. It maintains the existence of a close relationship between language, defined in terms of its ethnological peculiarities, and the collective, cultural view of the world, characteristic of the society using the language. Generally, it is emphasized that this relativity refers to semantically marked language segments only, i.e. basically to the lexico-semantic repertory as well as to some morphological categories (such as the various inflective types of tenses). This hypothesis resulted in a variety of proliferations providing both radical (as its structural echo claiming that we do not speek a language but it speaks through us) and "soft" interpretations (limited to the illustration of ethnic differences by lexical and grammatical examples).

Some radical interpretations of the relativistic hypothesis suggest that language is a tool creating the whole cultural reality, which contains only those phenomene, categories, features, etc., that can be named by the language.

The second example of the creative power of language to be considered here relies on a purely grammatical concept of "creativity". It occurs, especially, in certain formal grammatical constructions following artificial grammars constructed for the purpose of formalized languages, on the grounds of logic syntax. Natural languages are creative due to their grammars having a certain, even infinite, "generative power", i.e. formally there is a potentially infinite set of sentences: properly, correctly formulated formulae. However they are also creative owing to the possibility of constructing sentences (acceptable within the frames of the obligatory grammatical rules and lexical repertory) which, so far, have never been uttered. Evidently, this is of consequence to the cognitive power of language mentioned in the previous example.

The third example refers to particular non-communicational functions ascribed in traditional language communication schemes to linguistic utterances, e.g. the poetic function. R. Jakobson defined it as "expectation of message only". From this angle one considers utterances in which the message is less important than the way they are constructed, the words they use and put upon and of how their words sound. Thus the hierarchy of functions is restricted, or even reversed: the poetic function substitutes or even outpaces communication. Now, mainly the appearance of (aesthetic) values contributes to the creative aspect of language. It is a procedure analogous to all other arts in which a work bestowed with artistic, aesthetic values emerges from material.

The reversal of the hierarchy of linguistic utterances — their functions — can be achieved differently though, again, referring to aesthetic values, sometimes called supra-aesthetic. Although poetic function is still related to message itself, semantic values are at least secondary. Aesthetic concepts following B. Croce tend to overestimate another function, i.e. the expressive one. Here language becomes a means of expression — exteriorization of the unique, creative "inside", psyche, self — rather than a means of communication between its participants. Consequently, for this approach to language and communication the efficiency of speech acts becomes less important. They are treated instrumentally, almost as means conveying expression. Such valuating categories as "beauty", "originality" and "uniqueness" become much more important. Grammatical requirements of correctness, agreement with intersubjective, compulsory principles becomes a burden, a troublesome demand limitting the creative, original linguistic constructions. And thus we arrived at the conclusions concerning the non-professional character of language. As already mentioned, the study refers to the dichotomy of the professional and non-professional in culture. Hence art, statically and disregarding its genetic origins, is an example of the former while customs of the latter. Language, as the present study attempted to demonstrate, provides a complex problem because in certain situations it is undoubtedly a form of non-professional culture. What obscures the image is the fact that communication between people is not the sole function realized by linguistic utterances. Due to the illocutional and perlocutional effects we enter the sphere of customs: language can offend, insult or flatter. This is still within the non-professional cultural sphere. However, considering the possibility of using language as literary material, we enter the sphere of art, i.e. professional culture, with its clear division into senders and receivers. The same refers to substantial numbers of performative utterances, especially those supervised by legal, political and religious rules (certain performative formulae are valid only when uttered by priests or clerks).

Evidently, the above summarized complications result from the characteristic omnipresence of language in culture as well as from its being a separate, peculiar form of symbolic culture. The dependence is mutual. The transposition of other forms of social consciousness into the linguistic sphere relies mainly on an "interference" of the latter into the hierarchy of aims defined by the normative element.

It can be stated that language viewed as isolated and autonomous becomes a form of symbolic culture with the purpose of communication at the top of the hierarchy. However, the hierarchy can be changed, reversed — when affected by normative components regulating social practice and related to other forms of social consciousness. Thus it may occur that the choice of aims realized *via* linguistic utterances may depend on customs, religion, magic, law, art, etc. Here, linguistic constructions are treated instrumentally as means, or one of them, of realizing such activities as marriage, conjuring up of good weather or the expelling of illness. Though an elementary grammatical and orthoepic correctness is also demand, its aims is not communication limited to linguistic semantics.

It is virtually impossible to imagine a sphere of culture, considering its characteristically social practice, as capable of functioning without language. If that is true, the classification of languages as non-professional form of symbolic culture depends on whether it appears as either the original means of communication or as literary material, i.e. an element of custom or religion. It is possible to classify the uses of language on a "foreign" ground, regarding the sphere entered by language, i.e. professional or non-professional culture.

Translated by Ewa Kębłowska-Ławniczak

Grzegorz Banaszak

CONTEMPORARY MUSICAL CONSCIOUSNESS IN THE PERSPECTIVE OF THE SOCIO-PRAGMATIC THEORY OF CULTURE

The sphere of actions connected with the creation and reception of music can be regarded as a kind of symbolic-cultural social practice.[1] This means that respecting a determined set of beliefs by participants of this practice is a necessary condition for the occurrance of effects belonging to the objective scope of its functioning. This set comprises first of all normative beliefs pointing out the aims of musical creation and directival beliefs establishing the ways of realization of these aims. They constitute together the scope of social consciousness that can be named musical culture or social musical consciousness. I will also use the abbreviated term "musical consciousness" in a sense synonymous with the former ones. The musical consciousness understood in this way constitutes the socio-objective regulator of musical practice determining the sense and form of musical production and enabling them to perform objective functions connected with needs addressed to musical practice by other domains of social life.

The aim of this paper is to characterize generally the contemporary musical consciousness. I will try to use the suggestions presented here to argue that reflection on music conducted on the basis of the assumed theory of culture offers a chance of solving certain traditional musicological problems and enables to constitute a cognitive perspective oriented at a complete and systematic investigation of phenomena belonging to the scope of musical culture.

1. The Variants of Social Musical Consciousness

Contemporary musical consciousness is a diversified domain. It comprises some types of states of affairs functioning as leading values which hardly could be reduced to a more general sense actualized within all manifestations of musical practice. These values often coexist in symbiosis as

---

1. I refer here to the observations of the socio-pragmatic theory of culture. Basic concepts and assumptions are contained in J. Kmita, *O kulturze symbolicznej* (On symbolic culture), Warsaw 1982.

relatively equally valuable components of musical sense understood in a complementary way. However, one of them is often given priority over the other ones, reducing them to an instrumental role or attributing them the status of a not very important side effect of the creative act. Therefore, the analysis of contemporary musical consciousness must take into consideration its different variants. Some of them, connected with traditionally understood music, were shaped within many centuries of its development, whereas other, produced in recent years, are connected with the "art of tone" understood so differently from the traditional one that it is controversial to attribute the name "musical" to the consciousness constituted by them.

First, I will try to characterize traditional variants of social musical consciousness starting with their simplest manifestations of which every one designates one specific type of value to be the sense.

2. Traditional Musical Consciousness

The first variant of the traditional musical consciousness, which could be called the communicative-correspondence musical consciousness, is connected with understanding music as a specific way of "talking about the world". According to it, the composer's aim is to communicate through musical means certain visions which are intended by their authors to constitute specific images of the world.[2]

Within the so-called programme music the realization of the communicative-correspondence sense is conducted similarly to the way used in traditional visual arts.[3] The representing structure consists in certain sequences of tones to which reference in the form of represented reality is attributed by analogy to the images of concrete extramusical phenomena present in objective experience. As opposed to works of fine art referring to visual characterizations, programme music compositions are based on audially perceivable similarities between appropriately interpreted sound structures and extramusical phenomena taken in the perspective of objective experience. Specific imitations of rain, the groans of dispair or the uproar of battle are some of the generally known examples of "musical

---

2. I limit myself only to a general characterization of the considered type of consciousness referring to the theoretical approach to artistic communication as it was presented by J. Kmita. Therefore, a closer analysis of the semantic-musical problems which constitute the source of basic musicological disputes has to be postponed.

3. An analysis of this sphere of artistic practice and the consciousness regulating it is contained in: W. Ławniczak, *O poznawaniu dzieła sztuki plastycznej* (On investigating a work of fine arts), Warsaw/Poznań 1983.

images" resembling concrete phenomena of the extramusical world. Insofar as this semantics functions in a nonconventionalized way (i.e. it assigns references to a sequence of tones in a nonautomatic manner requiring reflection to model these references) and also refers to worldview beliefs which give the presented phenomena a practically non-perceivable "metaphysical" dimension, a metaphorical stratum of musical composition is constituted that can be identified with the musically communicated vision of the world. These visions being the aim of programme music oscillate either in the symbolic and fantastic direction which is characteristic for the majority of programme compositions created within the romantic tradition, or in the objective and realistic direction that is typical for contemporary manifestations of the programme production.

The type of musical communication presented above is rather a peripheral phenomenon in the discussed sphere of artistic practice. Composers make use of it to a limited degree introducing elements called programme or illustrative ones into a work based on different principles of communication. When characterizing this different way of communication, let us first pay attention to the specific character of represented reality. It does not constitute an image of concrete phenomena that refers to the perspective of common experience, but it is a specifically musical reality — a world of sound constructs which on the basis of semantic rules are enriched with extrasound characteristics that are specific for extramusical states of affairs. When listening to music, one perceives a complex whole in which the crucial role is played by the system of references of appropriate sound structures interpreted semantically by referring to certain elements of objective or psychological experience. However, musical semantics makes use of experience in a rather peculiar way because it employs its selected elements by referring them to properties abstracted from the concrete. These properties are characterized by abstract concepts which can be identified with a complex system of judgements.[4] If a definite sound construction being an element of a musical representing structure satisfies some of these judgements, it may become by analogy a sign of appropriate characteristics. Musical semantics "situates" the images of these characteristics on the sound constructs that result from a specific transformation of the representative structure. It consists in omitting those qualities of the structure that are irrelevant for the intended form of represented musical reality. In other words, the sound objects constituting the representative stratum "enter" into the represented reality appropriately modified and modelled according to their usefulness

4. See J. Kmita, *Kultura i poznanie* (Culture and cognition), Warsaw 1985, pp. 64 ff.

as carriers of definite extrasound contents. This is the second and more important component of the represented reality. In the practice of musical perception these components merge into one musical reality.

The musical represented reality is treated within the communicative-correspondence type of consciousness only as a means enabling realization of the main aim which consists in communicating a specific vision of the world. This vision is achieved through neutralization of the concreteness of the represented reality by symbolic and metaphoric semantic inter-pretation. As in the case of non-programme music, the concretness of this reality consists in linking the extrasound characteristics with concrete sound constructs. Therefore, abstracting from the sound basis is the first step of metaphoric interpretation. The next steps may contain, if necessary, further transformation of the contents separated from the basis and connected with extrasound characteristics which would allow to give them a more general symbolic meaning. Besides, it would allow to enrich them with a "metaphysical dimension" obtained through reference to worldview beliefs that co-designate the considered characteristics. In this way, an abstract vision of the world unconnected with any concrete sphere of phenomena is created. It is often stated in such a sense that musical compositions contain specific visions of transitoriness, threat, dialectic nature of the world, etc. The recovering of links which allow to pass to the vision that is at least partially made concrete, permits obviously a whole class of possible interpretations. Therefore, one can say that musical communication is characterized by universality and ambiguity that are not met in traditionally representing works. The listeners to music who feel the need of getting this ambiguity under control, often refer to musically represented reality and render it similarly to interpretations used in programme music. This act is often effective as it enables grasping a general similarity between certain sound structures and some phenomena or processes from extramusical reality which is often consciously created by the composer. Additionally, the titles of compositions and the data concerning the context of their creation are usually used as interpretative hints. However, one can participate in musical culture consciously maintaining the universality and nondefiniteness of musical sense. Then, it is treated as an expression of contents defined often as archetypic, as an embodiment of the stable elements of consciousness that cannot be articulated but can only be the subject of recurring attempts at ap-proximation.

The above characterized communicative-correspondence perspective considers musical compositions as sets of specific images referring to the world of psychic life, and communication of the visions contained in these images is regarded to be the aim of musical activity. However, there is a tradition of thinking about music where its sense is regarded in categories of a particular kind of usefulness; the variant of social musical consciousness based on it can therefore be called a pragmatic musical consciousness. The core of this variant of consciousness comprises various states of affairs connected with the influence of music on the listeners, in particular the possibility of causing psychic reactions called aesthetic experiences. In such a case the primary aim of musical creativity is to build compositions which would yield experiences of particular kind resulting from contemplations of purely acoustic properties of the sound structure. More often, aesthetic experiences occur as a result of following a "musical story" constituted on the basis of semantic rules. However, the world of a musical composition built in such a way is consciously neutral as far as correspondence is concerned. In other words, it is not important as an image of extramusical world, but only as a specific musical "action" created with an intention of maximizing psychic experiences, mainly of an aesthetic nature. While working on a composition which should evoke such experiences from states of affairs that can be presented on the basis of musical semantics, a composer does not pay too much attention to the so-called relation to reality. Sometimes, he simply consciously avoids any perceivable similarities with the contents of images pertaining actual relationships between phenomena, assuming that a work of art should be an artificially modelled and richer alternative of the "common" reality.

Musical production oriented at maximizing aesthetic experiences is the main, although not the only, manifestation of pragmatic musical consciousness. This consciousness regulates also musical acts tending towards aims that are more closely connected with the practical sphere of life. Particularly, it refers to the so-called applied music which includes among others, dance music and marches. Besides, some contemporary para-artistic orientations bordering on musical culture and other spheres of culture also refer to the pragmatic musical tradition (e.g. those which assume that being a means of nonverbal communication and aesthetic expression music serves to integrate a given community).

The third variant of traditional musical consciousness is connected with the sphere of professional-artistic sense characterized by J. Kmita.[5] This sense is realized through the fulfillment of definite professional criteria whose concrete forms depend on the worldview beliefs concerning the role of an artist and the so-called sense of art existing in a given society. The fulfillment of these criteria manifest simultaneously that certain artistic values are being respected, or more generally — it is a manifestation of an

5. J. Kmita, *Kul.ura i poznanie,* op. cit., pp. 176 ff.

artistic group membership, similarly as a perfect performance of any type of work communicates that the value lying in this performance is respected and one is a worthy representative of a given professional group. Contemporary musical production is in many cases oriente mainly at the realization of such a professional-artistic sense which is particularly manifested in convictions identifying the sense of music with creation of acoustic constructions as sets of structurally subtle sound wholes. The sphere of musical syntax, specifically autonomized and raised to be the main component of music, becomes the central point of interest. Musical constructions realized within this circle of thinking and sometimes called "pure forms" are additionally treated as constructs with peculiar aesthetic values. The professional-artistic attitude also characterizes a whole range of productions connected with the usage of modern means of musical articulation (e.g. electronic sound synthesis or elements of the so-called concrete music). The manifestation of combinatory ingeniousness or perfection in making use of new means is for many composers an autonomously understood prior sense of their activities although not necessarily declared. The examples discussed here would belong together to the professional-artistic variant of musical consciousness.

The traditional variants of musical consciousness characterized so far concentrate on one distinguished kind of value monopolizing the sphere of musical sense. However, this sense is often understood, as it was mentioned at the beginning, as a complex and hierarchically ordered system, a combination of the earlier considered values. For example, when one attempts to obtain the communicative-correspondence effect, the syntactic aspect of the composition is not treated purely instrumentally but it is assumed that a musical production should be both a vision of the world and a valuable construction from the professional-artistic point of view. However, this is not only limited to the fulfillment of elementary requirements of professional correctness, but is manifested in the creation of a musical structure that exceeds this minimum and is interesting as an autonomously and extrasemantically understood creative construction. The two values taken into consideration here can be treated as equivalent, but it may happen that one of them is attributed a distinguished meaning. It can be added that after a closer investigation of relations of the second type one may observe that the "distance" between these values either takes nearly equivalent form, or acquires a dimension which reduces one of these values to the role of an aspect of a musical work which is taken into consideration but is not very important. This last case approximates the "pure" communicative-correspondence variant of musical consciousness or the "pure" professional-artistic variant, but they cannot be identified. Thus for example, composers who consequently base on beliefs constituting the professional-artistic variant, completely neutralize the correspondence message of a work existing for them as "pure form" only. Composers who take into consideration both the professional-artistic and the communicative-correspondence values, always "see" these two aspects, even when an accidental meaning is attributed to one of them. To summarize the above opinions, let us assume that three types of complex musical sense based on the discussed values can be distinguished. One of them corresponds to the situation of their equivalence, the two remaining ones with two other possible combinations. Detailed problems connected with the "distance" between values constituting these combinations will not be taken into account in the following discussion.

A complex musical sense may also be either a constitution comprising the communicative-correspondence and pragmatic values, or a constitution consisting of pragmatic and professional-artistic values, or finally — a whole taking into consideration all three kinds of values. When considering the possible ways of ordering the above combinations of values, one obtains further types of complex musical senses.

Normative beliefs pointing out various types of complex musical senses together with the corresponding directival beliefs, constitute succeeding variants of traditional musical consciousness. Thus, this consciousness occurs as a set of these variants, each of which is a socio-subjective regulator of relatively different musical acts. It seems to me that reference to detailed musicological analysis would confirm and illustrate the thesis that all the possibilities considered here were realized in musical practice.

Musical consciousness is combined through musical practice with the sphere of objective social requirements which are functional determinants of this practice and indirectly of the consciousness regulating it. Undertaking actions based on different variants of musical consciousness enables to fulfill various kinds of these requirements. Variants, in which a priviledged position is occupied by communicative-correspondence values, allow musical practice to play the role of a worldview valorization which is realized through communicating a vision of the world combining a certain domain of practically perceivable values with corresponding "ultimate" values. Because of the already mentioned specific character of the musical visions of the world, this valorization is usually ambiguous; it enables the creation of worldview images referred to various spheres of "life" values. Musical acts oriented subjectively at achieving professional-artistic values also function in a worldview and valorizing manner. However, the valorization function is not performed here through the mediation of musical visions of the world but through reference to various kinds of myths expressing the artistic activity of a composer in a context of defined worldview values. In such a case, artistic actions themselves undergo valorization which may also expand onto the sphere of acts connected with the perception of music. In such a case superiority is given to the community of listeners who accept the same artistic values. The actions of composers and audience centred around the professional-artistic values besides being manifestations of respecting these values, integrate the community of artists and audience, and at the same time distinguish it from all "noninitiated". The integrative-differentiating function is also connected with the musical practice oriented at realization of values earlier included in the pragmatic set. However, it seems that offering means enabling the participants of social practice to achieve certain psychic states is the basic socio-objective function connected with this kind of sense. Social practice which in most cases is realized in the context of the so-called "commonness" does not satisfy psychic needs (e.g. for contacts with aesthetic or "metaphysical" values) of a certain group of its participants which may potentially threaten its effectiveness (e.g. because of partial engagement or because of attempts to modify certain aspects of this practice which may cause disintegrations). Pragmatically oriented artistic activity makes it possible to fulfill the individual needs by producing works causing various psychic experiences and in this way it relieves other domains of social practice, as far as this aspect is concerned, and increases the chances of their undisturbed functioning. The earlier discussed function of worldview valorization and the function defined above can be considered complementarily. The first one sanctions practice in the worldview way, whereas the other one protects it by proposing a supplementary way of "metaphysical" enrichment of the sphere of ordinariness. The latter function gains particular importance when the first one is not effective enought.

Now, let us investigate the relationship between the attitude sketched above and some controversies traditionally connected with studies on musical culture. For example, the dispute about the semantic status of music has lasted for a long time, resulting in attitudes which on the one hand treat it as a specific means of communication, and on the other in categories of "pure form". In turn, the attitudes of the first type differ in solving questions concerning the object and mode of musical com-munication. In a slightly different context, a controversy occurs whether music describes or causes psychic experiences.[6] When analysing contrary

---

6. Controversies and attitudes connected with them are discussed in works by M. Piotrowski, *Autonomiczne wartości muzyki* (Autonomous values of music), Poznań 1984, and "Znak — symbol — oznaka; O heteronomicznych kategoriach semiotyki muzycznej" (Sign — symbol — symptom; On heteronomous categories of musical semiotics), *Muzyka* 1/1985.

opinions articulated during these disputes, one can observe that they are an expression of an objectivizing usage of normative and directival judgements belonging to different variants of musical culture (musical social consciousness).[7] Every author "sees" music in the context of normative and directival beliefs defining his own way of participation in musical culture and treats the values respected by himself as certain objectivized facts, and the rules used by himself — as objectivized regularities which govern music in a universal way. From the point of view accepted in this paper, the discussed opinions — after "subjectivizing" them — can be recognized as more or less adequate verbalizations of different variants of musical social consciousness.

I would like to end at this point the considerations concerning traditional musical consciousness and devote some remarks to new nontraditional types of this consciousness, where metamusical consciousness holds a distinguished position. To avoid terminological complications the terms "artistic consciousness" and "artistic activity" or "musical consciousness" and "musical compositions" will sometimes be used in some contexts in a broader meaning comprising also a metaartistic sphere. Besides, this convention seems to be in agreement with some general intuitions concerning the way in which the word "artistic" is understood.

3. Metamusical Consciousness

Examining contemporary creative realizations considered to be artistic, one may distinguish a certain subclass which is homogenous as far as the sense and performed functions are concerned and simultaneously different in these aspects from the traditional artistic practice. This is an activity which gives up using the potential of act for communicating visions referred to the outer world, it abandons also the production of aesthetic "pure forms" and the evocation of aesthetic experiences. Although it employs means of communication used within the traditional artistic practice, its aim — declared by artists and recognized by critics and art theoreticians — is to transmit different kinds of beliefs concerning the so-called artistic values, their social functions or artistic means and the context of their application. In comparison with the traditional artistic activities it seems to be on a higher level, and the artistic practice itself with its currently respected or only projected consciousness background, becomes the object of penetration. Referring to the well known terminological tradition, one can speak in this case about metaartistic activity and

7. About objectivizing usage of cultural judgements in humanistic investigations see J. Kmita, *Kultura i poznanie*, op. cit., pp. 49 ff.

a similar term can be attributed to the consciousness regulating it.

The metaartistic consciousness often regulates activities that are very similar to "common" artistic acts oriented at the realization of the communicative-correspondence values. However, the difference is that instead of worldview valorization of extraartistic "life" values, facts concerning the ways in which artistic practice functions are valorized. The visions communicated through artistic means establish relationships between various manifestations of "artistic life" and worldview values, to great extent taken from beliefs concerning the so-called sense of art or the position of an artist and his activity within society and culture. Because of the specific context of contemporary artistic practice, the valorization taken into account here usually assumes the form of contest or rejection. Its main orientation is to deny myth of an artist and by means of mockery attack the traditional sphere of artistic *sacrum*. Such a metaartistic sense can be already found in Duchamp's famous "Fountain" where a urinal is provocatively raised to the dignity of a work of art and aimed at the historically developed form of the so-called aesthetic taste, contesting an aesthetic-contemplative perception of art. The change of the position of art in the age of consumption, technology and mass media is the "topic" of many productions within the sphere of pop-art. The struggle against the ideology of exclusive artistic professionalism connected with the programme of destruction of the so-called fine arts, is the worldview context necessary for understanding many of the Fluxus group manifestations.

The type of metaartistic consciousness mentioned above is connected mainly with the actions within contemporary visual arts. Because of the specific character of musical communication it is of little importance for the musical practice. Metamusical consciousness is usually a manifestation of another trend of metaartistic thinking which refers to traditional pragmatic and professional-artistic senses, transforming them however in a characteristic way. The metaartistic acts undertaken on the basis of this kind of thinking do not refer to worldview beliefs and are separated from them in a programme manner. Such a worldview neutralization is assumed for example by a composer who states that,

> the creation of original sound products thanks to the invention of a very special way of violin making, becomes the most important matter. The next step is to choose sounds and make their samples from which a further choice would be done. Finally, it is a problem of combining them and their mutual relationships.[8]

Many artists and critics call attempts belonging to this trend of metaartistic

---

8. From the works of the Group of Musical Studies ORTF (elaborated on the basis of a work by P. Scheffer), in: J. Patkowski and A. Skrzyńska (Eds.), *Horyzonty muzyki* (The horizons of music), Cracow 1970.

295

actions the "investigation of art". It involves a wide range of possibilities. Here are some declarations highlighting this type of activity: exploration of new artistic means, experiments concerning the nature of their influence, inquiry into the borders of hearer's perceptive dispositions, an attempt to create a new context of using certain artistic techniques. Without evaluating the effectiveness of the undertaken actions in relation to the planned results, one can generally state that this activity is concentrated on the practically perceivable aspects of artistic activity. The convictions communicated through the creation of objects that have to exemplify the contents of the regarded beliefs, concern the artistic means and the context of their usage. In this way, the so far unconscious capabilities of the used means are discovered and besides, their new variants are projected. The function of the worldview valorization of artistic practice characteristic for the first of the discussed trends of metaartistic consciousness is replaced by what may be called a practical-artistic function and which consists in a specific reconstruction of the hitherto artistic experience and projection of its new forms. Using an analogy from the domain of science, it could be said that the first variant of metaartistic consciousness functions in relation to artistic practice similarly as the philosophy of cognition entangled in worldview beliefs in relation to scientific practice. In turn, the second variant seems to be related to a "technologically" conducted methodology of science; it becomes a sort of "artistic methodology" referring to art and conducted through artistic means.

It happens quite often that works of contemporary music realize simultaneously both the metaartistic and the traditional artistic sense, e.g. the communicative-correspondence one. Then the musical communicative structure is subordinated to a two-fold type of semantics. On the one hand, it may be interpreted traditionally and then it refers to the represented reality and the vision of the world "appearing" through it, or on the other hand, it refers to an interpretation respecting its metaartistic status. In order to read the second sense, the traditional semantics has to be suspended in a way, "put into brackets". Then, the artistic construction itself or more precisely the class of constructions similar in their essential aspects to the presented one, together with an appropriate context of their creation and potential functioning, become the reference in the second type of semantics. Thus, the assumptions of semantics consisting of worldview and common-experience beliefs pertaining to the extramusical world are not engaged in the perception of the metaartistic communicative senses. It becomes necessary to make use of an appropriate "knowledge about music" which refers to the artistic domain, and would allow to understand the practical and maybe worldview implications of the interpreted work.

The two discussed communicative planes can cause many misunderstandings in the interpretation and evaluation, particularly of those productions which are characterized by an apparent dominance of the metaartistic sense. A traditional reference could be constituted, but is treated by the artist as being of little or no importance. From the point of view of a traditionally oriented hearer such a reference is the expected communicative sense of the work, and as a result the composition turns out incomprehensible or uninteresting, causing disapproval or even disgust at an artistic extravagance. It often happens that for various reasons such a production wins approval but this is based on an interpretation that levels down the basic metaartistic sense. Cage's famous composition 4'33 is an example of a production which practically has no musical structure. Its provocative sense seems to be of a profoundly metamusical character and among others lies in showing a case of a "musical composition" which does not include any sound. Such an example is an extreme variant of a musical work which usually is a composed combination of sounds and pauses. But even when referring to this production, it often happens that one tries to make use of something similar to traditional interpretative categories and states for example that the noises produced by the audience watching an inactive pianist are just the music.[9] There have been examples of such an interpretation. They are met quite often and are even more possible when the production, metaartistic in intentions, allows to perceive any traditionally understood "representation". This is so because authors of metaartistic productions do not have at their disposal means which could be employed for example when using metalanguage within a methodological discourse. Therefore, they cannot prevent a hearer from employing a traditionally oriented aesthetic-contemplative attitude and looking for a sense that refers directly to the extramusical world. A composition with the dominance of a metaartistic sense is obviously only just one manifestation of the characterized two-level communication. A wide range of contemporary musical production is represented by constructs which transfer equivalently treated artistic and metaartistic senses or creations oriented at the traditional sense which however contain an "addition" of metaartistic meaning that is recognizable by those more interested.[10]

9. An interpretation of this realization of Cage presents J. Szerszenowicz, "Nowa muzyka — nowe środki oddziaływania" (New music — new means of influence), *Studia Filozoficzne* 1-2/1982.

10. For example, M. Bristiger makes the following statement about the composition

4. Paramusical Consciousness

Observing contemporary "musical life" one can notice the occurrance of creative propositions which exceed the horizon of notions traditionally connected with music. The intentions accompanying them and the means used within them, situate them at the border between music and other spheres of culture. However, new types of senses contain elements of traditional musical senses or at least refer to them genetically, and the ways of their realization remain in perceivable relationships with the traditional musical experience. After attributing the name of paramusical consciousness to the consciousness regulating these activities, let us present some of its manifestations. Thus, for instance, there is a group of activities either based on musical compositions or realized as planned actions, or specific verbal messages referring to musical associations. The aim of such activities is to form the listeners' sensitiveness to music or to initate certain thought processes which are to result in creative behaviour. Paramusical activities are sometimes oriented at eliminating the border between musicians and listeners, and consist in arranging events that are occasions for a spontaneous creation of various musical actions. These actions are sometimes attributed a sense which brings them closer to the worldview sphere of symbolic culture. Another group of activities which could also be considered as paramusical is constituted by acts oriented at introducing musical elements to the life environment.[11]

---

by L. Berio which is usually interpreted in traditional categories, "In fact, 'Circles' are an attempt to create a new, so far unknown attitude of music to word. Luciano Berio has been fascinated by this problem for many years formulating it again and again in new ways in his succeeding musical works (...). What function does word perform in relation to music under such conditions? And what is the relationship between these two systems of expression? What is the sense of permanent oscillation between singing, *Sprech-stimme* and *Sprechgesang*, of levelling the semantic stratum of a text by destroying the integrity of word, of separating particular phonetic elements and making use of their specific expressive abilities, of darkening a text by a melismatic extension of a syllabe and lightening a text by a syllabic elaboration? The novelty of Berio's aesthetic proposal is manifested in the way he solves the problem". In turn, Berio presents the effects of his work stating, "The real aim considered is neither in an opposition nor mixture of two systems of expression, but in the creation of a relationship of continuity, the creation of an opportunity of passing imperceptibily from one to the other without manifesting the differences between the perceptive logico-semantic attitude (which we reserve for verbal communication) and the perceptive attitude of a musical type." (M. Bristiger, in: *Horyzonty muzyki,* op. cit.

11. The description of various activities exceeding the traditional musical perspective is presented by J. Szerszenowicz, "W stronę antymuzyki czy nowej muzyczności" (Towards antimusic or new musicalness), *Studia Filozoficzne* 7/1984.

Without going into a closer characterizations of paramusical activities one can state however, that these activities perform mainly the socially integrating function and the educational-cultural function to the extent in which the projects connected with them have been at least partially realized, whereas the valorizing and worldview function connected with the traditional musical function is fulfilled by them to a considerably smaller degree. Thus, the social functions which have been distinctly of marginal importance within the context of traditional musical practice, gain crucial meaning within the paramusical activity. The phenomenon characterized here is a manifestation of developmental processes concerning the whole artistic culture. These processes consist not only in obliterating the borders between various domains of art but also in "fusing" elements of artistic culture with elements belonging to other realms of symbolic culture.

Finally, I would like to present some general opinions concerning the profits of using the perspective of the socio-pragmatic theory of culture in the studies on music. First of all, it is possible, as I have already partially mentioned, to avoid the limitations characteristic for the musicological reflection which consist in objectivising usage of norms and directives of a particular variant of musical consciousness. Referring oneself to the subjectivelly understood culture, one can treat musical culture in the subject-variant way which allows to overcome the traditional musicological disputes and enables complete studies on norms and directives belonging to various types of musical consciousness. These investigations can make use of certain earlier observations conducted in an objectivizing way and treat them as an objectivized registration of beliefs belonging to a definite variant of musical experience. The socio-pragmatic theory of culture also shows how to explain the fact of social acceptance of beliefs reconstructed on its assumptions. This perspectively gives a chance of obtaining results that would bring musicology closer to those domains of humanistic investigations that have already reached a theoretical status. It is also of importance that this theory has at its disposal a conceptual apparatus which allows to situate musical phenomena in a broader cultural context. This also enables to exceed the rather hermetic musicological concepts and offers an opportunity of referring to cognitive observations concerning other domains of culture, which seems to be of particular importance in the case of the analyses of paramusical consciousness.

Translated by Stefan Wiertlewski

Anna Zeidler

VALORIZATION OF TRADITION AS A MEANS OF PRESERVING THE CONTINUITY OF CULTURE

In the foreword to her book symptomatically entitled *Between the present and the future time* almost entirely devoted to reinterpretations of various parts of philosophical tradition, H. Arendt justifies the selected method of philosophizing by the peculiarity of the spiritual situation in which we live. In order to do this, she elaborates on one of Kafka's miniature parables, the hero of which, "He", is entangled in a struggle between two forces (that of the past and that of the future) and fights both of them and each of them separately, aware of his existence in a "time gap" and dreaming in vain about "taming" or "mastering" it the need to "settle" in the time "between", "conditioned by what exists no longer and what does not exist yet", was shared by individuals almost since the beginning of the human thought. It could be connected with the topos of life in harmony with the world, enlivened in the tradition of German classical philosophy.

The peculiarity of modern situation seems to consist in the fact that the world perceived in the "time gap" has become "more of a battlefield than a home".

> The difficulty (...) lies in the fact that we do not seem properly fit or prepared for this conceptual effort, for settling in the gap between the past and the future. During the long periods of our history, the thousands of years which passed since the origins of Rome and which were determined by Roman concepts, this gap was bridged by something that since the Roman times has been called tradition. It is no longer a mystery for anyone that together with the progress of the modern times, this tradition has become much weaker. When its continuity was finally interrupted, the gap between the past and future time ceased to be experienced by only several people for whom thinking was the primary occupation. It has become a very real and painful reality for everyone. It means that it has become a political fact, "political" in the peculiar sense in which this term is used by the author of *Human Fate*.[1]

Kafka's metaphor can be interpreted as an image of a situation in which a common feeling is the sense of unfitness of tools we have at our disposal to grasp the continuity of culture; the sense of "disinheritance" as one of the most significant manifestations of a deep structural crisis of historical formation.

1. H. Arendt, *Between past and future*, New York 1961, p. 14.

There are three solutions to the situation described by H. Arendt: leaving the battlefield in order to submerge in Heideggerian anonymous Self (participation in the area of a broadly understood mass culture, together with the reduction of the old world of values characteristic for it), an attempt of re-constructing one's "being" in the name of Heideggerian "authenticity", and a continuation of the struggle to defeat the mentioned "time gap": an interpretational-reinterpretational construction of the continuity of culture. The last solution is preferred by the modern, post-Heideggerian hermeneutics, represented by Ricoeur and Gadamer.

The fact that the continuity of culture is not — as it used to be — given, but requires a peculiar spiritual activity of individuals ("exercises in thinking") is supposed to present — according to H. Arendt — a peculiar "justification" of the method of practising philosophy, adopted by her and also by other scholars.

"History differs from prehistory in violating a certain commonly accepted sense", said J. Patocka, searching for the genesis of the contemporary situation in the moment of passing to the societies "with a history".

Assuming different premises, external in relation to "thinking", Habermas characterizes the indicated critical state of matters as an effect of a long lasting historical process, described by M. Weber as "disenchanting the world". In modern societies the growth of significance and scope of purposeful-rational actions is accompanied by a growing degradation of "traditional images of the world and objectivizations", which

lose their power and validity (1) as a myth, as a common religion, as an old ritual, as justifying metaphysics, as an unquestioned tradition (i.e. as all those forms of legitimization which offered the individuals the sense of the continuity of tradition and naturalization in the world — A.Z.). They are, however, transformed into (2) subjective ethics and beliefs ("protestant ethics") and finally become a material of (3) a construction, with the help of which tradition is criticized and the liberated contents of tradition are reorganized, according to the principles of formal legal relations.[2]

The processes indicated by Habermas, characteristic of the transition to the societies of a modern type, have resulted in the minimization of the role of worldview in regulating the practice of everyday life,[3] which has become a direct premiss of the modern sense of the crisis of culture and the lack of its "natural" continuity, so dramatically described in the statements quoted above. They somehow justify the concentration of modern humanistic sciences upon the problems of interpretation either "from the

2. J. Habermas, "Technik und Wissenschaft als 'Ideologie'" (Polish translation), in: *Czy kryzys socjologii?* (Whether a crisis of sociology?), Warsaw 1977, p. 363-364.
3. J. Kmita, *O kulturze symbolicznej* (On symbolic culture), Warsaw 1982.

outside" or by means of a characterization of non-conceptual determinants of the indicated state of matters. I am recalling them here in order
to present one of the fundamental ideas of that outline. It can be reduced to
a statement that the growth of interest in the problems of interpretation in
modern humanistic sciences (in particular, in the area of reflection on art)
should not be explained either by coincidence or fashion on the one hand,
or — on the other hand — by some internal logic of development of
knowledge itself. It is undoubtedly governed by the mechanism of
historical necessity, indicated by Habermas, which is, however, perceivable far beyond the sphere of internal analyses of the contents and
form of modern humanistic reflection. In its various disciplines, the
growth of the significance of interpretational problems is recorded at
different times, what is connected with a varied speed of changes occurring
in the areas investigated by cultural practices.

In aesthetics, for example, the problem of the continuity of tradition,
both in the worldview-artistic aspect and in a more global scope — in the
aspect of the formula of art as an autonomous discipline of social practice,
constituting a clear conceptual context of the problems of interpretation,
has re-appeared with an unincidentally strong influence during the
expansion of the second avantgarde (the so-called neoavantgarde) in a
much more clear way that the first consequences which affected art as a
result of "disenchanting the world" (i.e. losing the support of worldview
systems respected commonly and in a relatively stable way). As it has been
observed by Adorno, art can no longer claim for itself enchantment in a
"disenchanted" world, though it must somehow ("critically") assimilate
this situation. The institutional strengthening of artistic criticism as a
practice which — through interpretation — enables the functioning of art
in communicational circulation is clearly related with that situation.

The relation between exposing the theory and practice of interpretation
on the one hand and the situation of particular cultural disciplines on the
other is in a way realized by the representatives of modern humanisitic
sciences. In order to become convinced about it, it is sufficient to take a
look at the history of hermeneutics — a discipline which traditionally
focuses on interpretation and encompasses areas that are parts of various
cultural practices (from religion and law to art). Its appearance and
subsequent mutations, connected with annexing constantly new areas of
culture (including science) — up to the claims of universality put forward
today — are not incidentally associated with the subsequent stages of the
process of "disenchantment" of first the magic, then religion, and finally
worldview *en block,* and thus also art. This relation is also stressed by the
representatives of hermeneutics, who are traditionally far from explaining
the form of cultural beliefs in terms of their external determinations. For

example, discussing the problem of alegorical interpretation in ancient hermeneutics, Gadamer says that "such an interpretation has already been used in the times of sophistry, i.e. since the moment in which the world of values of the Homer epos lost its power".[4]

A direct point of reference for modern art and aesthetics is that stage of "disenchantment" which was most distinctly indicated by Nietzsche, who ascertained the change of morality into a "moral interpretation of phenomena" and of which an equally diliged and critical observer was the founder of modern hermeneutics, W. Dilthey. The tendencies which were synthetically expressed by the statement concerning "God's death" (i.e., as it was expressed by Camus, finding him dead in the soul of the epoch) made Dilthey undertake an attempt to constitute hermeneutics as a valid method of *Geisteswissenschaften* (including the knowledge of art as a specific discipline of *Geist,* thanks to which hermeneutics entered the area of aesthetics, in order to "incorporate" it in its later mutations). Dilthey's essay entitled *The origin of hermeneutics,* published in 1900, is a "model" manifestation of those tendencies.

Contrary to various anti-Diltheyan declarations of later representatives of hermeneutics, this is not far from the point in which — thanks to radicalization carried out by Heidegger and the universalization of hermeneutics — art is treated as one of the most important disciplines of hermeneutic experience. Gadamer in *Wahrheit und Methode* and in his later essays explicitly puts forward the theory and practice of interpretation as the principal task of all knowledge of art. This proposition harmonizes with the "critical" tendencies in the 20th century artistic practice (particularly the literary one), the tendencies which were so highly evaluated by Adorno, who believed them to be a continuation of "the true essence of art".

Now I would like to take a closer look at how the indicated tendencies are realized in practice, taking as a starting point Gadamer's attempt of interpretation of one of the oldest of aesthetic categories — the category of mimesis. This will serve the purpose of understanding the situation in modern art and defending the idea of continuity of artistic practice and the symbolic culture in general. An additional value of that example is placing the interpretational activities of the author against a broader historical context. Elaboration of certain intuitions in this respect will allow us for a more precise perception of the tendencies which I have originally characterized as functional rights of the presently common sense of the

4. H.G. Gadamer, "Hermeneutik", in: *Historisches Wörterbuch der Philosophie,* vol. 3, Basel 1974.

significance of interpretational problems in the research of art or the symbolic culture as a whole.

The task assumed by the author of *Wahrheit und Methode* is to understand the status of avantgarde practices, mainly those which subject the plane of artistic presentation to destruction. In particular, he is interested in the phenomenon of non-figurative plasticity, which — at a first glance — "rejects all schematic possibilities of understanding", thus becoming a convenient experimental area, in which the scope of validity of older aesthetic concepts can be verified. It can be easily noticed that the author passes from the analysis of the chronologically nearest tradition further into "the depth of history", where he intends to find premises allowing him for a conceptualization of the phenomenon of modern non-figurative plasticity and other tendencies parallel to it in the area of other disciplines of artistic practice.

This apparently paradoxical behavior is not surprising if we recall Gadamer's concept of speech as a medium of hermeneutic experience and the idea of the history of concepts as philosophy, connected with it. According to this concept, the analysis of the history of a concept is always a task aimed at discovering its "live" semantics, i.e. the way of functioning in "live speech", concealed in history by the "alienated, fossilized language". "Live speech" seems to be that form of cultural communication which had existed before the separation of common experience from the sphere of worldview and, later, science.

The starting point for Gadamer's analysis of the concept of mimesis is at first its common, everyday meaning, functioning in the contemporary "universal consciousness", i.e. — from his perspective — in the fossilized language of the alienated aesthetic experience. Yet, he hastily acknowledges that neither identifying mimesis with imitation nor the peculiar mutations of this category in the form of concepts of expression and sign "can be a match for the new phenomenon". It is then necessary to reach backwards, to the philosophical aesthetic concepts, which "are certainly able to solve the mystery of modern painting in the best way".

The first philosopher to whom Gadamer turns is Kant. Yet, it is immediately clear for every reader of *Wahrheit und Methode* that he will not find anything useful in Kant's aesthetics. It is the thought of Kant, placing art in the transcendentally viewed subjectiveness, that becomes in a way responsible for the process described as the alienation of aesthetic experience. Using a whole range of arguments, Gadamer indicates that Kant's thinking has initiated a new paradigm, in which a work of art has become an object of a purely aesthetic contemplation, aesthetic experience, the world of a "beautiful appearance" separated from life, i.e. from the entire historical experience of the recipients. A symptom of that is the

304

possibility of exhibiting and watching paintings in museums and galleries.[5]

From the Gadamer's perspective the participation in art is to consist in placing art again in the world, i.e. relating it to the truth and ethicality, making a work of art an element of "infinite" conversation allowing the recipient to better understand himself, his times, and history. The isolational-subjectivist dimensions of Kant's aesthetics, particularly its later transformations (e.g. that of Schopenhauer), are responsible for the form in which both the old and modern painting appears in the "universal" (common) consciousness.

On the basis of Gadamer's approach we may say, quite "externally" in relation to the concept that is interesting to us here, that Kant's aesthetic paradigm has become a peculiar rationalization of that stage of development of the artistic practice in which it separates itself from the original magical-religious context, gains autonomy, and in this sense becomes "a world for itself", at the same time constructing the institutional framework of its own independence.

In this context we cannot be surprised by the subsequent step taken be the philosopher, namely reaching back to Aristotle. Even the fact that neither Aristotle nor Plato, to whom Gadamer also refers, knew aesthetics as an independent philosophical discipline makes it possible to view them as closer to hermeneutic ideals than the representatives of the so-called "modern philosophical thought".

Analyzing the functioning of the category of mimesis in Aristotle's thinking, Gadamer observes that it used to be equiped in much more elaborate senses than the subsequent "imitation", connected with the growing role of the common image of the world superceding the magical-religious image. An analysis of contexts in which the term "mimesis" occurs in Aristotle's writings (in *Politics, Nicomachean Ethics, Poetics*), his perfidious, as Gadamer calls it, dialogue with Plato, induce one to identify "imitation" with "recognition". In Aristotle's concept, this "recognition" is supposed to concern both the "solid form of things" and oneself.

This would put us much closer to understanding the status of non-figurative painting, in which we do "recognize" something, if not for the fact that Aristotle's concept of "recognition" assumes the existence of a binding tradition, within the scope of which "everybody understands one another and meets himself". It is a tradition which was constituted by myth and which provided a natural background for the emancipating art. Yet, as we know, the world of myth became disintegrated during the historical process of "disenchanting" culture.

---

5. H.G. Gadamer, *Warheit und Methode,* 4. Auf. Tübingen 1975 and *Die Aktualität des Schönen. Kunst als Spiel, Symbol und Fest,* Stuttgard 1977.

305

Even the Christian art — one has to admit openly — lost its mythical power some 150 years ago. It was not the revolution of modern painting, but the end of the last monumental European style — barocco — that became the true end. Together with it ended the natural imagery of Western tradition — its humanistic heritage and Christian message.[6]

That heritage, although it does not constitute the natural world of the life of modern man, can also be (to a smaller or greater degree) individually remembered and so it can stimulate the participation in both the old and modern art. To the degree to which we still perceive its traces, Aristotle's "recognition" emanates a certain truth. But what traces can be found in modern non-figurative art, asks sceptically Gadamer.

Before we take a look at the philosopher's further searches, let us make several digressions. The main interest here is non-figurative painting and, secondly, similar tendencies in modern art. If we agree with the thesis that presently the interpretational context of the fine arts is to a large degree constituted by literature, the thesis on the residual role of myth can be somehow weakened, and thus also assume that Aristotle's "recognition" is still functioning in a much stronger sense than it is assumed by Gadamer. In the autothematic-"critical" trend of modern literature, a myth is no longer a subject of faith, although it is still present as the subject of reflection, discussion, intellectual treatment, and even play.

As long as one cannot do without a Christian or ancient dress, it cannot be only a dress, something exclusively formal. (...) as long as the "utilization" of mythology (with all the consequences of the fact that it is being "used" and not "lived in") is a notorious and common feature of literature, the temperature of the myth has not dropped completely.[7]

The above diagnosis given by Mieletinski, related with a fast development of "mythologism" in the 20th century literature in connection with a clearly literary-like character of artistic criticism, makes it possible to weaken Gadamer's negative conclusions. It is well known, however, because of the type of coexistence with art desired in hermeneutics, that the rejection of Aristotle's concept is connected here also with the fact that it constitutes in fact the expression of emancipation tendencies of the artistic practice within the possibilities provided by the ancient world, or — in other words, that it will initiate thinking about art in the categories developed (in an extreme form) by Kant's paradigm. And so, an apparently more familiar concept for Gadamer is that of Plato, a thinker who sanctioned the "disintegration" of the practical world and the world

6. H.G. Gadamer, "Kunst und Nachahmung" (Polish transl.), in: H.G. Gadamer, *Rozum, słowo, dzieje* (translated from *Kleine Schriften*), Warsaw 1979, p. 137.
7. E. Mieletynski, Poetyka mitu/The poetics of a myth/;/translated from Russian/, Warsaw 1981, p. 346-347.

of ideas, thus originating the history of European metaphysics (and therefore also Kant's paradigm, placed within its framework and subjected to criticism).

In order to support our thesis, let us refer to a historian and sociologist of culture, who explains the paradox mentioned above in the following way.

> Plato, who opposed the tendency of art to become separated as a distinguished discipline, tried to reduce to minimum the imitational element in art, while Aristotle, who became a theoretical advocate for that tendency, not only did not make such efforts, but considered imitation to be the essence of art, its most important property. It has turned out that stressing the imitational character of art not only did not hamper justifying the necessity of its distinguishing from the objective reality, the entire practical-life process, but on the contrary, made it possible to find constantly new arguments indicating the existence of such a necessity. What is more, the theory of mimesis, the theory of the imitational character of art, originated and developed as a theoretical form of realizing, justifying, and vindicating the process of science being distinguished as a peculiar and self-sufficient discipline.[8]

The ascertainment quoted above allows for a better understanding of the subsequent, even deeper withdrawal of Gadamer, this time to the stage in which the possibility of art merely began to emerge, i.e. to art's hypothetical earliest beginnings. The author of *Wahrheit und Methode* seems to be telling that the origins of that stage may allow us to find such a sense of the concept of mimesis which will save modern painting in the role of a component of our entire life experience. As I have already mentioned, a very helpful perspective in this respect appears to be that of Plato, particularly as the criticism of the observed emancipation tendencies of art, moving it further from the truth, appreciated very highly also by Gadamer. Analyzing the destructive influence of tragedy and comedy (connected above all with the fictionalization of a mythical story and thus questioning the ethical messages entangled in it), Plato has commented upon the representatives of imitational art in the following way:

> (...) since the time of Homer all poets have been imitating and creating images of courage and other things of which they have been writting, though none of them has come close to truth.[9]

The suggestion to banish poets from the country, accompanied by a desire to reconstruct the earlier ("true") way of functioning of the elements of art in life, is known to have been connected with idealizing ancient Greece and the Egyptian caste system. Let us again recall Dawydow, according to whom

8. J. Dawydow, *Sztuka jako zjawisko socjologiczne* (Art as a social phenomenon), Warsaw 1971, p. 243.
9. These problems are dealt with in Plato's *Pheadrus, Republic and Philebus*.

Plato (...) has grasped the exceptionally dramatic situation experienced in his times by the ancient artistic culture. Separated from life, art has lost some of its essence, role, and significance it had once had when being a component of a syncretic and whole system of life forms in the brave times of ancient Greence described by Homer (...). The price art had to pay for becoming independent was its transformation into a peculiar discipline considered by Plato, not without satisfactory grounds, to be a discipline of an individual's false, unreal, imagined life, so much different from its real, social life activity. In that sense the synthesis of arts which became embodied in the ancient tragedy, summarizing the process of the formation of ancient art, was no longer a real synthesis, i.e. it did not integrate art with other practical areas of social life, but rather it provided an imagined integration which opposed these areas. Ever since then there has appeared a problem of the relation of art with life, the necessity to search for the threads which bind art with other areas of human life (...).[10]

Plato is known to have evaluated music the highest, although even in music he has finding "destructive" tendencies. Yet, it was to provide a kind of model of the organization of social life, order in general. This element has been used by Gadamer, who follows Plato in his identification of the most primitive and at the same time most general sense of the category of mimesis with the idea of order. In his formulation of that idea, he refers to Pythagoreans, continuing the idea of music as the basis of the agreement "between things in nature and the best management of the universe".

Pythagorean concept of mimesis as the order of the world, sounds, the visible world, and human soul, generalized as all presentation of the order, "a certificate of a spiritual ordering energy" — the sense of the category lost in the history of making it abstract, is supposed not only to save the continuity of the aesthetic-artistic tradition (as it can be applied to both non-figurative painting and similar tendencies in other disciplines of artistic practice), but also — surprisingly — to acknowledge an extremely important role performed in contemporary life by that totally condemned modern art. In the world which not only "crowded out visible forms of ritual and cult" but also destroyed a thing,

each work of art is still something that performs the role once performed by that thing, something in the existence of which the order shines and is confirmed.[11]

To be more precise, it is not exactly the work of art as a separate being that becomes the model in constructing one's own life (to such a degree to which we do not want to yield to the power of "monologized" culture), but rather its "understanding" acquisition, the incorporation of it into the scope of one's own life experience. According to the model of art as a game, we cannot speak separately about a work of art and its recipient, because then we remain within the framework of alienated aesthetic consciousness

10. J. Dawydow, *Sztuka ...*, op. cit., p. 300.
11. H.G. Gadamer, "Kunst ...", op. cit., p. 140.

(Kant's paradigm), which eliminates the truth as a sort of normative idea of all participation in art.

Gadamer's method implies, that mimesis no longer appears as an outdated form of conceptualization of art, and — what more — avantgarde praxis does not seem so revolutionary as declared in programmes of its promoters.

In fact Gadamer considers "the genuine question of art" which consists — according to his opinion — in "coexistence of the past and the present". An acceptance of this claim enables us to understand why art becomes so interesting subject of analyses on present day status of cultural tradition. We can also oppose Ricoeur's opinion that the author of *Wahrheit und Methode* is "enslaved by tradition" and recall Habermas's rebellious attitude from *Erkentniss und Interesse*.[12]

Translated by Krzysztof Sawala

12. "Ethics and culture. Habermas and Gadamer in dialogue", *Philosophy Today* 17/1973.